Developing Service-Oriented AJAX Applications on the Microsoft® Platform

Daniel Larson

PUBLISHED BY
Microsoft Press
A Division of Microsoft Corporation
One Microsoft Way
Redmond, Washington 98052-6399

Library of Congress Control Number: 2008935429

Printed and bound in the United States of America.

1 2 3 4 5 6 7 8 9   QWT   3 2 1 0 9 8

Distributed in Canada by H.B. Fenn and Company Ltd.

A CIP catalogue record for this book is available from the British Library.

Microsoft Press books are available through booksellers and distributors worldwide. For further information about international editions, contact your local Microsoft Corporation office or contact Microsoft Press International directly at fax (425) 936-7329. Visit our Web site at www.microsoft.com/mspress. Send comments to mspinput@microsoft.com.

Microsoft, Microsoft Press, Active Directory, ActiveX, IntelliSense, Internet Explorer, MS, MSDN, Outlook, SharePoint, Silverlight, SQL Server, Virtual Earth, Visual Studio, Windows, Windows Live, Windows Server, and Windows Vista are either registered trademarks or trademarks of the Microsoft group of companies. Other product and company names mentioned herein may be the trademarks of their respective owners.

The example companies, organizations, products, domain names, e-mail addresses, logos, people, places, and events depicted herein are fictitious. No association with any real company, organization, product, domain name, e-mail address, logo, person, place, or event is intended or should be inferred.

This book expresses the author's views and opinions. The information contained in this book is provided without any express, statutory, or implied warranties. Neither the authors, Microsoft Corporation, nor its resellers, or distributors will be held liable for any damages caused or alleged to be caused either directly or indirectly by this book.

Acquisitions Editor: Ben Ryan
Developmental Editor: Devon Musgrave
Project Editor: Valerie Woolley
Editorial Production: ICC Macmillan, Inc.
Technical Reviewer: Per Blomqvist; Technical Review services provided by Content Master, a member of CM Group, Ltd.
Cover: Tom Draper Design

Body Part No. X15-12282

Dedication

To Sallina—the bride of my youth, my inspiration, my muse.
You are all that I long for, all that I desire, all that I need.
With more than words can express—thank you.
I would be nothing without your love.

To Violet—you are more than we could have ever expected.
You are a true blessing, a gift from God to your mother
and to me. And to your siblings, we're waiting
for you with greatest expectations.

Contents at a Glance

Table of Contents

What do you think of this book? We want to hear from you!

Microsoft is interested in hearing your feedback so we can continually improve our books and learning resources for you. To participate in a brief online survey, please visit:

www.microsoft.com/learning/booksurvey

What do you think of this book? We want to hear from you!

Microsoft is interested in hearing your feedback so we can continually improve our books and learning resources for you. To participate in a brief online survey, please visit:

www.microsoft.com/learning/booksurvey

Foreword

This book is going to give you a ton of technical information about building AJAX applications with Microsoft technologies. But before you dive into the details, spend a few minutes with me here talking about why you want to do it and some ways to think about it.

AJAX, by name, has been popular for a few years. The technology, though, has been in use for quite a long time. Early versions of Microsoft's Outlook Web Access pioneered the space to some extent. Although this was limited to Internet Explorer and used proprietary extensions, the implementation started to demonstrate what could be done in a Web application and that not every feature required a page view. Since then, many more applications have adopted the techniques.

AJAX has since become a buzzword. If your application doesn't use it, developers say, "This would be so much better with AJAX." Marketers say, "We need some AJAX." Technical press say, "It's not very AJAXy." And the technical geek crowd say, "It's so Web 1.0." But your users won't use that word. In fact, they've most likely never even heard of AJAX unless they're technical folks themselves. Aunt Sylvia doesn't worry herself with any of this. Ask her what a "page view" is, and she'll give you one of those "why do I care about this?" looks.

What users will notice is their experience, and this is where great applications can take advantage of AJAX. Enhancing the user experience and driving efficiency (for the user or your application) are certainly noble goals, and AJAX can certainly help satisfy these goals.

Much of this book will discuss service-oriented architecture and how to go about designing services to work well with your Web application. Even in the absence of AJAX, designing your application in this way will yield dividends in the future, and with the introduction of technologies like Windows Communication Foundation (WCF), this is easier than ever. Service design forces you to think about how to carve up your application into discrete chunks, and it will get you thinking about how to group functionality in ways that will reduce the communication between your application and the browser.

Many AJAX applications will offload processing from the server to the browser, and it's here that you must be careful. You have a few variables to work with as you do your design:

- Server CPU (database, application server, Web server)
- Network utilization
- Client CPU (in the browser)

That's pretty much it. There are other variables, such as local browser storage and such, but these three are the most important ones. As you turn dials in your application, a shift occurs between these variables.

Server CPU is pretty straightforward—you understand your database and your application logic, and you have a general idea about what's expensive and what's not. Hopefully, by designing your services cleverly, you've carved up the problem into smaller, more manageable chunks, which makes CPU management across a server farm somewhat easier to plan.

Network utilization is important to think about. In today's world of high-speed data connections, it's easy to forget your users who might be on the road with some sort of cellular connection. Some 3G networks, for example, can be quite fast in terms of throughput, but they may have dreadful latencies. The only way you'll know how this affects your application is to try it. Test!

Client CPU is a bit of a wildcard. As of this writing, the spread in JavaScript execution performance between the top four desktop browsers is a factor of 10. So the fastest browser in common use will process JavaScript a full 10 times faster than the slowest (according to published tests). Not to mention mobile browsers, which can be dramatically slower yet. Test on all of the browsers you can! I've used an application that is as smooth as silk on one browser but that on another browser brings the client computer to its knees for seconds at a time. This is hard to predict—test!

At NewsGator, our enterprise product line makes use of AJAX, using many of the techniques described in this book, including service-based architecture. This approach has allowed us to deliver the user experience we want, limit the number of certain expensive API calls back to the server, deliver asynchronous updates to users, and even increase the usability of some built-in SharePoint capabilities by eliminating long page loads.

You're in the business of building Web applications or you wouldn't be reading this book. Make them the best they can be—functional, responsive, intuitive, and attractive. Use AJAX to solve problems; use it to make things better for the user. It's one more tool in your toolbox, and it's a powerful one.

Greg Reinacker
CTO and Founder
NewsGator Technologies, Inc.

Acknowledgments

While it goes without saying, I owe all that I am to my Lord, Jesus Christ. Thank you for all that You are and have done in my life.

While I wrote this book myself, I actually had a very talented team that worked with me to refine the content. My peer review team consisted of extremely talented developers and Microsoft MVPs. If the book makes any sense at all, I owe it to my peer review team for helping form the content. Folks on this team include Mikhail Dikov, Darrin Bishop, Al Pascual, Alvin Bruney, and Morgan Everett. Also, big thanks to Mark Collins, Nick Swan, Todd Baginski, and Sahil Malik for feedback on various chapters. I'd like to thank Sahil Malik for his excellent writing about Windows Communication Foundation (WCF) and SharePoint. I'd also like to thank the following friends at Microsoft for their continued support: April Spence, Lawrence Lliu, Paul Andrew, and Melissa Travers.

I'd also like to send a shout-out to Ted Pattison: thanks for letting me write *Inside Windows SharePoint Services 3.0* with you. This book is a continuation of our chapter on AJAX Web Parts, and I wouldn't be writing this without our last book project.

I'd also like to thank Ben Ryan for picking up this book project, especially with the current flood of AJAX books on the market. I trust this book will be unique in your library!

On the editing side—John Pierce was the man responsible for the polish—John, I'm amazed at your editing skills and the readability that you've added. Per Blomqvist was responsible for the technical review and provided invaluable feedback on the technical content. If the code runs, we can thank Per! Additional thanks to Devon Musgrave for helping me start the book out and providing those early edits. I'd like to thank the entire Microsoft Press team for making this happen—you've truly made this a great experience and you've helped me write a great book. I wouldn't want to write a book without you!

In the community, I owe a lot to friends like Joe Mayo, Roy Ogborn, and the Denver community of Microsoft Developers, led by fine folks like Chris Wallace, to whom I owe a great deal of thanks for getting me started with Microsoft technologies. When I first arrived in Denver, I was just learning .NET 1.0, and a lot of people in the Denver community have contributed to my success. A special thanks to Roy Haschenberger and family for your support throughout the years. And Amos, thanks for buying my book.

I'd like to especially thank the NewsGator Enterprise developer team for helping to refine this architecture over the last few years and for giving me a playground to implement these concepts. A big thanks to Lane Mohler, Sherstin Lauman, Brian Agnes, Josh Aragon, and Tom McIntyre on the NewsGator Enterprise developer team, and Brian Kellner, Ashley Roach, Karyn German, and Greg Reinacker in NewsGator Management for supporting this effort through NewsGator Enterprise and NewsGator Social Sites. This book is largely about the architecture patterns we've developed and refined at NewsGator by developing services first and AJAX applications second. I'd also like to send a shout-out to the other AJAX developers at NewsGator: "Was that a postback?"

Finally, I'd like to thank my wife for her support in this project. Sallina, you're an amazing wife and I couldn't have written this without your support. This book is for our children; they will never have to write postback code.

Introduction

AJAX has fundamentally changed how we build and consume Web applications. Reloading pages, posting forms, and even Web site navigation have changed drastically since I first started building Web pages back in 1992. Today, customers expect rich Internet applications with live data, not just pages of static information. This is especially true as more and more business applications are moved to the Internet and browsers such as Google's Chrome browser are developed to optimize rich Internet applications.

A few years ago AJAX was a novel concept. Most of us had seen AJAX used in dramatic ways in applications like Google Maps and Microsoft's Windows Live Local, but only a few developers understood how to use it in their own applications. It was magic then, but today it's expected, and applications without AJAX feel unresponsive, clunky, and outdated.

It's also important to note that AJAX isn't a term for the user experience. While you may get some of the user experience benefits of AJAX without developing a service-oriented application, you won't get the flexibility and longevity of the purist AJAX approach. One thing I don't cover in this book is the Update Panel, a Web control introduced with ASP.NET AJAX that implements "magic" AJAX-like behavior with the ASP.NET postback model.

Rather than the user experience, AJAX describes the architecture pattern: asynchronous JavaScript and XML. Another way to describe this pattern is this: "Write Web services, and then write a JavaScript library to use them." It is this approach that I take in this book, which is also dubbed *service-oriented AJAX*.

Service-oriented AJAX takes the approach of starting with the Web service API. The API implements the core functionality of the application and exposes the application to multiple clients. With this approach, you can easily swap out the JavaScript application with alternate clients, such as Flash or Silverlight, or even remote Windows or Macintosh clients. Because we're taking a service-oriented approach, the same services can be extended to implement a remote API as well as the JavaScript API that our AJAX application will use. While the *X* in AJAX stands for XML, the data format isn't important, and WCF supports both XML and JavaScript-serialized (JSON) data streams.

In this book, I use the Microsoft AJAX Library—the client-side library for ASP.NET AJAX—to implement the client runtime. The Microsoft AJAX Library is utilized throughout the book but is covered in detail in Chapters 4 through 8. It is the Microsoft AJAX Library that is used to build the client runtime, which will make asynchronous Web service calls to the backend through the JavaScript library.

When I first started implementing this pattern several years ago, I used a combination of ASMX Web services and HTTP handlers to implement the API, and I used the Microsoft ASP.NET AJAX extensions to integrate JavaScript support on these services. But then came

Windows Communication Foundation (WCF) and then the WCF Web programming model introduced in the Microsoft .NET Framework 3.5. This changed everything and enabled further abstraction through which the service developer doesn't need to identify how the service will be exposed—the same service can be extended using a great number of bindings and behaviors, and it can be called from everything from JavaScript clients to TCP/IP bindings or even message queue integration.

Just as a poorly designed ASP.NET application is difficult to maintain, a clumsily built AJAX application can be a developer's nightmare. Switching to AJAX does have its challenges: browser compatibility issues, accessibility issues, and architectural challenges with moving the user interface logic from the server to the client. In essence, we're moving the user interface from a compiled language such as C# or Visual Basic.NET in ASP.NET to JavaScript, an interpreted language that runs on the client. But with a properly built service-based architecture, your back-end application will be more flexible and secure than you could have imagined, and it will be built for the future. Your application won't be tied to a front-end technology such as ASP.NET, AJAX, or Silverlight—it will be built to be consumed as services. This will free up your front-end programming a great deal—you will be able to add features and integrate multiple components with much less effort than with traditional Web applications.

Armed with a proper understanding of service-based AJAX architecture and Microsoft's rich frameworks for Internet applications, including ASP.NET AJAX and WCF, developers can create enterprise-class applications that are quicker to write, more maintainable than traditional Web applications, and future-proof. The main application won't be tied to the user interface but will remain in compiled code on the server. On the back end, you'll use WCF to expose application data through services that will be consumed by multiple applications, not just your AJAX application. WCF is another technology that is geared toward the future—it is built to decouple the application from the interface, so as technology evolves you won't be stuck with an outdated service platform.

AJAX development will use your existing skills and knowledge of ASP.NET, but it does require a fresh approach to Web development. This book is aimed to help you take your existing developer skills and use them to build fresh applications using the service-oriented AJAX architectural pattern.

Who This Book Is For

This book is written for the intermediate to advanced Web developer using Microsoft technologies. It's written to guide your transition from ASP.NET to ASP.NET AJAX using WCF Web services. This book is written with some C#, but primarily JavaScript. Visual Basic.NET developers should be able to translate the C# code with ease, as the focus of the book is architectural. Compiled code samples in this book are written with C# and compiled against the 3.5 SP1 framework using Visual Studio 2008, but you'll also find a lot of JavaScript.

Some basic knowledge of C#, ASP.NET, Web development, and the .NET Framework is required. Knowledge of WCF is not required but will be helpful. I'll cover the basics of WCF for AJAX developers and point you to some great references along the way.

What This Book Is About

This book is about developing software with the service-oriented AJAX pattern, using the Microsoft 3.5 .NET Framework and Microsoft enterprise servers.

Part I, "AJAX and WCF." This section introduces the service-oriented AJAX architecture pattern and WCF as the technology platform for Web services.

- Chapter 1, "Service-Oriented AJAX Fundamentals," introduces the service-oriented architecture pattern for AJAX applications. It gives an overview of the pattern and simple examples to get you started.

- Chapter 2, "The AJAX Application Server: Service Orientation and the Windows Communication Foundation," introduces WCF as a Web service technology platform and focuses on the service-oriented principles of modern software architecture.

- Chapter 3, "The AJAX Application Server: Windows Communication Foundation's Web Programming Model," describes the WCF Web programming model and the REST architecture pattern, as well as syndication support in the WCF framework.

Part II, "Practical AJAX." This section focuses on programming the client-side, service-oriented AJAX application using the Microsoft AJAX Library.

- Chapter 4, "The AJAX Runtime with the Microsoft AJAX Library," introduces the Microsoft AJAX Library and focuses on the core runtime controls and deployment.

- Chapter 5, "The Microsoft AJAX Library," looks at the Microsoft AJAX Library in-depth and focuses on the core runtime, including core namespaces, base type extensions, and the JavaScript type system.

- Chapter 6, "AJAX Application Services with *Sys.Services*," covers AJAX-enabled application services for authentication, profile, and authorization using the ASP.NET AJAX framework.

Part III, "Applied AJAX." This section focuses on implementing object-oriented JavaScript control libraries and applications with the Microsoft AJAX Library while utilizing service-oriented Web service frameworks.

- Chapter 7, "Building an AJAX Class Library with Components," explains the JavaScript *Component* model for object-oriented development using the Microsoft AJAX Library.

- Chapter 8, "Building AJAX Controls," explains the JavaScript *Behavior* and *Control* model for object-oriented development using the Microsoft AJAX Library.

- Chapter 9, "AJAX and XSLT," explains basic XSLT and how to use XSLT for client-side rendering in service-oriented AJAX applications.

- Chapter 10, "AJAX and Browser History," describes the history management capabilities of the client-side AJAX framework utilizing the Microsoft AJAX Library.

- Chapter 11, "Extending SharePoint with Service-Oriented AJAX," covers how to deploy Web services to Windows SharePoint Services 3.0 and Microsoft Office SharePoint Server 2007, and how to deploy service-oriented AJAX applications within the Web Part framework.

The book also includes an appendix, "WCF Support in SharePoint," an online-only document available at *http://www.microsoft.com/mspress/companion/9780735625914*.

What Won't Be Covered

This book is written to explain the service-oriented AJAX architecture pattern—and is not a comprehensive reference to the complete Microsoft AJAX Library, ASP.NET, and WCF. I'll explain enough of these technologies to get you started with the pattern and make the book a readable reference. You might need to refer to MSDN documentation and use your favorite Web search engine to supplement these concepts with comprehensive reference material.

Because I'm taking an AJAX-purist approach with the service-oriented AJAX architecture pattern, I won't include any documentation on the Update Panel. The Update Panel is a pseudo-AJAX approach that provides only some of the benefits of AJAX, but it's primarily used to extend legacy code with AJAX-like behavior. It doesn't fit the architectural pattern of a service-oriented framework, and it's not something I recommend for new development. There are plenty of excellent references on the Update Panel—this book isn't one of those.

I also don't cover accessibility in this book. This isn't because it's not important—it's very important. Frankly, there wasn't enough time, and I'm not an expert at this. Instead, I'll leave it to you to use the service-oriented AJAX pattern to implement accessible solutions. Because the architectural pattern implements services to provide data streams, it should be simple enough to implement alternate user interfaces that are accessible to screen readers and alternate input devices, but I will leave that to accessibility experts to document.

Next, I don't provide a large number of usability tips in this book, even though it's an important subject. I'll leave it to you to take the service-oriented AJAX architectural pattern to implement usable applications. When users do something, it's important to let them know that the system is processing their actions. If you're loading data that may take a while, be sure to let users know that their data is loading and give them an opportunity to cancel long-running tasks.

Finally, I'm not going to cover any preview technology or betas in this book. There is a lot to anticipate, including the next version of ASP.NET AJAX (available through technology previews at *www.codeplex.com/aspnet*) and browser advancements, including Internet Explorer 8. Also, cross-site XML HTTP requests will be available in future browsers that will allow Web service calls to remote Web applications, whereas the pattern in this book makes Web service calls to the same Web application that hosts the JavaScript runtime and Web page.

The Author's Blog

My blog is at *http://daniellarson.spaces.live.com,* where I frequently write about AJAX, SharePoint, speaking engagements, fatherhood, and life as a software developer. Keep up and keep in touch through my blog!

Companion Content

This book features a companion Web site that makes available to you all the code used in the book. This code is organized by chapter, and you can download it from the companion site at this address: *http://www.microsoft.com/mspress/companion/9780735625914.*

Hardware and Software Requirements

You'll need the following hardware and software to work with the companion content included with this book:

- Microsoft Windows Vista Home Premium Edition, Windows Vista Business Edition, Windows Vista Ultimate Edition, Windows XP Professional, Windows 2003 Server Standard, Windows 2003 Server Enterprise, Windows 2008 Server Standard, or Windows 2008 Server Enterprise.

- Microsoft Visual Studio 2008 Standard Edition with Service Pack 1, Visual Studio 2008 Enterprise Edition with Service Pack 1, or Microsoft Visual C# 2008 Express Edition and Microsoft Visual Web Developer 2008 Express Edition with Service Pack 1.

- Microsoft .NET 3.5, Service Pack 1, available at *http://msdn.microsoft.com/vstudio/ cc533448.aspx.*

- Microsoft SQL Server 2005, Service Pack 2; Microsoft SQL Server 2005 Express Edition, Service Pack 2; Microsoft SQL Server 2008 Express Edition; or Microsoft SQL Server 2008.

- 1.6 GHz Pentium III+ processor, or faster.

- 1 GB of available, physical RAM.

Additionally, Chapter 11, "Extending SharePoint with Service-Oriented AJAX," requires Windows SharePoint Services 3.0 running on Microsoft Windows Server 2008 or Microsoft Windows Server 2003.

This book was written using Windows Server 2008.

Find Additional Content Online

As new or updated material becomes available that complements your book, it will be posted online on the Microsoft Press Online Developer Tools Web site. The type of material you might find includes updates to book content, articles, links to companion content, errata, sample chapters, and more. This Web content is available at *www.microsoft.com/learning/ books/online/developer*, and is updated periodically.

Support for This Book

Every effort has been made to ensure the accuracy of this book and the contents of the companion CD. As corrections or changes are collected, they will be added to a Microsoft Knowledge Base article.

Microsoft Press provides support for books and companion CDs at the following Web site:

http://www.microsoft.com/learning/support/books/.

Questions and Comments

If you have comments, questions, or ideas regarding the book or the companion CD, or questions that are not answered by visiting the sites above, please send them to Microsoft Press via e-mail to

mspinput@microsoft.com.

Or via postal mail to

Microsoft Press
Attn: *Developing Service-Oriented AJAX Applications on the Microsoft Platform* Editor
One Microsoft Way
Redmond, WA 98052-6399.

Please note that Microsoft software product support is not offered through the above addresses.

Part I
AJAX and WCF

Chapter 1
Service-Oriented AJAX Fundamentals

After completing this chapter, you will

- Understand the architectural principles of service-based AJAX development.

- Understand the role of the ScriptManager control and the Microsoft AJAX Library in the client-side JavaScript runtime.

- Be able to use basic techniques for AJAX programming with ASP.NET AJAX 3.5.

- Be able to implement simple services for AJAX using Windows Communication Foundation (WCF).

- Be able to call simple Web services from an AJAX application.

Service-Based AJAX: Architecture Overview

Programming a service-based AJAX application requires a new approach to Web development and a fundamental change in how you conceive and build applications. In a traditional ASP.NET application, you create page-based Web Forms applications. I'll call this "classic ASP.NET." The classic ASP.NET Web Forms architecture is monolithic: in classic ASP.NET, you create functionality for a form-based user interface. With service-oriented AJAX applications, your functionality is no longer tied to a page or Web form. It is instead based on Web services that can be called from any page or application. Even the JavaScript components that form the AJAX application aren't tied to a page; they exist as components that can be used in many pages and applications and loaded as they are needed.

 Note A service-based AJAX application is implemented with JavaScript components programmed against Web services. Service-based AJAX development applies the principles of service orientation to Web application development.

While you have many architecture choices for AJAX applications, the service-based architectural style fits well and offers the greatest amount of flexibility, reusability, and extensibility. With advances in Web service technologies through Windows Communication Foundation (WCF) and JavaScript support for network services in the ASP.NET AJAX Extensions, Microsoft has created a rich platform for developing not just a service-oriented architecture but also service-based AJAX applications.

With a service-based application, you have a clean separation of the API layer and the user interface. To create this separation using the Microsoft .NET 3.5 Framework, you first write an API by using WCF Web service technologies, and then you write the AJAX user interface with browser-based client technologies. The client application is built on the ASP.NET AJAX Extensions by using JavaScript and dynamic HTML. The service-based AJAX application is a client-side runtime that renders the user interface and calls back-end services, with a reusable, tested, and secure service-oriented back end exposed through WCF endpoints. This architecture is a good fit with Microsoft servers such as Microsoft Office SharePoint Server and third-party enterprise servers such as NewsGator Enterprise Server. Seldom do applications in the enterprise run as isolated applications; because the AJAX architecture is service based, it is also an ideal choice for integration with third-party applications.

Three goals of service-based AJAX are to decouple the user interface from the back end, to create reusable services, and to create reusable AJAX components. Because of this decoupling, the application can evolve as a user interacts with it. Additional AJAX components can be loaded as they are needed, and views can navigate through data sets as the user browses data. What used to happen in a classic ASP.NET application that spanned multiple pages can happen in one client runtime that is dynamically loaded and destroyed as necessary during the page execution. And because all the components are programmed against Web services, you have a lot of opportunities for reuse. This is a great shift from traditional server-side ASP.NET development. Unlike the monolithic page-based programming model, service-based AJAX development is divided into server-based API programming and client-based component development that consumes the service-oriented API. Figure 1-1 illustrates this architecture and demonstrates the service-based AJAX architecture pattern.

With this architecture, it is easy to swap out the AJAX interface or add additional client applications—including Microsoft Silverlight, Adobe Flash, and Microsoft Windows Presentation Foundation applications or even Macintosh clients—all connected through Web services. It is also simple to use both services and client components in multiple contexts throughout your application. To show you how the basic architecture fits together, I'll first describe the ASP.NET AJAX client runtime. I'll then illustrate a service-based back-end system using Web services in WCF.

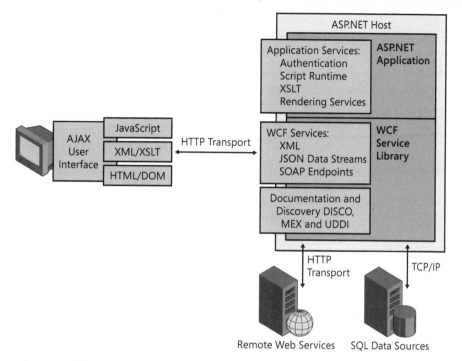

FIGURE 1-1. The service-based AJAX architecture pattern, with JavaScript clients talking to WCF service endpoints.

The Client-Side Runtime

A fundamental principle of AJAX is to perform as much processing as possible on the client. This includes rendering, data retrieval, and loading multiple applications throughout the life cycle of the page. Where the life cycle of classic ASP.NET pages could be very short, the page life cycle can be very long with an AJAX application. Your users might not reload the page all day because the data can be constantly refreshed without reloading the page.

> **More Information** ASP.NET AJAX 3.5 builds on the JavaScript framework included with ASP.NET 2.0 AJAX Extensions but includes support for browser history (the Back button) through the *Sys.Application* object and support for dynamic data services with the ADO.NET Entity Framework. It is also integrated with Microsoft Silverlight controls, which can be used to implement the AJAX user interface.

The ASP.NET AJAX client runtime is based on the Microsoft AJAX script library, which is defined in MicrosoftAjax.js. Additional components and special-purpose libraries designed for using the ADO.NET Entity Framework and the Silverlight browser runtime are defined in MicrosoftAjaxDataService.js, SilverlightControl.js, SilverlightMedia.js, and

SilverlightPlugin.js. You can view the script library for reference from the installation directory at %ProgramFiles%\Microsoft ASP.NET 3.5 Extensions\MicrosoftAjaxLibrary. These scripts are compiled into the *System.Web.Extensions* assembly and are included through the ScriptManager control. Each script has an associated *.debug* script that is used when debugging compilation is set in web.config. The debug scripts are much more readable than the release scripts and provide support for JavaScript IntelliSense through Microsoft Visual Studio 2008.

More Information Microsoft's ASP.NET AJAX client-side library is separate from ASP.NET and may be manually added to HTML pages, but in that case you don't get all the benefits of simple configuration and deployment. For more information about deploying ASP.NET AJAX in non-Windows environments, see *http://ajax.asp.net/docs*.

To understand the client runtime with ASP.NET AJAX, we'll first look at script inclusion through the ScriptManager control and then cover basic application management through the JavaScript *Sys.Application* object. Finally, we'll look at client-side rendering and asynchronous data operations.

The ASP.NET AJAX ScriptManager Control

The ScriptManager control (*System.Web.UI.ScriptManager*) is used by ASP.NET AJAX to render script references during initial page rendering. This control is one of the few ASP.NET server controls that you use in a client-centric Web application. When the ScriptManager control is placed on the page, it includes references for the Microsoft AJAX script library. You also use the control to include script references for your own script libraries, including JavaScript proxies for Web services and XML endpoints that enable integration between JavaScript components and back-end services.

Tip The ScriptManager control also references the more verbose and readable debug JavaScript files while the application is running in debug mode, which improves your debugging experience. The debug scripts are stricter than the release scripts because you might want to handle exceptions more liberally while in release mode but catch all errors while testing in debug mode.

Page Life Cycle and *Sys.Application*

The client-side page life cycle is important to know when building ASP.NET AJAX client applications, much as the server-side life cycle was important to know in classic ASP.NET when building server controls. Specifically, you should care most about the life cycle of the ASP.NET AJAX object *Sys.Application*, which is responsible for the client-side AJAX application runtime. Its methods and events are analogous to the server-side *Page* and *Control* life cycle in classic ASP.NET. Because you must load the client-side runtime in the form of script libraries (the ASP.NET AJAX library plus any custom libraries implemented in your code), you need to ensure that these libraries are loaded before calling any dependent scripts. You don't want to call any client-side functions that aren't yet loaded within your client-side page load method. To account for this, the *Sys.Application* object is created when the client page loads, and it manages the application context as the AJAX library loads and fires events during its life cycle. You will often add handlers to these events to initialize your components.

The three main application events to handle are *init, load,* and *navigate.* You can also handle the *unload* and *disposing* events, although this is less common. To initialize your page with default content, use the *init* event. The *init* event is raised after all scripts have been loaded and is used to enable default object creation. The *load* event is raised after the *init* event has been handled and the objects in the application have been created and initialized. Ideally, you would initialize your components in *init* and process initial data loading tasks in the *load* handler. The *navigate* event is new in the 3.5 extensions and is used in conjunction with history points, which we'll talk about later in the book. During the life cycle of the client runtime, you use the *navigate* event and *Sys.Application* to manage navigational history as the client loads new application contexts and data streams. Table 1-1 lists the events raised by *Sys.Application* and describes when and why you should handle these events.

TABLE 1-1 *Sys.Application* Life Cycle Events

Event	Description
init	Raised after all initial scripts have been loaded but before custom components and objects have been created. Use the *init* event to create your custom components.
load	Raised after all the objects in the application have been created and initialized using the *init* event. Use the *load* event after creating your components to handle initial data retrieval and other client-side page loading tasks.
unload	Raised when the user navigates off the page, reloads the page, or closes the browser. This event is raised just before disposing of the components in the client application.
disposing	Raised as the application disposes of all resources, just before the end of the browser application instance.
navigate	Raised when the user navigates using the back or forward buttons of the Web browser. Handle this event to implement support of backward and forward navigation in your AJAX application.

To add a handler to *Sys.Application* events, use the *add_* function that corresponds with the event. For example, to add a custom function named *onAjaxInit* to the application's *init* event, use the following command in your script:

```
Sys.Application.add_init(onAjaxInit);
```

Likewise, the *add_load* and *add_disposing* methods can be used to handle those events:

```
Sys.Application.add_load(onAjaxLoad);
Sys.Application.add_disposing(onAjaxDisposing);
```

A complete example of a Hello World Web page using the *Sys.Application* object is shown in Listing 1-1.

Note In the following examples, I sometimes use inline script in the page to make the sample code readable. For production code I always use separate script files to implement the client runtime. These files are reusable, organized per component, cached by the browser, and loaded as needed during the client lifetime.

Tip Code for this book is available online at *http://www.microsoft.com/mspress/companion/ 9780735625914*. The code for this chapter is in the file Chapter 1.zip. Where appropriate, I'll list the file name in the listing heading so that you can locate the sample in the Visual Studio solution. The solutions require Visual Studio 2008 (Express, Professional, or Standard), SQL Server 2005 Express or SQL Server 2008 Express, and the Microsoft .NET Framework 3.5 Service Pack 1.

LISTING 1-1. The basic page life cycle with ASP.NET AJAX (*Web/HelloWorld.aspx*).

```
<%@ Page Language="C#" AutoEventWireup="true" %>
<html xmlns="http://www.w3.org/1999/xhtml">
<head runat="server">
    <title>ASP.NET AJAX: Fundamentals</title>
</head>
<body>

    <form id="form1" runat="server">
    <asp:ScriptManager ID="AspxScriptManager" runat="server"/>
    <div id="MainContent">
        Loading...
    </div>
    </form>

    <script language="javascript" type="text/javascript">
        function onAjaxLoad(){
            //  $get(id) is the ASP.NET AJAX equivalent of
            //  document.getElementbyID(id);
            $get('MainContent').innerHTML = 'Hello World';
        }
        function onAjaxInit(){
            $get('MainContent').innerHTML = 'Get ready, here I come!';
        }
        function onAjaxDisposing(){
            alert('Goodbye cruel world!');
        }

        Sys.Application.add_init(onAjaxInit);
        Sys.Application.add_load(onAjaxLoad);
        Sys.Application.add_disposing(onAjaxDisposing);
    </script>
</body>
</html>
```

Because the *Sys.Application* life cycle is event-based, multiple handlers can be added to each event. By using event handlers for component creation and initialization, you can build multiple components and deploy them independently without tying your component to a single page or a single page's *Load* method. For example, you might define a group chat component in the JavaScript library *chat.js* and a stock ticker component in the JavaScript library *stockticker.js*. Because the application model accepts multiple event handlers for *init* and *load*, you can add handlers to the *init* and *load* events from both script libraries. As long as components and script libraries use event handlers for initialization, they can be loosely tied to the page. However, a *pageLoad* method can be used to handle loading a page for page-based scripts and is called after the *Sys.Application init* and *load* event handlers are processed.

> **Tip** The AJAX Web Form template for Visual Studio 2008 uses the *pageLoad* method for initialization, which is not a best practice. Avoid using *pageLoad*. Add event handlers to *init* and *load* for more robust, maintainable code.

Web Requests with *Sys.Net.WebRequest*

One of the main components of the AJAX architecture pattern is client-side data loading with JavaScript Web requests. Handling your own Web requests can be complex—you have to check the browser's implementation of the *XMLHttpRequest* object, which might be implemented as a native object or a version of Microsoft's ActiveX object using MSXML, and you have to handle multiple ready-state changes until the request is complete. It can be quite complex, and the *XMLHttpRequest* object is not implemented consistently across various browsers. Thankfully, the Microsoft AJAX Library includes the *Sys.Net.WebRequest* object to perform this task. This JavaScript class is the main component you use for network operations. In its implementation, *Sys.Net.WebRequest* wraps the *XMLHttpRequest* object in a cross-browser fashion, but we care only that it can make Web requests for us. That is the beauty of the ASP.NET AJAX library—the gory implementation details are hidden, and you don't need to worry about browser compatibility. *Sys.Net.WebRequest's* interface is similar to the *System.Net.WebRequest* class in the .NET Framework. With this class you don't need to handle the implementation details of the AJAX call, you just make a call to a URL and pass in a response handler.

All network calls (Web service methods or simple HTTP requests) made with JavaScript are asynchronous. This means that you have to implement a callback handler whenever you make a Web request or call a Web service. Any time you make an AJAX Web request—either a GET request through *Sys.Net.WebRequest* or a Web service call using WCF proxies—you need to handle the response with an asynchronous callback.

To perform a Web request using *Sys.Net.WebRequest*, create a new *WebRequest* object, set the URL by using the method *set_url*, add a completed event handler callback method by using *add_completed*, and call the *invoke* method. You can also pass in an arbitrary user context object that is passed to the callback method. The user context object can be any object, but typically you will use the user context object to reference a DOM object or include instructions for processing the callback. You can also specify the type of request by using the *set_httpVerb* method of *Sys.Net.WebRequest*, usually the verb "GET" or "POST", and a request body by using the *set_body* method for posting data to the server. The following example creates a simple GET Web request, passing in the *ajaxDataCallback* event handler (an arbitrarily-named function) as the callback method and setting a user context object through the *WebRequest*'s *set_userContext* method. If you do not specify the verb, the "GET" verb is used as the default.

```
var req = new Sys.Net.WebRequest();
req.set_url('Example.xml');
req.set_httpVerb('GET');
var context = { targetElementID : 'MainContent', exampleData : 'Hello, world!'};
req.set_userContext(context);
req.add_completed(ajaxDataCallback);
req.invoke();
```

To process the response, the callback method accepts the parameters *webRequestExecutor* and *userContext* as in the following example. Notice that the user context object is the same object that was passed into the request and is not changed during execution.

```
function ajaxDataCallback(webRequestExecutor,userContext){
    alert(userContext.exampleData);
}
```

The *webRequestExecutor* parameter is an object of the JavaScript type *Sys.Net.WebRequestExecutor* and contains the server response, including HTTP headers, HTTP status information, and the body of the response. For clarity, I recommend using the term *response* rather than *webRequestExecutor*, which will make your code easier to understand. You can also get information about the request by retrieving the request object with the *get_webRequest* method. In the callback, you can obtain the XML contents of an XML document through the *get_xml* method, or the text contents of the response through the *get_responseData* method. If the response type is XML, you get an XML DOM object from *get_xml*; otherwise *get_xml* returns *null*. If the response contains a JSON-formatted string, you can use the *get_object* method, but *get_object* will throw an exception if the data is not a JSON-formatted string. Listing 1-2 contains a complete code sample for making a simple Web request using the *Sys.Net.WebRequest* object and an asynchronous callback handler.

LISTING 1-2. A simple Web request using *System.Net.WebRequest* (Web/SimpleWebRequest.aspx).

```
<%@ Page Language="C#" AutoEventWireup="true"  %>
<html xmlns="http://www.w3.org/1999/xhtml">
<head>
    <title>ASP.NET AJAX: Fundamentals: Simple Web Request</title>
</head>
```

```
<body>
  <form id="form1" runat="server">
    <asp:ScriptManager ID="AspxScriptManager" runat="server"/>
  </form>
  <script language="javascript" type="text/javascript">
        function OnAjaxLoad(){
            var req = new Sys.Net.WebRequest();
            req.set_url('Example.xml');

            // userContext is an arbitrary object passed to the callback.
            var context = new Object();
            req.set_userContext(context);

            req.add_completed(ajaxDataCallback);
            req.invoke();
        }

        function ajaxDataCallback(response, userContext){
            // Include "debugger" to break into Visual Studio or Firebug:
            debugger;

            // For an XML response, use get_xml()
            var xml = response.get_xml();
            alert(xml);

            // For a text response, use get_responseData()
            var text = response.get_responseData();
            alert(text);

            // If the response is a JSON serialized object, use get_object:
            try{
                // This will work only with a JSON response, not XML:
                var responseObject = response.get_object();
                alert(responseObject);
            }catch(e){ /* This error is expected for non-JSON responses */ }

            // All requests include a status code and description:
            var statusCode = response.get_statusCode();
            var status = response.get_statusText();
            alert(statusCode + ':' + status);
        }

        Sys.Application.add_load(OnAjaxLoad);
  </script>
</body>
</html>
```

Client-Side Rendering

Because AJAX moves rendering logic to the client, you can load data when you need it,
reload portions of your interface when required, and maintain a responsive interface as the

user interacts with the page. There are many different ways to render content on the client: you can write HTML through JavaScript, you can use JavaScript templates, or you can use Extensible Stylesheet Language Transformations (XSLT). I'll use XSLT throughout this book in most client-side controls because it is often the simplest, most flexible rendering technique and also scales well. Alternatively, you can construct your own DOM elements or ASP.NET AJAX client controls through script or even use a combination of all of these techniques.

> **Note** DOM, or Document Object Model, is the JavaScript model that enables working with an HTML document. A DOM element is any HTML element in the browser's document and can be accessed through the document JavaScript object.

Throughout this book, you'll learn how to create data-driven DOM controls by using various rendering methods, but we'll look at some simple examples here to get you started. Because of the flexibility of transforming standard XML messages with XSLT, this is a favorite technique among AJAX developers. XSLT can be loaded when needed using the ASP.NET AJAX JavaScript class *Sys.Net.WebRequest*, or it can be stored in a JavaScript variable in simple cases. Because XSLT support isn't included in the ASP.NET AJAX library, you have to include your own transformation method. A simple method is shown in Listing 1-3, which takes a DOM element and applies a transform to the XML.

LISTING 1-3. A simple XSLT function for JavaScript.

```
XmlTransform = function (xml, xsl, control){
    if (!window.XSLTProcessor){ // ie
      var content = xml.transformNode(xsl);
      control.innerHTML = content;
   }else{  // MOZZILA
      var processor = new XSLTProcessor();
      processor.importStylesheet(xsl);
      var content = processor.transformToFragment(xml, document);
      control.appendChild(content);
   }
 }
```

Under most circumstances when you use XML with XSLT transforms, you load the XSLT at the same time as you load the XML and you transform it when you have both the XML and XSLT ready, caching the XSLT to use again. You can also load XSLT as the user interacts with the page, which lets you bring in new data-bound AJAX controls. You'll see examples of wrapping this functionality into DOM-based ASP.NET AJAX controls in Chapter 8, "Building AJAX Controls," but for now I will simply extend the DOM element with *expando* properties. Expando properties are arbitrary JavaScript properties that are added to elements at run time through script. In this case, we'll store the XML and XSLT as properties of the element and perform the transformation when we have the data. Listing 1-4 demonstrates this simple technique by loading the data and the XSLT and performing a simple XSLT transform during the client-side page execution in response to a user action. You can do this many times throughout the life cycle of the page to render data as the user requests it or with a client-side timer function. For this simple example, I've used static XML files on the server.

LISTING 1-4. XSLT can be used to render data on the client (*Web/SimpleXmlTransform.aspx*).

```
<%@ Page Language="C#" AutoEventWireup="true"  %>
<html xmlns="http://www.w3.org/1999/xhtml">
<head id="Head1" runat="server">
    <title>ASP.NET AJAX: Fundamentals: Simple XML Transform</title>
</head>
<body>
    <form id="form1" runat="server">
    <asp:ScriptManager ID="AspxScriptManager" runat="server"/>
    <div id="MainContent">
       <a href=javascript:loadXml();>
          Click to load data.
      </a>
    </div>
    </form>
    <script language="javascript" type="text/javascript">
        function loadXml(){
            var context = $get('MainContent');
            var xmlReq = new Sys.Net.WebRequest();
            xmlReq.set_url('SampleRSS.xml');
            xmlReq.add_completed(xmlCallback);
            xmlReq.set_userContext(context);
            xmlReq.invoke();

            var xsltReq = new Sys.Net.WebRequest();
            xsltReq.set_url('SampleRSS.xslt');
            xsltReq.add_completed(xsltCallback);
            xsltReq.set_userContext(context);
            xsltReq.invoke();
        }

        xmlCallback = function(executor, context, args1, args2, args3){
            var control = executor.get_webRequest().get_userContext();
            var xml = executor.get_xml();
            // control.xml is an expando property, storing the xml for latter use
            control.xml = xml;
            if (control.xslt != null)
                XmlTransform(control.xml, control.xslt, control);
        }

        xsltCallback = function(executor, context, args1, args2, args3){
            var control = executor.get_webRequest().get_userContext();
            var xslt = executor.get_xml();
            // control.xslt is an expando property, storing the xslt for latter use
            control.xslt = xslt;
            if (control.xml != null)
                XmlTransform(control.xml, control.xslt, control);
        }
```

```
        XmlTransform = function (xml, xsl, control){
            for(var i=0; i< control.childNodes.length; i++){
                control.removeChild(control.childNodes[i]);
            }control.innerHTML = '';
            if (!window.XSLTProcessor){ // ie
             var content = xml.transformNode(xsl);
             control.innerHTML = content;
           }else{  // MOZZILA
             var processor = new XSLTProcessor();
             processor.importStylesheet(xsl);
             var content = processor.transformToFragment(xml, document);
             control.appendChild(content);
           }
         }
      }
   </script>
  </body>
  </html>
```

With the Web request in Listing 1-4, a simple XSLT file is used to render the page elements. Listing 1-5 displays a simple XSLT file for transforming an RSS formatted XML document. You'll learn more about RSS and other syndication formats in Chapter 3, "The AJAX
Application Server: Windows Communication Foundation's Web Programming Model," as
syndicated formats are an ideal data scheme for loosely coupled systems.

LISTING 1-5. A simple XSLT file for rendering RSS items (*Web/sampleRSS.xslt*).

```
<xsl:stylesheet
    xmlns:xsl="http://www.w3.org/1999/XSL/Transform"
    version="1.0">
 <xsl:strip-space elements="true"/>
 <xsl:output omit-xml-declaration="yes" method="html" />
 <xsl:template match="/rss/channel">
   <h3>
     <xsl:value-of select="title" disable-output-escaping="yes" />
   </h3>
   <xsl:apply-templates select="item" />
 </xsl:template>
 <xsl:template match="item">
   <div>
     <xsl:value-of select="description" disable-output-escaping="yes"  />
   </div>
 </xsl:template>
</xsl:stylesheet>
```

In the XSLT in Listing 1-5, the rendering logic creates an *H3* element for the XPath item */rss/
channel* and then creates a *DIV* element for each item in the channel. Listing 1-6 defines a
simplified RSS document that could be used as the data source for the AJAX component. In
Chapter 3 we'll look at built-in support for RSS generation in the .NET 3.5 Framework.

LISTING 1-6. A simplified RSS document. RSS is an ideal format for loosely coupled systems.

```
<rss version="2.0">
  <channel>
    <title>Over-simplified RSS channel</title>
    <item>
      <title>An example RSS item</title>
      <description>
        RSS is an ideal format for loosely coupled systems.
      </description>
    </item>
  </channel>
</rss>
```

Note As an alternative to XSLT, you might want to explore JavaScript template frameworks, such as the *prototype* JavaScript library (*http://www.prototypejs.org/api/template*). JavaScript templates will be an integrated part of ASP.NET AJAX in future releases and can be downloaded from the ASP.NET CodePlex site (*http://codeplex.com/aspnet*).

Introducing Windows Communications Foundation

At the core of the service-based AJAX application architecture is the data services layer. This layer exposes the back-end system through Web services and XML endpoints. To build data services for AJAX with ASP.NET 2.0, I would use a combination of SOAP-based ASMX Web services and HTTP handlers for simple XML data streams. With the 3.5 release of the .NET Framework, you can use Windows Communication Foundation, or WCF, to provide data services that are built from the ground up with service orientation in mind. Service orientation describes the architectural commitment to provide message-based applications that are loosely coupled, well defined, and abstracted from implementation details. A service-based AJAX application is built to reflect many of the principles of service-orientation.

WCF services in the .NET 3.5 Framework were built with AJAX applications in mind and include a flexible communications architecture that targets the ASP.NET AJAX library. WCF supports simple XML endpoints (also known as *POX*, or Plain Old XML), SOAP messages, and data serialization with JSON, the JavaScript Object Notation syntax. Because WCF is integrated with the ASP.NET AJAX Extensions through behaviors, ASP.NET AJAX can generate JavaScript proxies for WCF Web services that make consuming the services from AJAX applications easy and maintainable.

More Information For in-depth coverage of WCF as a service-oriented architecture platform, I recommend the book *Pro WCF: Practical Microsoft SOA Implementation* (APress, 2007).

WCF is a technology first introduced with the .NET 3.0 Framework. It is simpler to implement than classic ASP.NET ASMX Web services and includes a more flexible programming model. I'll discuss WCF in detail in Chapter 2, "The AJAX Application Server: Service Orientation and the Windows Communication Foundation," and Chapter 3, but for now let's look at some simple examples to get started. You'll see that programming WCF is straightforward and perhaps the easiest way yet for Microsoft developers to expose back-end data as XML.

> **Tip** While this book uses WCF to implement the services layer, you can also use the same tech-
> niques to program against ASP.NET 2.0 Web Services by applying the *ScriptService* attribute to
> each Web service. For POX endpoints with ASP.NET 2.0, you can use HTTP handlers implemented
> with the *IHttpHandler* interface.

To get started, first create a new WCF Service Library, or simply a class library with references to *System.ServiceModel* and *System.ServiceModel.Web*. The service library is basically a class library, but it also lets you test your WCF endpoints directly, without a Web application. I generally prefer to create a class library containing WCF service classes and interfaces and reference that class library from the ASP.NET Web application project.

Because services are defined outside ASP.NET in service libraries, you can host these services in multiple ASP.NET Web applications or WCF hosting environments. To add a service library to an ASP.NET Web application, simply add a reference to the WCF class library in the Web project. In the next section, we'll look at defining the service endpoints and registering them with ASP.NET through the web.config file.

XML Endpoints with WCF

The simplest Web service endpoint is known as Plain Old XML (POX), which is a Web service without the SOAP message wrapper. While SOAP-based Web services offer rich semantics for remote procedure calls and are extensible through the WS-* specifications, SOAP is not always the best solution for data retrieval for Web applications. In fact, Web services called from JavaScript proxies using ASP.NET AJAX do not use SOAP at all. Instead they use a simple POST implementation. POX endpoints offer several architectural advantages and can make use of Web caching technologies implemented by proxies and modern Web browsers. In Chapter 3, you'll see detailed examples of the REST (Representational State Transfer) architectural pattern that builds on POX endpoints, but first let's look at using basic WCF endpoints to build POX services for AJAX applications.

To build a simple XML endpoint with WCF, create a new class in the WCF Service Library project. In this example, I created a class named *SimpleXmlService* with a single *HelloWorld* method that returns an XML element. WCF services are defined through attributes, much like the use of the *WebService* and *WebMethod* attributes to define Web services in classic ASP.NET. In WCF, you use the attribute *ServiceContract* to define a WCF service class and the attribute *OperationContract* to define any WCF service method. It is important to note that you must also include the *AspNetCompatibilityRequirements* attribute to allow the WCF service to run in ASP.NET.

In the service code shown in Listing 1-7, the *SimpleXmlService* class defines a method that returns an *XmlElement* and includes the *ServiceContract* and *AspNetCompatibilityRequirements* attributes on the class. The *HelloWorld* method has both an *OperationContract* attribute and a *WebGet* attribute. The *WebGet* attribute allows WCF to expose the method through an HTTP GET endpoint, meaning that you can simply access the XML through a URL.

LISTING 1-7. A simple XML WCF service (*Web/SimpleXmlService.cs*).

```
using System;
using System.ServiceModel;
using System.ServiceModel.Activation;
using System.ServiceModel.Web;
using System.Xml;

namespace WcfFundamentals
{
    [ServiceContract(Namespace="SimpleXmlService")]
    [AspNetCompatibilityRequirements(
        RequirementsMode = AspNetCompatibilityRequirementsMode.Allowed)]
    public class SimpleXmlService
    {
        [WebGet]
        [OperationContract]
        public XmlElement HelloWorld()
        {
            var doc = new XmlDocument
            {
                InnerXml = "<message>Hello XML World!</message>"
            };
            return doc.DocumentElement;
        }
    }
}
```

 Tip Throughout this book I'll use C# 3.0 syntax, compiled to run against the .NET 3.5 Framework. If this syntax is new to you, I recommend picking up Joe Mayo's book *C# 3.0 Unleashed: With the .NET Framework 3.5* (Sams Publishing, 2008).

Because I defined *SimpleXmlService* as an XML endpoint that is exposed through a URL, I can use the general purpose *Sys.Net.WebRequest* object to get the XML. I don't need to use a JavaScript Web service proxy to access the data. The Hello World Web request page in Listing 1-8 demonstrates a simple Web request to the XML endpoint and renders the response message on the page. In a real application, this request might be executed many times during the page's life cycle or in response to user actions. Because the application is service-based (however simple it may be), you can reuse the service in multiple applications.

LISTING 1-8. The Hello World Web request page demonstrates a simple AJAX network request (*Web/SimpleXmlWebRequest.aspx*).

```
<%@ Page Language="C#" AutoEventWireup="true" %>
<html xmlns="http://www.w3.org/1999/xhtml">
<head id="Head1" runat="server">
    <title>ASP.NET AJAX: Fundamentals: Simple XML Web Request</title>
</head>
<body>
    <form id="form1" runat="server">
    <asp:ScriptManager ID="AspxScriptManager" runat="server"/>
    <div id="MainContent">
        Loading...
    </div>
    </form>

    <script language="javascript" type="text/javascript">
        function OnAjaxLoad(){
            var req = new Sys.Net.WebRequest();
            req.set_url('SimpleXmlService.svc/helloworld');
            req.add_completed(ajaxDataCallback);
            req.invoke();
        }

        function ajaxDataCallback(response){
            var content = $get('MainContent');
            var xml = response.get_xml();
            if (xml == null)
                Sys.Debug.fail('Could not load the message!');

            var messageNodes = xml.getElementsByTagName('message');
            if (messageNodes.length == 1)
                if (messageNodes[0].textContent) // ff
                    content.innerHTML = messageNodes[0].textContent;
                else //ie
                    content.innerHTML = messageNodes[0].text;
        }

        Sys.Application.add_load(OnAjaxLoad);
    </script>
</body>
</html>
```

Now that you've seen simple XML endpoints, it's time to look at updating data in an AJAX application. Just as you use services for data retrieval, you can use services to update data. WCF makes exposing these methods to the AJAX client through JavaScript proxy classes quite easy. With WCF, JavaScript proxy classes are generated by the ASP.NET AJAX runtime through behaviors enabled in web.config.

Tip In the same way that you can build Web service proxies for C# class libraries in Visual Studio by adding a Web reference, you can use JavaScript proxy classes for JavaScript class libraries. The proxies allow you to call a native JavaScript method rather than worrying about the Web service message semantics and network operations. JavaScript proxy classes are generated dynamically by the ASP.NET AJAX framework by adding a service reference to the ScriptManager control.

Updating Data with WCF Services

While SOAP or POST based Web services aren't always the ideal mechanism for loading data, they are an ideal mechanism for method calls, especially complex data input or modification. And with WCF, you don't really need to make this distinction—the same WCF method can be exposed as a simple XML endpoint (POX) or a SOAP endpoint. The code in the service doesn't need to change. You also don't need to make any commitments to AJAX or any other client technology—your services layer will be completely separate from the AJAX interface. In fact, you can choose to expose your WCF application over alternate transports such as MSMQ, TCP/IP channels, or even SMTP.

Note A wiki is a notepad-like application for collaboration on the Web, designed for speed and ease of use. Throughout the book, we'll use wikis as examples of AJAX applications, and we'll be building a knowledge base application as a case study using wiki techniques. For more information on wikis, see *http://en.wikipedia.org/wiki/Wiki*.

For the first example, I'll create a simple Web service that remembers a message in application state. I'll start off by defining a data class named *WikiData*. This data class is the starting point for the WCF service—it defines the message returned by the service. To define the data structure, you use the *DataContract* and *DataMember* attributes. The *WikiData* class has a *DataContract* attribute to define the namespace of the elements, and *DataMember* attributes to define the XML-serialized elements. The *WikiData* class is defined in Listing 1-9. By defining this contract, you can program any client application against this data format.

LISTING 1-9. The *WikiData* data contract (*WcfFundamentals/WikiData.cs*).

```
using System.Runtime.Serialization;

namespace WcfFundamentals
{
    [DataContract(Name = "WikiData", Namespace = "ServiceOrientedAjax.Examples")]
    public class WikiData
    {
        [DataMember]        public string Title { get; set; }

        [DataMember]
        public string Body { get; set; }
    }
}
```

The *DataContract* defined in Listing 1-9 will output the following XML format:

```
<WikiData xmlns="ServiceOrientedAjax.Examples"
        xmlns:i="http://www.w3.org/2001/XMLSchema-instance">
    <Body>Hello WCF World!</Body>
    <Title>example</Title>
</WikiData>
```

After defining the data contract, the next task is to implement the service. You can create the
service using a Visual Studio template or by defining a class marked with the *ServiceContract*
attribute, which identifies a class as a WCF service implementation. Each method that it
exposes as a Web service endpoint must be marked with the *OperationContract* attribute.
The *OperationContract* attribute is similar to the *WebMethod* attribute used with ASP.NET
Web Services and defines a method that is exposed through WCF endpoints.

Because I defined the data class *WikiData* with the *DataContract* attribute, I can use *WikiData* as
the return type of the Get request and also as the input parameter on the Set operation. Listing
1-10 defines a simple WCF service that uses the *WikiData* data contract defined in Listing 1-9.

LISTING 1-10. A simple wiki WCF class using the *WikiData* data contract (*WcfFundamentals/SimpleWikiService.cs*).

```csharp
using System;
using System.ServiceModel;
using System.ServiceModel.Activation;
using System.ServiceModel.Web;
using System.Web;
using System.Runtime.Serialization;

namespace WcfFundamentals
{
    [ServiceContract(Namespace = "ServiceOrientedAjax.Examples")]
    [AspNetCompatibilityRequirements(RequirementsMode =
        AspNetCompatibilityRequirementsMode.Allowed)]
    public class SimpleWikiService
    {
        [OperationContract]
        public void SetWiki(WikiData wiki)
        {
            HttpContext.Current.Application[wiki.Title] = wiki.Body;
        }

        [OperationContract][WebGet]
        public WikiData GetWiki(string title)
        {
            WikiData wiki = new WikiData{
                Title = title,
                Body = (string)HttpContext.Current.Application[title]
                        ?? "Hello WCF World!"
            };
            return wiki;
        }
    }
}
```

After defining the WCF service, you need to define the endpoint in the ASP.NET application through a service (SVC) file and web.config. The service file is a simple text file that is used by ASP.NET to activate the WCF service endpoint. The service file should contain the following reference to the *SimpleWikiService* WCF endpoint:

```
<%@ ServiceHost Service="WcfFundamentals.SimpleWikiService" %>
```

After ensuring that the service endpoint is defined in an SVC file, you must also define its endpoint and behaviors in web.config. Behaviors can apply to multiple endpoints and can change how the client accesses the WCF endpoint. In this example, I defined both a POX endpoint and a JSON-enabled endpoint with *enableWebScript*. These additional behaviors are enabled through the *behaviorConfiguration* element.

To enable ASP.NET AJAX to build a JavaScript proxy class for the service, you can specify the *enableWebScript* behavior, which can be mapped to multiple WCF endpoints. The following example defines the *JsonBehavior* behavior configuration (the name "JsonBehavior" is arbitrary), which includes the *enableWebScript* behavior:

```
<behaviors>
  <endpointBehaviors>
    <behavior name="JsonBehavior">
        <enableWebScript />
    </behavior>
  </endpointBehaviors>
</behaviors>
```

The *enableWebScript* behavior also converts the default response from XML format to JSON format, using JavaScript object notation to define the data. This format can be easier to work with when manually processing the data and not using an XSLT transformation. Because WCF abstracts endpoint behavior from implementation, you can define both an XML endpoint and a JSON endpoint in web.config without any changes to the service. The endpoint is mapped to a URL and defines how the client accesses the service. It's important to realize that this mapping is performed through configuration and not during service development, as you'll see in the following example.

To define an additional endpoint that provides JSON data, you can use web.config to map an endpoint to a behavior configuration. For example, I mapped an additional endpoint to *SimpleWikiService.svc/json*, which will be a JSON-enabled endpoint with the same implementation as the *SimpleWikiService.svc* endpoint. To define the endpoint, create a *service* element with a child *endpoint* element. The *endpoint* element defines the address, behavior configuration, binding, and contract for the service. The *address* of the endpoint is relative to the .svc file that activates the WCF service, and *behaviorConfiguration* defines additional behaviors for the endpoint. The following example defines the service endpoints for *SimpleWikiService*, with an additional endpoint mapped to "/json" that uses the *JsonBehavior* configuration:

```
<services>
    <service name="SimpleWikiService">
```

```
        <endpoint address=""
            binding="webHttpBinding" contract="SimpleWikiService" />

        <endpoint address="json" behaviorConfiguration="JsonBehavior"
            binding="webHttpBinding" contract="SimpleWikiService" />
    </service>
</services>
```

The data contract specified in Listing 1-9 will output the following JSON data stream when accessed through an endpoint with the *enableClientScript* behavior:

```
{"d":{"__type":"WikiData:ServiceOrientedAjax.Examples",
    "Body":"Hello WCF World!","Title":"example"}}
```

This JSON-formatted data stream contains the same content as the XML output defined by the data contract. Because JSON streams are easier to work with in script if you're not applying an XSLT transformation, Microsoft chose this as the default behavior for script-enabled Web services.

Because we have the *enableWebScript* behavior defined in web.config for the /json endpoint, the ASP.NET AJAX runtime will generate a JavaScript proxy for the service. This proxy is all you need to call the WCF service and handle its response. To examine the JavaScript proxy manually, use the WCF endpoint and add the "/jsdebug" switch to the end of the URL, such as *http://localhost/ajaxfundamentals/simplewikiservice.svc/json/jsdebug*. The proxy will contain the correct JavaScript syntax details for calling the Web service through the ASP.NET AJAX JavaScript framework, including serialization objects for calling and retrieving the data. For now though, all you need to know is that the proxy generates static (not instance) JavaScript methods for each WCF operation. The public methods call instance methods of the proxy that you won't call directly. For each Web service operation, three parameters are added to the method parameters: *onSuccess*, *onFailed*, and *userContext*. Because all network calls are made asynchronously, you must pass in callback handlers for the response. The *userContext* object is passed unchanged to the callback and generally contains a pointer to the AJAX component that called the method, although you can pass any object as the user context.

Following is the main public proxy methods that are generated for our WCF endpoint, with the methods *GetWiki* and *SetWiki*. Although the actual proxy contains more code, the JavaScript functions that correspond to the public service methods are generally the only methods you will need to call.

```
GetWiki:function(title,succeededCallback, failedCallback, userContext) {
    return this._invoke(this._get_path(),'GetWiki',true,{title:title},
        succeededCallback,failedCallback,userContext); }}

SetWiki:function(wiki,succeededCallback, failedCallback, userContext) {
    return this._invoke(this._get_path(), 'SetWiki',false,{wiki:wiki},
        succeededCallback,failedCallback,userContext); }
```

To use this code in our AJAX application, you need to reference the JavaScript proxy classes generated by ASP.NET AJAX. To do this, you use the ScriptManager control, defining a reference to SimpleWikiService.svc in the *Services* node. To add a *ServiceReference*, add a *ServiceReference* node with the *Path* parameter to your WCF endpoint, as in the following example:

```
<asp:ScriptManager ID="AspxScriptManager" runat="server" >
    <Services>
        <asp:ServiceReference Path=" SimpleWikiService.svc/json" />
    </Services>
</asp:ScriptManager>
```

The full code for our simple WCF-based Web application is shown in Listing 1-11. Building on these simple principles, later in the book you will develop components that encapsulate client-side logic and enable deployment across multiple contexts throughout multiple applications.

LISTING 1-11. Using WCF operations for AJAX back-end services (*Web/SimpleWikiPage.aspx*).

```
<%@ Page Language="C#" AutoEventWireup="true"  %>
<html xmlns="http://www.w3.org/1999/xhtml">
<head id="Head1" runat="server">
    <title>ASP.NET AJAX: Fundamentals: Simple Wiki with WCF</title>
</head>
<body>
    <form id="form1" runat="server">
    <asp:ScriptManager ID="AspxScriptManager" runat="server" >
        <Services>
            <asp:ServiceReference Path="SimpleWikiService.svc/json" />
        </Services>
    </asp:ScriptManager>
    <div id="MainContent" onclick="editMessage">
        Loading...
    </div>
    <br />
    <span    style="border:solid 1px silver;"
             id="editButton"
             onclick="editMessage();" >
        Edit
    </span>

    <div id="EditorRegion" style="display:none;">
        <textarea id="TheEditor" rows="10" cols="80" ></textarea>
        <br />
        <span style="border:solid 1px silver;" onclick="save();" >
            Save
        </span>
    </div>

    </form>

    <script language="javascript" type="text/javascript">
```

```
        var wikiName = 'default';

        function OnAjaxLoad(){
            var userContext = new Object();
            ServiceOrientedAjax.Examples.SimpleWikiService.GetWiki(
                wikiName, getMessageSuccess, onMessageFailure, userContext);
        }

        function editMessage(){
            $get('EditorRegion').style.display='';
            $get('editButton').style.display='none';
            $get('MainContent').style.display='none';
            $get('TheEditor').value = $get('MainContent').innerHTML;
            $get('TheEditor').enabled= true;
        }

        function getMessageSuccess(wikiData, userContext){
            var EditorRegion = $get('EditorRegion');
            EditorRegion.style.display='none';
            var content = $get('MainContent');
            content.innerHTML = wikiData.Body;
            content.style.display='';
        }

        function save(){
            var msg = $get('TheEditor').value;
            var userContext = new Object();
            userContext.msg = msg;
            userContext.title = wikiName;
            var wiki = new Object();
            wiki.Title=wikiName;
            wiki.Body = msg;
            ServiceOrientedAjax.Examples.SimpleWikiService.SetWiki(
                wiki, onSaveSuccess, onMessageFailure, wiki);
            $get('TheEditor').enabled= false;
        }

        function onSaveSuccess(response, wiki){
            getMessageSuccess(wiki,null);
        }

        function onMessageFailure(ex, userContext){
            var content = $get('MainContent');
            content.innerHTML = ex;
        }

        Sys.Application.add_load(OnAjaxLoad);
    </script>
</body>
</html>
```

Listing 1-11 defines a simple wikilike application. To initialize the page, we use the *OnAjaxLoad* event handler method to load the data with the *GetWiki* JavaScript proxy method. When the user clicks the Edit button, we hide the display and show a data input form, allowing the user to edit the contents of the wiki item. When the user is finished editing, we save the content using the *save* method, which calls the *SetWiki* method. Because we have a JavaScript proxy to our WCF methods, we don't have to worry about the semantics of the call; we simply call our JavaScript methods. Because the network operations of the Web service proxy are asynchronous, we pass in the *onSaveSuccess* method as the callback handler.

With these simple examples, you've seen the fundamentals of AJAX applications using a service-based architecture and Microsoft's ASP.NET AJAX framework, utilizing WCF as the services layer and the Microsoft AJAX Library on the client. With these building blocks you can build very powerful and robust AJAX applications.

Summary

In this chapter, you learned about the basic architectural differences between traditional ASP.NET programming and client-side AJAX programming with ASP.NET AJAX against a service-based architecture. You learned the basic principles of service-based programming and how to create basic WCF endpoints for ASP.NET AJAX.

With these basic skills you should be able to write simple client-side AJAX—but we'll take this to the extreme throughout this book as we look at an AJAX-friendly service infrastructure based on service-oriented WCF applications and object-oriented AJAX components that use Microsoft's AJAX JavaScript library.

But first, a robust AJAX front-end application requires a robust back-end application. In the next two chapters, we'll look deeper into WCF fundamentals, service orientation, and the WCF Web programming model before moving on to client-side AJAX programming with the Microsoft AJAX Library.

Chapter 2
The AJAX Application Server: Service Orientation and the Windows Communication Foundation

After completing this chapter, you will

- Understand the principles of service orientation and how to incorporate service orientation in an application platform for AJAX components.

- Understand the fundamentals of Windows Communication Foundation (WCF) endpoints, bindings, and behaviors.

- Understand how to implement contract-based services with WCF.

- Understand how to deploy WCF services to an ASP.NET application.

In Chapter1, "Service-Oriented AJAX Fundamentals," you learned about foundational AJAX runtime components using JavaScript, ASP.NET AJAX, basic AJAX Web requests, and simple service endpoints in Windows Communication Foundation (WCF). You also learned about some of the benefits of service orientation and of separating an end-user application from back-end architecture. In this chapter we will look at service orientation and back-end architecture in more detail. You'll also learn how to implement an application as a service-oriented Web application. We'll use WCF services hosted in an ASP.NET application, and these services will be the core application platform for the AJAX application.

The Benefits of WCF as the AJAX Services Platform

WCF serves as the plumbing for AJAX-enabled Web services and provides a unified programming model for communication between servers and clients. Although WCF is a flexible runtime that can be hosted in many environments other than ASP.NET, including services hosted over TCP/IP or other LAN protocols, we'll look at WCF purely as a Web services platform. The examples I describe in this chapter and throughout the book run in Internet Information Services (IIS) under an ASP.NET hosting application.

By using a service-based architecture you gain tremendous potential for the reuse of an AJAX application, and you can free your application from the monolithic page-based development model that is typical of pre-AJAX Web applications. As a side benefit, an investment in the service platform architecture lets you use the same Web services for remote clients. Whether you decide to expose services to remote applications or use tightly coupled services as the basis for your AJAX application, the service-based AJAX architecture pattern enables reuse, rapid development, and the greatest flexibility for your AJAX application by separating it from the service platform. And because services are not tied to the end-user application, the service application tends to have a much longer lifetime as a product than the end-user application does. You can also add new services and platform enhancements without having to refactor the client application. You can upgrade the back-end platform with new data access technologies, such as enhancements to Language Integrated Query (LINQ) or Microsoft SQL Server, without affecting the service interfaces. Figure 2-1 highlights the role of WCF in the AJAX application architecture.

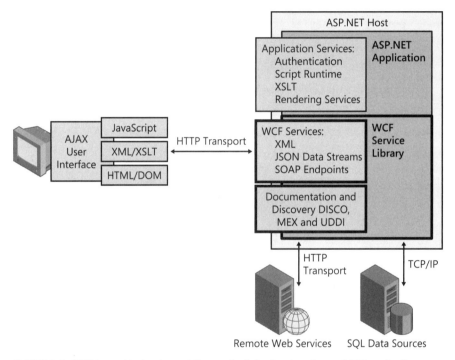

FIGURE 2-1. WCF is used to implement the service infrastructure for an AJAX application.

While I primarily discuss using WCF for service implementations, WCF is just one way to implement services. In place of WCF you could use ASMX Web services or ASP.NET with HTTP handlers to implement XML endpoints, as I'll discuss at the end of this chapter. There is no right or wrong way to implement the service layer, but we will mainly use the .NET 3.5 Framework implementation of WCF because of its rich support for service orientation and its ability to separate the Web programming model from the service implementation.

More Information This book is not meant to be a comprehensive reference about WCF. I cover enough about WCF to show how to implement the AJAX back end. For a comprehensive reference on WCF, I recommend Justin Smith's book *Inside Windows Communication Foundation* (Microsoft Press, 2007).

Service Orientation and Service-Based AJAX Applications

Service orientation is an architectural approach that defines an application solely by its service interfaces. This approach also describes an architectural commitment to provide message-based applications that are loosely coupled, well defined, and abstracted from implementation details. The example of a service-orientated application that I describe in this chapter is built to reflect the following tenets of service-oriented software:

- The boundaries between applications are explicit

- Services are developed and deployed autonomously

- Services expose well-defined messages

For an AJAX application, following these tenets means that the service won't be tightly joined to a JavaScript client or to the service's use in the local Web application. The services are available to any remote application as well as to the local AJAX application.

 More Information For in-depth information about service-oriented architecture (SOA) and service orientation, I recommend reading "The Four Tenets of Service Orientation," at *http://www.bpminstitute.org/articles/article/article/the-four-tenets-of-service-orientation.html*, and Wikipedia's SOA reference at *http://en.wikipedia.org/wiki/Service-orientation*.

Service orientation is the principle that enables a service-based AJAX application. It lets an AJAX developer deliver multiple components based on common services and data schemas. Service orientation and schema-based programming also simplify the development of controls and client-side rendering, enabling developers to create common controls and common rendering techniques for standardized data schemas. As an example, when you write XSLT for rendering logic, you base it on a schema and you can reuse the XSLT in multiple contexts.

Our *service-based* AJAX application will sit on top of a *service-oriented* application architecture. Because AJAX integration is loosely coupled through run-time behaviors, you don't need to write much AJAX support into the service code. The AJAX application is developed on top of the service interface, which has AJAX-enabling behaviors added to it through configuration. Following this strategy, you can add remote client applications to the same service and reuse service endpoints for multiple AJAX components. Ideally you won't have an AJAX-based service application but a service-based AJAX application instead.

 More Information For a guide comparing ASP.NET 2.0 ASMX Web services to WCF Web services, see the MSDN topic "Comparing ASP.NET Web Services to WCF Based on Development," at *http://msdn2.microsoft.com/en-us/library/aa738737.aspx*.

WCF Fundamentals

WCF lets developers build service-oriented applications on the Windows platform using a unified programming model. You can use the same service-oriented programming model with WCF to develop outward-facing Web service applications, intranet Web services, peer-to-peer intranet applications, or server-to-server distributed applications. The WCF program-ming model is flexible because it provides a layered approach to services, based on channels, bindings, contracts, endpoints, and behaviors. Through the layered approach, behaviors are added to an endpoint during configuration, and multiple endpoints with alternative behav-iors and bindings can be created in the hosting application. The constant is the programming model—regardless of the binding or behavior, the service programming model is unified. Figure 2-2 shows the layered approach to WCF programming.

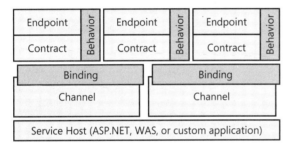

FIGURE 2-2. WCF uses a layered approach to service programming.

Service contracts are created by applying contract attributes to an interface. The inter-face is then implemented by a class that defines the implementation. There is nothing "special" about a service class, and it does not inherit a base class such as the ASMX Web service class—it is just a type that implements the service interface that is marked with WCF attributes.

Endpoints expose service contracts through a URI (Uniform Resource Identifier) such as *http://knowledgebase/dataservice.svc*, which in ASP.NET is based on an SVC file deployed to the Web application. Bindings are applied to the endpoint and specify which protocol to use, either a simple Web binding, a Web Service binding using SOAP, or a custom binding. The binding is used by the hosting application to create service channels with a bound protocol. In specifying the transport mechanism and protocol for communication, the binding separates the service from the transport technology. Within an ASP.NET Web application, the bindings you use most often include *wsHttpBinding*, which is an HTTP binding for SOAP Web services, and *webHttpBinding*, which is an HTTP binding for simple Web services without SOAP. An AJAX client most often uses *webHttpBinding*, and remote clients most often use *wsHttpBinding*. Silverlight 2.0 and other ASMX-compatible clients use the basic binding, *basicHttpBinding*.

In the following sections I'll describe contracts, endpoints, bindings, and behaviors in more detail. First, however, let's look at simple examples using a *HelloWorld* implementation and then at a more complete example of an application that we'll carry into later chapters.

WCF Contracts

Service-oriented applications are based on contracts. Contracts define the data schema and operational contracts for the service and the interface for remote clients. The contract is all that a remote application will know about—it will not know about the internals or implementation details of the service. With SOAP-based Web services, contracts are exposed by Web Service Description Language (WSDL). With .NET Web services, including ASMX (ASP.NET 1.1 and ASP.NET 2.0 Web services) and WCF services, WSDL is generated by the service run-time and is used by Visual Studio or svcutil.exe to generate proxy classes for remote clients. The great part about WSDL is that you don't really need to read it, even though it plays an important role in the service-oriented architecture: it's just plumbing that our tools create and consume. More information about WSDL and svcutil.exe is available on *http://msdn.microsoft.com/aa347733.aspx* and in the book references cited in this chapter.

A service contract is defined in code through attributes applied to the service interface. Although you can apply service interface attributes to a concrete class, the service interface should always be defined as an *interface* type to provide the most maintainable code. Using an interface keeps your code more stable for remote clients because it is easier to catch breaking changes at compile time. For example, the following code defines a simple interface for a HelloWorld service with a single method, *Hello*:

```
public interface IHelloWorld{
        string Hello();
}
```

To use this interface as a WCF service, you need to add the *ServiceContract* and *OperationContract* attributes. The attribute *ServiceContract* is applied to an interface or class to enable it as a WCF service. The attribute *OperationContract* is applied to service methods. The following example enables the *IHelloWorld* interface to be used as a WCF service contract:

```
[ServiceContract]
public interface IHelloWorld{
        [OperationContract]
        string Hello();
}
```

Tip If you've implemented Web services using ASMX in .NET 2.0, you're already familiar with the attribute-based model. The WCF *ServiceContract* attribute is similar to the ASMX *WebService* attribute, and the WCF *OperationContract* attribute is similar to the ASMX *ServiceMethod* attribute.

The *ServiceContract* attribute also has the parameters *Name* and *Namespace*, which are used to further identify the contract. The *OperationContract* has the *Name* attribute. The *Name* and *Namespace* parameters specify the XML name and namespace of the service and operation in the WSDL contracts. The XML namespace is a conceptual URI that identifies your service and XML schema. These URIs are similar to .NET namespaces, but they are applied to XML to disambiguate data schemes. They do not have to be real URLs; they are most often based on the developer's public URL. For example, Microsoft defines the XML namespace for Simple List Extensions at the URI *http://www.microsoft.com/schemas/rss/core/2005*. This isn't a "real" URL because no page is present at that location. Instead it is an *identifier*. These namespaces might not seem important to the casual developer, but they are critical in service-oriented architectures. If you don't define an XML namespace, the namespace *http://tempuri.org* is assigned. It's a best practice to always define the XML name and namespace on the contract, as in the following example applied to *IHelloWorld*:

```
[ServiceContract(Name="HelloWorld", Namespace="http://example.com/exampleServices")]
public interface IHelloWorld{
        [OperationContract(Name="Hello")]
        string Hello();
}
```

In defining the service interface, you define the public service contract that is used for generating WSDL and for exposing the service class through WCF. The contract has nothing to do with implementation; it only specifies the operation and the data schema. By implementing an interface you can guarantee that you won't break any service clients. Published interfaces of a public API are considered immutable, but you can always add additional interfaces. To complete the Hello World example, examine the interface *IHelloWorld* in Listing 2-1. In addition to the previously published *Hello* method, I've added the *Goodbye* method. The addition of the second method is not a breaking change for client applications. Additionally, the *WebGet* attribute is applied to these methods, which I'll discuss briefly in the following section about *WebServiceHostFactory* and in depth in Chapter 3, "The AJAX Application Server: Windows Communication Foundation's Web Programming Model."

> **Tip** Code for this book is available online at *http://www.microsoft.com/mspress/companion/9780735625914*. The code for this chapter is in the file Chapter 2.zip.

LISTING 2-1. The *IHelloWorld* contract defines the service and its operations (*ExampleServices/IHelloWorld.cs*).

```
using System;
using System.ServiceModel;

namespace ExampleServices
{
    [ServiceContract (Name="HelloWorld",
            Namespace="http://example.com/exampleServices")]
    public interface IHelloWorld
    {
```

```
        [WebGet]
        [OperationContract(Name="Hello")]
        string Hello();

        [WebGet]
        [OperationContract(Name="Goodbye")]
        string Goodbye();
    }
}
```

As I mentioned previously, applying the *ServiceContract* attribute to the interface lets the interface be used as a service contract. Each method exposed to the service must be marked with the *OperationContract* attribute. Listing 2-2 defines the HelloWorld service that implements the *IHelloWorld* contract. I'll use this service in the following sections to demonstrate endpoints, bindings, and behaviors. Because the service plumbing is handled in the interface, the service class can handle implementation without additional service markup.

LISTING 2-2. The HelloWorld service implements the *IHelloWorld* interface (*ExampleServices/HelloWorld.cs*).

```
using System;
using System.ServiceModel;
using System.ServiceModel.Activation;

namespace ExampleServices
{
    public class HelloWorld : IHelloWorld
    {
        public string Hello()
        {
            return "Hello, world!";
        }

        public string Goodbye()
        {
            return "Goodbye, cruel world!";
        }
    }
}
```

Because I implemented an interface for the service that is separate from the implementation of the service itself, I have more maintainable code over the lifetime of the application. I know that code modifications in the *HelloWorld* class do not break the service contract at compile time. The WCF service endpoint enables access to the service interface and class through configuration settings.

WCF Endpoints

Endpoints define the address or URI at which a service is available. An endpoint is enabled through a service host that creates service channels and bindings. The service host is used to run a service, configure its endpoints, and apply security settings. The host can be created through a console application, a service application, Windows Process Activation Service (WAS), IIS, or ASP.NET. In this book I will describe ASP.NET-hosted services.

In ASP.NET, service host files let ASP.NET create and run the WCF service hosts. The service host file simply defines the service activation endpoint and is roughly equivalent to an ASMX Web service file for ASP.NET 2.0. The service host file in ASP.NET uses the .svc file extension and is deployed to the ASP.NET file system.

The ASP.NET service host file activates the service and passes the call to the WCF runtime. The service host file defines the service implementation class (not the interface) and is further configured through the web.config file, where the interface, binding, and behaviors are also configured. The following service host file defines the service *ExampleServices.HelloWorld*, which will be hosted using *ServiceHostFactory* and the generic *ServiceHost* host class:

```
<%@ ServiceHost Service="ExampleServices.HelloWorld" %>
```

 Tip The *ServiceHost* and *ServiceHostFactory* classes are generally handled by the ASP.NET runtime and are configured through web.config and .svc files. You won't need to create or instantiate these classes in ASP.NET hosted WCF.

If you do not specify additional details, the service host used will be the generic *ServiceHost*, and *ServiceHostFactory* will be used to create it. The *ServiceHost* and *ServiceHostFactory* classes require configuration in web.config, as discussed in the following sections. In ASP.NET you can also specify *WebServiceHostFactory* or *WebScriptServiceHostFactory* as the host factory, an approach that does not require additional configuration but is also less flexible. The following SVC file creates a *WebServiceHost* using *WebServiceHostFactory* and requires no configuration in web.config:

```
<%@ ServiceHost Service="ExampleServices.HelloWorld"
    Factory="System.ServiceModel.Activation.WebServiceHostFactory"%>
```

WebServiceHostFactory creates a host running in the ASP.NET application and applies *webHttpBinding* and *webHttpBehavior* to the endpoint. You need to add the *WebGet* attribute to any GET-enabled endpoints to take advantage of *webHttpBehavior*, which exposes the Web service over HTTP GET requests. I'll talk more about GET and *webHttpBehavior* in Chapter 3.

Likewise, the *WebScriptServiceFactory* class creates a host running in the ASP.NET application and applies *webHttpBinding* and *enableWebScriptBehavior* to the endpoint. The following SVC file creates a *WebScriptServiceHost* using *WebScriptServiceHostFactory* without any changes to web.config:

```
<%@ ServiceHost Service="ExampleServices.HelloWorld"
    Factory="System.ServiceModel.Activation.WebScriptServiceHostFactory"%>
```

> **Important** While the *WebServiceHostFactory* and *WebScriptServiceFactory* classes don't require configuration entries in web.config, they are less flexible in how you can define endpoints.

If you are using the generic *ServiceHost* host (which is the default if you do not use the *ServiceHostFactory* classes discussed previously), you must also define the service in web.config. The SVC file serves as the activation point and the configuration file specifies the relative endpoint address, interface, binding, and behavior. We'll talk about bindings and behaviors next. For now, *wsHttpBinding* specifies that the endpoint uses SOAP, as opposed to *webHttp-Binding*, which specifies the simple URL protocol.

The following service configuration from web.config specifies that the *HelloWorld* type should expose the *IHelloWorld* interface through *wsHttpBinding* when it is accessed from the URL *"HelloWorld.svc/soap"*. Notice that the endpoint address defined is relative to the SVC file.

```
<service name="ExampleServices.HelloWorld">
    <endpoint address="soap" binding="wsHttpBinding"
            contract="ExampleServices.IHelloWorld" />
</service>
```

WCF Bindings

A binding defines the transport mechanism of the service. This mechanism binds the service to a SOAP protocol or a Web request–based protocol. For AJAX services, you use the *webHttpBinding* binding, which enables simple HTTP access. (We'll look at the Web programming model of WCF using simple GET and POST requests in the next chapter.) The *webHttpBinding* binding also enables *WebScriptEnablingBehavior,* which automatically builds JavaScript proxies for WCF services. As I mentioned previously, you typically use *wsHttp-Binding* when exposing your service to remote clients through SOAP, but you usually use *webHttpBinding* when exposing services to the JavaScript client. Additionally, Silverlight 2.0 uses *basicHttpBinding,* which is also used to maintain compatibility with ASMX Web service clients.

The following endpoint definition adds to the previous example by adding an endpoint that uses *webHttpBinding* and is defined at the URL *HelloWorld.svc/ajax.*:

```
<service name="ExampleServices.HelloWorld">
    <endpoint address="soap" binding="wsHttpBinding"
            contract="ExampleServices.IHelloWorld" />
    <endpoint address="ajax" binding="webHttpBinding"
            contract="ExampleServices.IHelloWorld" />
</service>
```

WCF Behaviors

Behaviors in WCF enable extensions to the service. Behaviors can be scoped to a service, an endpoint, a contract, or an operation. A WCF behavior is custom code that is applied to the service call by modifying the run-time operation. For example, *WebScriptEnablingBehavior* allows a WCF method to accept calls from the JavaScript client. It also generates a JavaScript proxy when accessed through the */js* or */jsdebug* endpoints, making the WCF operation simple to call from AJAX code.

Behaviors are defined in web.config in the node *configuration/system.serviceModel/behaviors*. Many behaviors are possible, including behaviors you write yourself, but the behaviors we care about most enable discovery of the service and AJAX integration of the endpoint.

> **More Information** In this book we'll only look at built-in WCF behaviors, but you can create your own behaviors as well. For more information about custom WCF behaviors, see Aaron Skonnard's article at *http://msdn2.microsoft.com/en-us/magazine/cc163302.aspx*.

On the service level, the *serviceMetaData* behavior enables the generation of WSDL and Metadata Exchange (MEX), which lets clients consume the service. This behavior, defined in *serviceBehaviors*, is specified as

```
<serviceMetadata httpGetEnabled="true" />
```

The *serviceDebug* element helps a developer debug the service by displaying error messages in SOAP faults, something that you will want to enable so that your AJAX client can handle exceptions. The *serviceDebug* element is defined as

```
<serviceDebug includeExceptionDetailInFaults="true" />
```

The *serviceDebug* element has the optional attributes *httpHelpPageEnabled* and *httpHelp-PageUrl,* which enable help pages for the service.

The following configuration creates a service behavior (with the name *ExampleServicesBehavior*) that can be applied to services to enable service metadata and service debugging information:

```
<serviceBehaviors>
    <behavior name="ExampleServicesBehavior">
        <serviceMetadata httpGetEnabled="true" />
        <serviceDebug httpHelpPageEnabled="false" includeExceptionDetailInFaults="true" />
    </behavior>
</serviceBehaviors>
```

After defining the service behavior configuration, you can apply it to multiple services. The following code applies our behavior configuration to the *ExampleServices.HelloWorld* service.

```
<service name="ExampleServices.HelloWorld" behaviorConfiguration="ExampleServicesBehavior">
  <endpoint address="soap" binding="wsHttpBinding"
          contract="ExampleServices.IHelloWorld" />
  <endpoint address="ajax" binding="webHttpBinding"
          contract="ExampleServices.IHelloWorld" />
</service>
```

The other behavior that is most important to AJAX development is the endpoint behavior *enableWebScript*. The *enableWebScript* behavior is defined in the type *System.ServiceModel. Description.WebScriptEnablingBehavior* and enables dynamic generation of JavaScript service proxies and JavaScript integration support for service endpoints. The following configuration defines the *ExampleAjaxBehavior* configuration, which includes the *enableWebScript* behavior. *ExampleAjaxBehavior* is an arbitrary name that is assigned to the endpoint in the endpoint configuration.

```
<behaviors>
    <endpointBehaviors>
        <behavior name="ExampleAjaxBehavior">
            <enableWebScript />
        </behavior>
    </endpointBehaviors>
</behaviors>
```

To apply the *ExampleAjaxBehavior* configuration to a service endpoint, add the *behavior-Configuration* attribute to the endpoint, as in the following example. You can apply the *enableWebScript* behavior only to *webHttpBinding*. All other bindings cause a failure upon service activation. The following configuration adds the *ExampleAjaxBehavior* to the "ajax" endpoint that uses *webHttpBinding*.

```
<service name="ExampleServices.HelloWorld" behaviorConfiguration="ExampleServicesBehavior">
    <endpoint address="soap" binding="wsHttpBinding"
            contract="ExampleServices.IHelloWorld" />
    <endpoint address="ajax" binding="webHttpBinding"
            behaviorConfiguration="ExampleAjaxBehavior"
            contract="ExampleServices.IHelloWorld" />
</service>
```

Important The *webHttpBinding* binding is required for services exposed to the ASP.NET AJAX runtime with the *enableWebScript* behavior. The *enableWebScript* behavior applied to a service configured with *wsHttpBinding* results in an activation failure.

I previously listed the code for the HelloWorld service in Listings 2-1 and 2-2. Listings 2-3 and 2-4 contain the SVC and web.config sample configuration code for the HelloWorld service implementation. The service is implemented in the ExampleServices.dll assembly, referenced through the ExampleService.SVC file, and finally configured through the web.config file.

LISTING 2-3. The ExampleServices.svc service activation file is deployed to the ASP.NET Web application (*Web/ExampleService.svc*).

```
<%@ ServiceHost Service="ExampleServices.HelloWorld"  %>
```

LISTING 2-4. The service is configured with endpoints, bindings, and behaviors in web.config (*Web/web.config*).

```
<configuration>
  <!-- ASP.NET configuration omitted... -->
  <system.serviceModel>
    <serviceHostingEnvironment aspNetCompatibilityEnabled="true" />
    <behaviors>
      <serviceBehaviors>
        <behavior name="ExampleServicesBehavior">
          <serviceMetadata httpGetEnabled="true" />
          <serviceDebug httpHelpPageEnabled="false"
              includeExceptionDetailInFaults="true"  />
          <serviceAuthorization principalPermissionMode="UseAspNetRoles" />
        </behavior>
      </serviceBehaviors>
      <endpointBehaviors>
        <behavior name="ExampleAjaxBehavior">
          <enableWebScript />
        </behavior>
      </endpointBehaviors>
    </behaviors>

    <services>
      <service name="ExampleServices.HelloWorld"
        behaviorConfiguration="ExampleServicesBehavior">

        <endpoint address="soap" binding="wsHttpBinding"
                  contract="ExampleServices.IHelloWorld" />

        <endpoint address="ajax" binding="webHttpBinding"
                  behaviorConfiguration="ExampleAjaxBehavior"
                  contract="ExampleServices.IHelloWorld" />
      </service>
    </services>
  </system.serviceModel>
</configuration>
```

Although more configuration might be required to deploy WCF services rather than ASP.NET 2.0 Web services, the flexibility that configuration gives you lets you change endpoints, bindings, and behaviors without recompiling code. For example, in ASMX Web services, the attribute *ScriptService* must be applied to the compiled Web service class, whereas with WCF services you can simply attach the *enableWebScript* behavior in configuration. With ASMX Web services you cannot expose client script proxies through configuration.

ASP.NET Runtime Support for WCF Services

Service orientation describes platform-neutral and message-based software, making HTTP an ideal protocol for service-oriented applications and ASP.NET the ideal platform for hosting true service-oriented WCF applications. WCF services can be deployed in an ASP.NET application running in side-by-side mode, which means that they execute outside the ASP.NET integrated pipeline, or WCF can run as an integrated part of the ASP.NET pipeline through ASP.NET Compatibility mode. ASP.NET Compatibility mode enables integration with ASP.NET platform services, but as a side effect can also introduce tight coupling with the ASP.NET runtime. Although these conditions can be less than ideal for intranet software, where you might want to use TCP/IP for performance reasons, the HTTP protocol is an ideal transport for Web services deployed in a true service-oriented fashion to remote clients not tied to a specific platform. ASP.NET Compatibility mode has nothing to do with consumers of the service; it only specifies the compatibility level of the service runtime. When compatibility mode is enabled in the ASP.NET web.config file, WCF services run in ASP.NET Integrated Pipeline mode. ASP.NET Integrated Pipeline mode lets the service run within the ASP.NET pipeline and have full access to HTTP runtime objects through the *HttpContext.Current* property. For example, you might want to use ASP.NET authentication and the *HttpContext. Current.User* property to access the ASP.NET user principal, or you might want direct access to HTTP headers within certain Web services. When developing services for an AJAX application, it's ideal to run in ASP.NET Compatibility mode.

 Tip Tying your service to the HTTP protocol does not detract from its service-oriented nature because the HTTP protocol is the one protocol that can cross nearly all platform and network boundaries with ease.

To set WCF to enable compatibility mode and run in the ASP.NET integrated pipeline, include the *serviceHostingEnvironment* element with the *aspNetCompatibilityEnabled* attribute set to *true*. Here is an example:

```
<system.serviceModel>
    <serviceHostingEnvironment aspNetCompatibilityEnabled="true" />
    <!-- WCF configuration here. -->
</system.serviceModel>
```

> **Tip** The requirement for an explicit compatibility setting is built into WCF to maintain a loose coupling with the transport mechanism. WCF doesn't have to use the HTTP transport. It can also use TCP, MSMQ, or other transport protocols. When developing primarily for the ASP.NET AJAX application client, you can add this dependency on the ASP.NET runtime by enabling or even requiring ASP.NET Compatibility mode.

Without ASP.NET Compatibility mode, a WCF service running in the ASP.NET application does not run within the ASP.NET HTTP pipeline. WCF services run in side-by-side mode. The Web request is intercepted by the WCF runtime and processed completely outside the ASP.NET HTTP pipeline. In side-by-side mode, *HttpContext.Current* is always *null,* and the WCF service cannot access the ASP.NET infrastructure. If nothing is specified in web.config, side-by-side is the default mode.

For your service to run in ASP.NET Compatibility mode, it must be marked with the *AspNetCompatibilityRequirements* attribute. The following attribute applied to a service class (the implementation class, not the interface) allows the service to be activated in ASP.NET Compatibility mode:

```
[AspNetCompatibilityRequirements(
    RequirementsMode = AspNetCompatibilityRequirementsMode.Allowed)]
```

Possible values for *RequirementsMode* are *Allowed, NotAllowed,* and *Required.* You want to use the value *Allowed* if your service supports activation in ASP.NET Integrated Pipeline mode and in side-by-side execution outside the ASP.NET pipeline. *Allowed* is the preferred configuration for maximum flexibility. However, if your service's execution requires the ASP.NET runtime (for example, through extensive use of the HTTP protocol), use the *Required* value. Finally, if you develop a service that won't be compatible with the ASP.NET integrated HTTP pipeline, use the *NotAllowed* value to be explicit. If you do not specify ASP.NET compatibility requirements, the default behavior is the same as specifying *NotAllowed.*

> **Important** You must allow ASP.NET compatibility through the *AspNetCompatibilityRequirements* attribute on the service class (not the service interface, as other WCF attributes). If you don't, the service will not be activated and will throw an exception.

Case Study: Introducing the Knowledge Base Reference Application

Throughout the rest of this book, I'll use a knowledge base application to demonstrate service design principles and AJAX architecture patterns. A knowledge base is simply a specialized database application used for knowledge management. In this chapter, I'll describe a generic knowledge base service application that's not tied to a specific end-user application. Access to the knowledge base is enabled through a service-oriented WCF application. When discussing WCF, I'll use the case study as a reference application for building AJAX-friendly services. In later chapters, I'll demonstrate how to develop AJAX components based on the services built in the first few chapters.

Although the application is simple—because it is built to demonstrate service principles, WCF technologies, and AJAX implementations—this architecture is the same basic architecture we use at NewsGator for major commercial applications. Customers might or might not use the slick AJAX user interface that we've provided, but many customers develop applications that integrate our Web services API, and most customers use additional client or server applications connected through the API. One particular value of NewsGator's product line is the Web services platform which is also at the core of integrated applications that run on Windows and Macintosh desktops, Microsoft Office applications, and Microsoft Office SharePoint Server instances. While the technology platforms vary drastically, each application is integrated through the Web services platform, either with NewsGator Online Web services or instances of NewsGator Enterprise Server running inside the corporate firewall.

The sample knowledge base application uses catalogs of data entry items and stores multiple versions of each data entry so that multiple users can edit items. This allows the data to be used for versioned documents, including wikis, blogs, and general purpose data. Each catalog exposes a feed of recently posted items and a search interface, although users can also search multiple catalogs on the basis of content, title, and tags. (A tag is simply a keyword associated with a data item.) Figure 2-3 shows the basic database schema for the knowledge base application. This schema also serves as the basic data model exposed through WCF contracts in the sample application.

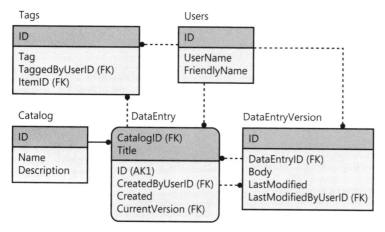

FIGURE 2-3. The knowledge base reference application database schema.

To implement the knowledge base application, I defined a single data access class that implements data access code to persist the knowledge base data to SQL Server. In a production application, code for this purpose would typically be implemented in an assembly separate from the service interfaces to further isolate the service endpoints from the implementation details. For our purposes, the data access class is as simple as possible and removes the implementation details from our code samples so that we can focus on the WCF components for our AJAX application. Figure 2-4 displays the class diagram for the *DataAccess* class. In the following section, I'll describe the principles of contract-based programming and service-oriented WCF development.

FIGURE 2-4. The *DataAccess* class implements the business logic for the service application.

More Information The full code for the *DataAccess* class is available as part of the chapter's sample code. Go to *http://www.microsoft.com/mspress/companion/9780735625914* to download the code.

Contract-Based Service Programming

WCF services are based on contracts. Contracts are defined for both services and messages, and data contracts can be defined for the message schema. Data contracts are not required for simple types, XML types such as *XmlDocument,* or for types that use the *XmlSerializer* class. A contract can also be expressed through a universal contract by using the *Message* type, which describes the entire message.

In the first service contract example, I defined a catalog service that enables the creation of catalogs and lists available catalogs. In the data model, the catalog is the root-level item that data entries belong to. It is an abstract concept that could be exposed as a blog, wiki, or general purpose list. To keep it simple, I defined the catalog with a simple string definition. Listing 2-5 defines the *ServiceContract* for the catalog service by defining the *ICatalogService* interface. Because the service returns a simple string result and not a complex type, I did not need to define a data contract for this service.

LISTING 2-5. The *CatalogService* message contract uses simple strings to identify catalogs (*KnowledgeBase/ICatalogService.cs*).

```
using System;
using System.Collections.Generic;
using System.ServiceModel;
using System.ServiceModel.Web;

namespace KnowledgeBase
{
    [ServiceContract(Name = "CatalogService",
        Namespace = "http://knowledgebase/CatalogService")]
    public interface ICatalogService
    {
        [OperationContract]
        void Create(string catalog);

        [OperationContract]
        List<string> GetCatalogs();
    }
}
```

To implement the service, I created a class that implements the *ICatalogService* interface, using object-oriented classes in the business logic to handle the implementation. Because we're using the security principal *HttpContext.Current.User*, I marked the class with the *AspNetCompatibilityRequirements* attribute and set the compatibility level to *Required* by using *AspNetCompatibilityRequirementsMode.Required*. Listing 2-6 contains the implementation of the concrete *CatalogService* class.

LISTING 2-6. The *CatalogService* implementation is lightweight and handles the service logic while deferring business logic to the implementation (*KnowledgeBase/CatalogService.cs*).

```
using System;
using System.Collections.Generic;
using System.Web;
using KnowledgeBase.Implementation;
using System.ServiceModel.Activation;

namespace KnowledgeBase
{
```

```
    [AspNetCompatibilityRequirements(
        RequirementsMode=AspNetCompatibilityRequirementsMode.Required)]
    public class CatalogService : ICatalogService
    {
        public void Create(string catalog)
        {
            var dataImplemenation =
                new DataAccess(HttpContext.Current.User);
            dataImplemenation.Create(catalog);
        }

        public List<string> GetCatalogs()
        {
            var dataImplemenation = new
                DataAccess(HttpContext.Current.User);
            return (dataImplemenation.GetCatalogs());
        }
    }
}
```

Implementing Data Schema Through WCF Data Contracts

As I mentioned, data contracts are not needed for simple types such as the string ex-ample I used for catalogs, nor are they required for types that serialize to XML, such as *XmlDocument*. For complex types, however, you should write a data contract. These con-tracts form the message contracts when they are joined with the service contracts. The data contract formalizes the data structure and defines the data schema of the message. Applied to AJAX development, you can program the JavaScript client against the data type defined by *DataContract*, or you can build XSLT style sheets that render the schema. To define the data contract in WCF, you use attributes in the *System.Runtime.Serialization* namespace, specifically *DataContractAttribute* applied to the class and *DataMemberAttribute* applied to each field that will be serialized to the message stream. Listing 2-7 lists the data contract for the *DataItem* type. The data contract defines the XML name *Item* and the namespace *http://knowledgeBase*.

LISTING 2-7. The *KnowledgeBase DataItem* data contract defines a complex XML type (*KnowledgeBase/DataItem.cs*).

```
using System;
using System.Collections.Generic;
using System.Runtime.Serialization;
using System.ServiceModel;

namespace KnowledgeBase
{
    /// <summary>Represents an item in a knowledgebase.</summary>
    [DataContract(Name = "Item", Namespace = "http://knowledgebase")]
```

```
public class DataItem
{
    [DataMember(Name="Title", Order=1)]
    public string Title { get; set; }

    [DataMember(Name="Body", Order=2)]
    public string Body { get; set; }

    private string format = "wiki";
    [DataMember(Name = "Format", Order = 3)]
    public string Format {
        get { return this.format; } set { this.format = value; } }

    [DataMember(Name = "Version", Order = 4)]
    public int Version { get; set; }

    [DataMember(Name = "LastModifiedBy", Order = 5)]
    public string LastModifiedBy{ get; set; }

    [DataMember(Name = "LastModified", Order = 6)]
    public DateTime LastModified { get; set; }

    [DataMember(Name = "Created", Order = 7)]
    public DateTime Created { get; set; }

    [DataMember(Name = "CreatedBy", Order = 8)]
    public string CreatedBy { get; set; }

    private List<string> tags = new List<string>(0);
    [DataMember(Name = "Tags", Order = 9)]
    public List<string> Tags {
        get { return this.tags; } set { this.tags = value;  } }

    [DataMember(Name = "Catalog", Order = 10)]
    public string Catalog { get; set; }
}
}
```

The WCF runtime uses the data contract shown in Listing 2-7 to generate the XML schema definition (XSD) shown in Listing 2-8. This XSD definition is referenced by WSDL files and allows remote clients to program against the XML schema of the WCF data contract.

LISTING 2-8. The data contract will generate an XSD in the WSDL files (*Auto generated WSDL resource*).

```
<?xml version="1.0" encoding="utf-8"?>
<xs:schema elementFormDefault="qualified" targetNamespace="http://knowledgebase"
xmlns:xs="http://www.w3.org/2001/XMLSchema" xmlns:tns="http://knowledgebase">
  <xs:import
      schemaLocation="http://localhost:8080/Web/DataService.svc?xsd=xsd3"
      namespace="http://schemas.microsoft.com/2003/10/Serialization/Arrays"/>
  <xs:complexType name="Item">
    <xs:sequence>
```

```
        <xs:element minOccurs="0" name="Title" nillable="true" type="xs:string"/>
        <xs:element minOccurs="0" name="Body" nillable="true" type="xs:string"/>
        <xs:element minOccurs="0" name="Format" nillable="true" type="xs:string"/>
        <xs:element minOccurs="0" name="Version" type="xs:int"/>
        <xs:element minOccurs="0" name="LastModifiedBy"
            nillable="true" type="xs:string"/>
        <xs:element minOccurs="0" name="LastModified" type="xs:dateTime"/>
        <xs:element minOccurs="0" name="Created" type="xs:dateTime"/>
        <xs:element minOccurs="0" name="CreatedBy" nillable="true" type="xs:string"/>
        <xs:element minOccurs="0" name="Tags" nillable="true" type="q1:ArrayOfstring"
            xmlns:q1="http://schemas.microsoft.com/2003/10/Serialization/Arrays"/>
        <xs:element minOccurs="0" name="Catalog" nillable="true" type="xs:string"/>
      </xs:sequence>
    </xs:complexType>
    <xs:element name="Item" nillable="true" type="tns:Item"/>
  </xs:schema>
```

Finally, the data contract in listing 2-9 is serialized into the following XML:

```
<Item xmlns="http://knowledgebase" xmlns:i="http://www.w3.org/2001/XMLSchema-instance">
  <Title>Test</Title>
  <Body>Test Wiki Content</Body>
  <Format>wiki</Format>
  <Version>8</Version>
  <LastModifiedBy>Daniel Larson</LastModifiedBy>
  <LastModified>2008-02-24T23:32:05.407</LastModified>
  <Created>2008-02-24T23:26:01.203</Created>
  <CreatedBy>Daniel Larson</CreatedBy>
  <Tags xmlns:a="http://schemas.microsoft.com/2003/10/Serialization/Arrays">
    <a:string>Test</a:string>
  </Tags>
  <Catalog>Default</Catalog>
</Item>
```

To render this data contract on the client, you could use XSLT or DOM-based JavaScript code built against this data schema. Any service that uses the *http://knowledgebase/Item* object could use the same common rendering logic.

Listing 2-9 defines the data service interface for the main CRUD (create, read, update, delete) operations. In the data service example, the *DataItem* is passed into and out of the service, letting any client that understands the *item* element defined in the *http://knowledgebase* XML namespace consume the service.

LISTING 2-9. The service contract definition for *IDataService* uses the *DataItem* data contract (*KnowledgeBase/IDataService.cs*).

```
using System;
using System.ServiceModel;
using System.ServiceModel.Activation;
using System.ServiceModel.Web;
using System.ServiceModel.Syndication;
```

```
namespace KnowledgeBase
{
    [ServiceContract(Namespace="http://knowledgebase/",
            Name="DataService")]
    public interface IDataService
    {
        [WebGet]
        [OperationContract(Action="Get")]
        DataItem GetData(string catalog, string title);

        [OperationContract(Action="Save")]
        void SaveData(DataItem data);

        [OperationContract(Action = "Delete")]
        void Delete(DataItem data);
    }
}
```

To implement the service, you simply create a class that implements the service contract interface. Keep in mind that the service class can implement several interfaces. Later we'll define additional endpoints that use the same service implementation. Listing 2-10 defines the service implementation for the *IDataService* interface.

LISTING 2-10. The service implementation for *IDataService* implements the interface and uses minimal logic to process incoming messages (*KnowledgeBase/DataService.cs*).

```
using System;
using System.ServiceModel.Web;
using System.ServiceModel;
using System.ServiceModel.Activation;

using KnowledgeBase.Implementation;
using System.Security.Principal;
using System.Web;

namespace KnowledgeBase
{
    [AspNetCompatibilityRequirements(
        RequirementsMode=AspNetCompatibilityRequirementsMode.Required)]
    public class DataService : IDataService
    {
        public DataItem GetData(string catalog, string title)
        {
            if (string.IsNullOrEmpty(title))
                title = "default";
            if (string.IsNullOrEmpty(catalog))
                catalog = "default";
            var dataImplementation =
                new DataAccess(HttpContext.Current.User);
            return dataImplementation.GetData(catalog, title);
        }
```

```
        public void SaveData(DataItem data)
        {
            var dataImplementation =
                new DataAccess(HttpContext.Current.User);
            dataImplementation.SaveData(data);
        }

        public void Delete(DataItem data)
        {
            var dataImplementation =
                new DataAccess(HttpContext.Current.User);
            dataImplementation.Delete(data);
        }
    }
}
```

In the previous examples, I demonstrated contract-based programming techniques for WCF by using simple types and through complex types that use a data contract. I also kept the service implementation as minimal as possible, leaving the details to object-oriented code that is implemented through a data access class in the sample code. After defining the contract and implementation, I can now expose the endpoints through SVC files and the ASP.NET web.config file to begin using them in the ASP.NET AJAX application and remote clients.

The first step in defining the endpoints is to define some common behavior configurations. You don't want to have one behavior configuration per endpoint because that gets messy very quickly—instead, define some common configurations that can be used by your services. I've found generally that one service behavior configuration and two endpoint behavior configurations suffice. Listing 2-11 defines the service metadata and *serviceDebug* configurations that should apply to all the services. It also shows a JavaScript-enabled configuration that we will apply to our endpoints.

LISTING 2-11. The behavior configuration for our example application includes service behaviors and endpoint behaviors, enabling integration with ASP.NET AJAX client applications.

```
<behaviors>
  <serviceBehaviors>
    <behavior name="MetaDataBehavior">
      <serviceMetadata httpGetEnabled="true" />
      <serviceDebug httpHelpPageEnabled="true"
          includeExceptionDetailInFaults="true" />
    </behavior>
  </serviceBehaviors>
  <endpointBehaviors>
    <behavior name="ExampleAjaxBehavior">
      <enableWebScript />
    </behavior>
  </endpointBehaviors>
</behaviors>
```

After defining the behavior configurations for AJAX services, you can then define the endpoints with a combination of address, binding, and behavior configurations. Listing 2-12 shows the behavior configuration for the *DataService* endpoint using the binding *webHttp-Binding* and the *ExampleAjaxBehavior* behavior configuration. Although the service is defined with *webHttpBinding*, which uses the simple HTTP protocol without SOAP, the service could be exposed at another endpoint with an alternative binding, such as *wsHttpBinding*, enabling SOAP-based client access.

LISTING 2-12. The endpoints are defined in web.config by applying behavior configurations, bindings, and addresses for each service endpoint

```
<serviceHostingEnvironment aspNetCompatibilityEnabled="true" />
<services>
  <service name="KnowledgeBase.DataService"
             behaviorConfiguration="MetaDataBehavior">

    <endpoint address="" behaviorConfiguration="ExampleAjaxBehavior"
             binding="webHttpBinding"
             contract="KnowledgeBase.IDataService" />

    <endpoint contract="IMetadataExchange" binding="mexHttpBinding" address="mex" />

  </service>
</services>
```

The service host file must also be deployed to the Web application to enable the endpoint. Keep in mind that nothing ties the service host file to a particular endpoint configuration; that work is performed through configuration in web.config. When ASP.NET processes the SVC service activation file, it processes the WCF service in an HTTP handler implementation. Here is the service host file for *KnowledgeBase.DataService*:

```
<%@ ServiceHost Service="KnowledgeBase.DataService" %>
```

Note With WCF applications deployed in ASP.NET, you can also define services inline in the SVC file or in the *app_code* directory, although this approach isn't as maintainable or as flexible as keeping your services in an assembly. By implementing your services in an assembly, you can share your services across multiple service-host applications.

WCF Security and Authorization with ASP.NET

When running WCF services in an ASP.NET application with the ASP.NET integrated pipeline (with ASP.NET compatibility enabled), you share ASP.NET authentication, authorization, session, and roles. This means that you use the same ASP.NET authentication mechanisms as in

ASP.NET 2.0, although you will usually authenticate the AJAX client through AJAX-enabled Web services rather than a login form. The user is authenticated in the ASP.NET runtime before the WCF service is processed.

Within code running through the ASP.NET pipeline, the user principal is accessed through the *HttpContext.Current.User* property. *HttpContext.Current* is always *null* in a side-by-side hosted WCF application that is not run through the ASP.NET integrated pipeline, as well as in any service exposed outside HTTP. To write code that accesses the user principal in applications that can be hosted both in the ASP.NET pipeline and in pure WCF hosting environments, check for an instance of *ServiceSecurityContext* through the *ServiceSecurityContext. Current* property. *ServiceSecurityContext* will be *null* in an ASP.NET service, but the *HttpContext.Current* property is *null* in a non-ASP.NET WCF service. Listing 2-13 demonstrates this technique to get the security principal.

LISTING 2-13. Checking both *ServiceSecurityContext* and *HttpContext* ensures compatible service code in all environments (excerpt from *KnowledgeBase/DataService.cs*).

```
protected IPrincipal GetUser()
{
    ServiceSecurityContext sec = ServiceSecurityContext.Current;
    if (sec != null)
        return new GenericPrincipal(sec.PrimaryIdentity, null);
    else if (HttpContext.Current != null)
        return HttpContext.Current.User;
    else
        return null;
}
```

Web Services for AJAX Using ASP.NET 2.0 ASMX

Prior to WCF, the Microsoft AJAX framework was integrated with ASP.NET 2.0 ASMX Web services using the *System.Web.Extensions* assembly. Although I don't recommend using ASMX Web services for new development (because they are not as flexible or robust as WCF services), enabling AJAX integration support on an existing ASMX Web service application is a trivial task.

ASMX 2.0 services are built using a programming model similar to WCF services, using attributes to define service behavior. The attributes *WebServiceBinding*, *WebService,* and *WebMethod* are used to describe the service, and the base class *WebService* is used as a base implementation class. The code examples in this section compare ASP.NET 2.0 Web services to WCF services and demonstrate how to enable services with scripts by using attributes defined in *System.Web.Extensions*.

ASMX 2.0 introduced interface-based programming similar to the approach taken by WCF. Listing 2-14 shows a simple interface for *DataService* using ASMX attributes rather than WCF attributes. Conceptually, this is the same interface used in previous samples, defining web methods within the service binding.

LISTING 2-14. The *WebService* and *WebMethod* attributes are used to define an ASMX Web service (*KnowledgeBase.Compatibility/IDataService.cs*).

```
using System;
using System.Web.Services;
using System.Web.Script.Services;

namespace KnowledgeBase.Compatibility
{
    [WebServiceBinding(
        Namespace = "http://knowledgebase/",
        Name = "DataService",
        ConformsTo = WsiProfiles.BasicProfile1_1,
        EmitConformanceClaims = true)]
    // WCF: [ServiceContract(Namespace = "http://knowledgebase/",
    //          Name = "DataService")]
    public interface IDataService
    {
        [WebMethod(MessageName="GET")]
        // WCF: [OperationContract(Action = "Get")]
        DataItem GetData(string catalog, string title);

        [WebMethod(MessageName = "Save")]
        // WCF: [OperationContract(Action = "Save")]
        void SaveData(DataItem data);

        [WebMethod(MessageName = "Delete")]
        // WCF: [OperationContract(Action = "Delete")]
        void Delete(DataItem data);
    }
}
```

ASMX 2.0 Web services include support for script-enabled access through the *System.Web. Extensions* assembly. Instead of the behavior-based model that WCF uses, ASMX uses the attributes *ScriptService* and *ScriptMethod*. *ScriptService* enables JavaScript support through a script proxy method on the Web service, and *ScriptMethod* is used optionally on the Web service method to further define script behavior.

Although ASMX 2.0 supports a pure interface-based model, when using the *ScriptService* attribute you must define it on the class and you must also explicitly include the *WebMethod* attribute on all script-enabled methods in the class (not just in the interface). Listing 2-15 demonstrates the data service exposed through an ASMX service.

LISTING 2-15. The script-enabled ASMX 2.0 Web service is defined through the *ScriptService*, *WebService*, and *WebMethod* attributes (*KnowledgeBase.Compatibility/DataService.cs*).

```csharp
using System;
using System.Collections.Generic;
using System.Linq;
using System.Text;
using System.Web.Services;
using KnowledgeBase.Implementation;
using System.Web.Script.Services;

namespace KnowledgeBase.Compatibility
{
    [ScriptService]
    [WebService(Namespace = "http://knowledgebase/", Name = "DataService")]
    public class DataService : WebService, KnowledgeBase.Compatibility.IDataService
    {
        [WebMethod(MessageName = "GET")]
        public DataItem GetData(string catalog, string title)
        {
            var dataImplementation = new DataAccess(this.User);
            return dataImplementation.GetData(catalog, title);
        }

        [WebMethod(MessageName = "Save")]
        public void SaveData(DataItem data)
        {
            var dataImplementation = new DataAccess(this.User);
            if (data == null) throw new ArgumentNullException("data");
            if (data.Catalog == null)
                data.Catalog = "Default";
            dataImplementation.SaveData(data);
        }

        [WebMethod(MessageName = "Delete")]
        public void Delete(DataItem data)
        {
            var dataImplementation = new DataAccess(this.User);
            dataImplementation.Delete(data);
        }

        public void CreateData(DataItem entry) {
            throw new NotImplementedException();
        }
    }
}
```

While ASMX 2.0 Web services give you much of the functionality of WCF, the programming model is not as flexible and requires compiled configuration. You cannot choose to enable or disable script behaviors through configuration, and you cannot use a pure interface-based approach because the *WebMethod* attribute must be applied to the concrete class to enable script support. Regardless, if you have an existing ASP.NET 2.0 Web service applica-tion, you can easily enable script proxies through *System.Web.Extensions* and the *ScriptService* attribute.

Summary

In this chapter, you learned how to apply the principles of service orientation to the back-end services application that will serve as the core application server for the AJAX applica-tion. You also looked at *WebScriptingBehavior* and how to enable JavaScript support through configuration. Finally, you saw how to enable JavaScript support in legacy ASP.NET 2.0 ASMX services through *System.Web.Extensions* and the attributes *ScriptService* and *ScriptMethod*. By now you should understand the basics of WCF programming and be able to integrate a simple service library hosted in ASP.NET. In the next chapter we'll build on this foundation and look at additional Web service programming techniques using WCF's Web programming model.

Chapter 3

The AJAX Application Server: Windows Communication Foundation's Web Programming Model

After completing this chapter, you will

- Understand the Web programming model for Windows Communication Foundation (WCF) in the Microsoft .NET 3.5 Framework.

- Understand how to use *WebGet* and *WebInvoke* to provide Web-style services.

- Understand HTTP verbs, headers, and status codes.

- Understand the architectural principles of Representational State Transfer (REST).

- Understand how to use WCF syndication services to generate syndicated feeds.

- Understand how to implement HTTP handlers to process the raw HTTP context.

WCF and the Web Programming Model

WCF was introduced in the .NET 3.0 Framework. It was designed to provide a unified programming model for communications, whether peer to peer, server to server, or even distributed .NET applications. WCF in the .NET 3.5 Framework adds support for the Web programming model through the *System.ServiceModel.Web* assembly, enabling the use of AJAX applications and Web client technologies such as the ASP.NET AJAX JavaScript client, Microsoft Silverlight, Adobe Flash, and syndicated feed consumers. The Web programming model is built on top of the HTTP protocol, and it is much simpler than the SOAP protocol because it is based on standard HTTP requests. And because the Web programming model is based on standard HTTP, it is by nature accessible to the widest variety of clients, including Web browsers with no additional client framework.

 Note The Web programming model refers to a simple request and response model that uses the HTTP protocol without the semantics of SOAP.

The WCF Web programming model exposed through the *System.ServiceModel.Web* assembly consists of classes that implement Web-style services that use HTTP verbs and scripting behaviors for JavaScript integration. *Web-style* services are Web services that are accessible through pure browser technology. They can be called using the URL-based protocol, as opposed to a SOAP-based framework. In WCF documentation, the use of Web-style services is also known as the *Web programming model*. Although the *System.ServiceModel.Web* assembly provides additional functionality, including a robust framework for syndication, its main purpose is to support Web services through the Web programming model. This simplicity is central to the AJAX application frameworks that you'll develop using the service-based approach introduced in this book. Table 3-1 lists the key classes and types defined in the *System.ServiceModel.Web* assembly. We'll look at these classes and types in depth throughout the chapter.

TABLE 3-1. Key *System.ServiceModel.Web* Types

Type	Description
WebGetAttribute	Maps GET requests to WCF service methods.
WebInvokeAttribute	Maps HTTP verbs other than GET to WCF service methods.
WebOperationContext	Wraps the WCF *OperationContext* object and provides access to the HTTP context through a service-oriented programming model. Provides access to instances of *IncomingWebRequestContext*, *IncomingWebResponseContext*, *OutgoingWebRequestContext*, and *OutgoingWebResponseContext*.
IncomingWebRequestContext	Provides access to the HTTP context of the incoming request through a service-oriented programming model.
OutgoingWebResponseContext	Provides access to the HTTP context of the outgoing response through a service-oriented programming model.

Tip *OutgoingWebRequestContext* and *IncomingWebResponseContext* are used only by WCF client applications and are not used in the WCF service implementation.

Enabling the Web Programming Model

The Web programming model is enabled through the WCF behavior *WebHttpBehavior* and the WCF binding *WebHttpBinding*. Because WCF uses a configuration-based programming model, the behavior and binding are applied to the endpoint through web.config settings, as demonstrated in Listing 3-1.

Tip Code for this book is available online at *http://www.microsoft.com/mspress/companion/9780735625914*. The code for this chapter is in the file Chapter 3.zip.

LISTING 3-1. *WebHttpBehavior* and *WebHttpBinding* enable the Web programming model.

```
<system.serviceModel>
  <serviceHostingEnvironment aspNetCompatibilityEnabled="true" />
  <behaviors>
    <endpointBehaviors>
      <behavior name="RestBehavior">
        <webHttp />
      </behavior>
    </endpointBehaviors>
  </behaviors>

  <services>
    <service name="KnowledgeBase.DataService">
      <endpoint address="rest" behaviorConfiguration="RestBehavior"
                binding="webHttpBinding"
                contract="KnowledgeBase.IRestDataService" />
    </service>
  </services>
</system.serviceModel>
```

The *WebGet* and *WebInvoke* attributes enable the service to be exposed through the Web programming model. Both *WebGetAttribute* and *WebInvokeAttribute* are *IOperationBehavior* attributes. WCF attributes that implement *IOperationBehavior* are passive and have no effect on the service on their own—the attributes only define metadata on the service method that can be consumed through behaviors. A behavior, such as *WebHttpBehavior*, that consumes the *IOperationBehavior* attributes can process this metadata. This technique lets you use *WebGet* and *WebInvoke* on service interface methods without tying the implementation to the Web programming model. The same Web service can be exposed through *WebHttpBinding* and through "traditional" SOAP-based Web services by using *wsHttpBinding*, as discussed in Chapter 2, "The AJAX Application Server: Service Orientation and the Windows Communication Foundation." I'll talk more about *WebGet* and *WebInvoke* throughout this chapter because they are central to the Web programming model.

Accessing the Current Web Context from WCF

The Web context gives you full access to the incoming request and outgoing response, including HTTP headers, status, and verbs. To access the current Web context from a WCF operation, you need to access the property *WebOperationContext.Current*. *WebOperationContext* exposes the current Web request and response and is the preferred method of working with the HTTP context through the WCF programming model. Because the WCF programming model is based on contracts and messages, you generally don't have direct access to the HTTP response, as you would with a "raw" HTTP handler in ASP.NET. If you need direct access to the response, you can implement a stream-based handler to return text or binary data such as images, but this is an exception to the rule and shouldn't be used for data-oriented services.

You need to work with *WebOperationContext* for direct access to HTTP headers or other properties of the request and response when working with REST services. The *WebOperationContext* class and its *IncomingWebRequestContext* and *OutgoingWebResponse-Context* classes are shown in Figure 3-1.

FIGURE 3-1. *WebOperationContext* provides access to the *IncomingWebRequestContext* and the *OutgoingWebResponseContext* classes.

> **Tip** Because the *System.ServiceModel.Web WebOperationContext* class is oriented toward contract-based service programming, you should use its class heirarchy instead of the ASP.NET *HttpContext* class when working with WCF services.

To access the HTTP response so that you can set HTTP headers or status, use the *Outgoing-WebResponseContext* class, which is exposed through the property *WebOperationContext.Current.OutgoingResponse*. This class does not expose the response stream because you return an object from the service operation, and this object is serialized to the response stream. However, you might want to set HTTP headers or the HTTP status code in a Web application, in which case you would use *OutgoingWebResponseContext*. The following code sample uses *OutgoingWebResponseContext* (through the property *OutgoingResponse*) to set an HTTP header and the HTTP status code of the response:

```
WebOperationContext.Current.OutgoingResponse.Headers[
        HttpResponseHeader.CacheControl] = "Private";
WebOperationContext.Current.OutgoingResponse.StatusCode = HttpStatusCode.OK;
```

Tip Even though the *WebOperationContext* class replaces most of the functionality of *HttpContext*, you still need to use the *HttpContext* class to access the *User* security principal when running WCF in integrated pipeline mode (enabled through ASP.NET compatibility configuration). The *User* principal is not exposed through *WebOperationContext*. The property *HttpContext.Current.User* accesses the authenticated *User* principal from an ASP.NET integrated service.

The REST Architectural Pattern and WCF

The WCF Web programming model is based on REST (Representational State Transfer) principals, which are a stricter subset of the Web programming model. In many cases in the WCF documentation, the terms Web programming model and REST are interchangeable. In fact, the WCF Web programming model itself was built to support REST architectures.

Tip REST is an ideal mechanism for AJAX data retrieval using simple HTTP transports without the need for a SOAP envelope.

The REST architectural pattern is based on the premise that resources are represented by a unique human-readable URL. I introduced the concept of POX (Plain Old XML) Web service endpoints in Chapter 1, "Service-Oriented AJAX Fundamentals." POX endpoints are a subset of the full REST pattern. The full REST pattern defines methods for data creation, retrieval, updates, and deletion using standard HTTP verbs. In the REST pattern, the GET verb is always used for read-only data access instead of a Web service POST, which by definition is not cacheable. Because GET requests can take advantage of Web caching technologies, including server caching, browser caching, and even proxy caching, REST-style endpoints for data access have specific advantages over other endpoint implementations, whether you implement the full REST pattern or not. As you build your back-end service architecture, you might find that a mixture of REST services (especially for data retrieval) and SOAP-based Web services is ideal.

Tip Internet standard protocols such as the Atom publishing protocol are based entirely on REST services, making REST an essential pattern for the modern Web developer to know.

The REST architectural approach bases resources on URI identifiers and uses the standard HTTP verbs GET, PUT, POST, and DELETE. In a typical REST implementation, GET is used for data retrieval, POST is used to create new items, PUT to update existing items, and DELETE to delete an item.

In Chapter 1 I also introduced the *Sys.Net.WebRequest* JavaScript class, which is the class you use to access REST Web services using JavaScript code. The *Sys.Net.WebRequest* JavaScript class is used to perform simple Web requests in an asynchronous pattern. To recap, the following JavaScript code sample (Listing 3-2) creates a *WebRequest* instance using the ASP.NET AJAX library and asynchronously executes a GET request for the WCF service endpoint "example.svc/hello". Upon completion, the method *onCompletedHandler,* passed in with the *add_completed* method, is called, which can then be used to process the response asynchronously. The callback handler is called for both successful operations and failed operations.

LISTING 3-2. The *Sys.Net.WebRequest* JavaScript type is used to call REST endpoints.

```
function OnAjaxLoad()
{
    // Creates a new WebRequest object
    var request = new Sys.Net.WebRequest();

    // Used to send arbitrary value-typed data
    var userContext = new Object();
    request.set_userContext = userContext;

    // Sets the request endpoint
    request.set_url('example.svc/hello');

    // Adds the callback handler for the response
    // The callback handler contains the parameters response and userContext
    request.add_completed(onCompletedHandler);

    // Specifies the HTTP verb (GET is the default verb)
    request.set_httpVerb('GET');

    // Sets the content type header
    request.get_headers()["Content-Type"] = "application/xml";

    // Invokes the method asynchronously
    // The completed callback handler is called upon completion
    request.invoke();
}

function onCompletedHandler(response, userContext)
{
    // Process the response here
    // response is the WebRequestExecutor that contains the HTTP response
    // userContext is the object passed to request.set_userContext
}
```

Using *WebGet* for Data Retrieval

GET requests are mapped to service methods using the *WebGet* attribute. By applying the *WebGet* attribute, you indicate that the method is a data retrieval operation and can be exposed through the GET verb. The following code shows the *WebGet* attribute applied to a data-retrieval interface method, specifying the response format JSON:

```
[OperationContract]
[WebGet(ResponseFormat=WebMessageFormat.Json)]
DataItem GetData(string catalog, string title);
```

HTTP GET methods are central to REST architecture. In the REST pattern, the URL requested identifies the resource and the HTTP verb specifies the action. The GET verb is special and should only be used for retrieving data; a GET request should never update data on the server. GET endpoints should be a resource that can be bookmarked and cached, and, ideally, be readable. Content retrieved with GET can (and will) be cached on proxy servers and in the client browser, which offers a significant advantage for AJAX Web applications. Utilizing the client's Web browser's cache can dramatically improve AJAX performance by reducing network traffic and load time. We'll look at implementing cache support in the section "Client-Side Caching with GET" later in this chapter. The *WebGet* attribute applied to WCF methods also supports the passing of parameters through the URI template, which I'll discuss in the next section.

 Tip Methods exposed through *WebGet* and *WebInvoke* are not exposed through the AJAX runtime's JavaScript proxy and must be called through the JavaScript type *Sys.Net.WebRequest*.

Readable URLs and URI Templates

A core principle of REST is that a URI identifies a resource. A resource is simply requested by its URI, and you can perform actions on the object by applying HTTP verbs to the URI. For example, the URL *user.svc/daniel.larson/profile* could be used to identify the user profile for Daniel Larson. The URI is built using a readable, path-based approach, as opposed to a query string–based approach, which would be something like *user.svc/profile?user=daniel. larson*. Note that a URL with query string arguments does not provide a unique URL for the resource, because query strings are unordered pairs. A uniquely identifiable URL is built by using the path that identifies the resource. For example, the following URL could uniquely define the "welcome" entry in the "fundamentals" data catalog:

"feed.svc/fundamentals/topics/welcome"

A URI template is a special type of formatted string that is used to extract variables from the path. You can also use it to build sets of structurally similar URLs that differ only by the resource's logical primary key—such as a URL that defines *items posted by* that contains the *author* variable as part of the path. Named variables are defined in the path in curly braces. The URL consists of path and query segments, each of which can be used within the URI template, with the query attributes being defined as unordered pairs. For example, the following URI templates define a set of URLs that we'll use to retrieve data from the knowledge base application:

- "feed.svc/{catalog}/topics/{title}"

- "feed.svc/{author}/"

- "feed.svc/{author}/tags/{tag}"

> **Tip** Using a URI template with the *WebGet* or *WebInvoke* attribute in a service interface that is run through *WebScriptBehavior* causes a service-activation error. As a result, you might want to place REST-style methods in an isolated interface.

Ideally, the query string (as opposed to the path) should not be used to uniquely identify a resource but should be used only to filter a resource's data set. For example, the path *feed.svc/daniel.larson* can be used to identify a feed of items published by Daniel Larson (rather than the query-string based URL of *feed.svc?author=daniel.larson*), and data filters can further be applied by using query parameters. For example, the URL *feed.svc/daniel.larson?filter=today* specifies only items published today. The query string is not used to uniquely identify the resource (or *list* of resources) but only to filter the data.

You won't need to work directly with the *UriTemplate* class when writing WCF services using the *WebGet* and *WebInvoke* attributes, but you can use the class directly when parsing or building URLs in code. URI templates allow you to parse path information from a URI as method parameters. For example, the path *DataService.svc?catalog=Default&title=Hello* could be converted to the URI *DataService.svc/Default/Hello* by applying the following URI template to the *WebGet* attribute:

```
[OperationContract]
[WebGet(UriTemplate = "{catalog}/{title}", ResponseFormat = WebMessageFormat.Json)]
DataItem GetData(string catalog, string title);
```

To use URI templates, you need to define them on an interface that is not exposed through an endpoint configured with the *enableWebScript* behavior. The Web scripting behavior is not compatible with *UriTemplate*, which means you must create a dedicated interface for the REST endpoints. Fortunately, you can use the same service class and expose it through the alternative REST interface. In the following examples, I've defined endpoints through the *IRestDataService* interface, which is shown in Listing 3-3 and configured through the following web.config endpoint configuration:

```
<service name="KnowledgeBase.DataService">
    <endpoint address="rest"
        behaviorConfiguration="PoxBehavior" binding="webHttpBinding"
        contract="KnowledgeBase.IRestDataService" />
</service>
```

LISTING 3-3. The *WebGet* attribute with a *UriTemplate* is used to pass parameters to WCF methods (*Knowledgebase/IRestDataService.cs*).

```
using System;
using System.ServiceModel;
using System.ServiceModel.Web;

namespace KnowledgeBase
{
    [ServiceContract(Namespace = "http://knowledgebase/", Name = "Data")]
    interface IRestDataService
    {
        [WebGet(UriTemplate = "{catalog}/{title}")]
        [OperationContract(Action = "Get")]
        DataItem GetData(string catalog, string title);
    }
}
```

To access the "Hello" data entry in the "Default" catalog, you could simply use the URL *http://knowledgebase/DataService.svc/rest/Default/Hello*.

> **Tip** URI templates are a key component in building REST services using WCF.

Using the *UriTemplate* Class to Build URLs

The *UriTemplate* class allows you to build and parse URLs using URI template strings. It is not tied to the WCF networking stack but contained in the assembly *System.ServiceModel.Web*. *UriTemplate* defines the *BindByName* and *BindByPosition* methods to build templates with named or ordered arguments. The following code demonstrates a URI template that defines a feed with an author and a tag.

```
string template = "feed.svc/{author}/{tag}";
UriTemplate uriTemplate = new UriTemplate(template);
Uri prefix = new Uri("http://knowledgebase");
Uri url = uriTemplate.BindByPosition(prefix, "daniellarson","ajax");
```

The *UriTemplate* class can also be used to parse arguments passed in the URL. You use the *Match* method to retrieve arguments from the URL, as in the following code:

```
string template = "feed.svc/{author}/{tag}";
UriTemplate uriTemplate = new UriTemplate(template);

Uri incomingUrl = new Uri("http://knowledgebase/feed.svc/daniellarson/ajax");
UriTemplateMatch results = uriTemplate.Match(
        new Uri(incomingUrl.GetLeftPart(UriPartial.Authority)),
        incomingUrl);
```

```
if (results != null){
    string author = results.BoundVariables["author"];
    string tag = results.BoundVariables["tag"];
    Console.WriteLine("{0} : {1}", author, tag);
}
```

Finally, the *UriTemplate* class can be used in situations in which you cannot pass arguments by using a *UriTemplate* parameter, such as WCF services with the Web scripting behavior or when you are building URLs to access remote services.

Supporting REST Service Actions with *WebInvoke*

As I mentioned earlier, in the Web programming model, the GET verb is special, indicating a read-only data retrieval operation. All other HTTP verbs specify an action and can be mapped to a WCF method by using the *WebInvoke* attribute. The *WebInvoke* attribute by default maps to the POST verb, although any HTTP verb other than GET can be specified in the parameter. To map an HTTP verb to WCF, specify the verb in the parameter, as in the following example of an interface method:

```
[OperationContract]
[WebInvoke(Method = "PUT",
        UriTemplate = "update",
        RequestFormat = WebMessageFormat.Json,
        ResponseFormat = WebMessageFormat.Json,
        BodyStyle = WebMessageBodyStyle.Bare)]
    void Update(DataItem entry);
```

The *WebInvoke* attribute includes the following parameters that affect the endpoint. These attribute parameters are also common in the *WebGet* attribute.

- **BodyStyle** Determines the style of the incoming and outgoing messages using the *WebMessageBody* enumeration. *WebMessageBodyStyle.Bare* is the default, which is the behavior you want most often and indicates that the result of the service method is written directly to the body of the response. Other choices are *WebMessageBodyStyle. Wrapped,* in which the request and response are wrapped, *WebMessageBodyStyle. WrappedRequest,* and *WebMessageBodyStyle.WrappedResponse*.

- **RequestFormat** Specifies the request format with the *WebMessageFormat* enumeration, although the request format can be inferred by the request's Content-Type HTTP header regardless of the *RequestFormat* specified in the *WebInvoke* or *WebGet* attribute.

- **ResponseFormat** Specifies the response format when invoked using the *webHttp-Binding* binding and *webHttp* behavior. The value is either *WebMessageFormat.Xml* or *WebMessageFormat.Json*. This value cannot be overridden through the AJAX request or inferred through the Content-Type HTTP header as with *RequestFormat*.

When calling a service from client code (JavaScript), you must specify the content type using the *Content-Type* HTTP header; otherwise, the WCF endpoint won't understand the request and an exception will be thrown by the service. To set the content type, use the *get_headers* method of the *Sys.Net.WebRequest* instance that is invoking the method. The Content-Type header is case sensitive in the ASP.NET AJAX library. The WCF content type for XML is *"application/xml"*, and the content type for JSON is *"application/json"*. The following JavaScript code sets the content type as XML by using the *WebRequest* class's *headers* property:

```
var request = new Sys.Net.WebRequest
request.get_headers()["Content-Type"] = "application/xml";
```

Tip The two choices for supported content types are *"application/xml"* and *"application/json"*. If you need to support additional content types using WCF services, you must implement a *WebContentTypeMapper*. For more information, see the MSDN example at *http://msdn2. microsoft.com/en-us/library/bb943479.aspx*.

Warning While HTTP headers are not case sensitive, the *Sys.Net.WebRequest* Content-Type header is. If you don't specify the header using the case-sensitive header "Content-Type", the AJAX JavaScript framework will overwrite it before the request.

The POST verb specifies that a Web request is sending data to the server, and it is generally considered the optimal way to update a data source using standard Web browser technology. POST requests send a message payload in the body of the post and are used to post a message from the client to the server. In the following example, we'll use the JavaScript object *Sys.Net.WebRequest* to post content to the sample endpoint. By using the *set_httpVerb* method, you can specify the HTTP POST method and you can also send a message payload in the body of the request. Listing 3-4 demonstrates an HTTP POST to a WCF service using XML.

LISTING 3-4. To post an XML message to WCF, use the XML schema from the data contract and the "application/xml" content type.

```
// Saves the Item using the XML data contract
function Save(){
    var data = new Object();
    data.Title = $get('TitleDiv').innerHTML;
    data.Body = $get('DataInput').value;

    var xml = String.format(  // - MS JS method similar to c# string.Format()
    '<Item xmlns="http://knowledgebase">
        <Title>{0}</Title>
        <Body>{1}</Body>
        <Format>wiki</Format>
    </Item>', data.Title, data.Body);

    var userContext = new Object();
    var request = new Sys.Net.WebRequest();
```

```
        var url = 'DataService.svc/rest/save';
        request.set_url(url);
        request.add_completed(onSaveSuccess);
        request.set_httpVerb('POST');
        request.set_userContext = userContext;
        request.get_headers()["Content-Type"] = "application/xml";
        request.set_body(xml);
        request.invoke();
    }
```

In most cases, creating a JavaScript object is far easier than creating XML on the client, especially when considering the differences between browsers in the XML DOM. However, JavaScript objects exist only in memory and must be serialized before they can be passed across network services. To serialize the object as a string, you can use the AJAX class *Sys. Serialization.JavaScriptSerializer*. This JavaScript type defines the methods *serialize* and *deserialize*. To serialize the object, simply call *Sys.Serialization.JavaScriptSerializer.serialize(object)* on the JavaScript object. In most cases you should avoid writing JSON by hand and use the client-side AJAX framework and the server-side WCF framework to handle the serialization.

> **Note** To post a JavaScript object to a Web service, pass a JSON-serialized object to the request along with the Content-Type header "application/json". The client-side AJAX library provides the class *Sys.Serialization.JavaScriptSerializer*, which can serialize or deserialize objects to and from JSON.

Listing 3-5 shows a *Save* method that posts a JavaScript object to the WCF service defined at *DataService.svc/rest/save*.

LISTING 3-5. *Sys.Serialization.JavaScriptSerializer* provides JSON serialization for JavaScript objects that can be posted to a REST endpoint.

```
// Saves the Item using a JavaScript object
function Save(){
    var data = new Object();
    data.Title = $get('TitleDiv').innerHTML;
    data.Body = $get('DataInput').value;
    var json = Sys.Serialization.JavaScriptSerializer.serialize(data);

    var userContext = new Object();
    var request = new Sys.Net.WebRequest();
    var url = 'DataService.svc/rest/save';
    request.set_url(url);
    request.add_completed(onSaveSuccess);
    request.set_httpVerb('POST');
    request.set_userContext = userContext;
    request.get_headers()["Content-Type"] = "application/json";
    request.set_body(json);
    request.invoke();
}
```

HTTP Header Processing with the HEAD Verb

The HEAD verb is used only to process HTTP headers and does not receive a response body. Because HEAD requests are only processed on the server by returning HTTP headers, they are the most lightweight Web request that you can make. These requests are useful for simple methods, such as authorization checks or session "keep-alive" methods, for which there is no need to fully process the request or return a response. Implementing a simple "keep alive" service can be useful in AJAX applications to maintain authentication sessions or to check whether the current Web context's state is still valid. Because one goal of a rich Internet application is to provide client functionality similar to a Windows application, you might want to provide a method that calls a keep-alive method on a set interval so that the user's authentication session does not expire if his browser is idle but still left open. It can be annoying to replace a desktop application with a Web application only to have it time out on you after a long-running session. You might also use a keep-alive approach to return an HTTP header indicating an invalid state, which might occur if another user deletes the item that is being viewed during a long-running page lifetime. Listing 3-6 defines a "keep-alive" service that accepts a HEAD request for the *Ping* method.

LISTING 3-6. Use the HEAD method to process a simple request using HTTP headers (*ExampleServices/ KeepAlive.cs*).

```csharp
using System;
using System.Net;
using System.ServiceModel;
using System.ServiceModel.Web;
using System.ServiceModel.Activation;

namespace ExampleServices
{
    [ServiceContract]
    interface IKeepAlive
    {
        [WebInvoke(Method = "HEAD", BodyStyle = WebMessageBodyStyle.Bare)]
        [OperationContract]
        void Ping();
    }

    [AspNetCompatibilityRequirements(RequirementsMode =
        AspNetCompatibilityRequirementsMode.Required)]
    public class KeepAlive : ExampleServices.IKeepAlive
    {
        public void Ping()
        {
            WebOperationContext.Current.OutgoingResponse.StatusCode =
                HttpStatusCode.OK;
            return;
        }
    }
}
```

To call a WCF HEAD method from the JavaScript client, invoke *WebRequest* using the HEAD verb. In the callback, check the response status code for 200 (OK). If the status code is not OK, you can perform additional actions. I'll discuss HTTP status codes in more detail in the next section. For now, it is enough to know that the status code 200 indicates success. Listing 3-7 demonstrates a JavaScript *WebRequest* call that uses the HEAD verb to check for the response status code property.

LISTING 3-7. The HEAD verb is used for processing HTTP headers and can be used to implement a keep-alive call (*Web/KeepAlive.aspx*).

```
var headRequest = new Sys.Net.WebRequest();
headRequest.set_url('KeepAlive.svc/ping');
headRequest.set_httpVerb('HEAD');
headRequest.add_completed(headSuccess);
headRequest.invoke();

function headSuccess(response, userContext){
    var OK = 200;
    if (response.get_statusCode() != OK){
        var statusText = response.get_statusText();
        alert(statusText);
    }
}
```

HTTP Status Codes

HTTP status codes are used to indicate success or failure and include standard error codes used by the HTTP protocol. HTTP status codes are returned as integers and are encapsulated in the .NET Framework enumeration *System.Net.HttpStatusCode*. The AJAX framework does not include a client-side enumeration of HTTP status codes, so you will usually handle status codes yourself. Although there are more than 50 status codes, the main ones to discuss are OK (200), Forbidden (403), Unauthorized (401), Not Modified (304), and Internal Server Error (500). Status codes are also arranged in ranges: the 200 range indicates success, the 300 range indicates redirection, the 400 range indicates failure or authentication issues, and the 500 range indicates server errors. The most relevant HTTP status codes are listed in Table 3-2.

TABLE 3-2. Common HTTP Status Codes

Code	Description
2XX Success	**Responses in the 200 range indicate success.**
200 OK	Request was successful.
201 Created	Indicates that the POST was successful and the item was created on the server.
204 No Content	Indicates success and that the response is intentionally blank.

TABLE 3-2. **Common HTTP Status Codes**

Code	Description
3XX Redirection	**Responses in the 300 range indicate request redirection.**
301 Moved	Indicates that the resource has been moved to a new URI. Browsers (including AJAX clients) will redirect the request to the URI indicated in the *LOCATION* HTTP header.
304 Not Modified	Indicates that the resource has not been modified since the last response, and redirects the client request to the client cache.
4XX Client Errors	**Responses in the 400 range indicate an error in the request.**
400 Bad Request	Indicates a bad request.
401 Unauthorized	Unauthorized. Returns an *AUTHORIZATION* HTTP header indicating an authentication protocol that the client can use.
403 Forbidden	Indicates the requested object is forbidden and cannot be accessed by the client. Use Forbidden to explicitly deny access to a resource.
404 Not Found	Indicates there is no resource at the URI requested. This status code is usually returned by the Web server (IIS) and not service code.
410 Gone	Indicates that the resource has been deleted. This status code is usually returned by service code to indicate that the resource requested does not exist.
5XX Server Errors	**Responses in the 500 range indicate an error in the response.**
500 Internal Server Error	Indicates a generic server error.
501 Not Implemented	Indicates that the request (the URI and HTTP verb combination) is not implemented by server code.

With normal responses, the 200 (OK) value is returned. You can check for the status code 200 (OK) in your AJAX callback functions to determine success for HTTP calls. The 403 (FORBIDDEN) status specifies that the server refuses to process the request for the current security principal, whereas the 401 (UNAUTHORIZED) status specifies an unauthenticated or not properly authorized response. The general purpose 500 (Internal Server Error) status is perhaps the most useful error response for AJAX applications. It usually specifies additional data in the status description. From the WCF service, the status description is returned through the *WebOperationContext.Current.OutgoingResponse.StatusDescription* property.

> **Tip** The AJAX callback will receive a 200 (OK) status code from 304 (NOT MODIFIED) responses as the request is redirected to the client cache response, which has a 200 (OK) status. I'll talk about NOT MODIFIED and the client cache later in this chapter.

When making Web requests using the JavaScript class *Sys.Net.WebRequest*, the completed callback handler is used for both success and failure responses. The completed callback handler is added with the *add_completed* method prior to calling *invoke*. The callback handler receives the *Sys.Net.WebRequestExecutor* type as the response and can be used to retrieve the status code, status description, response headers, and the actual response. To indicate success, the server responds with a 200 (OK) status. Any other status is either a failure or requires additional action. To handle the status code on the client, use the *get_statusCode* method of *WebRequestExecutor*. This is a different error-handling strategy than is used with Web services exposed through the Web scripting behavior discussed in Chapter 2, where the JavaScript proxy generates a success callback and a failure callback. Instead, all responses are processed in a common callback function. Listing 3-8 demonstrates a common error-handling strategy for Web requests. First the status code is retrieved using *response.get_statusCode*. If the status code is not 200 (OK), you must implement error handling accordingly.

LISTING 3-8. The *get_statusCode* and *get_statusText* methods of the *WebRequestExecutor* JavaScript type return the status code and description from the server (*Web/Rest.aspx*).

```
function onSaveCompleted(response, obj){
    // Process the status. Could be 200 OK,
    // 403 forbidden, 404 not found, 410 gone
    var status = response.get_statusCode();
    if (status != 200){
        var statusText = response.get_statusText();
        var errMsg = String.format('ERROR: {0} replied "{1}" ({2}).',
            url, statusText, status);
        Sys.Debug.trace(errMsg);

        switch(status){
            case 410:
                alert('Content has been removed.');
                break;
            case 404:
                alert('Could not find resource.');
                break;
            case 403:
                alert('Access forbidden.');
                break;
            default:
                alert(errMsg);
        }
        return;
    }

    var result = response.get_responseData();
    var content = $get('MainContent');
    if (content != null)
        content.innerHTML = result;
}
```

Listing 3-8 demonstrates error handling within the callback function for a save operation. You might want to further abstract the data retrieval and response handling with a custom networking library implemented on top of *Sys.Net.WebRequest*. You could use such a library to provide common infrastructure such as friendly error handling and more robust support for client-side caching.

Client-Side Caching with GET

One of the biggest advantages of the HTTP GET verb is its support for client-side caching in the HTTP protocol. Client-side caching is built into all modern Web browsers and can dramatically improve the performance of your AJAX application. Client-side caching is based on the URI of the request—the browser stores a cache file for each URL. For Internet Explorer on Windows Vista, the files are stored in %HOMEPATH%\AppData\Local\Microsoft\Windows\ Temporary Internet Files. These cache files have the attributes *Name, Internet Address, Type, Size, Expires, Last Modified, Last Accessed,* and *Last Checked.* The *Last Modified* and *Expires* attributes are the only attributes that you can explicitly set on the server.

> **Tip** Because caching is unique for each URI, you might want to build a compilation key into your JavaScript application that is unique for each build to prevent the use of data from a previous build. For a related solution, see the ScriptRuntimeControl code sample in Chapter 4, "The AJAX Runtime with the Microsoft AJAX Library."

The GET response can specify additional metadata about the response stream, indicating cache policy; specifying if, how long, and where the content can be cached; and the date that the item was last modified on the server. The Last-Modified HTTP header indicates the date that the item was last changed on the server and is sent from the server to the client and back to the server in the incoming If-Modified-Since header. Because the Last-Modified header is rounded to the second, it cannot be used for precise date and time measurement. The ETag HTTP header is also sent from the server to the client and back to the server. It is an opaque token that is returned with the next request, which makes it a better candidate for a cache key if you can rely on a last-modified date from the data source.

By setting a cache policy and a last-modified date, a Web browser can successfully cache the data on the client. For most data, it is ideal to use the client-side cache but have the browser check with the server for a fresh copy of the data on each request. This enables the server to send a 304 (NOT MODIFIED) response if the server data has not changed, without the risk of having out of date data. The data query for the last updated date in a database table is usually much more efficient than querying the entire data set and processing the response. The server can detect that there is no new data and return a "not modified" response (HTTP status 304), bypassing additional processing and serialization of the data.

> **Tip** Client-side caching using the ETag or the Last-Modified header is best used for data that is changed relatively infrequently but requested often.

To force the browser to always ask the server if the server has a fresh copy of the data, expire the data using the Expires HTTP header, as in the following code:

```
WebOperationContext.Current.OutgoingResponse.Headers
    [HttpResponseHeader.Expires] = DateTime.UtcNow.AddYears(-1).ToString("r");
```

> **Tip** If you do not explicitly expire the response, the browser might cache the data indefinitely, depending on the browser's cache settings.

To return the date that the server data was last modified, use the Last-Modified header as in the following code, which sets the header to the current universal time. Note that the value used is the local time. The framework will convert this to universal time.

```
WebOperationContext.Current.OutgoingResponse.LastModified = DateTime.Now;
```

The Last-Modified header value is returned to the server in the HTTP header If-Modified-Since. This value is the date-time stamp in GMT (universal) format that is passed from the Web service in the Last-Modified header. To get this value from the request, use the following code in the Web service:

```
string lastModClientString =
    WebOperationContext.Current.IncomingRequest.Headers["if-modified-since"];
```

To return a "not modified" value to the client, set the HTTP status code to 304 (specified by the .NET type *HttpStatusCode.NotModified*) as in the following example:

```
WebOperationContext.Current.OutgoingResponse.StatusCode = HttpStatusCode.NotModified;
```

When you return a 304 (NOT MODIFIED) response to the client, the browser intercepts the 304 response and returns a 200 (OK) status with a copy of the cached data that is redirected from the browser's cache. This means that for a simple AJAX client, you won't be able to tell from the HTTP status alone whether a response is from the browser's cache or from the server.

The If-Modified-Since header specifies a conditional response, not a partial response. Either the full data set requested should be returned or the 304 (NOT MODIFIED) status with an empty response stream. A subset of data reflecting the *if-modified-since* date should not be returned. For a subset of data, use an alternative mechanism to request the filtered data set, such as a query string filter. Listing 3-9 demonstrates simple caching logic with the LAST-MODIFIED and IF-MODIFIED-SINCE HTTP headers.

LISTING 3-9. To implement client-side caching, return 304 (*HttpStatusCode .NotModified*) to utilize the browser cache (*ExampleServices/CacheSample.cs*).

```
using System;
using System.ServiceModel;
using System.ServiceModel.Web;
using System.ServiceModel.Activation;
using System.Web;
using System.Globalization;
using System.Net;

namespace ExampleServices
{
```

```
[AspNetCompatibilityRequirements(
    RequirementsMode = AspNetCompatibilityRequirementsMode.Allowed)]
[ServiceContract]
public class CacheSample
{
    [WebGet][OperationContract]
    public string Demo()
    {
        string lastModClientString =
            WebOperationContext.Current.IncomingRequest.Headers
            ["if-modified-since"];
        if (lastModClientString != null)
        {
            DateTime lastMod = DateTime.MinValue;
            DateTime tempDateTime = DateTime.MinValue;
            if (DateTime.TryParse(lastModClientString,
                    CultureInfo.InvariantCulture,
                    DateTimeStyles.AssumeUniversal, out tempDateTime))
                lastMod = tempDateTime.ToUniversalTime();

            if (DateTime.UtcNow - lastMod < TimeSpan.FromMinutes(1))
            {
                WebOperationContext.Current.OutgoingResponse.StatusCode =
                    System.Net.HttpStatusCode.NotModified;
                return null;
            }
        }

        // DO NOT USE HttpContext.Current,
        // instead use WebOperationContext.Current

        WebOperationContext.Current.OutgoingResponse.Headers
            [HttpResponseHeader.CacheControl] = "Private";

        WebOperationContext.Current.OutgoingResponse.LastModified =
            DateTime.Now.AddMinutes(1);

        // Expire the content to force a request
        WebOperationContext.Current.OutgoingResponse.Headers
            [HttpResponseHeader.Expires] =
            DateTime.Now.AddYears(-1).ToString("r");

        return DateTime.Now.ToString("r");
    }
}
}
```

Although the code sample in Listing 3-9 uses a hard-coded last-modified expiration time of 1 minute, you would ideally check the last-modified date against the server data source's last-modified date. If you are using a back-end database, you should always use the database time as the last-modified time stamp, which allows you to pass in a last-modified time to the data query.

> **Tip** When converting local time to universal time with the .NET Framework, always check that the time to be converted is not in the future. If it is, an *ArgumentOutOfRangeException* is thrown. This exception is a common bug on distributed systems where the time might not be perfectly synchronized.

Introducing WCF Syndication Services

Syndication is a mechanism by which applications publish their data in a standardized XML format. By publishing in a standardized feed format, a server application enables remote clients to access your data streams through loosely connected channels, and the data can take on a life of its own in the remote system. Syndicated content is defined by *items* in a syndicated *feed*. Remote clients can subscribe to a remote feed and store the data locally, often aggregated with multiple feeds. This enables loosely coupled integration across all sorts of applications and platforms. With syndicated feeds, your data is no longer restricted to your application or even to clients of your application—it can take on a life of its own in aggregation systems and intranet and Internet data repositories. With built-in syndication support in Windows, the Office system, Windows SharePoint Services, and countless client and server applications, syndicated feeds enable users to consume data as they want.

The two most widely used standardized XML specifications for syndicated feeds are RSS and Atom. RSS, or Really Simple Syndication, defines a channel of repeating items. Each item has a title, description, and link, making it an ideal format for sharing news on the Web. Because of the simplicity of RSS, it is the most widely used syndication format today and the standard syndication format used by Windows Live services and the 2007 Microsoft Office System. The schema of RSS is inferred; all elements of the RSS specification are defined without a namespace. Any extensions to the RSS specification are added through elements and attributes defined in custom namespaces.

> **More Information** The full RSS specification is available at *http://www.rssboard.org/rss-specification*. Only a subset of the RSS specification is implemented by the default WCF feed generator; the full RSS specification requires custom extensions.

A simple RSS document is shown in Listing 3-10. The XML document exists outside an XML namespace, and any custom elements are defined in explicit namespaces. This feed was generated by using the WCF syndication framework and contains Atom elements using the *a10* prefix, defined in the namespace *http://www.w3.org/2005/Atom*. While the RSS specification defines items such as pubDate to specify the publishing date, the WCF syndication implementation favors Atom standards and includes the Atom equivalent defined in the *Atom* namespace, which is perfectly legal according to the RSS specification.

LISTING 3-10. RSS is a (really) simple syndication format that defines a channel of repeating items.

```
<rss version="2.0" xmlns:a10="http://www.w3.org/2005/Atom">
  <channel>
    <title>Recently Posted: Default</title>
    <description>Recently Posted items for Default</description>
    <item>
      <a10:author>
        <a10:name>Daniel Larson</a10:name>
      </a10:author>
      <title>Test</title>
      <description>Test Wiki Content</description>
      <pubDate>Sun, 24 Feb 2008 23:26:01 -0700</pubDate>
      <a10:updated>2008-02-24T23:32:05-07:00</a10:updated>
    </item>
  </channel>
</rss>
```

Note With support for offline synchronization, users can read an RSS feed from my Web site whenever they want, regardless of their Internet connection. Syndicated feeds are also archived and processed in online data stores such as NewsGator Online and Technorati, where the data is saved, tagged, and analyzed by the mass population of the Internet. You can subscribe to my feed at the URL *http://feeds.feedburner.com/daniellarson*.

The Atom syndication format is similar to RSS but offers richer semantics and is defined in the *Atom* XML namespace. The Atom format defines a *feed* element with multiple *entry* elements, all of which are defined in the XML namespace *http://www.w3.org/2005/Atom*. Listing 3-11 lists the same syndicated document defined in Listing 3-10 but instead expresses it in the Atom format.

LISTING 3-11 The Atom feed expresses a feed of multiple entries.

```
<feed xmlns="http://www.w3.org/2005/Atom">
  <title type="text">Recently Posted: Default</title>
  <subtitle type="text">Recently Posted items for Default</subtitle>
  <id>uuid:256307b6-5e6b-40d8-9a28-74bb1aa25a2a;id=1</id>
  <updated>2008-02-26T01:27:55Z</updated>
  <entry>
    <id>uuid:256307b6-5e6b-40d8-9a28-74bb1aa25a2a;id=2</id>
    <title type="text">Test</title>
    <published>2008-02-24T23:26:01-07:00</published>
    <updated>2008-02-24T23:32:05-07:00</updated>
    <author>
      <name>Daniel Larson</name>
    </author>
    <content type="text">Test Wiki Content</content>
  </entry>
</feed>
```

By using syndicated feeds as foundational components of your AJAX architecture, you can use the same code for syndication as you use for your application services. Wherever you have lists of repeating items, a feed can be a good architectural fit for the message.

To create your first WCF syndication service, define a service method that returns a *SyndicationFeedFormatter* object. To make it easy for you, Visual Studio 2008 includes a template for a Syndication Feed Library project type, although you will probably want to include syndication feeds as part of your main WCF service library.

> **Note** The *SyndicationFeedFormatter* is an abstract class that serializes a feed into XML using RSS, Atom, or a custom serialization format. You generally return an instance of *Atom10FeedFormatter* or *Rss20FeedFormatter*, although WCF provides support for custom syndication formats through custom classes that inherit from *SyndicationFeedFormatter*.

Within your implementation, create a *SyndicationFeed* object containing a list of *SyndicationItem* items. As the last step, return a *SyndicationFeedFormatter* instance, which will usually be an *Rss20FeedFormatter* or, preferably, the *Atom10FeedFormatter*. The *SyndicationFeedFormatter* takes the feed as an input parameter and serializes it with the formatter. Listing 3-12 demonstrates the simplest of feed generators using *SyndicationFeed*, *SyndicationItems*, and *Atom10FeedFormatter*.

LISTING 3-12. The Hello World syndication feed (*KnowledgeBase/FeedDemoService.cs*).

```
using System;
using System.Collections.Generic;
using System.ServiceModel.Syndication;
using System.ServiceModel.Web;
using System.ServiceModel.Activation;
using System.Globalization;
using System.Net;

namespace KnowledgeBase
{
    [AspNetCompatibilityRequirements(RequirementsMode =
            AspNetCompatibilityRequirementsMode.Required)]
    public class FeedDemoService : IFeedDemoService
    {
        public SyndicationFeedFormatter CreateFeed(string title)
        {
            SyndicationFeed feed = new SyndicationFeed(title,
                "A WCF Syndication Feed for " + title, null);
            List<SyndicationItem> items = new List<SyndicationItem>();

            // Create a new Syndication Item.
            SyndicationItem item = new SyndicationItem("An item",
                "Item content", null);
            items.Add(item);
```

```
            feed.Items = items;
            return new Atom10FeedFormatter(feed);
        }
    }
}
```

The WCF syndication programming model is based on the Atom specification. The main syndication objects also map to items in the Atom specification, making Atom the preferred syndication format for WCF services. The syndication object model consists of the following core objects.

- **SyndicationFeed**   Defines the top-level feed object, *feed* in Atom 1.0 or *rss* in RSS 2.0. The feed contains metadata about the feed and a collection of *SyndicationItems*.

- **SyndicationItem**   Defines the individual feed item, *item* in RSS 2.0 or *entry* in Atom 1.0. Items are contained in the *channel* element in RSS 2.0 or as child elements of *feed* in Atom 1.0. *Items* contain collections of categories expressed through the *SyndicationCategory* class and generally have an *author, link,* and *date published.*

- **SyndicationPerson**   Represents the content's author or a contributor. *SyndicationPerson* defines the properties *Email, Name,* and *Uri* and is a common object that is serialized either as the Atom *author* element or *contributor* element, depending on which collection it is added to.

- **SyndicationCategory**   Represents a *tag* applied to content and is typically a string applied by the content author to categorize the content. However, the category can also specify a label or schema that can apply special meaning to the tag.

- **SyndicationLink**   Specifies a link from a syndicated item and is most often used to link to the resource that the syndicated item represents or to include an associated file such as a podcast or document in an item. *SyndicationLink* properties include *MediaType,* which specifies the MIME type of the attachment, *RelationshipType,* which defines the relationship of the link (alternate, related, self, enclosure, or via), *Title,* and *Uri.*

> **More Information**   For a full reference on *System.ServiceModel.Syndication,* see the MSDN topic *http://msdn2.microsoft.com/en-us/system.servicemodel.syndication.aspx.*

To extend the syndication engine with custom elements, you can use the class *Syndication-ElementExtension.* Examples of common extensions include Microsoft's Simple List Extensions (SLE 1.0; see *http://msdn.microsoft.com/bb190612.aspx*) or GeoRSS extensions (see *http://www.georss.org*), which encode items with geographical data and are typically used to create mashups with mapping services such as Microsoft Virtual Earth.

To create a feed that supports extensions, you can use a loosely typed access model by creating extension objects as needed, or you can create classes that derive from *SyndicationFeed* and *SyndicationItem*. The latter is the preferred mechanism and should be considered for any commercial syndication implementation. Although I won't go into detail on syndication customization, you can read the MSDN topic "Syndication Extensibility" at *http://msdn2.microsoft.com/bb924494.aspx* for documentation on syndication extensibility.

Syndication feeds are most often used to display recently posted items, especially in an aggregated fashion when results come from various feeds. The sample application's data access class defines a method *GetRecentlyPosted,* which returns a list of recently posted syndication items from the specified catalog. Listing 3-13 demonstrates the addition of the syndicated feed to the *DataService* class by returning an item of type *SyndicationFeed-Formatter.* The *SyndicationFeedFormatter* object automatically serializes into the response stream when accessed through *WebHttpBinding.*

LISTING 3-13. The syndication feed is useful for generating feeds for external consumers (*KnowledgeBase/DataService.cs*).

```csharp
using System;
using System.ServiceModel.Web;
using System.ServiceModel;
using System.ServiceModel.Activation;

using KnowledgeBase.Implementation;
using System.Security.Principal;
using System.Web;
using System.ServiceModel.Syndication;
using System.Collections.Generic;

namespace KnowledgeBase
{
    [AspNetCompatibilityRequirements(
            RequirementsMode=AspNetCompatibilityRequirementsMode.Required)]
    public class DataService : IDataService, IKnowledgeBaseFeedServer
    {
        // previous code omitted...

        public SyndicationFeedFormatter CreateRecentlyPostedFeed(string catalog)
        {
            SyndicationFeed feed =
                new SyndicationFeed("Recently Posted: " + catalog,
                "Recently Posted items for " + catalog, null);

            DataRetrieval knowledgeBase =
                new DataRetrieval(HttpContext.Current.User);
            List<SyndicationItem> items = knowledgeBase.GetRecentlyPosted(catalog);
            feed.Items = items;

            HttpContext.Current.Response.Cache.SetExpires(
                DateTime.Now.AddYears(-1));
```

```
            WebOperationContext.Current.OutgoingResponse.LastModified =
                DateTime.UtcNow;

            SyndicationFeedFormatter formatter = new Atom10FeedFormatter(feed);
            return formatter;
        }
    }
}
```

By implementing an additional interface for the feed generator, you can support a friendly REST interface for the catalog's recently posted feed. Listing 3-14 defines the interface for the feed server that can be added to *DataService*. Notice that I'm using the *UriTemplate* class to pass in the catalog and title parameters and the *ServiceKnownType* attribute to specify the well-known return type. *ServiceKnownType* is required by the WCF runtime and is used to maintain compatibility with SOAP-based service clients, although WCF will serialize the feed into XML through the *WebHttp* behavior.

LISTING 3-14. The knowledge base recently posted interface uses the *UriTemplate* and *SyndicationFeed* implementations (*KnowledgeBase/IKnowledgeBaseFeedServer.cs*).

```
using System;
using System.ServiceModel.Syndication;
using System.ServiceModel;
using System.ServiceModel.Web;

namespace KnowledgeBase
{
    [ServiceKnownType(typeof(Atom10FeedFormatter))]
    [ServiceContract]
    interface IKnowledgeBaseFeedServer
    {
        [OperationContract]
        [WebGet(UriTemplate = "{format}/{catalog}",
                BodyStyle = WebMessageBodyStyle.Bare)]
        SyndicationFeedFormatter CreateRecentlyPostedFeed(
            string format, string catalog);
    }
}
```

In the previous code samples, I demonstrated only the feed generation capabilities of the WCF syndication framework. The syndication framework also includes support for parsing syndicated feeds and support for parsing RSS 2.0 and Atom 1.0 into the common syndication object model.

I also described the Atom syndication format because it is the basis of the syndication engine. The Atom protocol contains more than just the syndication specification, however. It is also a rich protocol for publishing content using the REST programming model, which makes it an ideal protocol for collaborative data input in AJAX applications.

> **More Information**   For more information on the Atom publishing protocol, see
> *http://atomenabled.org.*

Implementing REST Web Services Using ASP.NET 2.0 HTTP Handlers

A Web service is defined as an endpoint that returns data using standard HTTP mechanisms. Although .NET developers have generally associated Web services with SOAP-based services, you've already seen examples of REST services and POX (Plain Old XML) services using WCF. At times, however, you might want to process the raw HTTP request and response, and WCF might not be the best solution. For example, in Windows SharePoint Services 3.0, WCF services aren't supported through the out-of-the-box application. You might choose to implement HTTP handlers for performance reasons, or perhaps the service you're providing doesn't fit well with the WCF programming model. HTTP handlers can be mapped to any URL (including wildcards) through Internet Information Services (IIS) and web.config, which offers flexibility but less abstraction than the WCF model.

An HTTP handler gives you full control over request and response processing and is simply a class that implements the *IHttpHandler* interface. The HTTP handler has no runtime overhead, making it the most lightweight implementation possible to process a Web request. This is ideal in certain cases, but it does not give you the flexibility or abstraction of the WCF framework. Regardless, an HTTP handler does play a role in service-based AJAX applications and is an interface you should learn about as a Web application developer. The *IHttpHandler* interface is shown in Listing 3-15. It allows you to implement the processing of the request and response through raw access to the current instance of *HttpContext*.

LISTING 3-15. The *IHttpHandler* interface processes the raw HTTP context.

```
namespace System.Web
{
    public interface IHttpHandler
    {
        bool IsReusable { get; }
        void ProcessRequest(HttpContext context);
    }
}
```

There are only two methods to implement with the *IHttpHandler* interface—*IsReusable* and *ProcessRequest*. *IsReusable* specifies that the ASP.NET runtime can reuse the object for multiple requests. It should be set to *false* for any handler that implements any type of state, such as private fields or properties. If the method doesn't use state and one instance can be reused for multiple requests, you can gain a performance boost by setting *IsReusable* to *true*. *ProcessRequest* passes in the current HTTP context through the *HttpContext* class, which gives you full access to the request and the response.

To write a simple HTTP handler, implement the *IHttpHandler* interface and process the request and response streams in the *ProcessRequest* method. As you can see in the Hello World HTTP handler example in Listing 3-16, implementing the *IHttpHandler* interface is a trivial task, but it can be a powerful tool for building endpoints because it gives you complete control over the process.

LISTING 3-16. The *IHttpHandler* interface is used to process the entire HTTP context (*ExampleServices/ HelloHandler.cs*).

```
using System;
using System.Web;

namespace ExampleServices
{
    public class HelloHandler : IHttpHandler
    {
        public bool IsReusable { get { return true; } }
        public void ProcessRequest(HttpContext context)
        {
            context.Response.Write("Hello World!");
        }
    }
}
```

 More Information If your handler uses any type of asynchronous methods, such as for input/output operations or data access, consider using the *IHttpAsyncHandler* for asynchronous processing in ASP.NET. For more information about implementing asynchronous handlers, see the MSDN topic "Creating an Asynchronous HTTP Handler" at *http://msdn2.microsoft.com/en-us/library/ms227433.aspx*.

To enable your handler in the Web site, you must register it in web.config in the *httpHandlers* node. You must register the type and assembly for the handler, as well as the HTTP verb (or multiple verbs, including wildcards) that it will respond to. Here is the web.config entry for our *HelloHandler* class, using the URL *helloworld.aspx*.

```
<httpHandlers>
    <add verb="GET" path="HelloWorld.aspx"
        type="ExampleServices.HelloHandler, ExampleServices" validate="false"/>
</httpHandlers>
```

> **Tip** When registering an HTTP handler, you must register it with a file extension that is handled by the ASP.NET framework. You can use any extension as long as it is mapped to the ASP.NET process in IIS. In Windows SharePoint Services 3.0, all file extensions are configured to be processed by ASP.NET and you will not have this constraint for services running under the SharePoint application.
>
> You can also specify which file extensions are processed by ASP.NET in IIS. In IIS 7.0 you can open the Web site's Handler Mappings section, where you can specify the executable to handle the request with a script map. To process all requests through the ASP.NET engine, specify the "*" request path mapping and use the path to your ASP.NET DLL, *aspnet_isapi.dll.*

Instead of registering HTTP handlers in web.config directly, you can map wildcards to an *IHttpHandlerFactory* interface. For example, you can map all the files in a subdirectory to a handler factory with the following configuration. This web.config file would be deployed in a subdirectory such as "/feeds".

```
<httpHandlers>
    <add verb="*" path="*"
        type="ExampleServices.FeedHandlerFactory, ExampleServices" validate="false"/>
</httpHandlers>
```

The *IHttpHandlerFactory* interface is a simple factory interface that enables you to specify which HTTP handler should process a request. If mapping requests to services through configuration isn't practical because of your hosting environment, the HTTP handler factory can be a great alternative. When it is more practical to use code than configuration to decide which service should handle a URL endpoint, an HTTP handler factory might be your best architectural option.

Listing 3-17 shows the *IHttpHandlerFactory* interface. The *GetHandler* method uses the current HTTP context as well as physical path information to let your code determine which handler to return.

LISTING 3-17. The *IHttpHandlerFactory* interface is used to return an HTTP handler for processing a request.

```
namespace System.Web
{
    // Defines the contract for IHttpHandler class factories
    public interface IHttpHandlerFactory
    {
        // Returns an instance of the IHttpHandler interface.
        IHttpHandler GetHandler(HttpContext context,
            string requestType, string url, string pathTranslated);

        // Enables a factory to reuse an existing handler instance.
        void ReleaseHandler(IHttpHandler handler);
    }
}
```

To implement the handler, inherit from *IHttpHandlerFactory* and choose which handler to return in the *GetHandler* method. The *UriTemplate* class can be useful for parsing URLs and determining which handler to call based on the URI. In the following code samples, I use the *UriTemplate* class to determine the handler for an endpoint and return a syndication feed using the syndication library from the *System.ServiceModel.Web* assembly. This is the same endpoint functionality as shown in Listing 3-14, but it is expressed through an ASP.NET HTTP handler implementation. Listing 3-18 demonstrates the handler factory that uses the *UriTemplate* to determine the endpoint.

LISTING 3-18. To implement the *IHttpHandlerFactory*, implement logic to choose which handler to return based on the path translated, URL requested, and verb (*ExampleServices/FeedHandlerFactory.cs*).

```
using System;
using System.Web;

namespace ExampleServices
{
    public class FeedHandlerFactory : IHttpHandlerFactory
    {
        public IHttpHandler GetHandler(HttpContext context,
            string requestType, string url, string pathTranslated)
        {
            // Use a simple UriTemplate to determine the handler to return.
            UriTemplate template = new UriTemplate("feed.aspx/{catalog}");
            Uri baseAddress = new Uri(
                context.Request.Url.GetLeftPart(UriPartial.Authority) +
                context.Request.ApplicationPath);
            UriTemplateMatch results = template.Match(baseAddress,
                context.Request.Url);
            if (results != null)
            {
                string catalog = results.BoundVariables["catalog"];
                return new RecentlyPostedFeedHandler(catalog);
            }

            else
                return new ExampleXmlHandler();
        }

        public void ReleaseHandler(IHttpHandler handler)
        {
            // Use this method to free up any state to enable reuse
            // for the handler instance.
        }
    }
}
```

The *IHttpHandler* interface is used to return *IHttpHandler* implementations, deferring the decision to run time rather than configuration. In this case, I've provided a *UriTemplate* implementation to determine the handler and to parse the service parameters, an approach that is similar to using the *WebGet* attribute with *UriTemplate* in WCF technologies. You can see here that the code is very similar to the WCF implementation, although slightly more processing is required. Listing 3-19 completes the HTTP handler sample by implementing an Atom feed that uses the same code as previously implemented in WCF.

LISTING 3-19. To implement *IHttpHandler*, handle the HTTP context directly (*ExampleServices/RecentlyPostedFeedHandler.cs*).

```
using System;
using System.Text;
using System.Web;
using KnowledgeBase;
using System.Xml.Serialization;
using System.ServiceModel.Syndication;
using System.Xml;
using KnowledgeBase.Implementation;
using System.Collections.Generic;

namespace ExampleServices
{
    public class RecentlyPostedFeedHandler : IHttpHandler
    {
        public bool IsReusable
        {
            get { return false; }
        }

        public string Catalog { get; set; }
        public RecentlyPostedFeedHandler(string catalog) { this.Catalog = catalog; }

        public void ProcessRequest(HttpContext context)
        {
            // Creates a new feed using the WCF Syndication library.
            context.Response.ContentType = "text/xml";
            SyndicationFeed feed =
                new SyndicationFeed("Recently Posted: " + this.Catalog,
                "Recently Posted items for " + this.Catalog, null);

            DataAccess knowledgeBase = new DataAccess(HttpContext.Current.User);
            List<SyndicationItem> items =
                knowledgeBase.GetRecentlyPosted( this.Catalog);
            feed.Items = items;
            SyndicationFeedFormatter formatter = new Atom10FeedFormatter(feed);
            XmlWriter outputWriter = new XmlTextWriter(context.Response.Output);
            formatter.WriteTo(outputWriter);
            HttpContext.Current.Response.Cache.SetLastModified(DateTime.UtcNow);
            HttpContext.Current.Response.Cache.SetCacheability(
                HttpCacheability.Private);
            outputWriter.Flush();
        }
    }
}
```

While less abstracted than WCF services and tightly coupled to the HTTP runtime and ASP.NET, HTTP handlers can play an important part in AJAX service architectures, both for implementing services and for providing AJAX infrastructure components. HTTP handlers are the most lightweight HTTP processing mechanisms available using the .NET Framework.

Summary

In this chapter, we looked at the WCF Web programming model and support for the HTTP protocol, including the REST architecture pattern. You learned about using the GET verb for data retrieval and its architectural advantages for using client-side data caching with the Last-Modified HTTP header. We also looked at *WebInvoke* support for HTTP verbs specifying actions. Finally, we looked at alternative Web service technologies that target the AJAX client using ASP.NET 2.0 technologies.

In the next chapter, I'll introduce Microsoft's ASP.NET AJAX client-side JavaScript runtime, and then we'll start building components and controls for AJAX applications in the following chapters, all using the service techniques we've covered in this chapter.

Part II
Practical AJAX

Chapter 4
The AJAX Runtime with the Microsoft AJAX Library

After completing this chapter, you will

- Understand the ScriptManager server control and its role in deploying an AJAX application.

- Understand object-oriented JavaScript and the Microsoft AJAX Library.

- Understand and be able to utilize the Microsoft AJAX Library's JavaScript type system.

In the first three chapters, we've looked at programming service-oriented AJAX applications using Windows Communication Foundation (WCF) to implement the back-end server. In this chapter we'll start looking at client applications that use the ASP.NET AJAX client-side runtime, also known as the Microsoft AJAX Library, and the ASP.NET ScriptManager control.

Note The Microsoft AJAX Library refers to the client-side JavaScript framework of ASP.NET AJAX. ASP.NET AJAX includes both the client runtime as well as the server runtime.

Programming for the client runtime is a dramatic shift for most ASP.NET developers. We're used to compiled code, drag-and-drop controls, and the Microsoft .NET Framework. We're also used to object-oriented design patterns and principles, base classes, and inheritance. At first the JavaScript language can seem quite primitive to an ASP.NET developer. But with a little understanding of the JavaScript programming model and its rich support for inheritance and design patterns, you'll be able to use JavaScript and the Microsoft AJAX Library to develop component-based application frameworks, utilizing the same modern object-oriented programming principles that you're used to in managed code. Microsoft's AJAX library is built specifically with .NET developers in mind and adds a type system on top of the loosely typed JavaScript language.

Understanding the Client-Side Programming Model

The client-side programming model is based on the Document Object Model (DOM), which is the browser's interpretation of the HTML rendered on the Web page. Although the DOM programming model is similar in all Web browsers, it varies and is subtly different based on the underlying browser engine—for example, the Gecko engine is used by FireFox and Netscape browsers, the IE Engine is used by Internet Explorer, Webkit by Safari and Chrome, and Opera has its own engine as well. These variations make the DOM a problematic technology to deal with in applications that target all browsers, but the variations are limited in scope and generally deal with operations that are performed on XML or document nodes. The Microsoft AJAX Library's DOM extensions handle cross-browser issues very well, so whenever you are working with the AJAX library you can be assured that your code works across browsers. In the following chapters, I'll describe cross-browser framework classes, including *Sys.UI.DomElement* and *Sys.UI.DomEvent*, in more detail.

> **Tip** Whenever you program against the DOM directly, be aware of the subtle differences between DOM implementations and test with the versions of the browsers that you plan to support. It is common for modern applications to support Internet Explorer 7 and FireFox 2.0 at a minimum, although many organizations are still using Internet Explorer 6.

On top of the DOM sits JavaScript, which is relatively consistent across all modern browsers, although newer features of JavaScript 1.8 are not implemented in Internet Explorer. JavaScript 2.0 is also a work in progress and will be available in the releases of browsers after Internet Explorer 8 and Firefox 3.0; however, JavaScript 2.0 will have only minor changes and will retain the same loosely typed nature of JavaScript 1.2. Because JavaScript is the one language that is consistent across all Web browsers and is implemented in a robust and consistent manner in all Web platforms, it has become the language of the Web and will not be replaced any time soon.

The Microsoft AJAX Library itself is implemented with the JavaScript language and includes a type system, cross-browser support for DOM functionality, network libraries, a component model, and a control framework. Because the DOM and browser network libraries that use multiple implementations of *XmlHttpRequest* vary from browser to browser, the Microsoft AJAX Library's cross-browser implementation and abstraction is one of its chief benefits.

Finally, on top of the Microsoft AJAX Library, an application developer can extend, build, and integrate AJAX frameworks and custom AJAX applications programmed to use Web services and other data sources. To put this all into an architecture diagram, Figure 4-1 depicts the client-side programming model of the Microsoft Ajax Library.

The AJAX Application		
Custom AJAX Frameworks		AJAX Control Toolkit
Microsoft AJAX Library 3.5	Web Service Proxies	Control Infrastructure
	Application Services	Component Infrastructure
	Network Library	DOM Extensions
	Type System (Namespace, Classes, Inheritance Model)	
	Base Type Extensions	
JavaScript Language		
Browser DOM Model		

FIGURE 4-1. The AJAX application runtime is built on the DOM using JavaScript. It is implemented through the Microsoft AJAX Library, custom frameworks, and custom applications.

Deploying the Runtime with ASP.NET Server Controls

In a pure AJAX application architecture, server-based controls are avoided in favor of using a pure client runtime. The one server control you do use, however, is the ScriptManager, which is used to deploy the client runtime to the page. The ScriptManager control also performs a small bit of script injection to specify the authentication status of users when you use it with application services, a capability that I'll discuss in the Chapter 6, "AJAX Application Services with Sys.Services." Although you can include the AJAX library's JavaScript files manually, you'll generally gain better results by letting ASP.NET handle script registration through this simple control.

Only one instance of the ScriptManager control can be included on a page. If more than one instance occurs, ASP.NET throws an *InvalidOperationException*. The consequences of this restriction mean that if you're using master pages, you cannot include a ScriptManager on the master page and on the content page. Instead, you should use the ScriptManagerProxy control on the content page, which adds script references to the main ScriptManager control at compile time.

> **Tip** The ScriptManager control is also used to enable partial rendering through the Update Panel, a pseudo-AJAX technique I will not cover in this book.

When you use master pages, the master page should contain the ScriptManager control and any scripts that are common to content pages. (Ideally, you will have only one page for the entire AJAX application, but this is rarely the case.) Listing 4-1 defines a simple master page that includes the ScriptManager control.

LISTING 4-1. The master page contains the ScriptManager control and any core libraries for your application (*Web/Master/Example.master*).

```
<%@ Master Language="C#" %>
<html xmlns="http://www.w3.org/1999/xhtml">
<head id="Head1" runat="server">
    <title>Service Oriented AJAX: Example Master Page</title>
    <asp:ContentPlaceHolder ID="head" runat="server">
    </asp:ContentPlaceHolder>
    <link href="../Style/StyleSheet.css" rel="stylesheet" type="text/css" />
</head>
<body>
    <form id="pageForm" runat="server">
    <div id="pageHeader">
        Service-Oriented AJAX on the Microsoft Platform
    </div>
    <div id="pageBody">

        <asp:ScriptManager ID="AjaxScriptManager" runat="server" />
```

```
            <asp:ContentPlaceHolder ID="MainMasterBody" runat="server">
                Application Content Goes Here
            </asp:ContentPlaceHolder>
        </div>
        </form>
    </body>
    </html>
```

When the ScriptManager control is defined on the master page, the ScriptManagerProxy control is used to access the ScriptManager and add script and service references from content pages. Listing 4-2 demonstrates a content page that adds the script JSBasics.js by using a ScriptManagerProxy.

LISTING 4-2. The content page contains custom application code (*Web/Default.aspx*).

```
<%@ Page Language="C#" MasterPageFile="~/Master/Example.master" %>

<asp:Content ID="Content1" runat="server" ContentPlaceHolderID=MainMasterBody>
    <asp:ScriptManagerProxy ID="ScriptManagerProxy1" runat="server">
        <Scripts>
            <asp:ScriptReference Path="~/SCRIPT/JSBasics.js " />
        </Scripts>
    </asp:ScriptManagerProxy>

    <div>Hello, Ajax Developers!</div>

</asp:Content>
```

A new capability in the 3.5 AJAX framework (included in .NET 3.5 service pack 1) is the ability to combine scripts. This capability reduces the number of network calls that a page is required to make for the page to be loaded. Both the ScriptManager and ScriptManagerProxy controls contain the *CompositeScript* tag, which allows you to generate a single script file from multiple scripts. While you might gain the benefits of fewer network calls on the initial download, the browser will cache the JavaScript on subsequent calls regardless, making this a trivial gain that makes it more difficult to debug. However, you might find it useful in certain situations to combine a portion of your scripts as a logical unit.

> **More Information** For more information on composite scripts, see the MSDN online documentation at *http://msdn.microsoft.com/system.web.ui.scriptmanager.compositescript.aspx*.

Compiled Script Resources

Using the ScriptManager control, you can reference compiled script resources instead of file-based script resources. This lets you deploy scripts in an assembly rather than through the file system. To include a compiled script resource, add the JavaScript file to a class library and choose *Embedded Resource* as the property of the file. You must then reference the script through the *System.Web.UI.WebResource* attribute, which makes the script resource accessible through the ASP.NET script resource handler. The name of the file will be the fully qualified resource name, as the following code sample demonstrates. As an example, to include the file DemoScript.js, add it to the root folder of the class library project and set its compile action to Embedded Resource. For an assembly named ScriptDemo, the resource name will be ScriptDemo.DemoScript.js. If the resource name is not in the root folder of the project, it needs to be changed to include the implied namespace based on the folder path. For example, placing the file in a Scripts folder would change the name to ScriptDemo.Scripts.DemoScript.js. The following attribute would be used to enable the compiled resource "DemoScript.js" to be accessible through the script handler:

```
[assembly: System.Web.UI.WebResource("ScriptDemo.DemoScript.js",
    "application/x-javascript")]
```

To reference this script in the ScriptManager, use the following entry, noting that the reference is to the named resource (the same name defined in the *WebResource* attribute) rather than a URL:

```
<asp:ScriptManager ID="AjaxScriptManager" runat="server"  >
    <Scripts>
        <asp:ScriptReference Assembly="ScriptDemo" Name="ScriptDemo.DemoScript.js" />
    </Scripts>
</asp:ScriptManager>
```

Tip Although you can include scripts that are compiled as resources, I've found that doing so makes debugging much more difficult. I recommend including all scripts as files rather than compiled resources.

The Script Manager Programming Model

The ScriptManager exposes a programming model, and it can be used from server-side code to generate script library references and to ensure that the client AJAX runtime is loaded and configured properly. You can implement a ScriptManager wrapper by creating a composite control that checks for the existence of a ScriptManager in the page and add either a reference or create a new instance of the ScriptManager if needed. Using the ScriptManager in a composite control has several important benefits. For example, you can control script caching and also ensure that one and only one ScriptManager is present in situations in which you might not control the entire page runtime. You may be developing components that are deployed to a portal runtime where you may not "own" the page, or you may even be developing controls that are deployed to customers in their own runtime. In these cases, you might want to write code that checks for the presence of the ScriptManager. The following C# code sample can be used within a server control to check for the existence of a ScriptManager and add a ScriptManager to its own controls collection if necessary:

```csharp
var scriptMan = ScriptManager.GetCurrent(this.Page);
if (scriptMan == null)
{
    scriptMan = new ScriptManager();
    this.Controls.Add(scriptMan);
}
```

Another benefit you gain from implementing a ScriptManager wrapper is control over script caching in the Web browser. Ideally, a script will be cached liberally by the client browser because JavaScript resources don't often change. However, a cache policy that is too liberal can cause you to find that older versions of your script files are cached on the client and that users need to clear their cache to receive updated code. One way to work around cache-related bugs is to use a cache key that is appended to a script's URL. The cache key can be generated in a variety of ways, including a string generated from the assembly signature (which changes with each compilation), the build number, or a custom key that identifies your release. Because script files are cached on the basis of their file name and query string, appending an arbitrary query string that changes with each build ensures that users are always using the latest versions of your scripts and not an earlier version from their cache.

To add a cache key to your script references, you can append a cache query string to the end of the path, as the following code demonstrates. You will also need to check whether the script has a path or is a compiled script resource reference, because the compiled assembly resource has a null *Path*, and setting it will cause an exception.

```csharp
foreach (ScriptReference script in this.Scripts){
    if (!string.IsNullOrEmpty(script.Path)){
        char seperator = script.Path.Contains("?") ? '&' : '?';
        script.Path = string.Format("{0}{1}cache={2}", script.Path, seperator, this.CacheKey);
    }
    this.ScriptManager.Scripts.Add(script);
}
```

For commercial applications, I almost always implement a wrapper for the ScriptManager. Not only does this approach protect me from cached scripts, but in Web Part applications it ensures that my code doesn't break my customer's application, where the customer might or might not already have a ScriptManager control. Listing 4-3 demonstrates a server control that can be used to encapsulate a client runtime. This control can be used in code or in markup using standard ASP.NET server control syntax.

LISTING 4-3. The ScriptManager control can be used in a server control to deploy custom script deployment logic (*AjaxControls/ScriptRuntimeControl.cs*).

```csharp
using System;
using System.Web.UI;
using System.ComponentModel;
using System.Web;
```

```csharp
using System.Drawing.Design;
using System.Globalization;
using System.Security.Permissions;
using System.Reflection;

namespace AjaxControls
{
    [NonVisualControl,
        ToolboxItemFilter("System.Web.Extensions, Version=3.5.0.0, Culture=neutral,
PublicKeyToken=31bf3856ad364e35",
        ToolboxItemFilterType.Require),
        DefaultProperty("Scripts"),
        ParseChildren(true),
        PersistChildren(false),
        AspNetHostingPermission(SecurityAction.LinkDemand,
            Level=AspNetHostingPermissionLevel.Minimal),
        AspNetHostingPermission(SecurityAction.InheritanceDemand,
            Level=AspNetHostingPermissionLevel.Minimal)]
    public class ScriptRuntimeControl : Control
    {
        private ScriptReferenceCollection _scripts;
        [Editor("System.Web.UI.Design.CollectionEditorBase, System.Web.Extensions.
Design, Version=3.5.0.0, Culture=neutral, PublicKeyToken=31bf3856ad364e35",
                typeof(UITypeEditor)),
            Category("Behavior"),
            PersistenceMode(PersistenceMode.InnerProperty),
            DefaultValue((string)null),
            MergableProperty(false)]
        public ScriptReferenceCollection Scripts
        {
            get
            {
                if (this._scripts == null)
                {
                    this._scripts = new ScriptReferenceCollection();
                }
                return this._scripts;
            }
        }

        private ServiceReferenceCollection _services;
        [PersistenceMode(PersistenceMode.InnerProperty),
            Category("Behavior"),
            Editor("System.Web.UI.Design.CollectionEditorBase, System.Web.Extensions.
Design, Version=3.5.0.0, Culture=neutral, PublicKeyToken=31bf3856ad364e35",
            typeof(UITypeEditor)),
            DefaultValue((string)null),
            MergableProperty(false)]
        public ServiceReferenceCollection Services
        {
            get
            {
                if (this._services == null)
                {
                    this._services = new ServiceReferenceCollection();
                }
```

```
                return this._services;
        }
    }

    private ScriptManager scriptMan;
    // A null-safe reference to the page's script manager.
    public ScriptManager ScriptManager
    {
        get
        {
            EnsureScriptManger();
            return scriptMan;
        }
    }

    protected override void CreateChildControls()
    {
        base.CreateChildControls();
        EnsureScriptManger();
    }

    // Make sure there is only 1 script manager on the page.
    private void EnsureScriptManger()
    {
        if (scriptMan == null)
        {
            scriptMan = ScriptManager.GetCurrent(this.Page);
            if (scriptMan == null)
            {
                scriptMan = new ScriptManager();
                this.Controls.Add(scriptMan);
            }
        }
    }

    private string cacheKey;
    /// <summary>A cache key for script paths</summary>
    /// <remarks>Ideally, this would be generated from the build.</remarks>
    public string CacheKey
    {
        get
        {
            if (cacheKey == null)
                cacheKey = Assembly.GetExecutingAssembly()
                        .ManifestModule.ModuleVersionId.ToString();
            return cacheKey;
        }
    }

    // Add any scripts and service references to the real script manager.
    protected override void OnPreRender(EventArgs e)
    {
        base.OnPreRender(e);
        this.EnsureChildControls();
```

```
            foreach (ScriptReference script in this.Scripts) {
                if (!string.IsNullOrEmpty(script.Path)) {
                    char seperator = script.Path.Contains("?") ? '&' : '?';
                    script.Path = string.Format("{0}{1}cache={2}",
                        script.Path, seperator, this.CacheKey);
                }
                this.ScriptManager.Scripts.Add(script);
            }

            foreach (ServiceReference proxy in this.Services)
            {
                this.ScriptManager.Services.Add(proxy);
            }

            // Common scipt manager cconfiguration:
            this.ScriptManager.EnableHistory = true;
        }
    }
}
```

The *ScriptRuntimeControl* demonstrated in Listing 4-3 wraps the ScriptManager and provides basic functionality for the client-side AJAX application while also adding a cache key to script URLs to prevent caching of earlier scripts. The cache key is dependent on the assembly's build, an ideal strategy if you implement a build server. Alternatively, you might want to use another algorithm to build the cache key, such as a file-dependent timestamp.

As shown in the previous examples, the ScriptManager control has a server side API that is useful for configuring custom JavaScript application deployment. You can also package a ScriptManager wrapper that automatically includes your client-side runtime by adding the script references in the *prerender* method. Now that we've covered the server-side interface of the ScriptManager control, let's take a detailed look at the client-side runtime.

Object-Oriented JavaScript Fundamentals

Most developers are used to writing simple functions in JavaScript, but JavaScript is also an object-based language that lends itself well to polymorphism and design patterns. Everything in JavaScript exists as an object, including functions, and these JavaScript objects are loosely typed and can be extended at run time. Instead of an inheritance based on class definitions, JavaScript objects inherit their behaviors through prototypes, and they can also be assigned behaviors at run time. To create an object in JavaScript, the *function* keyword is used to create an object constructor, which is called with the *new* keyword to create an object instance. Understanding the inheritance model of JavaScript is vital to implementing effective JavaScript libraries.

Important In JavaScript, objects inherit behavior, and behavior is assigned through a prototype or at run time after the object is instantiated.

In the following code, the function *DataItem* forms the class definition for the *item* object that is instantiated in the *pageLoad* function.

```
function DataItem(content){
    this._content = content;
}

function pageLoad() {
    var item = new DataItem('Hello world!');
}
```

Tip In JavaScript, method and class definitions are both defined with *function*, so it's important to use naming semantics that clearly identify what is a class definition and what is a function definition. The Microsoft standard for JavaScript class libraries is to use Pascal casing for class definitions (*MyClass*) and camel casing for method definitions (*myMethod*).

JavaScript's type system is *duck typed,* which means that the object is defined by its behavior: if it walks like a duck, swims like a duck, and flies like a duck, it probably is a duck. Because of its duck-typed nature, JavaScript doesn't require a class-based model of strong types. Likewise, formal interfaces aren't required because there isn't a need for explicit or implicit casting. Instead of working with inheritance hierarchies to build type libraries, JavaScript uses a model in which a prototype is used to assign common behavior to the type.

A JavaScript prototype is much like a class definition you write in C#, although a prototype is more flexible because it is not a static declaration, can be assigned to multiple types, and can assign unrelated behavior. All instances of a type inherit the behavior assigned to the prototype. For example, to implement the property *content*, you can implement *get* and *set* functions in the prototype as the following code demonstrates:

```
DataItem.prototype = {
    get_content : function(){return this._content;},
    set_content: function(){this._content = value;}
}
```

Tip Properties in JavaScript are implemented and accessed through *get_* and *set_* methods. This convention is common throughout the Microsoft AJAX Library.

As the preceding code sample demonstrates, prototype syntax is expressed with JavaScript-serialized object notation using colon-delimited name-value pairs. Commas rather than semicolons are used to separate function definitions, and colons are used to assign a function to a field. A function can be defined inline in a prototype, or a prototype can be used to assign an existing function to the instance method, as the following prototype demonstrates with the method *DataItem$GetWikiMarkup,* which is assigned to the instance method *getWikiMarkup.*

```
DataItem.prototype = {
    get_Content : function(){return this._content;},
    set_Content: function(){this._content = value;},
    getWikiMarkup : DataItem$GetWikiMarkup
}

function DataItem$GetWikiMarkup(){
    return ConvertToWiki(this._content);
}

function ConvertToWiki(htmlMarkup){
    // implementation of wiki converter
}
```

An alternative syntax can be used to assign the *getWikiMarkup* function to the prototype after the prototype definition. Using this approach, you can extend existing frameworks without modifying the source code. The following code demonstrates the assignment of *getWikiMarkup* to the prototype:

```
DataItem.prototype.getWikiMarkup = DataItem$GetWikiMarkup;
```

The Microsoft Ajax Library JavaScript Type Extensions

Building on the simple JavaScript type system, the Microsoft AJAX Library adds a type system through simple JavaScript conventions. The type system is defined using the *Type* AJAX class and is described in the following sections.

> **Tip** To best understand the AJAX library, you should open the source code for *MicrosoftAjax.debug.js* in Visual Studio. The JavaScript files are available in a stand-alone download from *http://ajax.asp.net.*

The JavaScript Type

The *Type* class defined in the Microsoft Ajax Library is a special kind of library component that extends the JavaScript *Function* class. (All JavaScript functions derive from *Function.*) In the Microsoft AJAX Library, the JavaScript *Type* class is defined by referencing the global JavaScript *Function* class, as the following line from the library's source code demonstrates:

```
window.Type = Function;
```

Because *Type* extends *Function,* all prototype methods of *Type* are available as instance methods of functions. This lets the Microsoft AJAX Library add a type system for namespaces, classes, and inheritance models similar to those found in managed languages such as C# and other .NET Framework languages.

> **Tip** Because a class does not exist in the JavaScript language, the term *class* (when speaking about JavaScript) refers to a function that is written as a logical class implementation and is designed to be called with the *new* operator, or a type that is defined using the Microsoft AJAX Library type system.

JavaScript Namespaces

With client-side script libraries, you should create namespaces as appropriate to organize classes, just as you would in compiled class libraries. The need for namespaces is especially true as you build larger client script libraries and interact with custom libraries from vendors or open source projects. To register a namespace, use the method *Type.registerNamespace*. This method creates a namespace object under which types in your namespace are created.

To create the namespace *SOAjax.Controls,* use the following script, which creates a root level namespace for *SOAjax* with a child namespace *Controls*:

```
Type.registerNamespace('SOAjax.Controls');
```

To see an example of how a namespace is registered in low-level code, you can look at the Microsoft AJAX Library itself. The following snippet defines the *Sys* namespace in the Microsoft AJAX Library. You should avoid using this syntax, but it is helpful as an illustration of exactly what a namespace is.

```
// from MicrosoftAjax.debug.js, demonstrating low-level namespace implementation
window.Sys = {
    __namespace: true,
    __typeName: "Sys",
    getName: function() {return "Sys";}
};
```

When you define JavaScript libraries, you should create namespaces to distinguish your types from other class libraries and to help organize your code in conceptual buckets. For example, consider the Microsoft AJAX Library—core objects are defined in *Sys*, network libraries are defined in *Sys.Net*, and UI libraries are defined in *Sys.UI.*

Types and Inheritance

The Microsoft AJAX Library extends the *object* type through the *registerClass* and *inheritsFrom* functions for working with classes and inheritance. These functions are used by the framework to manage the type system and inheritance chains. They are also used to assign base class behaviors to inheriting classes. The main reason to use inheritance is to make code reusable by assigning common behaviors through base classes. In JavaScript, you can also share methods between types through prototype assignment. Instead of building a complex type system for business objects and database persistence as you might in C#, the main reason to use inheritance in the AJAX library is to develop components and controls that are managed through the *Sys.Application* object. The classes you build in JavaScript will be used to encapsulate user interface functionality rather than business logic, which is handled through back-end services.

In the following code samples, I'll show you some simple extensions to DOM elements. You'll learn more about components and controls in the next section of the book, "Applied AJAX," but for now we'll use simple JavaScript classes to demonstrate inheritance. Because typically (but not always) you'll be using JavaScript class libraries to build out user interface libraries and not business logic, I'll focus on DOM-based programming.

To build a class definition, start out with a function. Because JavaScript is an object-based language, all functions are equivalent to class definitions and can be called with the *new* keyword to create a new object instance. A function can also be assigned to an object—in most cases you'll be creating functions that exist within a namespace, which is itself really just an object. For example, the following code creates the namespace *SOAjax.Examples* and creates the class *BaseControlExtension* as a member of the namespace.

```
Type.registerNamespace("SOAjax.Examples");
SOAjax.Examples.BaseControlExtension = function(domElement, args) { }
```

To assign methods to a type, you assign methods to its *prototype*. There are two syntaxes that you will see when working with the Microsoft AJAX Library, and either one is valid. The first syntax creates methods as functions and assigns the functions to the prototype. This syntax is optimal for large class libraries, such as the Microsoft AJAX Library's core framework, but is less readable. The following code sample uses this syntax to create a function *SOAjax$Examples$BaseControlExtension$init* and assign it to the *init* method using the prototype. Notice that the dollar sign is an arbitrary separator character used by convention throughout the AJAX library.

```
function SOAjax$Examples$BaseControlExtension$init(domElement, args) {
    Sys.Debug.trace('Example code.')
}
SOAjax.Examples.BaseControlExtension.prototype{
    init : SOAjax$Examples$BaseControlExtension$init
}
```

Another way to write this code is to assign the prototype method in the function declaration:

```
SOAjax.Examples.BaseControlExtension.prototype.init =
    function SOAjax$Examples$BaseControlExtension$init(domElement, args) {
        Sys.Debug.trace('Example code.')
    }
```

The standard syntax, which is also the preferred best practice for custom libraries because it is the most readable, defines methods directly in the prototype. The following code is syntactically equivalent to the earlier code samples but defines the method inline in the prototype.

```
SOAjax.Examples.BaseControlExtension.prototype{
    init : function(domElement, args) {
        Sys.Debug.trace('Example code.')
    }
}
```

To create a base class for a control extension (an object that will interact with a DOM element), you can create a base class (called *BaseControlExtension* here) that takes a *domElement* in its constructor and has an optional argument list. In this example, I also create an *init* method that creates a floating DIV element based on the location of the target element. I add a click handler that can hide the extension and dispose logic that deletes the class instance. Listing 4-4 demonstrates the base class that can then be implemented for specific use.

LISTING 4-4. The *BaseControlExtension* class forms a base class for DOM-based functionality (*Web/Script/ClientLibrary.js*).

```
Type.registerNamespace("SOAjax.Examples");
SOAjax.Examples.BaseControlExtension = function(domElement, args) {
    this.init(domElement,args);
}

SOAjax.Examples.BaseControlExtension.prototype = {
    target: null,
    extendedControl: null,
    timeOut: null,

    init: function(domElement, args) {

        this.target = domElement;
        this.target.control = this;

        this.extendedControl = document.createElement('DIV');
        Sys.UI.DomElement.setVisible(this.extendedControl, false);
        document.body.appendChild(this.extendedControl);

        // Sets the location of the DOM element, discussed in chapter 5.
        var loc = Sys.UI.DomElement.getLocation(this.target);
        var bounds = Sys.UI.DomElement.getBounds(this.target);
        Sys.UI.DomElement.setLocation(this.extendedControl,
            loc.x + 15, loc.y - bounds.height);
        Sys.UI.DomElement.setVisible(this.extendedControl, true);

        this.clickDelegate = Function.createDelegate(this, this.dispose);
        $addHandler(this.extendedControl, 'click', this.clickDelegate);
    },

    dispose: function() {
        this.target.control = null;
```

```
        document.body.removeChild(this.extendedControl);
        if (this.clickDelegate) delete this.clickDelegate;
    }
}
SOAjax.Examples.BaseControlExtension.registerClass(
    'SOAjax.Examples.BaseControlExtension');
```

In Listing 4-4, we created base functionality and registered the class with the AJAX library type system. To create a concrete class that implements the *BaseControlExtension*, we can create another class and register it with the type system as well. To register the *Tooltip* class with the type system and to inherit the base class functionality, use the *registerClass* method of the type itself, passing in the name of the class plus the type of the class you're inheriting from. The following syntax is used to register a concrete class as inheriting from a base abstract class:

```
concreteClass.registerClass('concreteClass', abstractClass);
```

For example, to register the *Tooltip* class as inheriting from *BaseControlExtension*, call the *registerClass* method of the *Tooltip* type as follows, passing in the type of the base class as a parameter:

```
SOAjax.Examples.Tooltip.registerClass('SOAjax.Examples.Tooltip',
    SOAjax.Examples.BaseControlExtension);
```

To override a method of the base class, define the method in the concrete class prototype. Within the method, you can call the base class method with the type's *callBaseMethod* function. The *callBaseMethod* function is a method of the defined type that also takes as parameters an instance parameter (usually *this*), the name of the method, and then optional parameters, which matches the base class's signature. Similar to the type's *registerNamespace* method, the *callBaseMethod* function is part of the type. For example, to call the *init* method of the *Tooltip*'s base class, the following syntax is used.

```
init: function(domElement, args) {
    SOAjax.Examples.Tooltip.callBaseMethod(this, 'init', [domElement, args]);
}
```

Listing 4-5 completes the earlier code sample by creating a *Tooltip* class that inherits from the base *BaseControlExtension* class and provides simple tooltip functionality.

LISTING 4-5. To create an inheriting class (a *concrete* class), use the *registerClass* method and the *callBaseMethod* function (*Web/Script/ClientLibrary.js*).

```
SOAjax.Examples.Tooltip = function(domElement, args) {
    this.init(domElement, args);
}
SOAjax.Examples.Tooltip.prototype = {
    init: function(domElement, args) {
        SOAjax.Examples.Tooltip.callBaseMethod(this, 'init', [domElement, args]);
```

```
        this.extendedControl.style.border = '1px solid black';
        this.extendedControl.style.backgroundColor = 'yellow';
        this.extendedControl.style.padding = '3px';
        this.extendedControl.innerHTML = args.message;
    },

    dispose: function() {
        SOAjax.Examples.Tooltip.callBaseMethod(this, 'dispose');
    }
}

SOAjax.Examples.Tooltip.registerClass('SOAjax.Examples.Tooltip',
    SOAjax.Examples.BaseControlExtension);
```

To use this control in a page, you can simply create a tooltip using the *new* keyword of the *Tooltip* class.

```
var tip = new SOAjax.Examples.Tooltip($get('TestDiv'), {message :'Hello, world'});
```

In JavaScript, it is best to avoid creating deep hierarchical class models, as you would in compiled languages such as C#, and focus on behavioral inheritance instead. A shallow class inheritance chain performs better, is more effective, and is easier to debug. Because of the loosely typed nature of JavaScript, in which objects are flexible, I favor a behavioral inheritance model and prefer to assign behaviors as needed. As a general rule, a goal in designing JavaScript type libraries is to create as few type definitions as possible and to create general purpose, reusable components that can extend HTML elements and browser functionality.

Now that you have an understanding of the type extensions of ASP.NET AJAX, we'll look more closely at the AJAX library's client framework in the next chapter. The client framework is a lightweight JavaScript runtime with support for most browser-oriented programming tasks, including DOM manipulation, network calls, components, and controls. You'll see that control implementation is missing from the framework and is left instead to third-party developers and the AJAX Control Toolkit, a collaboration between Microsoft and the ASP.NET community. The ASP.NET AJAX Control Toolkit can be downloaded from *www.codeplex.com/ajaxcontroltoolkit*.

Summary

In this chapter you learned about the basics of the client-side runtime with the ScriptManager control and the core type system of the Microsoft AJAX Library.

By now you should understand the basics of object-oriented JavaScript programming with the Microsoft AJAX Library's type system and be able to write simple JavaScript class definitions. In the following chapters we'll build on this foundation as we continue to explore the Microsoft AJAX Library and learn how to write components, behaviors, and controls using Microsoft's framework.

Chapter 5
The Microsoft AJAX Library

After completing this chapter, you will

- Understand and utilize the Microsoft AJAX Library.

- Understand the *Sys.Net* Network Library.

- Understand the document object model and the Microsoft AJAX extensions to programming the DOM through the Microsoft AJAX Library.

In Chapter 4, "The AJAX Runtime with the Microsoft AJAX Library," we looked at the basic AJAX runtime and how it utilizes the Script Manager and the ASP.NET AJAX programming model. We also looked at object-oriented JavaScript and at Microsoft's type extensions to the JavaScript language. Building on the core type system, the Microsoft AJAX Library is implemented in logical namespaces that provide functionality for the client-side AJAX application. In this chapter I'll explain the main namespaces and types, including the network library and the Document Object Model (DOM) programming model.

The Microsoft AJAX Library Client Framework

The Microsoft AJAX Library consists of a central framework of components, controls, and utilities, as well as a network stack and Web service proxies, all implemented in JavaScript. While the AJAX library is targeted toward AJAX applications, most of the library supports approaches to dynamically programming client browsers and can be used in any type of browser-based application, whether the application uses an AJAX programming model or a Web Forms programming model. Because an AJAX application often includes more code for manipulating the browser's user interface than a traditional Web application, where the rendering is done on the server, a robust framework of controls, utilities, and debugging support is needed for an AJAX application. Table 5-1 lists the key JavaScript namespaces in the Microsoft AJAX Library, which are all defined under the root namespace *Sys*.

 Tip Although the Microsoft AJAX Library does not parallel the Microsoft .NET Framework, it is conceptually similar in design and structure.

TABLE 5-1 JavaScript Namespaces in the AJAX Library

Namespace	Description
Sys	The root namespace for the Microsoft AJAX Library. Contains all fundamental classes and base classes, including the *Component* base class and the client runtime *Sys.Application* object.
Sys.Net	Contains the core network stack for Web service calls, wrapping the native *XMLHttpRequest* object in a browser-safe abstraction.
Sys.Serialization	Contains the *JavaScriptSerializer* class, which is used for data serialization for Microsoft ASP.NET AJAX client applications and has enhanced JSON-parsing capabilities.
Sys.Services	Contains types that provide script access in ASP.NET AJAX client applications to the ASP.NET authentication service, profile service, and role service. Use this namespace with Web services defined in *System.Web.ApplicationServices*.
Sys.UI	Contains types related to the user interface (UI), such as controls, events, and UI properties in the Microsoft AJAX Library. Use base classes in this namespace to implement custom client-side controls. Use the static DOM-related classes in this namespace to manipulate the client interface.

JavaScript Base Type Extensions

The AJAX library contains base type extensions that add functionality to the string, array, number, Boolean error, and object types. These extensions are useful when you are working with JavaScript primitive data types and when you are working with text in the browser. The base type extensions also provide support for the browser's current culture when used in a localized application.

To enable automatic localization of the Web application, add the following globalization node to *system.web* in web.config, and set the ScriptManager's *EnableScriptGlobalization* property to *true*.

```
<globalization culture="auto" />
```

The base type extensions described in the following sections can be used to simplify the JavaScript programming model and are also useful in localizing applications. The base type extensions appear in Microsoft Visual Studio IntelliSense when the JavaScript file contains the following script reference at the top of the file:

```
/// <reference name="MicrosoftAjax.js"/>
```

Array Extensions

The Microsoft AJAX Library adds static methods that simplify the programming model for working with JavaScript arrays through the *Array* static type. The JavaScript array is not static in length, as is a .NET array. It can change length, and it contains both stack and queue functionality. Table 5-2 lists extensions to the *Array* type. (These extensions are all static methods.)

TABLE 5-2 Array Extensions

Method	Description
Array.add(*array, item*)	Adds an item to the end of the array.
Array.addRange(*array, items*)	Copies all the elements of the additional array to the end of the array.
Array.clear(*array*)	Removes all items from the array.
Array.clone(*array*)	Returns a new array with copied elements from the existing array.
Array.contains(*array, item*)	Returns *true* if the item is found in the array, otherwise *false*.
Array.dequeue(*array, item*)	Removes and returns the first element from the array.
Array.forEach(*array, delegate*)	Runs the *delegate* code on each member of the array.
Array.indexOf(*array, item*)	Returns the index of the item in the array.
Array.insert(*array, index, item*)	Inserts the item into the specified location of the array.
Array.parse(*string*)	Returns an array from a string.
Array.remove(*array, item*)	Removes the item from the array.
Array.removeAt(*array, index*)	Removes the item from the array at the specified index.

More Information For more information on the native JavaScript *Array* object, see *http://msdn.microsoft.com/yyadtt0s.aspx.*

Boolean Extensions

The Boolean *parse* method returns *true* or *false* when parsing a string. *Boolean.parse* will only parse the case insensitive "true" or "false" strings, it will not parse 0 or 1. If the string cannot be parsed, an *Error.argumentOutOfRange* is thrown. Table 5-3 lists the *Boolean.parse* extension to the *Boolean* type.

TABLE 5-3 Boolean Extensions

Method	Description
Boolean.parse(*boolString*)	Returns a Boolean *true* or *false* by parsing a case insensitive "true" or "false" string.

Date Extensions

The *Date* extensions in the AJAX library offer localization support for date formats and include serialization support. Table 5-4 lists the *Date* extensions in the Microsoft AJAX Library. Where *date* is listed, the method is an instance method in which *date* is a *date* type. *Date.parseLocale* and *Date.parseInvariant* are static functions.

TABLE 5-4 Date Extensions

Method	Description
date.format(*formatString*)	Returns a date using the date format of the *formatString* parameter using the invariant culture.
date.localeformat(*formatString*)	Returns a date using the date format of the *formatString* parameter using the current culture.
Date.parseLocale(*dateString*, *formats*)	Parses the date string and returns a date using the optional array of formats. If the date string cannot be parsed, null is returned.
Date.parseInvariant(*dateString*)	Parses the date string and returns a date using the invariant culture. If the date string cannot be parsed, null is returned.

Date format strings can be obtained from the *culture* object's *dateTimeFormat* field, part of *Sys.CultureInfo*. Using culture-sensitive format strings ensures that the date rendered is appropriate for the culture. For example, 12/11/2008 means December 11 in the United States, but it means November 12 in the United Kingdom and elsewhere.

Sys.CultureInfo.CurrentCulture.dateTimeFormat.ShortDatePattern returns the string "M/d/yyyy" in the U.S. English culture. In the UK English culture, *ShortDatePattern* returns "dd/MM/yyyy".

> **More Information** For more information on the native JavaScript Date object, see *http://msdn.microsoft.com/t5580e8h.aspx*. For additional information on globalizing dates through script, see *http://msdn.microsoft.com/bb386581.aspx*.

Error Extensions

The *Error* type extensions of the AJAX library extend the native *Error* type by providing a richer API around exception details. Just as specific exceptions can be thrown in the .NET Framework, specific errors can be thrown in the AJAX Library, providing more meaningful errors than the general purpose *Error*. The *Error* type provides one factory method, nine methods to create specialized errors, and one utility method that adds exception details.

Creating Errors with *Error.create*

Error.create is a factory method that simplifies the process of creating an error. It is used by all the specialized error types in the AJAX library. The message of the error is used as the main parameter. Additional information passed into the *errorInfo* dictionary is added to the error object.

To raise an exception using *Error.create*, pass a display message and error details as parameters. The following code sample creates a generic error, passing a second object containing additional error information that could be used in debug code:

```
throw Error.create("Unexpected error.",
    { name: "SOAjax.Examples.Foo" , argument : "bar"});
```

The methods listed in Table 5-5 create specific errors. They are used within the AJAX library and are also useful for custom code. For each error, the method that creates the error is listed along with usage guidelines.

TABLE 5-5 Error Extensions

Method	Description
Error.argument (*paramName, message*)	Use when an argument is passed that is the wrong type, such as when a string is passed when a Boolean value is expected.
Error.argumentNull (*paramName, message*)	Use when a required parameter is null.
Error.argumentOutOfRange (*paramName, message*)	Use when an argument is passed that is outside the expected value range. For example, in a specialized method you might accept a string parameter with only known strings, or you might accept a parameter within a specific numeric range.
Error.argumentType (*paramName, message*)	Use when an argument is passed that is the wrong type, such as when a string is passed when a Boolean value is expected.
Error.argumentUndefined (*paramName, message*)	Use when a required argument is *not* passed. Similar to the argumentNull method, although the undefined exception is not thrown when a parameter is null, only when its argument is not passed.
Error.format()	Use when a formatting related exception occurs.
Error.invalidOperation()	Use when an operation is called that is invalid.
Error.notImplemented()	Use in a method that is stubbed out for future use but is not implemented. You can also use this in a base class method when you are expecting a concrete class to provide the implementation.
Error.parameterCount()	Use when there's an expected number of parameters that is not met.

> **More Information** For more information on the native JavaScript *Error* object, see *http://msdn.microsoft.com/t9zk6eay.aspx*.

Number Extensions

The number extensions in the AJAX library are used to support formatting and parsing, specifically with culture-specific formats. Table 5-6 lists the format extensions included in the Microsoft AJAX Library and describes when to use them.

TABLE 5-6 Number Extensions

Method	Description
Number.format(*number*)	Use to format numbers with the invariant culture.
Number.localeFormat(*number*)	Use to format numbers with the current culture.
Number.parseInvariant(*numericString*)	Use to parse numbers with the invariant culture.
Number.parseLocale(*numericString*)	Use to format numbers with the current culture.

Object Extensions

The *Object* extensions in the Microsoft AJAX Library are included to extend the library's type system and are used for classes registered with *Type.registerClass*. The extensions are instance methods and are listed in Table 5-7.

TABLE 5-7 Object Extensions

Method	Description
object.GetType()	Use to get the type of an object that was registered using the Microsoft AJAX Library's type system. Returns the type's constructor.
object.GetTypeName()	Use to get the type name of an object that was registered using the Microsoft AJAX Library's type system.

String Extensions

The AJAX library includes extensions to the *String* type that simplify string programming tasks. *String.format* and *String.localeFormat* are static methods of *String;* the other extensions are instance methods of *String* that can be used on any String object.

TABLE 5-8 String Extensions

Method	Description
String.format(*format,args*)	Creates a string from the format argument using the invariant culture, replacing each token with an item from the argument's array.
String.localeFormat(*format,args*)	Creates a string from the format argument using the current culture, replacing each token with an item from the argument's array. The current culture is used to format dates and numbers.
string.endsWith(*suffix*)	Determines whether the string instance ends with the given suffix. The comparison is made after trimming the end of the string and setting both strings to lowercase.
string.startsWith(*prefix*)	Determines whether the string instance starts with the given prefix. The comparison is made after trimming the start of the string and setting both strings to lowercase.
string.trim()	Removes leading and trailing white space from the string.
string.trimEnd()	Removes trailing white space from the end of the string.
string.trimStart()	Removes leading white space from the beginning of the string.

One of the most useful extensions is *String.format*, first introduced in .NET 1.0. With *String.format* you can define formatted text with replacement arguments, just as you can in server-side code with the .NET Framework's *string.Format* method. For example, the following script produces a string containing information about the current browser context. The first argument contains the format string, while the arguments passed in replace the numbered token parameters.

```
String.format('Browser: {0}; version {1}; supports debugger: {2}',
    Sys.Browser.name, Sys.Browser.version, Sys.Browser.hasDebuggerStatement)
```

In addition to the string extensions, the type *Sys.StringBuilder* is a core object for working with strings in the Microsoft AJAX Library and is logically an extension to *String*. Whenever you are building a complex string, consider using the *StringBuilder* class.

Sys.StringBuilder

The *Sys.StringBuilder* type uses an array of strings to implement a client-side JavaScript version of the *System.Text.StringBuilder* class. Because strings are immutable in JavaScript, just as they are in managed code languages such as C#, you are creating a new instance of the string each time it is modified. Working with an array of immutable strings is more efficient in JavaScript than is manipulating a single string variable at run time. This approach can be useful when a program is building HTML, XML, or JSON manually by looping through a result set. Listing 5-1 demonstrates the use of *Sys.StringBuilder* in the Microsoft AJAX Library's *SysNetWebRequest$_createQueryString* function.

> **Tip** Code for this book is available online at *http://www.microsoft.com/mspress/companion/9780735625914*. The code for this chapter is in the file Chapter 5.zip.

LISTING 5-1. *Sys.StringBuilder* is the ideal way to build strings when looping through a result set. The code sample is from *MicrosoftAjax.debug.js*.

```
function Sys$Net$WebRequest$_createQueryString(queryString, encodeMethod) {
    if (!encodeMethod)
        encodeMethod = encodeURIComponent;
    var sb = new Sys.StringBuilder();
    var i = 0;
    for (var arg in queryString) {
        var obj = queryString[arg];
        if (typeof(obj) === "function") continue;
        var val = Sys.Serialization.JavaScriptSerializer.serialize(obj);
        if (i !== 0) {
            sb.append('&');
        }
        sb.append(arg);
        sb.append('=');
        sb.append(encodeMethod(val));
        i++;
    }
    return sb.toString();
}
```

> **More Information** For full documentation of the global base type extensions, see the online documentation at *http://msdn.microsoft.com/bb397506.aspx*.

Global Types and Objects in the *Sys* Namespace

The *Sys* namespace is analogous to the *System* namespace in the .NET Framework. It contains the *Sys.Application* object that controls the AJAX library runtime and is the root namespace for the Microsoft AJAX Library. The types *Sys.Application*, *Sys.Debug,* and *Sys.Browser* are the principal global objects in the *Sys* namespace and are used in the basic application infrastructure.

Sys.Application

In Chapter 1, "Service-Oriented AJAX Fundamentals," I introduced the *Sys.Application* object, which is instantiated at the beginning of client execution and then used to initialize the client application. (If you are not familiar with *Sys.Application* and the basic client life cycle, review Chapter 1 to learn how this object works at the center of the client-side application runtime.) *Sys.Application* is an instance of the Microsoft AJAX *Sys._Application* class defined in MicrosoftAjax.debug.js. Its main task is to manage page components, history, and the current state of the JavaScript application. It is also a key JavaScript component for applications using the Update panel (a pseudo–AJAX ASP.NET technology).

Sys.Application has four events to which you can add handlers: *init, load, navigate,* and *unload.* You can use *Sys.Application* to control the order of these events when a page is loaded. To add page initialization or page loading functionality to a client, attach a function to the events as shown in the following examples, where *handler* is a custom function:

```
Sys.Application.add_init(handler);
Sys.Application.add_load(handler);
Sys.Application.add_navigate(handler);
Sys.Application.add_unload(handler);
```

Upon creation, *Sys.Application* fires the *init* event and then calls any event handlers (functions) added with the *add_init* method. After initialization, the *load* event fires and calls any event handlers added with the *add_load* method. Next, if a *pageLoad* function is defined on the page, *Sys.Application* calls the *pageLoad* function.

> **Tip** If you include JavaScript code in the ASPX page that references the Microsoft AJAX Library, it must be located after the page's form element, which is where the AJAX library runtime is included on the page. If code referencing the library is included in the page header, the library will not have been loaded when the code attempts to execute. Ideally, all significant JavaScript code will be external to the page in a JavaScript file.

A *pageLoad* function should be used to initialize the page if there is logic specific to the page, whereas discreet components should add handlers to the *init* and *load* events, typically in external scripts. Remember that both the *init* and *load* events fire before the *pageLoad* function is called and have the advantage of being able to call multiple event handlers. The *pageLoad* function should only be defined on the page itself, not in code libraries that can be deployed to multiple pages. Listing 5-2 and Listing 5-3 demonstrate the order of execution: initialization, the *load* event, and finally the *pageLoad* function.

LISTING 5-2. The *pageLoad* function is used to handle page loading (*Web/Sys.Application.aspx*).

```
<%@ Page Language="C#" %>
<html xmlns="http://www.w3.org/1999/xhtml">
<head>
  <title>Sys.Application Runtime Demo</title>
  <script type="text/javascript">
    function pageLoad() {
        Sys.Debug.trace('Page Load: pageLoad function on page.');
    }
  </script>
</head>
<body>
    <form id="form1" runat="server">
        <asp:ScriptManager ID="ScriptManager1" runat="server" >
            <Scripts>
                <asp:ScriptReference Path="SysApplication.js" />
            </Scripts>
        </asp:ScriptManager>
        <div style="width:100%; height:200px">
            <textarea cols="80" rows="10" id="TraceConsole"></textarea>
        </div>
    </form>

</body>
</html>
```

LISTING 5-3. *Sys.Application* is used to initialize the page runtime and library components through the events *init* and *load* (*Web/SysApplication.js*).

```
Type.registerNamespace('SysAppDemo');

SysAppDemo.Init = function() {
    Sys.Debug.clearTrace();
    Sys.Debug.trace(
        'SysAppDemo.Init: used to initialize SysAppDemo library component(s)');
}

SysAppDemo.Load = function() {
    Sys.Debug.trace(
        'SysAppDemo.Load: used to load SysAppDemo library component(s)');
}

// An init handler is used to initialize library components
Sys.Application.add_init(SysAppDemo.Init);

// A load handler is used to handle data loading for library components
Sys.Application.add_load(SysAppDemo.Load);
```

The output of Listings 5-2 and 5-3 is shown in Figure 5-1, demonstrating the order of execution.

```
SysAppDemo.Init: used to initialize SysAppDemo library component(s)
SysAppDemo.Load: used to load SysAppDemo library component(s)
Page Load: pageLoad function on page.
```

FIGURE 5-1. The application fires the *init* and *load* events before calling *pageLoad*.

Listings 5-2 and 5-3 demonstrate the usual way to include and instantiate script libraries. When the ScriptManager control loads scripts, it injects script elements into the DOM sequentially and waits for each script to be loaded before it continues. The *Sys.Application. notifyScriptLoaded* method is used to notify *Sys.Application* that a script has been loaded successfully. This method is the only reliable way across browsers for an application to know that a script was loaded. In compiled JavaScript resources, the ASP.NET AJAX runtime injects the following line, but you should include it in all file-based scripts.

```
Sys.Application.notifyScriptLoaded();
```

> **Important** In each JavaScript file that is to be added with the ScriptManager or through the *Sys.Application* object, include the JavaScript call *Sys.Application.notifyScriptLoaded();*.

As an alternative to loading scripts through the ASP.NET *ScriptReference* property of the ScriptManager control, you can load scripts using the *Sys._ScriptManager* class. The *Sys._ScriptManager* class can be used to load scripts after the page is loaded and can also be used to load scripts as needed throughout the page's life cycle.

Because ScriptManager blocks page rendering until all script resources are loaded, queuing up script references after the page loads can dramatically improve page-loading performance. This method is preferred for script libraries that enhance page functionality but aren't required for the initial page rendering. For example, consider a wiki page with a content area, tag cloud, and navigation controls. The navigation controls and initial content should be rendered as soon as possible as the page is loaded. The page itself will be very lightweight and render immediately, and the content will be rendered as soon as it is retrieved from a client cache or a back-end system. In this design, the scripts for the navigation controls and initial content should be included as *ScriptReference* elements of the ScriptManager. Secondary functionality, such as the tag cloud, user status, and social data, can be deferred into script libraries that are placed in a queue for loading after the initial rendering of the page.

To load scripts after a page loads, you need to get a reference to the *Sys._ScriptLoader* object through its *getInstance* method, queue up script references by using the *queueScriptRefer- ence* method, and then call the *loadScripts* method. You can queue up multiple scripts and pass a callback handler, or you can let the scripts handle their own initialization through the *Sys.Application init* and *load* events, which are fired again after the scripts are loaded. Keep in mind that event handlers that were called previously are not called again. The following example demonstrates how to use the *ScriptLoader* object to load secondary scripts after the core runtime is loaded.

```
function pageLoad() {
    var scriptloader = Sys._ScriptLoader.getInstance();
    scriptloader.queueScriptReference('DynamicLoadedScript.js');
    scriptloader.loadScripts(1000, null, null, null);
}
```

Another purpose of *ScriptLoader* is to load scripts in response to user actions during the lifetime of the page. With this technique, you can defer loading seldomly used functionality until a user needs it. Listing 5-4 demonstrates using *ScriptLoader* to load functionality as it is needed by the runtime.

LISTING 5-4. *Sys._ScriptLoader* can be used to load scripts after the page is loaded (*Web/ScriptLoader.aspx*).

```
<%@ Page Language="C#"%>
<html xmlns="http://www.w3.org/1999/xhtml">
<head>
    <title>Sys._ScriptLoader Demo</title>
    <script type="text/javascript">

    function pageLoad() {
        Sys.Debug.trace('Page Load: pageLoad function on page.');

        // To load scripts after the page load, uncomment the following lines:
//          var scriptloader = Sys._ScriptLoader.getInstance();
//          scriptloader.queueScriptReference('ScriptLoader_Demo.js');
//          scriptloader.loadScripts(1000, null, null, null);

        // To load scripts dynamically you can initiate the script load
        // through a handler:
        var target = $get('TestNode');
        $addHandler(target, 'click', loadScriptsDynamically);
    }
    </script>
</head>
<body>
    <form id="form1" runat="server">
        <asp:ScriptManager ID="ScriptManager" runat="server" />
        <div style="width:100%; height:600px">
            <textarea cols="80" rows="10" id="TraceConsole"></textarea>

            <div id="TestNode" style="cursor:pointer;">
                Click me to load scripts.
            </div>

        </div>
    </form>
```

```
    <script type="text/javascript">
        function loadScriptsDynamically(){
            var scriptloader = Sys._ScriptLoader.getInstance();
            scriptloader.queueScriptReference('ScriptLoader_Demo.js');
            scriptloader.loadScripts(1000, scriptLoadedCallback,
                scriptFailedCallback, scriptTimedOutCallback);
        }
        function scriptLoadedCallback(scriptLoader){
            // scriptLoader is of type Sys._ScriptLoader
            Sys.Debug.trace(
                'Scripts have been loaded successfully through the script loader.');
            Sys.Debug.assert(
                typeof(ScriptLoaderDemo.DynamicScriptType) == 'function',
                'Script did not load succesfully!');
        }
        function scriptFailedCallback(scriptLoader){
            Sys.Debug.traceDump(scriptLoader);
            Sys.Debug.fail('Script load failed.');
        }
        function scriptTimedOutCallback(scriptLoader){
            Sys.Debug.traceDump(scriptLoader);
            Sys.Debug.fail('Script load timed out.');
        }
    </script>
</body>
</html>
```

When script is loaded dynamically, the *init* and load *events* are raised once more when the script components, as shown in Listing 5-5.

LISTING 5-5. *load* and *init* can be used to initiate code in scripts after the page is loaded (*Web/ScriptLoader_Demo.js*).

```
/// <reference name="MicrosoftAjax.js"/>
Type.registerNamespace('ScriptLoaderDemo');

Sys.Debug.trace('Dynamically loaded script.');

ScriptLoaderDemo.Init = function() {
    Sys.Debug.trace(
        'ScriptLoaderDemo.Init: used to initialize library component(s)');
}

ScriptLoaderDemo.Load = function() {
    Sys.Debug.trace(
        'ScriptLoaderDemo.Load: used to load library component(s)');
}

ScriptLoaderDemo.DynamicScriptType = function() { }

// The init event will be raised to initialize dynamically loaded script
Sys.Application.add_init(ScriptLoaderDemo.Init);
```

```
// The load event will be raised to load dynamically loaded script components
Sys.Application.add_load(ScriptLoaderDemo.Load);

// Lets Sys.Application know that the script has loaded.
Sys.Application.notifyScriptLoaded();
```

Loading scripts dynamically is an advanced technique, but can add significant new capabilities to your AJAX application by loading components when needed rather than predetermining the JavaScript runtime at page load.

Sys.Debug

Sys.Debug provides debugging and tracing capabilities to a JavaScript application. This object is similar to *System.Diagnostics.Debug* in the .NET Framework. You can use this object to log events to the JavaScript console or the Visual Studio output window.

> **Note** In addition to Visual Studio's *output* window, the JavaScript console is available as a tab in FireBug (FireFox's free developer extension, available at *www.getfirebug.com*) or as the Script Console in the Internet Explorer Web Developer Extensions (available at *http://projects.nikhilk.net*).

The *Sys.Debug* object is instantiated by the Microsoft AJAX Library as an object of type *Sys._Debug*. This object is available in both debug and release scripts and can be set in script by the field *Sys.Debug.isDebug*. The value of *isDebug* is set to *true* in the debug script and to *false* in the release script. However, you can set *isDebug* to *true* or *false* through script. If you are using the Microsoft AJAX Library as a resource from the *System.Web.Extensions* assembly, debug scripts are enabled through web.config.

Debug scripts are enabled the same way that you enable debugging in an ASP.NET application—through the */configuration/system.web/compilation* node. To enable debug mode through web.config, find the *compilation* node under *system.web* and then set *debug="true"*. The following excerpt shows how to enable debug mode:

```
<configuration>
  <system.web>
    <compilation debug="true"/>
  </system.web>
<configuration>
```

Diagnostics with *Sys.Debug.trace*   You can write a trace message to the script console through the statement *Sys.Debug.trace*(message). This is perhaps the most useful way to quickly diagnose what is happening in the AJAX application. The script console is implemented in several ways. In FireFox, the script console is implemented in browser extensions such as Firebug (*http://www.getfirebug.com*), and in Internet Explorer the script console is implemented in browser extensions such as Web Development Helper (*http://projects.nikhilk.net*). When the Visual Studio debugger is attached to Internet Explorer, the trace is written to the output window, similarly to the .NET method *System.Diagnostics.WriteLine(*text*)*. You can also implement the script console as a text area in the page. Figure 5-2 demonstrates the trace output in Firebug's console, and Figure 5-3 demonstrates trace output written to the HTML script console as well as the Visual Studio output window in Internet Explorer and Visual Studio.

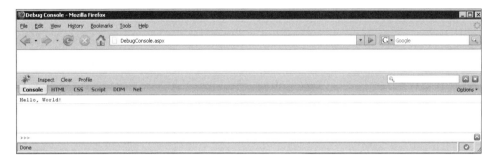

FIGURE 5-2. The Firebug debug console in Mozilla Firefox displays data from *the Sys.Debug.trace* method.

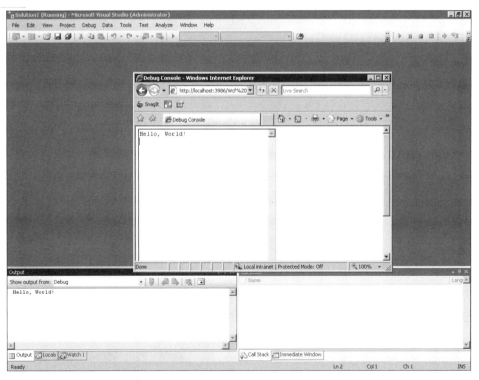

FIGURE 5-3. The Internet Explorer integrated debug environment with Visual Studio and the Debug Console.

To write an HTML script console that runs entirely in the browser, create a text area in the page with the ID "TraceConsole". This could also be created through debug scripts as demonstrated in Listing 5-6. This code sample shows the implementation of an HTML script console that runs in the browser for Internet Explorer only. To clear the TextBox trace console, use the method *Sys.Debug.clearTrace()*.

LISTING 5-6. A text area with the ID "TraceConsole" can be used with *Sys.Debug (Web/DebugConsole.aspx)*.

```
function initDebug(){
    if (Sys.Debug.isDebug){
        if (Sys.Browser.agent == Sys.Browser.InternetExplorer){
            var console = $get('TraceConsole');
            if (console == null){
                console = document.createElement('TEXTAREA');
                console.id = 'TraceConsole';
                document.body.appendChild(console);
            }
        }
    }
}

function pageLoad() {
    initDebug();
    Sys.Debug.trace('Hello, World!');
}
```

Diagnostics with *Sys.Debug.traceDump*(object, name)   *Sys.Debug.traceDump* dumps object fields to the script console. The *name* parameter is used only as a label in the trace output. This statement can be helpful in dumping out object state to diagnose errors. You can call this method from the browser's script console (Firebug for FireFox, or Web Development Helper for Microsoft Internet Explorer) or from the immediate window in Visual Studio. For example, to dump the *Sys.Application* object to the console, use the following code:

```
Sys.Debug.traceDump(Sys.Application);
```

Diagnostics with *Sys.Debug.assert*(condition, message, displayCaller)   Sys.Debug.assert is used to assert that the condition argument evaluates to true. If the condition is false, a dialog box displays the message through the JavaScript confirm function, giving you an opportunity to launch the debugger. If displayCaller is true, the dialog displays the full function body of the calling method.

For example, the following code is used to assert that the *Sys.Application* instance is initialized. If it is not initialized, it prompts the user to break into the debugger:

```
Sys.Debug.assert(Sys.Application.get_isInitialized(),
    'Expected an initialized Sys.Application!', true);
```

Diagnostics with *Sys.Debug.fail*()   *Sys.Debug.fail* is used to break into the script debugger after writing the message to the console. This is a simple wrapper for the *debugger* JavaScript statement, as the *debugger* statement does not exist in all browsers, although it is integrated in both Internet Explorer and FireFox browsers.

To break into the debugger, include the following code:

```
Sys.Debug.fail();
```

Sys.Browser

The *Sys.Browser* object is used to reference the current browser application instance, such as Internet Explorer or Firefox. *Sys.Browser.agent* is an object instance that is only useful to compare against *Sys.Browser.InternetExplorer, Sys.Browser.FireFox, Sys.Browser.Safari,* or *Sys.Browser.Opera* (the four major browsers). Listing 5-7 demonstrates a simple switch based on the current browser version.

LISTING 5-7. *Sys.Browser* can be used to implement browser-specific code.

```
function pageLoad() {

    switch(Sys.Browser.agent){
        case Sys.Browser.InternetExplorer:
            Sys.Debug.trace('We Love Redmond');
            break;
        case Sys.Browser.Firefox:
            Sys.Debug.trace('We Love Mountain View');
            break;
        case Sys.Browser.Safari:
            Sys.Debug.trace('We Love Cupertino');
            break;
        case Sys.Browser.Opera:
            Sys.Debug.trace('We Love Oslo');
            break;
    }
    Sys.Debug.trace(
        String.format('Browser: {0}; version {1}; supports debugger: {2}',
            Sys.Browser.name,
            Sys.Browser.version,
            Sys.Browser.hasDebuggerStatement) );
}
```

Sys.Browser can be used in your own applications, but it is mainly used in the AJAX library to determine browser capabilities. To see exactly how *Sys.Browser* is constructed, it's best to reference the source code, which is shown in Listing 5-8.

LISTING 5-8. *Sys.Browser* is used to determine the current browser application. The code sample is from the framework, defined in *MicrosoftAjax.debug.js*.

```
Sys.Browser = {};
Sys.Browser.InternetExplorer = {};
Sys.Browser.Firefox = {};
Sys.Browser.Safari = {};
Sys.Browser.Opera = {};
Sys.Browser.agent = null;
```

```
Sys.Browser.hasDebuggerStatement = false;
Sys.Browser.name = navigator.appName;
Sys.Browser.version = parseFloat(navigator.appVersion);
if (navigator.userAgent.indexOf(' MSIE ') > -1) {
    Sys.Browser.agent = Sys.Browser.InternetExplorer;
    Sys.Browser.version = parseFloat(navigator.userAgent.match(
        /MSIE (\d+\.\d+)/)[1]);
    Sys.Browser.hasDebuggerStatement = true;
}
else if (navigator.userAgent.indexOf(' Firefox/') > -1) {
    Sys.Browser.agent = Sys.Browser.Firefox;
    Sys.Browser.version = parseFloat(navigator.userAgent.match(
        / Firefox\/(\d+\.\d+)/)[1]);
    Sys.Browser.name = 'Firefox';
    Sys.Browser.hasDebuggerStatement = true;
}
else if (navigator.userAgent.indexOf(' AppleWebKit/') > -1) {
    Sys.Browser.agent = Sys.Browser.Safari;
    Sys.Browser.version = parseFloat(navigator.userAgent.match(
        / AppleWebKit\/(\d+(\.\d+)?)/)[1]);
    Sys.Browser.name = 'Safari';
}
else if (navigator.userAgent.indexOf('Opera/') > -1) {
    Sys.Browser.agent = Sys.Browser.Opera;
}
```

The Network Library in *Sys.Net*

The Microsoft AJAX Library provides a network stack for handling AJAX calls from the browser to local Web services. *Sys.Net.WebRequest* is the main class you'll use to implement AJAX functionality of this sort. It is a JavaScript version of the C# class *System.Net.HttpWebRequest* and is used to make network calls for which you need full control over the request object and response callback.

> **Note** Because of browser security, you can make network requests only to the same domain as the Web server that is hosting the AJAX page. This means that you cannot make remote Web requests—you can only access services on the Web server that is local to the Web application. Limiting network requests to the local Web server is a security implementation of the browser, not a limitation of the Microsoft AJAX Library. If scripts were able to make cross-domain calls, they would also be able to send data to remote resources. However, both images and scripts can be used to get and send data to remote servers. You can access remote script resources to load data by using a wrapped JSON message format known as JSONP, but this is a workaround and not part of the core library. A proposal for a cross-site XMLHttpRequest exists, but at the time of this writing it is only a working document.

To create a Web request, instantiate a new *Sys.Net.WebRequest* and set the URL and callback handler. The HTTP verb, request body, and HTTP headers can also be set, giving you full control over the network call. The *invoke* method initiates the call, and after the call is invoked you can get a *WebRequestExecutor* object by accessing the *executor* property. *Sys.Net.WebRequestExecutor* is the class that executes the actual request, and it is instantiated only after the request is invoked. The following code sample demonstrates a basic request and obtains a reference to the Web request executor after invoking the request:

```
var net = new Sys.Net.WebRequest();
net.set_url('example.WCF');
net.add_completed(callback);
net.invoke();
var networkCall = net.get_executor();
```

The *WebRequestExecutor* object is useful for canceling a network call. For example, you might be loading data in an AJAX call when a user changes his mind and decides to navigate to another area of data entry. In this case, you can call the *abort* method of the executor object, canceling the call. The callback is not processed on an aborted operation, although it is processed on an operation that times out. To cancel the network call, simply call *abort* on the executor as follows:

```
networkCall.abort();
```

A full code sample demonstrating a simple network call, a cancel operation, and the callback is shown in Listing 5-9

LISTING 5-9. Network requests are created using *Sys.Net.WebRequest* and executed with *Sys.Net. WebRequestExecutor (SysNet.aspx).*

```
// Processes the main page logic, demonstrating the network request.
function pageLoad() {
    // Create a new object to represent the application
    window.MyApplication = new Object();

    var context = {Method : 'pageLoad'};
    var net = new Sys.Net.WebRequest();
    net.set_url('timeout.aspx');
    net.set_timeout(1000);
    net.set_userContext(context);
    net.add_completed(callback);

    net.invoke();
    // Set our application's active network call to the current request,
    // so the user can cancel the request
    window.MyApplication.networkCall = net.get_executor();

    // Add a cancel handler to the CancelButton and display it.
    var cancelButton = $get('CancelButton');
    cancelButton.style.display='';
    Sys.UI.DomEvent.addHandler(cancelButton, 'click', abortRequest);
}
```

```
// Cancels the current web request. Could be called from a cancel button or by an
// impatient user
function abortRequest(){
    if (window.MyApplication.networkCall)
        window.MyApplication.networkCall.abort();
    window.MyApplication.networkCall = null;
}

// Processes the web request
function callback(response, method, context){
    // Adds intellisense to the method body:
    if (response == null){
        response = new Sys.Net.WebRequestExecutor(); throw 'Error';
    }

    // Clear the cancel button and the cancel handler.
    var cancelButton = $get('CancelButton');
    cancelButton.style.display='none';
    Sys.UI.DomEvent.removeHandler(cancelButton, 'click', abortRequest);

    // Clear the application's networkCall reference
    window.MyApplication.networkCall = null;

    // Get the response, if it's available:
    if (response.get_responseAvailable()){
        var xml = response.get_xml();
    }
    var timdOut = response.get_timedOut();
    var aborted = response.get_aborted();
    if (aborted){
        Sys.Debug.trace('aborted!!!');
    }
}
```

Additionally, each page includes an instance of *Sys.Net.WebRequestManager*, which is used to define global settings for Web requests, such as the timeout and callback handlers. If you need to define global settings or handlers on AJAX methods, use the *Sys.Net.WebRequestManager* object (which is actually an instance of the private class *Sys.Net._WebRequestManager*). To set the default timeout for Web requests, use the *defaultTimeout* property as follows:

```
Sys.Net.WebRequestManager.set_defaultTimeout(1000);
```

Finally, the network library also includes the *Sys.Net.WebServiceProxy* class, which is used as a base class for Web service proxies generated by script-enabled Windows Communication Foundation (WCF) or ASMX Web services. You will generally not use the *WebServiceProxy* class directly, but you'll use an implementation that calls your Web service through the auto-generated proxy. You can, however, use this class to call an arbitrary Web service, although the REST architecture is preferred if you are not generating a script proxy.

JavaScript Serialization with *Sys.Serialization*

The *Sys.Serialization.JavaScriptSerializer* class is used to serialize and deserialize JavaScript types into JSON objects. It is also used specifically to process date values serialized by ASP.NET AJAX server code. To serialize your JavaScript object into a JSON-formatted string, use the *serialize* method as follows:

```
var json = Sys.Serialization.JavaScriptSerializer.serialize(value);
```

Conversely, if you have a JSON string returned from a WCF service, you can use the *deserialize* method to get a JavaScript object from the JSON string, as the following code sample demonstrates:

```
var myObject = Sys.Serialization.JavaScriptSerializer.deserialize(value);
```

The *deserialize* method is not needed for general purpose deserialization but is used when the JSON string is generated from ASP.NET AJAX server serialization methods.

Application Services with *Sys.Services*

The *Sys.Services* namespace is used to integrate ASP.NET services such as authentication, profile, and roles with the client runtime. These services are integrated into the *Sys.Application* object and expose application services through integrated Web service proxies and script injection during the server-side page load. I'll discuss the *Sys.Services* namespace in depth in Chapter 6, "AJAX Application Services with Sys.Services."

Browser Extensions with *Sys.UI*

The *Sys.UI* namespace provides a framework for programming with DOM objects in the browser. It consists of base classes for control developers to implement as well as utility methods you can use to work with the DOM and DOM events.

> **Tip** The Control and Behavior classes are base classes used to build reusable components. I'll talk about both classes in further detail in Chapter 7, "Building an AJAX Class Library with Components," and Chapter 8, "Building AJAX Controls."

Programming DOM Elements with *Sys.UI.DomElement*

Sys.UI.DomElement is the main class that you'll use to work with DOM objects. It is useful for attaching event handlers and CSS style classes and for otherwise accessing or manipulating a DOM object. *DomElement* is a static class that contains utility methods for working with DOM elements.

Sys.UI.DomElement.getElementById(id, parent)   *Sys.UI.DomElement.getElementById* extends the basic JavaScript method *document.getElementById* with a second parameter: the parent element in which to search. Passing a second parameter limits the document's search scope and is more efficient than searching the entire document. Because this method is one of the most common JavaScript methods you'll use, it also has a shortcut method, *$get*.

For example, to get the document object "editButton" use the following code:

```
var editButton = $get('editButton');
```

If you know the scope of the search and already have a reference to the parent element, limit the scope of the search with the parent parameter, as the following code demonstrates:

```
var userStatusControl = $get('UserStatusControl');
if (Sys.Services.AuthenticationService.get_isLoggedIn()){
    var loginButton = $get('loginButton', userStatusControl);
    if (loginButton) Sys.UI.DomElement.setVisible(loginButton, false);
}
```

> **Tip** It's a best practice to check that the object exists before using it! Otherwise, you'll get the famous error message, *"Null is null or not an object."*

Sys.UI.DomElement.getLocation(*element*)   The *getLocation* method is used to get a *Sys.UI.Point* object that contains the element's x and y coordinates. The following code gets the target element's location:

```
var loc = Sys.UI.DomElement.getLocation(target);
```

The return object is of the type *Sys.UI.Point*, which is a simple data structure defined by the following code in the Microsoft AJAX Library:

```
Sys.UI.Point = function Sys$UI$Point(x, y) {
    this.x = x;
    this.y = y;
}
Sys.UI.Point.registerClass('Sys.UI.Point');
```

Sys.UI.DomElement.setLocation(*element, Sys.UI.Point*)   The *setLocation* method is used to set an element's *x* and *y* coordinates. The following code gets the target element's location by using *getLocation* and then sets the location to be 10 pixels offset in each direction:

```
var loc = Sys.UI.DomElement.getLocation(target);
Sys.UI.DomElement.setLocation(target, loc.x + 10, loc.y + 10);
```

Sys.UI.DomElement.getBounds(*element*)   The *getBounds* method is used to get the element's location, width, and height. This information can be useful when you want to position elements in relation to each other. For example, you might want to resize or reposition an element at run time in response to user actions or the size of the user's browser window. The following example shows how to get the bounds of an object using *getBounds*:

```
var bounds = Sys.UI.DomElement.getBounds(target);
```

The *getBounds* method returns an object of type *Sys.UI.Bounds*, a simple data structure similar to *Sys.UI.Point*. The following Microsoft AJAX Library source code defines *Sys.UI.Bounds*:

```
Sys.UI.Bounds = function Sys$UI$Bounds(x, y, width, height) {
    this.x = x;
    this.y = y;
    this.height = height;
    this.width = width;
}
Sys.UI.Bounds.registerClass('Sys.UI.Bounds');
```

To demonstrate the usefulness of *getBounds*, you can build a browser application that maintains UI elements such as navigation and header controls but that implements a scrolling region for the content. To implement this, you can get the window's height and set the content area to the height of the window minus the height of the header. Because you might be drawing the header and other controls dynamically, you can use the bounds of the header to determine the height and then set the height of the content area each time the user resizes the page. Figure 5-4 shows a simple user interface in which the content of the page is scrollable but the header and navigation placeholder are not.

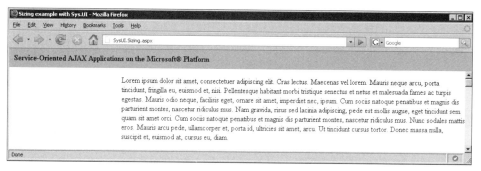

FIGURE 5-4. The *DomElement* class can be used to size and manage scrolling elements on the page.

To implement this functionality, the code in Listing 5-10 gets the height of the header and then calculates the height that the content *div* needs to be to allow scrolling.

> **Tip** Determining the window's height is straightforward in FireFox but not in Internet Explorer. In Internet Explorer, you must get the *document.body.parentNode's* height. The following code can be used to determine the height of the Web browser in both Internet Explorer and Firefox. Because each browser uses a slightly different version of the DOM model, you can simply determine whether the window implements the *innerHeight* property and use that if it does.
>
> ```
> var height;
> if (window.innerHeight){
>     height=window.innerHeight;
> }
> ```

```
else if (document.body.parentNode.clientHeight){
    height = document.body.parentNode.clientHeight;
}
else if (document.body.offsetHeight){
    height = document.body.offsetHeight;
}
```

LISTING 5-10. You can use *Sys.UI.DomElement* methods to maintain a scrolling region on the page (*Web/SysUI.Sizing.aspx*).

```
<%@ Page Language="C#" %>
<html xmlns="http://www.w3.org/1999/xhtml">
<head runat="server">
    <title>Sizing example with Sys.UI</title>
<script type="text/javascript">

function pageLoad() {
    $addHandler(window, 'resize', resizeElements);
    resizeElements();
}

function resizeElements(){
    var height;
    if (window.innerHeight){
        height=window.innerHeight;
    }
    else if (document.body.parentNode.clientHeight){
        height = document.body.parentNode.clientHeight;
    }
    else if (document.body.offsetHeight){
        height = document.body.offsetHeight;
    }
    var pageHeader = $get('pageHeader');
    var headerBounds = Sys.UI.DomElement.getBounds(pageHeader);
    var content = $get('MainContent');
    content.style.height = height - headerBounds.height + 'px';
}

</script>
    <style type="text/css">
        #pageHeader {padding:10px; background-color:Silver; font-weight:bold;
    </style>
</head>
<body style="padding:0px; margin:0px; overflow:hidden;" scroll="no" >
    <div id="pageHeader">
        Service-Based AJAX on the Microsoft Platform
    </div>
```

```
<table style="width:100%; height:100%" cellpadding="0" cellspacing="0">
    <tr valign="top">
        <td>
            <div id="NavigationPlaceholder" style="width:250px;"/>
        </td>

        <td>
            <div id="MainContent" style="overflow:auto;" >
                <p>
                    <!-- Content shortened. In practice, this would be the main
                        content region, containing the main text of the wiki
                        in our example application. -->
                    Lorem ipsum dolor sit amet, consectetuer adipiscing elit.
                </p>
            </div>
        </td>
    </tr>
</table>
<form id="form1" runat="server">
    <asp:ScriptManager ID="ScriptManager1" runat="server" />
</form>
</body>
</html>
```

Programming DOM Events with *Sys.UI.DomEvent*

Generally speaking, DOM events are anything that a user does while interacting with the browser's document. However, in the Microsoft AJAX Library the *Sys.UI.DomEvent* class wraps the browser event with a rich event object that is compatible across browsers. The *Sys.UI.DomEvent* can be used to handle mouse events, keyboard events, and browser events. To handle these events, use the *Sys.UI.DomEvent* class to add event handlers to DOM elements. Event handlers are functions that are called with a parameter of type *Sys.UI.DomEvent*. To add an event handler, use the *addHandler* method as follows:

```
Sys.UI.DomEvent.addHandler(target, 'click', domEventHandler);
```

Sys.UI.DomEvent.addHandler is also available through the shortcut reference *$addHandler*. The sample code above can be shortened to the following:

```
$addHandler(target, 'click', domEventHandler);
```

To demonstrate a simple event handler, you can dump the output of a DOM event to the trace log. Listing 5-11 demonstrates a simple event handler that logs the result of a DOM event to the trace console.

LISTING 5-11. *Sys.UI.DomEvent* can be used to add handlers and process DOM events (*Web/Sys.UI.DomEvent.aspx*).

```
<%@ Page Language="C#" %>
<html xmlns="http://www.w3.org/1999/xhtml">
<head>
    <title>Sys.UI.DomEvent Sample</title>
<script type="text/javascript">
function pageLoad() {
    Sys.Debug.clearTrace();
    var target = $get('TestNode');
    Sys.UI.DomEvent.addHandler(target, 'click', domEventHandler);
}

function domEventHandler(domEvent){
    if (domEvent == null){ domEvent = new Sys.UI.DomEvent();
        throw 'InvalidOperation';}
    Sys.Debug.traceDump(domEvent);
}
</script>

</head>
<body>
    <form id="form1" runat="server">
        <asp:ScriptManager ID="ScriptManager" runat="server"/>
    </form>
    <div id="TestNode" style="cursor:pointer;">Click me to test </div>
    <textarea cols="80" rows="10" id="TraceConsole"></textarea>
</body>
</html>
```

In practice, you'll use a DOM event to initiate AJAX calls such as loading data, saving data, or manipulating screen elements. Listing 5-12 demonstrates the *DomEvent* class and its properties in the event handler. The code also uses methods in *Sys.UI.DomElement* to manipulate the browser objects.

LISTING 5-12. The *DomEvent* class is used to process user actions (Web/*Sys.UI.DomEvent2.aspx*).

```
<%@ Page Language="C#" %>
<html xmlns="http://www.w3.org/1999/xhtml">
<head>
    <title>Sys.UI.DomEvent Sample 2</title>
    <style type="text/css">
        .superfly{ background-color:Yellow; }
        .superflied{  background-color:Lime; }
    </style>
    <script type="text/javascript">

function pageLoad() {
    var target = $get('TestNode');
    Sys.UI.DomEvent.addHandler(target, 'click', testMethod);
}
```

```
function testMethod(event){
    if (event == null){ event = new Sys.UI.DomEvent(); throw 'Invalid Operation';}
    var target = event.target;
    Sys.Debug.traceDump(event);

    Sys.UI.DomElement.addCssClass(target, 'superfly');
    Sys.UI.DomElement.toggleCssClass(target,'superflied');
    var bounds = Sys.UI.DomElement.getBounds(target);
    Sys.UI.DomElement.setLocation(target, bounds.x + 10, bounds.y + 10);

    var target2 = Sys.UI.DomElement.getElementById('TestNode2', target);
    Sys.UI.DomElement.setVisible(target2, !Sys.UI.DomElement.getVisible(target2));
}


    </script>
</head>
<body>
    <form id="form1" runat="server">
        <asp:ScriptManager ID="ScriptManager1" runat="server" />

        <div id="TestNode" style="cursor:pointer;">Click me to test
            <span id="TestNode2" style="display:none;">...no, really!</span>
        </div>
    </form>
</body>
</html>
```

With browser functionality implemented in *Sys.UI*, network operations implemented in *Sys.Net*, application functionality implemented in *Sys.Application*, debugging support implemented in *Sys.Debug*, and native and global JavaScript types enhanced and defined in the *Sys* namespace, the Microsoft AJAX Library makes client-side application programming a viable model. On top of this library you can develop components based on *Sys.Component*, behaviors based on *Sys.UI.Behavior*, and controls based on *Sys.UI.Control,* as you'll see in the following chapters. By using the library's type system and the ScriptManager control, you can package your application into discrete libraries and page runtime applications, and you can deliver your components to multiple applications as components.

Coding to Support Visual Studio IntelliSense

Visual Studio 2008 adds support for the JavaScript development environment through IntelliSense help for JavaScript class libraries. IntelliSense is enabled by adding script references at the head of the JavaScript file. Each file should list core libraries that it references in the form of script references. Script references can be named resources for compiled assemblies, such as the Microsoft AJAX Library itself, or path-based references. To add a reference to the AJAX library, include the following line at the top of your JavaScript file:

```
/// <reference name="MicrosoftAjax.js"/>
```

For assemblies other than the AJAX library, you need to include the assembly name in the script reference. For example, to include a reference to *MyLibrary.js* compiled into the assembly *MyAssembly.dll*, the following script reference would be added:

```
/// <reference assembly="MyAssembly" name="MyLibrary.js"/>
```

To add a reference to a custom library, include a reference with a path as follows:

```
/// <reference path="Controls/ApplicationRuntime.js"/>
```

Within the class library, IntelliSense will be enabled within the file for items that are declared *above* the line of code you're working on and also in any files referenced through script reference comments. Within an ASPX page, IntelliSense is enabled for all files that have been references through the ScriptManager control.

When the IDE parses for IntelliSense, it also does a round of error checking and will complain in the Error window if any errors are found. To force the IDE to update its JavaScript IntelliSense, press the keyboard combination CTRL-ALT-J.

The XML comments used in JavaScript are similar to those used in C#: three slashes precede a comment, and the comment uses standard comment elements defined by the Visual Studio IntelliSense engine. The standard elements are *summary* for class definitions, *value* for field definitions, *param* for method parameters, and *returns* for return types. JavaScript XML comments are always declared inside the method or class definition.

For each class definition, provide a summary of the class in its constructor method. The following example demonstrates the comments for a class constructor (in the *function* definition):

```
ExampleClassDefinition = function() {
    /// <summary>
    /// An example class, to demonstrate XML comments.
    /// </summary>
}
```

Properties are defined in the Microsoft AJAX Library by convention with *get* and *set* methods defined in the class prototype. Within the property, define the comment in the *get* method, as the following code demonstrates:

```
get_xml: function() {
    /// <value>Gets or sets the XML data</value>
    return this._xml;
},
set_xml: function(value) {
    this._xml = value;
}
```

The *value* element has the optional attributes *type, integer, domElement,* and *mayBeNull.* These attributes can be used to further define the value, although I generally prefer lightweight documentation with only the description defined. The following *value* element lists its optional attributes.

```
<value
    type="ValueType" integer="true|false" domElement="true|false"
    mayBeNull="true|false" elementType="ArrayElementType">Description</value>
```

Additionally, whenever arrays are passed, the following attributes can be added to *value*, *param*, or *returns* elements to specify the contents of the array elements: *elementType*, *elementInteger*, *elementDomElement*, and *elementMayBeNull*.

Events are defined by *add* and *remove* methods, which are explained in depth in Chapter 7 in the discussion of *Sys.Component*. For reference, you define the handler XML comments in the *add* method as the following code demonstrates:

```
add_render: function(handler) {
    /// <value>Bind and unbind to the render event.</value>
    this.get_events().addHandler('render', handler);
},
remove_render: function(handler) {
    this.get_events().removeHandler('render', handler);
}
```

For methods with parameters (including the constructor or *function*), the *param* element can be used to define the expected type of parameter. For example, the following code demonstrates the *param* definition for a method that expects a *Sys.UI.DomEvent* argument:

```
function testHandler(event){
    /// <param name="event" mayBeNull="false" optional="false"
    /// type="Sys.UI.DomEvent">The event from the user click</param>
}
```

The following *param* element lists its optional attributes:

```
<param name="parameterName" mayBeNull="true|false" optional="true|false"
    type="ParameterType" parameterArray="true|false" integer="true|false"
    domElement="true|false">Description</param>
```

IntelliSense within the method body is inferred through instantiation of the object. It doesn't matter what XML comments are provided for the method parameters. You won't get IntelliSense inside the method without creating a type inference through instantiation. When you know what type to expect in a method, set the parameter to an instance of the expected type in validation code that runs only if the argument is not passed. For example, the following *pageLoad* method adds the *testHandler* event handler to the *click* event of a DOM object. To enable IntelliSense within the body of the method, create an object and throw an error when the argument is null. Because the argument will never be null (unless there really is an error), the code will not be called under normal use, but you can implement the method body more quickly during development than by referring to external code documentation. The following example demonstrates how to create a type inference through object creation:

```
function pageLoad() {
    var target = $get('TestNode');
    Sys.UI.DomEvent.addHandler(target, 'click', testHandler);
}

function testHandler(event){
    ///<param name="event" mayBeNull="false" optional="false"
    /// type="Sys.UI.DomEvent">The event from the user click</param>

    // Type inference enables intellisense:
    if (event == null){ event = new Sys.UI.DomEvent(); throw 'Invalid Operation';}
    // intellisense is enabled for Event here, now known as a Sys.UI.DomEvent
}
```

Finally, for objects that return an item, the *returns* element should be used to specify the type of object that is returned. The following code sample demonstrates the XML comments for a method that returns a random DOM element. The *domElement=true* attribute is set, specifying that the method returns a DOM element.

```
function getRandomDomElement() {
    /// <summary>Gets a random DOM element</summary>
    /// <returns type="object" domElement="true" mayBeNull="true">
    ///    Returns a random DOM element.
    /// </returns>
    throw Error.notImplemented();
}
```

Tip Although XML comments add tremendous value in the form of documentation, I believe that the best code is the simplest code and that documentation should be lightweight. Because JavaScript is a loosely typed language, I prefer to keep strong references out of the documentation as well. I typically avoid the optional parameters for the elements and keep the code and the documentation as simple as possible.

Summary

In this chapter I described the Microsoft AJAX Library and its main namespaces and objects. By now, you should be familiar with the AJAX library and where to find classes and functionality within it. You should be familiar with the debugging support provided by *Sys.Debug*. Most importantly, I covered the functionality of *Sys.UI.DomElement* and *Sys.UI.DomEvent*, which are used to add functionality to a browser application. Building on this foundation, we'll look at application services using the *Sys.Services* application service layer from the Microsoft AJAX Library in the next chapter before moving on to building components and controls.

Chapter 6
AJAX Application Services with *Sys.Services*

After completing this chapter, you will

- Understand authentication, roles, and security in an ASP.NET AJAX application.

- Understand ASP.NET AJAX application services.

- Be able to integrate ASP.NET AJAX application services in a JavaScript application.

- Be able to extend and enhance application services with custom service implementations.

In Chapters 1, 2, and 3, I described how to use a service-oriented style of programming to develop service-based applications against services exposed through an AJAX-enabled Web binding. In Chapters 4 and 5, I covered the client runtime that utilizes the Microsoft AJAX Library, a robust application platform for client-side programming with JavaScript. In this chapter, I'll build on those foundations by describing how to add application services to the client application. These services supplement your application's API to provide AJAX functionality for authentication, authorization, and preferences.

More Information Application services are integrated on top of the ASP.NET provider model. For more information about ASP.NET providers, I recommend Dino Esposito's book *Programming Microsoft ASP.NET 3.5* (Microsoft Press, 2008).

Figure 6-1 illustrates the role of application services in Microsoft's AJAX application architecture. Application services are implemented in ASP.NET and exposed through Web services and integrated JavaScript proxies built into the AJAX library's *MicrosoftAjax.js* file. Application services are also integrated into the client runtime through the ScriptManager control, which recognizes the server-side authentication status on the initial page load, although the client-side authentication status can be updated throughout the lifetime of the page.

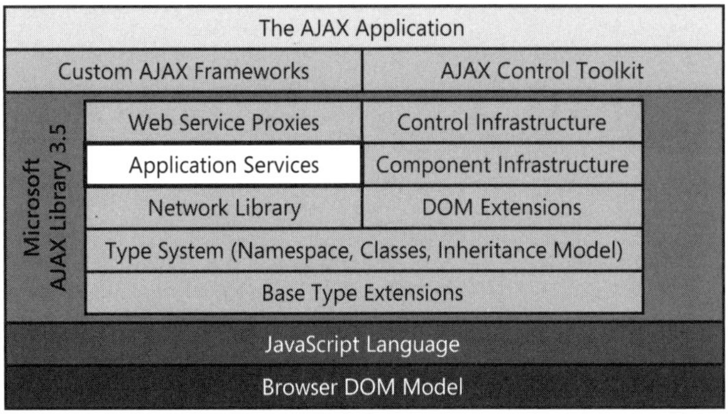

FIGURE 6.1. The role of application services in the AJAX application architecture.

ASP.NET AJAX Application Services with *Sys.Services*

ASP.NET AJAX includes the JavaScript namespace *Sys.Services* to provide application service functionality to the local Web application. The application services defined in *Sys.Services* are more than pure service proxies; they also contain logic used to incorporate initial state during server page loading and wrapper methods that add functionality to the application service proxies. While most proxy scripts are used only as proxies for Web services, application service proxies actually maintain application state. Rather than returning an object that encapsulates the application state returned from the Web services, the proxies themselves are the JavaScript objects that maintain their application state through the page's lifetime. This means that when you load values from authentication, roles, or profile services, the data is accessible at any time through methods of the proxy. You do not have to load it from the server or write your own wrapper object.

In the code samples in this chapter, I'll use the Forms Authentication provider for authentication, roles, and profiles. For a refresher on configuring forms-based authentication using ASP.NET, see the following sidebar "Enabling Forms-Based Authentication for ASP.NET." The chapter's code samples work equally well with Windows-authenticated applications or custom providers. You must still use aspnet_regsql.exe to configure the ASP.NET database for profiles, which is described in detail in the MSDN topic "Creating the Application Services Database for SQL Server" at *http://msdn.microsoft.com/library/x28wfk74.aspx*.

> ## Enabling Forms-Based Authentication for ASP.NET
>
> To enable forms-based authentication for the AJAX application, you follow the same steps as for ASP.NET 2.0 Web applications.
>
> First, use the ASP.NET tool aspnet_regsql.exe (located in *Windows\Microsoft.NET\ Framework\v2.0.50727*) to configure the database. Next, the database must be configured in web.config as LocalSqlServer. Be sure that the SQL connection string is defined

as the LocalSqlServer connection—either to an instance of SQL Express or an instance of SQL Server 2005 or 2008. The following XML shows the SQL connection to the authentication database for our AJAX application using SQL Server. If you are using a SQL Server Express instance and the aspnet database, you do not need to configure this connection string.

```
<connectionStrings>
    <clear/>
    <add connectionString="Data Source=localhost; Initial Catalog=enterprisewiki;
        uid=app;pwd=sekretpassword" name="LocalSqlServer" providerName="SqlClient" />
</connectionStrings>
```

After configuring the database and connection string, you can use the ASP.NET configuration tool in Visual Studio to create test users. Although I won't cover user-management functionality in this book, it is worth noting that user-management functionality in ASP.NET, such as password recovery and account creation, aren't yet directly exposed as AJAX controls. This functionality might best be integrated into an AJAX application as modal dialogs using "classic" ASP.NET 2.0. These topics are discussed at length in Dino Esposito's book *Programming Microsoft ASP.NET 3.5* referenced earlier in this chapter.

ASP.NET AJAX Script Initialization and *Sys.Services*

The ScriptManager server control is used to instantiate initial values for the core *Sys.Services* objects. It also provides initial state for authentication, role, and profile data during page loading through a technique I call *ASP.NET AJAX script initialization*. ASP.NET script initialization is used to set initial values from the server in a client-side framework. These values establish the initial state of known objects and cut down on the time required to initialize the page in the client. For application state such as authentication or profile data, this technique does away with the need for an initial Web service call to determine state that is already known when the script runtime is loaded.

In ASP.NET AJAX, the ScriptManager uses script initialization to tie authentication, role, and profile status to JavaScript *Sys.Services* objects without requiring an initial service call. During the lifetime of the page, the values can change and can be loaded from Web services as needed.

To utilize script initialization in your own code, use the *ClientScriptManager* class, which is exposed to ASP.NET server controls and pages as the property *Page.ClientScript*. The *ClientScriptManager* method *RegisterClientScriptBlock* is used to register startup scripts that run when the page is loaded. The following C# code demonstrates a simple script initialization technique you can use within the server code of the ASP.NET *Page* or *Control* classes in your application.

```
// Override the OnPreRender method of System.Web.UI.Control to initialize script values
protected override void OnPreRender(EventArgs e)
```

```
{
    base.OnPreRender(e);
    StringBuilder script = null;
    if (this.Page.User.Identity.IsAuthenticated) {
        // Perform any script initialization here
        script = new StringBuilder();
        script.Append(" Sys.Debug.trace('Authenticated script initialization'); ");
    }

    if (script != null && script.Length > 0)
    {
        this.Page.ClientScript.RegisterClientScriptBlock(
            this.GetType(), "Sys.Initialization", script.ToString(), true);
    }
}
```

With this technique, you can write initial script values that are set in JavaScript before the *Sys.Application init* or *load* client-side events are raised. When scripts initialized through the *RegisterClientScriptBlock* method are run on the client, all ScriptManager registered scripts will have been loaded by the JavaScript application.

The *ScriptManager* class uses a private method named *ConfigureApplicationServices* to perform ASP.NET AJAX script initialization for application services configured through the ScriptManager. This method is called during execution of the server-side *PreRenderComplete* event handler and initializes the state for the profile service, authentication service, and role service by writing JavaScript during the ASP.NET page execution. Listing 6-1 demonstrates the ScriptManager's implementation of script initialization. By looking at the method implementation, you can see that scripts for profiles, authentication, and roles are all rendered to the page by way of the *ClientScript* instance of the *Page*. (The type *IPage* in the ScriptManager source code is just an internal wrapper for the *Page* class.) The service manager classes *AuthenticationServiceManager*, *ProfileServiceManager,* and *RoleServiceManager* all handle their own script initialization by appending to a *StringBuilder* instance that contains initial script values. The script initialization of these objects is configured through properties of the ScriptManager, which I'll discuss throughout the rest of the chapter.

 Tip Code for this book is available online at *http://www.microsoft.com/mspress/companion/ 9780735625914*. The code for this chapter is in the file Chapter 6.zip. For authentication purposes, a demo user that ships with the example database has been configured with the username "user" and the password "password".

LISTING 6-1. The ScriptManager injects script for initial authentication, profile, and role states in its private method *ConfigureApplicationServices* (from *System.Web.Extensions.dll*).

```
// private method implementation from System.Web.UI.ScriptManager
private void ConfigureApplicationServices()
{
    StringBuilder sb = null;
    ProfileServiceManager.ConfigureProfileService(ref sb, this.Context, this,
        this._proxies);
```

```
    AuthenticationServiceManager.ConfigureAuthenticationService(ref sb,
        this.Context, this, this._proxies);

    RoleServiceManager.ConfigureRoleService(ref sb, this.Context, this,
        this._proxies);

    if ((sb != null) && (sb.Length > 0))
    {
        this.IPage.ClientScript.RegisterClientScriptBlock(typeof(ScriptManager),
            "AppServicesConfig", sb.ToString(), true);
    }
}
```

The internal methods *ProfileServiceManager.ConfigureProfileService, AuthenticationService-Manager.ConfigureAuthenticationService,* and *RoleServiceManager.ConfigureRoleService* are all used by ASP.NET AJAX to instantiate initial values for *Sys.Services* objects. The scripts generated by these methods are registered in a client script block with the page's *ClientScript* object. If the user is logged in, the ASP.NET AJAX runtime writes initialization script into the page, setting the *AuthenticationService* logged-in status to *true*. As the page loads, the ScriptManager renders the following script inline in the ASPX page. The method *Sys.Services. AuthenticationService._setAuthenticated* sets the application service proxy's initial state to *authenticated*.

```
<script type="text/javascript">
    if (typeof(Sys) === 'undefined')
        throw new Error('ASP.NET Ajax client-side framework failed to load.');
    Sys.Services._ProfileService.DefaultWebServicePath = 'Profile_JSON_AppService.axd';
    Sys.Services._AuthenticationService.DefaultWebServicePath =
        'Authentication_JSON_AppService.axd';
    Sys.Services.AuthenticationService._setAuthenticated(true);
    Sys.Services._RoleService.DefaultWebServicePath = 'Role_JSON_AppService.axd';
</script>
```

The authentication, profile, and role services for the JavaScript *Sys.Services* namespace are exposed through built-in HTTP handlers generated by the AJAX framework. To enable the built-in authentication, role, and profile application services used by *Sys.Services*, you must configure the web.extensions/scripting/webServices element in web.config. Here is an example configuration:

```
<system.web.extensions>
    <scripting>
      <webServices>
        <authenticationService enabled="true" />
        <profileService enabled="true"/>
        <roleService enabled="true"/>
      </webServices>
    </scripting>
  </system.web.extensions>
```

With this configuration, the HTTP handlers are exposed through the following application-relative endpoints:

- ~/Authentication_JSON_AppService.axd

- ~/Role_JSON_AppService.axd

- ~/Profile_JSON_AppService.axd

Keep in mind that these services are the internal implementations of application services defined in the *System.Web.Extensions* assembly. They are not meant to be called from remote services. Remote application services use the Windows Communication Foundation (WCF) classes defined in *System.Web.ApplicationServices*, which are not all fully compatible with the Microsoft AJAX Script Library version 3.5. In most cases, you do not need to use custom services for the main application services implementations, but you can create your own endpoints that adhere to the interface and are JSON-compatible, and you can set the paths to your services through properties of the ScriptManager.

The built-in ASP.NET AJAX application services respond only to the content-type "application/json" with the POST verb, so you cannot load these services over a GET call using a Web browser. The corresponding services in *System.Web.Extensions* are internal, sealed classes and aren't configurable or extendable by the user. As an alternative, you might want to use the services defined in *System.Web.ApplicationServices*. These services are designed with a more service-oriented nature in mind. I'll discuss these services at the end of this chapter. However, with the default application services that integrate with *Sys.Services*, no server programming is involved because the ASP.NET AJAX framework takes care of the implementation for you. In most cases, this might be all that you need to implement application services for AJAX, and you can use alternative authentication methods for remote clients.

> **Tip** In NewsGator's commercial applications, we deploy AJAX services in the ASP.NET Web application and configure the same services with alternative authentication schemes for external access. The strategy of deploying a service endpoint in multiple locations with alternative authentication schemes helps you develop services for the service-oriented architecture (SOA) platform and lets you reuse the same services for local AJAX applications.

JavaScript Authentication with *Sys.Services*

Sys.Services.AuthenticationService provides a JavaScript interface to ASP.NET authentication functionality. You can use the authentication service for an application that allows anonymous access but has enhanced functionality for logged-in users. In our sample application, I'll implement read-only wiki content for anonymous users, but logged-in users will have collaboration tools and can edit content. The *AuthenticationService* class extends the JavaScript proxy with basic authentication functionality for the JavaScript application and is integrated with the ScriptManager through script initialization during page loading.

The default authentication service works with ASP.NET forms-based authentication and is not an endpoint that is accessible over non-AJAX Web services. It is tightly coupled to the AJAX runtime and is not compatible with newer WCF *System.Web.ApplicationServices* endpoints discussed later in the chapter. However, you can provide your own endpoint that conforms to the interface, with a *Login* and a *Logout* method that are available over a JSON-enabled Web service accepting a POST command to *Login* and *Logout*.

> **Tip** You can provide a custom authentication service as long as it accepts the same JSON-formatted message as the Sys.Services.AuthenticationService proxy. To create your own authentication service, configure it to accept a JSON-formatted message and use the following JSON data structure. It should also set the authentication cookie on success.
>
> `{ userName:` *username*`, password:` *password*`, createPersistentCookie:` *isPersistent* `}`
>
> To set the custom endpoint that the *Sys.Services.AuthenticationService* should invoke, set the path in the ScriptManager or ScriptManagerProxy tag as follows:
>
> ```
> <asp:ScriptManagerProxy runat="server"
>     AuthenticationService-Path="services/Login.svc" />
> ```

The following code sample demonstrates a function for showing a login control for an anonymous user and a logout control for the logged-in user. This code could be called from the JavaScript page load event or during the client-side page's life cycle in response to the user logging in or out.

```
function showHideLogin(){
    var isLoggedIn = Sys.Services.AuthenticationService.get_isLoggedIn();
    var logincontrol = $get('loginControl');
    var logoutcontrol = $get('logoutControl');

    if (!isLoggedIn){
        // show the login UI
        logoutcontrol.style.display='none';
        logincontrol.style.display='';
    } else { // show the logout UI.
        logoutcontrol.style.display='';
        logincontrol.style.display='none';
    }
}
```

To log in, you can use the authentication service just like any other AJAX-enabled Web service. The following function can be assigned to a login button's *onclick* event:

```
function OnClickLogin(domEvent) {
    var username = $get('usernameInput').value;
    var password = $get('passwordInput').value;
    Sys.Services.AuthenticationService.login(username,
        password, false,null,null,OnLoginCompleted,OnFailed,null);
}
```

A complete code sample that uses the authentication service to implement AJAX authentication functionality is shown in Listings 6-2 and 6-3.

LISTING 6-2. Login controls can be implemented by HTML on the page. The controls call JavaScript methods for implementation (*Web/AuthenticationDemo.aspx*).

```
<%@ Page Language="C#" MasterPageFile="basic.master" %>

<asp:Content runat="server" ContentPlaceHolderID="MainMasterBody">
    <asp:ScriptManagerProxy runat="server">
        <Scripts>
            <asp:ScriptReference Path="AuthenticationDemo.js" />
        </Scripts>
    </asp:ScriptManagerProxy>

    <div style="display: none;" id="loginControl" class="loginControl">
        <div class="widgetTitle">Login</div>
        <div class="lightPadding">
            Username <br />
            <input type="text" id="usernameInput" /><br /><br />

            Password <br />
            <input type="text" id="passwordInput" /><br /><br />

            <button id="ButtonLogin" value="Login" type="button"
             title="Login">Login</button>
            <div id="loginFeedbackDiv">
            </div>
        </div>
    </div>

    <div id="logoutControl" class="loginControl" style="display: none;" >
        <button id="ButtonLogout" type="button" value="Logout"
            title="Logout">Logout</button>
    </div>

</asp:Content>
```

LISTING 6-3. To implement login functionality with *Sys.Services.AuthenticationService*, use the *login* and *logout* instance methods and implement custom callback handlers (*Web/AuthenticationDemo.js*).

```
/// <reference name="MicrosoftAjax.js"/>
// Provides the example client runtime for the authentication demo page

function pageLoad(){
    Sys.UI.DomEvent.addHandler($get('ButtonLogin'), 'click', OnClickLogin);
    Sys.UI.DomEvent.addHandler($get('ButtonLogout'), 'click', OnClickLogout);
    showHideLogin();
}

function showHideLogin(){
    var isLoggedIn = Sys.Services.AuthenticationService.get_isLoggedIn();
```

```
        var logincontrol = $get('loginControl');
        var logoutcontrol = $get('logoutControl');

        if (!isLoggedIn){   // show the login UI
            logoutcontrol.style.display='none';
            logincontrol.style.display='';
        } else {              // show the logout UI.
            logoutcontrol.style.display='';
            logincontrol.style.display='none';
        }
    }

    function OnClickLogin(domEvent) {
        if (domEvent == null){domEvent = new Sys.UI.DomEvent(null);
            throw Error.argumentNull;}

        var username = $get('usernameInput').value;
        var password = $get('passwordInput').value;
        Sys.Services.AuthenticationService.login(username,
            password, false, null, null, OnLoginCompleted, OnFailed, null);
    }

    function OnClickLogout(domEvent){
       Sys.Services.AuthenticationService.logout(
          null, OnLogoutCompleted, OnFailed, null);
    }

    // This is the callback function called if the authentication fails.
    function OnFailed(error, userContext, methodName) {
        var err = error.get_message();
        var timedOut = error.get_timedOut();
        var statusCode = error.get_statusCode();
        alert(err);
    }

    // The callback function called if the authentication completed successfully.
    function OnLoginCompleted(isLoggedIn, userContext, methodName) {
        showHideLogin();
        $get('passwordInput').value = '';
        if (!isLoggedIn)
            $get('loginFeedbackDiv').innerHTML = 'Unable to log in.';
        else
            $get('loginFeedbackDiv').innerHTML = '';
    }

    // This is the callback function called if the user logged out successfully.
    function OnLogoutCompleted(result) {
        showHideLogin();
    }

    Sys.Application.notifyScriptLoaded();
```

Upon logout, the authentication service always redirects the user after processing the custom *OnLogoutCompleted* handler. The following JavaScript is implemented by ASP.NET AJAX in the internal *_onLogoutComplete* handler:

```
// ASP.NET AJAX _onLogoutComplete implementation: always redirect when logging out
if (!redirectUrl) {
    window.location.reload();
}
else {
    window.location.href = redirectUrl;
}
```

However, because objects and methods in JavaScript are dynamic, you can assign a new function to the Microsoft AJAX Library's *Sys.Services.AuthenticationService._onLogoutComplete* method with your own implementation. To implement custom logout functionality without redirecting or reloading, you can implement the JavaScript code shown in Listing 6-4. This code assigns the *fixup_onLogoutComplete* method to the *_onLogoutComplete* method of *Sys.Services.AuthenticationService:*

LISTING 6-4. A custom implementation of the Microsoft AJAX Library's logout handler can be assigned at run time (*Web/AuthenticationDemo.js*).

```
// An instance method assigned to AuthenticationService:
//      Sys.Services.AuthenticationService._onLogoutComplete
fixup_onLogoutComplete = function(result, context, methodName) {
    var redirectUrl = context[0];
    var userContext = context[3] || this.get_defaultUserContext();
    var callback = context[1] || this.get_defaultLogoutCompletedCallback()
        || this.get_defaultSucceededCallback();
    this._authenticated = false;
    if (callback) {
        callback(null, userContext, "Sys.Services.AuthenticationService.logout");
    }
    if(redirectUrl) {
        window.location.href = redirectUrl;
    }
}

function fixup(){
    Sys.Services.AuthenticationService._onLogoutComplete = fixup_onLogoutComplete;
}
Sys.Application.add_init(fixup);
```

JavaScript Profile Data with *Sys.Services*

ASP.NET profiles are used to store user information and can be used to encapsulate user preferences. A profile should not be used to store security settings or critical business data because it is configured through the web.config file and isn't the most reliable form of data storage. To define a profile you must specify the provider and define the properties in web.config. Listing 6-5 demonstrates a simple profile definition in web.config. This profile defines the *startTopic* preference and the *Wiki.editorType* preference, which keep track of the user's startup topic and preferred editor.

LISTING 6-5. A profile is configured in web.config.

```
<profile enabled="true">
  <providers>
    <!-- Tip: use the strong name for the provider type! -->
    <add name="AspNetSqlProfileProvider"
        connectionStringName="LocalSqlServer"
        applicationName="/"
        type="System.Web.Profile.SqlProfileProvider, System.Web"/>
  </providers>
  <properties>
    <add name="startTopic" type="String" allowAnonymous="false" />
    <group name="Wiki">
      <add name="editorType" type="String" allowAnonymous="false" />
    </group>
  </properties>
</profile>
```

Sys.Services.ProfileService provides a JavaScript interface to ASP.NET profile functionality. Profile data can be loaded or saved through the profile service as needed. Building on the earlier example of the authentication service , the profile service can be called after a successful logon to get the current authentication principal's application preferences. Listing 6-6 demonstrates the profile loading logic, with the profile service's *load* method called after authentication.In the sample code, you can load the wiki application with the preferred starting page from the start topic last saved by the user.

LISTING 6-6. A profile is loaded through *Sys.Services.ProfileService.*

```
// The callback function called if the authentication completed successfully.
function OnLoginCompleted(isLoggedIn, userContext, methodName) {
    showHideLogin();
    $get('passwordInput').value = '';
    if (!isLoggedIn)
        $get('loginFeedbackDiv').innerHTML = 'Unable to log in.';
    else{
        $get('loginFeedbackDiv').innerHTML = '';
        Sys.Services.ProfileService.load(null, OnProfileLoaded,
            OnProfileFailed, null);
    }
}

function OnProfileLoaded(propertiesLoaded){
    if (propertiesLoaded == 0) return;
    var topicDiv = $get('Topic');
    topicDiv.innerHTML = Sys.Services.ProfileService.properties.startTopic;
```

```
    // TO DO: Load wiki with the preferred topic.
}

function OnProfileFailed(err, userContext, method){
    var error = err.get_exceptionType() + "-- " + err.get_message();
    alert(error);
}
```

To provide initial profile values in the server-side page load through script initialization, use the *ProfileService-LoadProperties* property in the ScriptManager through the *ScriptManager* or *ScriptManagerProxy* control, as in Listing 6-7.

LISTING 6-7. Script initialization is used to render initial profile values from the server on page loading when specified with the *ProfileService-LoadProperties* property.

```
<asp:ScriptManagerProxy runat="server"
       ProfileService-LoadProperties="startTopic,Wiki.editorType">
    <Scripts>
        <asp:ScriptReference Path="Sys.AuthenticationService.js" />
    </Scripts>
</asp:ScriptManagerProxy>
```

To save profile data, you can simply call the *save* method of *Sys.Services.ProfileService*. The callback handlers aren't required, and they aren't desirable in most cases because the user will not be waiting for the call to be completed and is unaware that the profile data is being saved. The following example saves the given topic to the profile's *startTopic* preference using the *save* method:

```
function saveStartTopic(topic){
    Sys.Services.ProfileService.properties.startTopic = topic;
    Sys.Services.ProfileService.save(['startTopic']);
}
```

Application Roles and *Sys.Services.RoleService*

Application roles are used in ASP.NET to aggregate permissions and to simplify security programming. Roles do not directly control security; they are only string-based attributes for a user that must be handled by application code. For example, before showing links to create new topics, you might check that a user has the *contributor* role, which includes the permissions *read* and *write*. Examples of roles in our wiki application are a*dministrator, contributor,* and *moderator.* The simplest way to configure roles with ASP.NET is to use the Web Site Administration Tool (WSAT). The WSAT for role management is shown in Figure 6-2.

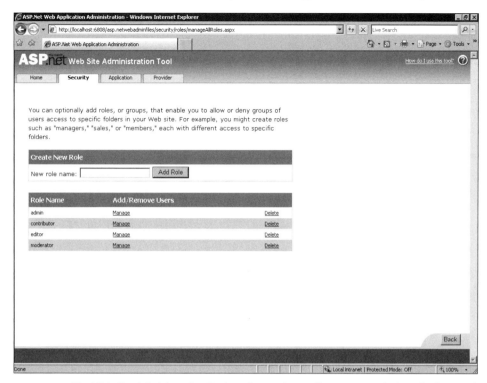

FIGURE 6-2. The Web Site Administration Tool can be used to easily manage Web site roles from within Visual Studio.

In server-side code, roles can be checked by using the *IPrincipal* interface, which is exposed through the *User* property of the *Page*, *Control*, or *HttpContext* instances. The *User* object in ASP.NET is defined as a type of the *IPrincipal* interface, which can be a generic user defined by any authentication provider or a Windows security principal using the Active Directory security principal of the calling user. Use the *IPrincipal* method *IsUserInRole* to determine whether a user has a given role.

In server-side code, you can use *IsInRole* to load optimized script libraries for application roles. For example, you might have a lightweight script library that is used for seventy percent of the users of your application, who are either anonymous Internet users or do not have contributor rights. The editing capabilities of the wiki could be exposed through a library that is defined in the contribute.js JavaScript file, and these capabilities could be rendered only if the user has the *contributor* role. The following C# code can be used on the server to determine whether a user is in the application role *contributor*. The code adds the wikiEditor.js file only if the user is a contributor.

```
<script runat="server">
// Example OnPreRender server-side Page method
protected override void OnPreRender(EventArgs e)
{
    base.OnPreRender(e);
    if (this.User.IsInRole("contributor"))
    {
        this.ScriptManagerProxy.Scripts.Add( new ScriptReference("wikiEditor.js") );
    }
}
</script>
```

> **Note** Roles can also be programmed on the server by using the static class *Roles*. The *Roles* class contains utility methods for working with the configured ASP.NET role provider.

Sys.Services.RoleService provides a JavaScript interface to roles application service. These roles are used to security trim the JavaScript user interface. On the server, roles are used to enforce security, but on the client, roles are used to configure the user interface. Security is always enforced on the server in the service implementation, as discussed in Chapters 2 and 3.

> **Tip** With the role service, a user can see indirectly all roles that she is a member of. Remember that all JavaScript methods and AJAX actions are exposed to the user and can be viewed through client-side debugging tools just like the ones you use to debug the application.

To load initial roles into the browser runtime during page load, set the ScriptManager's property *RoleService-LoadRoles* to *true* through the ScriptManager or ScriptManagerProxy control, as the following code demonstrates:

```
<asp:ScriptManagerProxy ID="ScriptManagerProxy" runat="server"
        RoleService-LoadRoles="true" >
    <Scripts>
        <asp:ScriptReference Path="Sys.RoleService.js" />
    </Scripts>
</asp:ScriptManagerProxy>
```

When *RoleService-LoadRoles* is set to *true*, the ScriptManager initializes the roles to the page through the ScriptManager's *ConfigureApplicationServices* method, mentioned earlier in the chapter. The following script is generated for a user with the *contributor* and *moderator* roles:

```
Sys.Services.RoleService._roles = Sys.Serialization.JavaScriptSerializer.deserialize(
    '[\"contributor\",\"moderator\"]');
```

> **Tip** Application roles are not case sensitive.

You can use the *isUserInRole* method to determine the status of a user's role at any time through JavaScript. The following code sample demonstrates a simple check on a user's membership in the contributor role:

```
var isContrib = Sys.Services.RoleService.isUserInRole('contributor');
```

The *RoleService* class differs from typical Web service proxies in that it saves the roles as an internal array, and it can be used to check role membership at any time without invoking a Web service call. In your JavaScript application code, you must know whether the ScriptManager has initialized the user's roles during page loading and that the user has not logged in or out since either the page was loaded or the last occurrence of the role service's *load* method. The role service knows only about the roles since the last time it was called. Therefore, you might want to load new role values after certain events occur, such as a successful login event, or after a certain time interval. While cached roles might be invalid, roles don't change very often—they only change when an administrator grants a greater degree of access or the user completes a specific operation, such as authentication.

To load new role values at any time in the client life cycle, call the *load* method of the *Sys.Services.RoleService* proxy class. The *load* method is not a direct call to the Web service endpoint, but a call to a wrapper method that lets the AJAX library persist the values of the call in the *RoleService* instance. Because *load* returns *null*, the parameters of the method include a callback handler, an exception handler, and the user-context object. Building on the earlier examples of authentication, Listing 6-8 demonstrates integrating the role service into the *OnLoginCompleted* JavaScript method.

LISTING 6-8. On successful login, you might want to load new role information for the current user before initializing the user interface for the logged-in user.

```
// The callback function called if the authentication completed successfully.
function OnLoginCompleted(isLoggedIn, userContext, methodName) {
    showHideLogin();
    $get('passwordInput').value = '';
    if (!isLoggedIn)
        $get('loginFeedbackDiv').innerHTML = 'Unable to log in.';
    else {
        $get('loginFeedbackDiv').innerHTML = '';
        Sys.Services.RoleService.load(rolesCompleted, rolesFailed, null);
    }
}

function rolesCompleted() {
    if (Sys.Services.RoleService.isUserInRole('contributor')) {
        //instantiate contributor controls on page
    }
    if (Sys.Services.RoleService.isUserInRole('moderator')) {
        //instantiate moderator controls on page
    }
}
```

Service-Oriented Application Services over WCF

With the default service proxies and the default server-side ASP.NET AJAX implementation, you can fully integrate application services on the client with little effort. These services, however, are designed only for the AJAX application and aren't meant to be used by remote clients. Ideally, it's a best practice to design the application with service orientation in mind. This way, service implementations can be used by remote clients without the need to rewrite the services. Fortunately, a service implementation designed for remote access is defined in *System.Web.ApplicationServices*, which is defined in the assembly *System.Web.Extensions*.

System.Web.ApplicationServices provides Web services for authentication, roles, and profile information, exposing the ASP.NET application services to remote and local clients. The services listed in Table 6-1 provide these services and can be included in your ASP.NET application through standard WCF configuration. These services are functionally equivalent to *System.Web.Security.AuthenticationService, System.Web.Profile.ProfileService,* and *System.Web.Security.RoleService*, and all but *AuthenticationService* share the same contract signature. This means that *ProfileService* and *RoleService* can be called using the *Sys.Services* JavaScript namespace by providing custom service path parameters to the ScriptManager. The WCF implementation is not compatible with *Sys.Services.AuthenticationService*, however.

TABLE 6-1. **Application Services Defined in *System.ServiceModel.ApplicationServices***

Type	Description
AuthenticationService	Enables access to ASP.NET forms authentication through the WCF service interface. A WCF version of *System.Web.Security. AuthenticationService*.
ProfileService	Enables access to the ASP.NET *Profile* store through the WCF service interface. A WCF version of *System.Web.Profile.ProfileService*.
RoleService	Enables access to ASP.NET *Roles* through the WCF service interface. A WCF version of *System.Web.Security.RoleService*.

To enable WCF application services, you must define them in web.config (in the same way that you enable standard WCF services) and include a SVC file that points to the service's host factory. Listing 6-9 defines the web.config entries you use to expose the application services to the local AJAX application or remote SOAP clients.

LISTING 6-9. WCF application services are defined in web.config the same way as standard WCF services (*Web/Services/web.config*).

```
<?xml version="1.0"?>
<configuration>
  <system.serviceModel>
    <services>
      <service
          behaviorConfiguration="AppServiceBehaviors"
          name="System.Web.ApplicationServices.AuthenticationService">
        <endpoint
            binding="basicHttpBinding"
```

```
                bindingNamespace="http://asp.net/ApplicationServices/v200"
                contract="System.Web.ApplicationServices.AuthenticationService"/>
      </service>

      <service
          behaviorConfiguration="AppServiceBehaviors"
          name="System.Web.ApplicationServices.RoleService">
        <endpoint
            binding="basicHttpBinding"
            bindingNamespace="http://asp.net/ApplicationServices/v200"
            contract="System.Web.ApplicationServices.RoleService"/>
      </service>

      <service
          behaviorConfiguration="AppServiceBehaviors"
          name="System.Web.ApplicationServices.ProfileService">
        <endpoint
            binding="basicHttpBinding"
            bindingNamespace="http://asp.net/ApplicationServices/v200"
            contract="System.Web.ApplicationServices.ProfileService"/>
      </service>
    </services>

    <behaviors>
      <serviceBehaviors>
        <behavior name="AppServiceBehaviors">
          <serviceMetadata httpGetEnabled="true"/>
          <serviceDebug includeExceptionDetailInFaults="true"/>
        </behavior>
      </serviceBehaviors>
    </behaviors>
    <serviceHostingEnvironment aspNetCompatibilityEnabled="true"/>
  </system.serviceModel>
</configuration>
```

SVC files must be deployed for each WCF service endpoint that implements an application service. Listings 6-10, 6-11, and 6-12 define the SVC files for application services, each of which uses the *ApplicationServicesHostFactory* class that generates the WCF endpoint.

LISTING 6-10. *AuthenticationService uses the ApplicationServicesHostFactory (Web/Services/Login.svc).*

```
<%@ ServiceHost Language="C#"
    Service="System.Web.ApplicationServices.AuthenticationService"
    Factory="System.Web.ApplicationServices.ApplicationServicesHostFactory" %>
```

LISTING 6-11. *RoleService uses the ApplicationServicesHostFactory (Web/Services/Role.svc).*

```
<%@ ServiceHost Language="C#"
    Service="System.Web.ApplicationServices.RoleService"
    Factory="System.Web.ApplicationServices.ApplicationServicesHostFactory" %>
```

LISTING 6-12. *ProfileService uses the ApplicationServicesHostFactory (Web/Services/Profile.svc).*

```
<%@ ServiceHost Language="C#"
    Service="System.Web.ApplicationServices.ProfileService"
    Factory="System.Web.ApplicationServices.ApplicationServicesHostFactory" %>
```

Unfortunately, the WCF authentication service is not fully compatible with the *Sys.Services. AuthenticationService* JavaScript class because the WCF method looks for a *username* parameter, whereas *Sys.Services.AuthenticationService* passes a *userName* parameter. (Notice the case difference.) Because of this difference, you must redefine the *Sys.Services. AuthenticationService* login method to pass the correct parameters. Listing 6-13 enables the *Sys.Services.AuthenticationService* to utilize the WCF *Sys-tem.Web.ApplicationServices. AuthenticationService* contract by passing the JSON parameter *username* rather than *userName*.

LISTING 6-13. To enable *Sys.Services* integration with the WCF *AuthenticationService* contract, you must redefine the login function (*Web/AuthenticationDemo_WCF.js*).

```
function WCF$login(username, password, isPersistent, customInfo, redirectUrl,
loginCompletedCallback, failedCallback, userContext) {
    this._invoke(this._get_path(), "Login", false,
        { username: username, password: password,
            createPersistentCookie: isPersistent },
        Function.createDelegate(this, this._onLoginComplete),
        Function.createDelegate(this, this._onLoginFailed),
        [username, password, isPersistent, customInfo, redirectUrl,
            loginCompletedCallback, failedCallback, userContext]);
}

Sys.Application.add_load(fixupWcf);
function fixupWcf(){}{
    if (Sys.Services.AuthenticationService.get_path().indexOf(".svc", 0) > 0)
        Sys.Services.AuthenticationService.login = WCF$login;
}
```

Using WCF endpoints for application services other than the authentication service is straightforward, but the WCF endpoints are not integrated with ASP.NET script initialization that is built into the basic implementation. If you need to use the WCF endpoints, you must develop your own script initialization code for the server. Listing 6-14 and Listing 6-15 demonstrate a WCF implementation of authentication, role, and profile services using WCF endpoints and custom script initialization.

LISTING 6-14. To use WCF services for AJAX application services, you must perform your own script initialization (*Web/AuthenticationDemo_WCF.aspx*).

```
<%@ Page Language="C#" MasterPageFile="basic.master" %>

<script runat="server">
```

```
    protected override void OnPreRender(EventArgs e)
    {
        base.OnPreRender(e);
        StringBuilder script = null;
        if (this.Page.User.Identity.IsAuthenticated) {
            // Perform any script initialization here
            script = new StringBuilder();

            var js = new System.Web.Script.Serialization.JavaScriptSerializer();
            var profileDictionary =
                new System.Collections.Generic.Dictionary<string, object>();

            ProfileBase profile = ProfileBase.Create(
                this.Context.User.Identity.Name, true);

            foreach (SettingsProperty prop in ProfileBase.Properties)
            {
                var value = profile.GetPropertyValue(prop.Name);
                if (value != null)
                    profileDictionary.Add(prop.Name, value);
            }
            var profileObject = js.Serialize(profileDictionary);
            script.AppendFormat(@"
            function onLoadDefaultProfile(){{
                var result = eval({0});
                Sys.Services.ProfileService._onLoadComplete(
                    result, new Object(), 'onLoad');
            }}
            Sys.Application.add_init(onLoadDefaultProfile);
            ", profileObject);

            var rolesForUser = Roles.GetRolesForUser();
            if ((rolesForUser != null) && (rolesForUser.Length > 0))
            {
                script.Append("Sys.Services.RoleService._roles = ");
                script.Append(js.Serialize(rolesForUser));
                script.Append(";\n");
            }
        }

        if (script != null && script.Length > 0)
        {
            this.Page.ClientScript.RegisterClientScriptBlock(
                this.GetType(), "Sys.Initialization", script.ToString(), true);
        }
    }
</script>

<asp:Content runat="server" ContentPlaceHolderID="MainMasterBody">
    <asp:ScriptManagerProxy ID="ScriptManagerProxy" runat="server"
            RoleService-Path="services/role.svc"
            ProfileService-Path="services/Profile.svc"
            AuthenticationService-Path="services/Login.svc" >
        <Scripts>
            <asp:ScriptReference Path="AuthenticationDemo_WCF.js" />
```

```
            </Scripts>
        </asp:ScriptManagerProxy>

        <div style="display: none;" id="loginControl" class="loginControl">
            <div class="widgetTitle">Login</div>
            <div class="lightPadding">
                Username <br />
                <input type="text" id="usernameInput" /><br /><br />

                Password <br />
                <input type="text" id="passwordInput" /><br /><br />

                <button id="ButtonLogin" value="Login" type="button"
                 title="Login">Login</button>
                <div id="loginFeedbackDiv">
                </div>
            </div>
        </div>

        <div id="logoutControl" class="loginControl" style="display: none;" >
            <button id="ButtonLogout" type="button" value="Logout"
                title="Logout">Logout</button>
        </div>

    </asp:Content>
```

LISTING 6-15. To integrate with WCF application services, you must redefine the *Sys.Services. AuthenticationService.login* method (*Web/AuthenticationDemo_WCF.js.*).

```
/// <reference name="MicrosoftAjax.js"/>
// Provides the example client runtime for the authentication demo page

function pageLoad(){
    Sys.UI.DomEvent.addHandler($get('ButtonLogin'), 'click', OnClickLogin);
    Sys.UI.DomEvent.addHandler($get('ButtonLogout'), 'click', OnClickLogout);
    showHideLogin();
}

function showHideLogin(){
    var isLoggedIn = Sys.Services.AuthenticationService.get_isLoggedIn();
    var logincontrol = $get('loginControl');
    var logoutcontrol = $get('logoutControl');
    if (!isLoggedIn){   // show the login UI
        logoutcontrol.style.display='none';
        logincontrol.style.display='';
    } else {
        // show the logout UI.
        logoutcontrol.style.display='';
        logincontrol.style.display='none';
    }
}
```

```
function OnClickLogin(domEvent) {
    if (domEvent == null){domEvent = new Sys.UI.DomEvent(null);
        throw Error.argumentNull;}

    var username = $get('usernameInput').value;
    var password = $get('passwordInput').value;
    Sys.Services.AuthenticationService.login(username,
        password, false,null,null,OnLoginCompleted,OnFailed,null);
}

function OnClickLogout(domEvent){
   Sys.Services.AuthenticationService.logout(
       null, OnLogoutCompleted, OnFailed, null);
}

// This is the callback function called if the authentication fails.
function OnFailed(error, userContext, methodName) {
    var err = error.get_message();
    var timedOut = error.get_timedOut();
    var statusCode = error.get_statusCode();
    alert(err);
}


// The callback function called if the authentication completed successfully.
function OnLoginCompleted(isLoggedIn, userContext, methodName) {
    showHideLogin();
    $get('passwordInput').value = '';
    if (!isLoggedIn)
        $get('loginFeedbackDiv').innerHTML = 'Unable to log in.';
    else
        $get('loginFeedbackDiv').innerHTML = '';
}


// This is the callback function called
// if the user logged out successfully.
function OnLogoutCompleted(result) {
    showHideLogin();
}


// An instance of AuthenticationService:
//     Sys.Services.AuthenticationService._onLogoutComplete
fixup_onLogoutComplete = function(result, context, methodName) {
    var redirectUrl = context[0];
    var userContext = context[3] || this.get_defaultUserContext();
    var callback = context[1] || this.get_defaultLogoutCompletedCallback()
        || this.get_defaultSucceededCallback();
    this._authenticated = false;
    if (callback) {
        callback(null, userContext, "Sys.Services.AuthenticationService.logout");
    }
    if(redirectUrl) {
        window.location.href = redirectUrl;
    }
}
```

```
function fixup(){
    Sys.Services.AuthenticationService._onLogoutComplete = fixup_onLogoutComplete;
}
Sys.Application.add_init(fixup);


// Only used for WCF services:
function WCF$login(username, password, isPersistent, customInfo, redirectUrl,
loginCompletedCallback, failedCallback, userContext) {
    this._invoke(this._get_path(), "Login", false,
        { username: username, password: password,
            createPersistentCookie: isPersistent },
        Function.createDelegate(this, this._onLoginComplete),
        Function.createDelegate(this, this._onLoginFailed),
        [username, password, isPersistent, customInfo, redirectUrl,
            loginCompletedCallback, failedCallback, userContext]);
}


function fixupWcf(){}{
    if (Sys.Services.AuthenticationService.get_path().indexOf(".svc", 0) > 0)
        Sys.Services.AuthenticationService.login = WCF$login;
}


Sys.Application.add_load(fixupWcf);
Sys.Application.notifyScriptLoaded();
```

Customizing WCF Application Services

Application services can be customized with authentication or provider logic through the
event-driven application model of ASP.NET 3.5. The *Authenticating* and *CreatingCookie*
events are both fired by the *System.Web.ApplicationServices.AuthenticationService* class.
These events can be handled through the *global.asax* ASP.NET file, which creates the server-
side application object. By handling the *Authenticating* event as shown in Listing 6-16, you
can provide custom authentication logic by using either a username/password combination or a custom authentication string that can be passed from the client and represent any
string-serialized data from the user's input. In addition to custom authentication logic, you
can also choose a new provider based on the login name.

LISTING 6-16. The *Authenticating* event can be handled to provide custom authentication (*Web/Global.asax*).

```
void Application_Start(object sender, EventArgs e)
{
    // Code that runs on application startup
    System.Web.ApplicationServices.AuthenticationService.Authenticating +=
        new EventHandler<System.Web.ApplicationServices.AuthenticatingEventArgs>
            (AuthenticationService_Authenticating);
}


void AuthenticationService_Authenticating(object sender, System.Web.
ApplicationServices.AuthenticatingEventArgs e)
```

```
{
    string username = String.Empty;
    string password = String.Empty;

    // You could pass in custom credentials
    string[] credentials;
    if(e.CustomCredential != null)
        credentials = e.CustomCredential.Split(new char[] { ',' });

    try
    {
        e.Authenticated = Membership.ValidateUser(e.UserName, e.Password);
    }
    catch
    {
        e.Authenticated = false;
    }
    e.AuthenticationIsComplete = true;
}
```

The profile service also fires events that you can handle to provide custom validation. To perform data validation on the server before data is saved, handle the *ValidatingProperties* event. Listing 6-17 demonstrates custom profile validation using this event.

LISTING 6-17. The *ValidatingProperties* event can be handled to provide custom server-side validation (*Web/Global.asax*).

```
void Application_Start(object sender, EventArgs e)
{
    // Code that runs on application startup
    System.Web.ApplicationServices.AuthenticationService.Authenticating +=
        new EventHandler<System.Web.ApplicationServices.AuthenticatingEventArgs>
            (AuthenticationService_Authenticating);

    System.Web.ApplicationServices.ProfileService.ValidatingProperties +=
        new EventHandler<
            System.Web.ApplicationServices.ValidatingPropertiesEventArgs>(
                ProfileService_ValidatingProperties);
}

void ProfileService_ValidatingProperties(object sender,
        System.Web.ApplicationServices.ValidatingPropertiesEventArgs e)
{
    if (String.IsNullOrEmpty((string)e.Properties["startTopic"])
        || ((string)e.Properties["startTopic"]).Contains(@"\") )
    {
        e.FailedProperties.Add("startTopic");
    }
}
```

Just as the authentication and profile services expose events to customize the service implementation, the role service can be configured using the *SelectingProvider* event. Listing 6-18 demonstrates a customization that uses EmployeesRoleProvider for all Fabrikam employees and the default AspNetProvider for all other cases.

LISTING 6-18. The *SelectingProvider* event of the role service can be used to return alternative role providers (*Web/Global.asax*).

```
void Application_Start(object sender, EventArgs e)
{
    // Code that runs on application startup
    System.Web.ApplicationServices.AuthenticationService.Authenticating +=
        new EventHandler<System.Web.ApplicationServices.AuthenticatingEventArgs>
            (AuthenticationService_Authenticating);

    System.Web.ApplicationServices.ProfileService.ValidatingProperties +=
        new EventHandler<
            System.Web.ApplicationServices.ValidatingPropertiesEventArgs>(
                ProfileService_ValidatingProperties);

    System.Web.ApplicationServices.RoleService.SelectingProvider +=
        newEventHandler<
        System.Web.ApplicationServices.SelectingProviderEventArgs>(
            RoleService_SelectingProvider);
}

void RoleService_SelectingProvider(object sender,
        System.Web.ApplicationServices.SelectingProviderEventArgs e)
{
    if (e.User.Identity.Name.IndexOf("@fabrikam.com") > 0)
    {
        e.ProviderName = "EmployeeRoleProvider";
    }
    else
    {
        e.ProviderName = "AspNetProvider";
    }
}
```

Summary

In this chapter you learned about application services using *Sys.Services* and the ASP.NET AJAX server-side implementation. You saw how ASP.NET AJAX uses script initialization to set initial JavaScript values on the server's page load method, and you learned how to inject your own initialization scripts. Finally, you learned how to use the WCF application services defined in *System.Web.ApplicationServices* to integrate services that support both local AJAX clients (through AJAX-enabled services) and remote SOAP-based clients. By now, you should be able to integrate application services into your AJAX application for authentication and roles. You should also be able to use the profile service to save and load user preferences during the execution of the application. In the next chapter we'll look at client-side programming with components, behaviors, and controls in the AJAX library.

Part III
Applied AJAX

Chapter 7
Building an AJAX Class Library with Components

After completing this chapter, you will

- Understand component-based development with the Microsoft AJAX Library.

- Understand property and event implementations with the Microsoft AJAX Library.

- Understand object-oriented AJAX programming using components.

- Learn how to use AJAX components in your AJAX applications.

In the three preceding chapters, I introduced the client-side runtime, described the Microsoft AJAX Library, and explored application services in the JavaScript namespace *Sys.Services*—specifically, using AJAX code for authentication, roles, and profile data. In this chapter, I'll build on these concepts and describe how to create a deployable application framework using AJAX controls and components in client-side libraries. These controls and components load data and interact with a service-oriented framework on the server.

The main goals of the AJAX JavaScript class library are portability, flexibility, maintainability, and above all, simplicity. You don't want to use massive amounts of JavaScript, with thousands of lines in each library file. You also want to avoid single-purpose components whenever possible so that you can reuse code in multiple contexts. Finally, you don't want to develop bloated applications that are slow to render and respond. To achieve these goals, you need to understand the limits of JavaScript and write your code appropriately.

 Tip Simplicity is a best practice in developing custom JavaScript class libraries. Keep your script library as simple as possible and use object-oriented designs to make your class interfaces simple and reusable.

The Microsoft AJAX Library provides a framework to help developers build object-oriented components for an AJAX application. This framework adds to the object-oriented JavaScript extensions to the type system that we looked at in Chapter 5, "The Microsoft AJAX Library." It also provides base class implementations for components, controls, and behaviors. These base classes include *Sys.Component*, *Sys.UI.Control*, and *Sys.UI.Behavior*. Both *Sys.UI.Control* and *Sys.UI.Behavior* are derived from *Sys.Component* and include the common functionality of the component infrastructure. A JavaScript component is an application object that is partially managed by the JavaScript *Application* object and includes base functionality such as creation and disposal services and a property and events framework. Figure 7-1 illustrates the role of the component infrastructure in an AJAX application. The component infrastructure is built into the Microsoft AJAX Library and is implemented through custom AJAX frameworks.

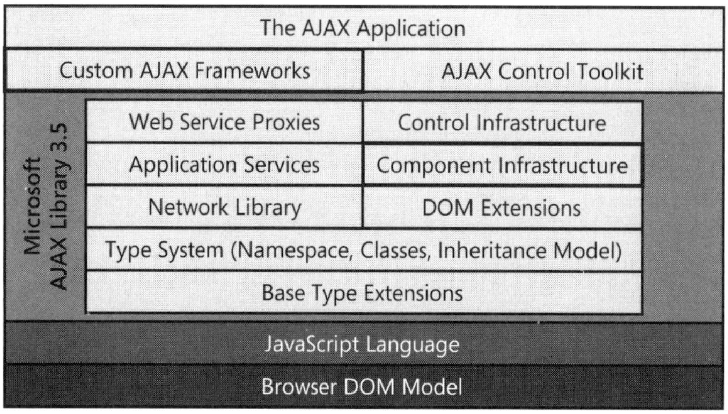

FIGURE 7-1. The component infrastructure is built into the AJAX library and implemented in custom AJAX frameworks.

Understanding Properties and Events in the AJAX Library

Before looking further into components and controls, I'll describe the fundamentals of properties and events in the AJAX library. After reviewing properties and events, I'll discuss how they are implemented in AJAX library components and how to use components to make AJAX applications more robust and maintainable. In the next chapter, we'll build on this foundation to develop controls and behaviors.

Properties

Properties are defined through a naming convention of the AJAX library and are not part of the JavaScript language. To define a property, use the *get_* and *set_* prefixes with the property name to define the property's function. For example, the following code block defines the property *text* in the *PropertyExample* class and creates an instance of the class before using the *text* property.

```
Type.registerNamespace("SOAjax.Examples");

SOAjax.Examples.PropertyExample = function() { }
SOAjax.Examples.PropertyExample.prototype = {
    _text: null,
    get_text: function() {
        /// <value>Used to get or set the text of the PropertyExample.</value>
        return this._text;
    },
    set_text: function(text) {this._text = text;}
}
```

```
var myObject = new SOAjax.Examples.PropertyExample();
myObject.set_text('Hello, World!');
Sys.Debug.trace( myObject.get_text() );
```

With this convention, the *text* property is defined, but it is not accessed through the syntax *myObject.text*. Instead, you gain access to the *text* property by using the statement *myObject.get_text*. A property should be documented inside the *get_* property method. The documentation is used to build Visual Studio IntelliSense for the property.

When you work with properties in the AJAX library to develop components, behaviors, or controls, you refer to the property using its name, and the AJAX library looks for the property's *get_* and *set_* methods. This mechanism applies to custom components as well as to components built into the AJAX library's base framework and the AJAX Control Toolkit on Codeplex.

> **Tip** Properties should be defined by creating accessor methods using lowercase field names with *get_* and *set_* prefixes. Private fields are used to store the property field and are defined through a naming convention that uses the underscore prefix. For example, the property *text* would be implemented by the private field *_text* that is accessed through the accessor methods *get_text* and *set_text*.

Events

Events play a key role in the AJAX library and enable the development of loosely coupled JavaScript component frameworks. Throughout this book, you've seen examples of using events with the *Sys.Application* object, including the *load*, *init*, and *dispose* events. Events can also be based on DOM events and user actions such as mouse events and keyboard events, as you saw in Chapter 6, "AJAX Application Services with *Sys.Services*," with the *$addHandler* function. You can define custom events in a JavaScript class by creating an event handler list and event binding methods using the AJAX library's naming conventions.

To support events, you must include an instance of *Sys.EventHandlerList* in your class. By convention, you need to include the event handler list in a *get_events* property method. The following code can be used to include the event handler list in a *get_events* property:

```
get_events: function() {
    if (!this._events) {
        this._events = new Sys.EventHandlerList();
    }
    return this._events;
}
```

To define an event, you must create *add_* and *remove_* methods to enable event binding, and you must call the event handler when the event fires. The *addHandler* and *remove-Handler* methods of *Sys.EventHandlerList* are used to add and remove event bindings. The

EventHandlerList class is used to aggregate event handlers into a single function so that multiple functions can be bound to a single event.

> **Tip** The *EventHandlerList* class is how the *Sys.Application* object supports multiple handlers for the *init* and *load* events.

To better understand the event handler list, refer to the AJAX library source code, which is shown in part in Listing 7-1. The list handler implements a simple dictionary of event names and functions. The *getHandler* method returns a dynamically created aggregate function that calls multiple handler functions for the event.

LISTING 7-1. The *Sys.EventHandlerList* class defines a dictionary of events and functions and supports the Microsoft AJAX Library event framework (excerpt from *MicrosoftAjax.debug.js*).

```
Sys.EventHandlerList = function Sys$EventHandlerList() {
    this._list = {};
}
function Sys$EventHandlerList$addHandler(id, handler) {
    Array.add(this._getEvent(id, true), handler);
}
function Sys$EventHandlerList$removeHandler(id, handler) {
    var evt = this._getEvent(id);
    if (!evt) return;
    Array.remove(evt, handler);
}
function Sys$EventHandlerList$getHandler(id) {
    var evt = this._getEvent(id);
    if (!evt || (evt.length === 0)) return null;
    evt = Array.clone(evt);
    return function(source, args) {
        for (var i = 0, l = evt.length; i < l; i++) {
            evt[i](source, args);
        }
    };
}
function Sys$EventHandlerList$_getEvent(id, create) {
    if (!this._list[id]) {
        if (!create) return null;
        this._list[id] = [];
    }
    return this._list[id];
}
Sys.EventHandlerList.prototype = {
    addHandler: Sys$EventHandlerList$addHandler,
    removeHandler: Sys$EventHandlerList$removeHandler,
    getHandler: Sys$EventHandlerList$getHandler,
    _getEvent: Sys$EventHandlerList$_getEvent
}
Sys.EventHandlerList.registerClass('Sys.EventHandlerList');
```

To include support for events in your class, create an *events* property that returns the *Sys. EventHandlerList* reference for the class and include *add_* and *remove_* methods for each supported event. For example, to define a *fire* event, include the methods *add_fire* and *remove_fire*, as shown in the following example:

```
add_fire: function(handler) {
    /// <summary>Adds a handler to the fire event.</summary>
    this.get_events().addHandler("fire", handler);
},
remove_fire: function(handler) {
    this.get_events().removeHandler("fire", handler);
}
```

To provide Visual Studio IntelliSense support for an event, add a summary of the event to the *add* method as the example demonstrates. Documentation is not needed for the *remove* method.

To fire the event from your class, get a handler method from the event handler list and call it. The *getHandler* method of the *EventHandlerList* will return a dynamically created method that will call each event handler that is added to the event. For example, the following code gets the handler for the *fire* event and calls it. Event handlers that were added to the class's *fire* event will be called from the method that is returned from *getHandler*. Notice the null reference checks in the code—because the event handler reference is lazily created, *this._events* will be null if there is no event.

```
fireEvent: function() {
    if (this._events) {
        var handler = this._events.getHandler("fire");
        if (handler) {
            handler(this, Sys.EventArgs.Empty);
        }
    }
}
```

Putting it all together, Listing 7-2 contains the full sample class for event binding. Take note of the internal reference of the event handler list and the *add_* and *remove_* methods for the *fire* event.

> **Tip** Code for this book is available online at *http://www.microsoft.com/mspress/companion/ 9780735625914*. The code for this chapter is in the file Chapter 7.zip.

LISTING 7-2. Events are bound through *add_* and *remove_* methods and are implemented by using the *Sys.EventHandlerList* class (*Web/Script/Examples.js*).

```
Type.registerNamespace("SOAjax.Examples");

SOAjax.Examples.EventExample = function() { }
SOAjax.Examples.EventExample.prototype = {
    /// <summary>
    /// An example of a class that demonstrates events.
    /// </summary>

    _text: null,
    _events: null,
    get_text: function() { return this._text; },
    set_text: function(text) { this._text = text; },

    get_events: function() {
        if (!this._events) {
            this._events = new Sys.EventHandlerList();
        }
        return this._events;
    },

    add_fire: function(handler) {
        /// <summary>Adds a handler to the example 'fire' event.</summary>
        this.get_events().addHandler("fire", handler);
    },
    remove_fire: function(handler) {
        this.get_events().removeHandler("fire", handler);
    },
    fireEvent: function() {
        if (this._events) {
            var handler = this._events.getHandler("fire");
            if (handler) {
                handler(this, Sys.EventArgs.Empty);
            }
        }
    }
}
```

Events are useful for building loosely coupled JavaScript components through handler functions in composite components or page implementations. To bind to the *fire* event, for example, create a method that handles the event in the page. Event handlers are passed the sender of the event plus any arguments. In the example in Listing 7-2, the *Sys.EventArgs. Empty* reference is used, specifying no arguments. The following code defines an event handler method that is bound to an instance of the *EventExample* class by adding the *onFire* handler method with the *EventExample.add_fire* method. The *fireEvent* method is then called, which fires the event, which is in turn handled by the *onFire* handler.

```
function onFire(sender, eventArgs){
    alert('Fire!');
}
```

```
var eventDemo = new SOAjax.Examples.EventExample();
eventDemo.add_fire(onFire);
eventDemo.fireEvent();
```

Custom event arguments can be used by your class by deriving from *Sys.EventArgs*. You might want to create a custom event arguments class to contain additional information. Listing 7-3 demonstrates a simple event arguments class that defines a *text* property.

LISTING 7-3. A custom event arguments class can be used to send additional information with the event (*Web/Script/Examples.js*).

```
SOAjax.Examples.TextEventArgs = function (text) {
    SOAjax.Examples.TextEventArgs.initializeBase(this);
    this._text = text;
}
SOAjax.Examples.TextEventArgs.prototype = {
    get_text: function() { return this._text; },
    set_text: function(val) { this._text = val; }
}
SOAjax.Examples.TextEventArgs.registerClass(
    'SOAjax.Examples.TextEventArgs', Sys.EventArgs);
```

Listing 7-4 demonstrates the use of the *SOAjax.Examples.TextEventArgs* class integrated with the previous sample code. You can use a custom event arguments class to pass data between components for loosely coupled, event-driven application objects.

LISTING 7-4. Custom event argument classes can be implemented to handle additional information in the event handlers (*Web/Script/Examples.js*).

```
SOAjax.Examples.EventExample = function() { }
SOAjax.Examples.EventExample.prototype = {
    /// <summary>
    /// An example class that demonstrates events.
    /// </summary>

    _text: null,
    _events: null,
    get_text: function() { return this._text; },
    set_text: function(text) { this._text = text; },

    get_events: function() {
        if (!this._events) {
            this._events = new Sys.EventHandlerList();
        }
        return this._events;
    },

    add_fire: function(handler) {
        /// <summary>Adds a handler to the example 'fire' event.</summary>
        this.get_events().addHandler("fire", handler);
    },
    remove_fire: function(handler) {
        this.get_events().removeHandler("fire", handler);
    },
```

```
        fireEvent: function() {
            if (this._events) {
                var handler = this._events.getHandler("fire");
                if (handler) {
                    // handler(this, Sys.EventArgs.Empty);
                    handler(this, new SOAjax.Examples.TextEventArgs(this.get_text()));
                }
            }
        }
    }

    function onFire(sender, eventArgs){
        Sys.Debug.assert(typeof(eventArgs.get_text)=='function',
            'Expected a get_text method of the event args class!')
        var text = eventArgs.get_text();
        Sys.Debug.assert(text != null, 'Expected text in the event args!');
        alert(text);
    }

    // Create an event demo object and exercise it:
    var eventDemo = new SOAjax.Examples.EventExample();
    eventDemo.set_text('Hello, AJAX nation!');
    eventDemo.add_fire(onFire);
    eventDemo.fireEvent();
```

While events and properties are useful in any JavaScript class, they are central to the AJAX component framework and are simplified in the *Sys.Component* base class by the base implementation. The *Sys.Component* base class contains the *EventHandlerList* class and the *get_events* method and contains a creation method that supports simple property and event binding. The *Component* class provides this infrastructure, which you would have to write yourself in custom classes, making the *Component* class an ideal base class for AJAX classes. In the next section, we'll look at component development using *Sys.Component*.

Developing Components Using the AJAX Library Framework

Among the challenges in developing AJAX applications are how to package applications into libraries and how to build true object-oriented frameworks. Although it's easy to build scripts that respond to events with functional programming, a functional approach can lead to un-maintainable and nonportable scripts. A design goal and best practice of AJAX programming is to create a number of reusable components that can work with many different back-end services. If developed with this goal in mind, your AJAX application can be deployed in many applications as long as the supporting Web services are also deployed.

For example, let's say your company wants to develop rich Internet applications but is also interested in the growing portal market and understands the need to develop applications for Microsoft Office SharePoint Server. Monolithic application frameworks are difficult to migrate from a controlled environment to a heterogeneous portal environment where they need to coexist with Web parts from multiple vendors. But, if you develop loosely coupled, component-based frameworks that are written against a portable Web service API, it is far simpler to port application components from a pure ASP.NET environment to a portal environment.

Component development is supported in the Microsoft AJAX framework through the *Sys.Component* base class, which provides support for properties and events and offers simple life-cycle management. The object *Sys.Application* is an implementation of the component class *Sys._Application*, a framework component class that is derived directly from *Sys.Component*. The following code sample from the AJAX library demonstrates how the *Sys.Application* object derives from *Sys.Component*. As the framework is loaded, the *Sys.Application* instance is created using the *Sys_Application* class, which fires events and controls the page life cycle.

```
Sys._Application.registerClass('Sys._Application', Sys.Component, Sys.IContainer);
Sys.Application = new Sys._Application();
```

To develop a custom component, you need to create a JavaScript class that derives from *Sys.Component*. Listing 7-5 defines a simple component with a *text* property. The *register-Class* method creates an inheritance chain so that *SOAjax.Examples.MyComponent* inherits from *Sys.Component* (as covered in Chapter 4, "The AJAX Runtime with the Microsoft AJAX Library").

LISTING 7-5. A component is based on the AJAX class *Sys.Component* (*Web/Script/Examples.js*).

```
Type.registerNamespace("SOAjax.Examples");
SOAjax.Examples.MyComponent = function() {
    /// <summary>
    /// An sample component class that demonstrates basic component implementation.
    /// </summary>
}
SOAjax.Examples.MyComponent.prototype = {
    initialize: function() {
        SOAjax.Examples.MyComponent.callBaseMethod(this, 'initialize');
    },

    _text: null,
    get_text: function() {
        /// <value>Gets or sets the component's text.</value>
        return this._text;
    },
    set_text: function(text) {
        this.raisePropertyChanged('text');
        this._text = text;
    },
```

```
    dispose: function() {
        // Use this to clear any handlers.
        SOAjax.Examples.MyComponent.callBaseMethod(this, 'dispose');
    }
}

SOAjax.Examples.MyComponent.registerClass('SOAjax.Examples.MyComponent',
    Sys.Component);
```

As Listing 7-5 demonstrates, the component is based on the AJAX class *Sys.Component*. Registering the class by using the *registerClass* method of the custom component type enables it to be derived from *Sys.Component* and inherit the base class's functionality. The advantage of using a component rather than a standard JavaScript class definition is that the component has a built-in event framework and creation support through the *Sys.Component. create* method (*$create*) that includes event and property binding. The *$create* method is kind of like a factory method that is used to create component instances.

> **Tip** If your class does not include properties or events, you probably don't need to implement a component.

Instead of using the standard constructor to create a component, you use the static *create* method of *Sys.Component*. The alias for *Sys.Component.create* is *$create*, which is the method that we'll use in the sample code. The method's signature is *$create(type, properties, events, references, element)*, where *type* is the JavaScript type and *properties*, *events*, and *references* are JSON-formatted objects containing bindable properties and events. By using *$create* and setting initial property and event bindings, you can build loosely coupled components that deliver functionality without sacrificing object-oriented design in JavaScript code. The following example creates a component using the *$create* method and sets the *text* property to "Hello, AJAX Nation!":

```
var example = $create(SOAjax.Examples.MyComponent, {text : 'Hello, AJAX Nation!'});
```

For more complicated components, you might need to use more verbose syntax, like the following code, which can be more readable when you have a larger number of properties to set:

```
var exampleProperties = {text : 'Hello, AJAX Nation!'};
var example = $create(SOAjax.Examples.MyComponent, exampleProperties);
```

$create performs eight tasks during the creation of the component. These tasks can be seen in Listing 7-6, which contains abbreviated source code from the AJAX library. First the component is created using the standard constructor, as in the following sample. The *element* variable is nullable and is used to assign a DOM element to the control if the component

is an implementation of *Sys.UI.Control*. The *$create* method is used for components and controls because controls inherit from *Component* but include support for DOM elements.

```
var component = (element ? new type(element) : new type());
```

Next the component's *beginUpdate* method is called, which in turn sets the component's *isUpdating* property to *true*.

```
component.beginUpdate();
```

Next, any properties passed into *$create* are set. In the example above, we pass in the property *text* with the value "Hello, AJAX Nation!". This property is then set during the creation of the object and has the same effect as calling *example.set_text('Hello, AJAX Nation')* after the object's creation. However, when properties are set during execution of the *$create* method, the values are available in the object's initialization code—in particular the component's *initialize* method. This makes it critical to use the *$create* method and property bindings if you're creating page components during the page's *init* or *load* events.

After setting the original properties, the component adds event handlers that are passed in the creation method. For example, you might want to add code that gets called in response to component events, much like the *init* event of the *Sys.Application* component.

Next, if the component implements an *id* property (exposed through *get_id*), the component is registered with *Sys.Application* so that it can be called using the *Sys.Application.find* method. This property is usually implemented in control classes but not in pure component classes.

The component then sets any references it might have. With an AJAX component, a reference is a special type of property that is used to refer to another AJAX object and enables reliable creation of composite components. A composite component uses multiple controls and components to implement functionality.

Finally, the *endUpdate* method is called, which sets the *updating* property to *false* and ensures the component is initialized. If the component is not initialized, the *endUpdate* method will call *initialize*. Here is the *endUpdate* method, which is called at the end of the *create* method:

```
function Sys$Component$endUpdate() {
    this._updating = false;
    if (!this._initialized) this.initialize();
    this.updated();
}
```

Examining the entire *$create* method will help you better understand the component creation process. Listing 7-6 contains the debug source code for the *$create* method from the Microsoft AJAX Library.

LISTING 7-6. The *$create* method is used to create and bind *Sys.Component* classes (excerpt from *MicrosoftAjax.debug.js*).

```
// $create component creation method from the Microsoft AJAX Library
var $create = Sys.Component.create = function Sys$Component$create(
    type, properties, events, references, element) {
    var app = Sys.Application;
    var creatingComponents = app.get_isCreatingComponents();
    component.beginUpdate();
    if (properties) {
        Sys$Component$_setProperties(component, properties);
    }
    if (events) {
        for (var name in events) {
            if (!(component["add_" + name] instanceof Function))
                throw new Error.invalidOperation(
                    String.format(Sys.Res.undefinedEvent, name));
            if (!(events[name] instanceof Function))
                throw new Error.invalidOperation(Sys.Res.eventHandlerNotFunction);
            component["add_" + name](events[name]);
        }
    }
    if (component.get_id()) {
        app.addComponent(component);
    }
    if (creatingComponents) {
        app._createdComponents[app._createdComponents.length] = component;
        if (references) {
            app._addComponentToSecondPass(component, references);
        }
        else {
            component.endUpdate();
        }
    }
    else {
        if (references) {
            Sys$Component$_setReferences(component, references);
        }
        component.endUpdate();
    }
    return component;
}
```

By examining the source code of the *Sys.Component.create* method in Listing 7-6, you can see how the framework performs property and event binding. You can also see how *Sys.Application* is used in the component creation process. Components that implement the page runtime should be created during the *Sys.Application.Init* event, in which case *Sys.Application* performs a second pass after object creation to set any component references. This step enables component code references for composite components while guaranteeing the creation state of each object.

Passing Context to Event Handlers

Working with object-oriented components requires an approach to JavaScript programming that is different from traditional functional programming in JavaScript. In the traditional model, a static function might be called in response to an event, but instead of stateless static functions, we'll be using object-oriented methods in which state and object-instance references are important. We want to bind instance methods to event handlers to create an object-oriented framework. The problem we encounter, however, is that by default, code fired by an event in JavaScript is called as an instance of the object that fired the event, even if a handler that is an instance method is added to the event through code such as *$addHandler(element, 'click', this.eventHandler)*. Before I demonstrate the correct method using *Function.createDelegate*, it's best to examine the default behavior.

A click handler that is bound to a DOM element runs under the context of the DOM element—the *this* keyword references the DOM element that was clicked to fire the event and not the instance of the class under which you expect to be executing. Consider the code in Listing 7-7. When you add an event handler, the following code is executed, passing the *this.testFunction* method as the handler.

```
// bad code example: "this" will not be "this"
$addHandler(this._testButton, 'click', this.testHandler);
```

Unfortunately, in the context of the handler method (*testHandler*), *this* no longer refers to the instance of the component that was passed with the method. Instead, *this* refers to the DOM element that was clicked to fire the event. To demonstrate this behavior, which will cause bugs in your application, examine the *SOAjax.Examples.ReferenceDemo* component class shown in Listing 7-7.

LISTING 7-7. Passing an instance method to an event handler yields unexpected results (*Web/Script/ Examples.js*).

```
SOAjax.Examples.ReferenceDemo = function() {
    /// <summary>
    /// An example component class that demonstrates reference passing.
    /// </summary>
}
SOAjax.Examples.ReferenceDemo.prototype = {
    initialize: function() {
        SOAjax.Examples.ReferenceDemo.callBaseMethod(this, 'initialize');
    },

    _testButton: null,
    get_testButton: function() {
        /// <value>Gets or sets the test button used for the example.</value>
        return this._testButton;
    },
    set_testButton: function(button) {
        this._testButton = button;
```

```
                // The handler for 'ButtonTest' will have a bad this reference,
                // referencing the DOM element not this component instance:
                $$addHandler(this._testButton, 'click', this.testFunction);
        },

        dispose: function() {
            $clearHandlers(this._testButton);
            SOAjax.Examples.ReferenceDemo.callBaseMethod(this, 'dispose');
        }
    }
    SOAjax.Examples.ReferenceDemo.registerClass(
        'SOAjax.Examples.ReferenceDemo', Sys.Component);

    function initComponents() {
        $create(SOAjax.Examples.ReferenceDemo, { testButton: $get('ButtonTest')} );
    }

    Sys.Application.add_init(initComponents);
```

When attaching an event handler to a DOM element, you must create a delegate with which to pass context. As in C#, JavaScript delegates are simply references to instance methods. The JavaScript delegate references an instance method and is created with the *Function.createDelegate* method, which is a method in the Microsoft AJAX Library. The *Function.Delegate* method is shown in Listing 7-8. It takes an instance and method parameter and returns a new function that calls the instance's method.

LISTING 7-8. *Function.createDelegate* creates a reference-aware method pointer to an instance method.

```
Function.createDelegate = function Function$createDelegate(instance, method) {
    return function() {
        return method.apply(instance, arguments);
    }
}
```

To create a handler that calls the current object, always use the *Function.createDelegate* method. The delegate is then used to call the current object instance. Without the delegate, the code in the handler does not execute from the object instance, and the *this* reference refers to the DOM object rather than the component object that the handler was created for. The code sample in Listing 7-9 builds on the earlier code listing of the *SOAjax.Examples.ReferenceDemo* component and demonstrates the *this* reference with and without the delegate.

LISTING 7-9. *Function.createDelegate* is used to create instance-method references for event handlers (*Web/Script/Examples.js*).

```
SOAjax.Examples.ReferenceDemo = function() {
    /// <summary>
    /// An example component class that demonstrates reference passing.
    /// </summary>
```

```
}
SOAjax.Examples.ReferenceDemo.prototype = {
    initialize: function() {
        SOAjax.Examples.ReferenceDemo.callBaseMethod(this, 'initialize');
    },

    _testButton: null,
    _testButton2: null,

    get_testButton: function() {
        /// <value>Gets or sets the test button used for the example.</value>
        return this._testButton;
    },
    set_testButton: function(button) {
        this._testButton = button;
        // The handler for 'ButtonTest' will have a bad this reference,
        // referencing the DOM element not this component instance:
        $$addHandler(this._testButton, 'click', this.testFunction);
    },
    testFunction: function() {
        debugger;
        Sys.Debug.traceDump(this)
    },

    get_testButton2: function() {
        ///<value>Gets or sets the testButton2</value>
        return this._testButton2;
    },
    set_testButton2: function(button) {
        this._testButton2 = button;
        // The handler for 'ButtonTest2' will have a reference to this component
        // because it is created with the createDelegate method.
        $addHandler(this._testButton2, 'click',
            Function.createDelegate(this, this.testFunction));
    },

    dispose: function() {
        $clearHandlers(this._testButton);
        $clearHandlers(this._testButton2);
        SOAjax.Examples.ReferenceDemo.callBaseMethod(this, 'dispose');
    }
}

SOAjax.Examples.ReferenceDemo.registerClass(
    'SOAjax.Examples.ReferenceDemo', Sys.Component);

function initComponents() {
    $create(SOAjax.Examples.ReferenceDemo,
        { testButton: $get('ButtonTest'), testButton2: $get('ButtonTest2') });
}

Sys.Application.add_init(initComponents);
```

Listing 7-9 demonstrates the *Function.createDelegate* method used to create an instance-method reference. Notice that the *dispose* method of the class is used to clean up any handlers so that handles to components that are removed from the page aren't kept alive.

Building an Application Services Component

In Chapter 6, we developed a login page by creating various methods that called *Sys.Services* in response to user actions. However, the code we ended up with wasn't very concise, object-oriented, or reusable. Basically, we had screen elements with JavaScript commands wired to them. While this is fine for demonstrating the *Sys.Services* Web service model, it isn't an approach you want to take with production code. Static JavaScript commands that handle DOM events can lead to unmaintainable "spaghetti" code, and you might soon find that you have a messy library of functions that are tied to specific page elements and must be recoded to be used in other contexts. You might also find that your AJAX implementation is slow and buggy compared to object-oriented server code. This doesn't need to be the case, because a properly developed component library goes far in helping you build a robust application framework.

To develop a component-based application, you need to define the central architecture and divide the client-side application into controls, components, and markup. In the next chapter you'll see how to build control classes to provide application functionality. First, however, we'll build an application services component that abstracts the authentication and authorization business rules from the page. In this model, the page JavaScript will tie together the application components and controls and bind them to DOM elements. The page will also bind event handlers of the application runtime to control implementations, letting the page respond to major events such as authentication or navigation. With this strategy, the components and controls can even be developed and tested independently.

Tip While it is out of the scope of this book, components and controls are ideally built using a test-driven approach. Christian Gross's excellent books on AJAX use this approach and are recommended reading for any AJAX application developer. These books are *Ajax Patterns and Best Practices* (Addison Wesley, 2006) and *Ajax and REST Recipes: A Problem-Solution Approach* (Addison Wesley, 2006).

For the application component, we'll develop a run-time component that wraps *Sys.Services* calls and fires authentication events that the page can respond to. Because we don't want to implement the HTML in JavaScript, we'll use static HTML in the page for the login controls, and we'll bind the controls to the application runtime. To start, the page HTML is included in Listing 7-10. The page consists of three main areas: navigation, login controls, and the chief content area, as shown in Figure 7-2. We'll use this basic page shell in this chapter for the application runtime component example. We'll build on this shell and application component when we add functional controls in the next chapter.

FIGURE 7-2. The application runtime in action.

LISTING 7-10. Simple HTML form elements can be used as login controls (*Web/Default.aspx*).

```
<%@ Page %>
<html xmlns="http://www.w3.org/1999/xhtml">
<head id="Head1" runat="server">
    <title>Service-Oriented AJAX</title>
    <link href="Style/StyleSheet.css" rel="stylesheet" type="text/css" />
</head>
<body>
  <form id="form1" runat="server">
    <asp:ScriptManager ID="AjaxScriptManager" runat="server"
            RoleService-LoadRoles="true"
            ProfileService-LoadProperties="startTopic"
            >
        <Scripts>
            <asp:ScriptReference Path="~/Script/SOAjax.js" />
            <asp:ScriptReference Path="~/Script/ApplicationRuntime.js" />
            <asp:ScriptReference Path="~/Script/Page.js" />
        </Scripts>
    </asp:ScriptManager>
    <div id="pageHeader">
        Service-Oriented AJAX on the Microsoft Platform

        <div id="logoutControl" class="loginControl" style="display: none;" >
            <button id="ButtonLogout" type="button" value="Logout">Logout</button>
            [Logged in]
        </div>

        <div style="display: none;" id="loginControl" class="loginControl">
            <div class="widgetTitle" id="loginLink">Login</div>
            <div class="lightPadding" id="loginUI" style="display: none;">
                Username <br />
                <input type="text" id="usernameInput" /><br /><br />

                Password <br />
                <input type="password" id="passwordInput" /><br /><br />

                <button id="ButtonLogin" value="Login" type="button"
                title="Login">Login</button>  
                <button id="ButtonCancelLogin" value="Cancel" type="button"
                title="Cancel">Cancel</button>
                <div id="loginFeedbackDiv">
```

```
                </div>
            </div>
        </div>
    </div>

    <div id="pageBody">
        <table style="width:100%; height:100%" cellpadding="0" cellspacing="0">
            <tr valign="top">
                <td width="150px" style="background-color:#EFEFEF; padding:15px;">
                    <div id="_EditControls" style="display:none;">
                        Logged-in controls
                    </div>
                    <div id="NavigationPlaceholder"
                        style="width:150px; background-color:#EFEFEF">
                        Navigation goes here...
                    </div>
                </td>
                <td width="100%">
                    <div id="MainContent" style="overflow:auto;" >
                        Service-Oriented AJAX on the Microsoft Platform:
                        Example Code.
                    </div>
                </td>
            </tr>
        </table>
    </div>
  </form>
</body>
</html>
```

Perhaps the first thing you'll notice when looking at the page is that it contains no embedded JavaScript. No *onclick* events are defined on buttons, and the login controls are implemented as simple form elements. We'll wire the HTML controls to the application component through the *$create* method after developing the component. The component itself fires the authenticated event, which can be handled by external event handlers, and contains properties that are used to bind the component to DOM elements on the HTML page.

In this manner, the application runtime is contained in a single component class, and it is bound to a set of DOM elements that make up the login user interface. When a user is successfully authenticated or logged out, the application runtime object fires events that the page can handle. For example, we want to display edit controls only when the user is authenticated.

For controls, we want to define the following properties, each of which corresponds to a DOM element on the page. Because the DOM elements aren't implementing the behavior, we don't need to create controls for these elements. We can simply access them from the application runtime component.

To create the login functionality, we'll define the following properties: *usernameInput, passwordInput, loginButton, cancelLoginButton, logoutButton, loginUI,* and *loggedinUI.* The *loginUI* and *loggedinUI* DOM elements represent DIV elements on the page that show a user interface for an anonymous user and a user who is logged in. These elements contain the controls for logging in or out, but they are used only to hide or show a group of controls. The input controls contain the user input values that the component accesses, and the buttom elements have event handlers added and bound to the component. Each property is defined with *get* and *set* methods that are called from the *Sys.Component's create* method ($create) if properties are passed. These methods are commonly referred to as *getters* and *setters,* where the *get_* and *set_* prefixes are used with the property name to define the method names.

To begin converting the authentication code to a component, we need to create a simple component called *SOAjax.Application.* This application component abstracts the authentication logic from the page, wraps the Web service authentication calls, and fires bindable events that the page can handle. Within the component, we start off by defining the private fields and public properties that reference DOM elements.

To define a property in the component's prototype, use the following syntax to create *get* and *set* methods, following the naming convention used by the Microsoft AJAX library:

```
propertyName = null,
get_propertyName: function() { return this._propertyName; },
set_ propertyName: function(val) { this._propertyName = val; },
```

To create events, all that is needed are *add* and *remove* methods, which are used to add or remove handler methods to events. Again, you must follow the naming convention used by the Microsoft AJAX library. The following syntax is used to create an event, where the name *eventName* is an arbitrarily named custom event:

```
add_eventName: function(handler) {
    this.get_events().addHandler("eventName", handler);
},
remove_eventName: function(handler) {
    this.get_events().removeHandler("eventName", handler);
}
```

Keep in mind that for both handlers and callbacks, *Function.createDelegate* is required to create instance references. To fire the event, a handler is obtained from the *Sys.EventHandlerList* instance (returned by calling *this.get_events* within a component) as discussed earlier in this chapter. The following code reviews the syntax to use for firing an arbitrary event from the class that contains the event:

```
// The following code fires the event eventName
var handler = this.get_events().getHandler("eventName");
if (handler) {
    handler(this, Sys.EventArgs.Empty);
}
```

Listing 7-11 defines a simple component class that contains properties for the relevant login controls on the page. The controls we have defined are *usernameInput* and *passwordInput* for credential input, *loginButton* and *logoutButton* (which we'll add click handlers to), and the *loginUI* and *loggedinUI* elements that can contain child DOM controls, including the login feedback element. We're not defining an AJAX library control itself for the authentication component because we'll use various DOM controls on the page within a single component.

LISTING 7-11. The application runtime component defines properties for bindable controls (*Web/Script/1. ApplicationRuntime.js*).

```
/// <reference name="MicrosoftAjax.js"/>

Type.registerNamespace('SOAjax');
SOAjax.Application = function() {
    /// <summary>
    /// A component that controls the page lifecycle, integrated with Sys.Services.
    /// </summary>
    SOAjax.Application.initializeBase(this);
}

SOAjax.Application.prototype = {
    usernameInput: null,
    passwordInput: null,
    loginUI: null,
    loggedinUI: null,
    logoutButton: null,
    loginButton: null,
    loginFeedbackDiv: null,

    initialize: function() {
        SOAjax.Application.callBaseMethod(this, 'initialize');
    },

    get_usernameInput: function() {
        ///<value>The authentication username text input element</value>
        return this.usernameInput;
    },
    set_usernameInput: function(control) { this.usernameInput = control; },

    get_passwordInput: function() {
        ///<value>The authentication password input element</value>
        return this.passwordInput;
    },
    set_passwordInput: function(control) { this.passwordInput = control; },

    get_loginButton: function() {
        ///<value>The login button element</value>
        return this.loginButton;
    },
    set_loginButton: function(control) {
        this.loginButton = control;
    },
```

```
        get_cancelLoginButton: function() {
            ///<value>The cancel login button element</value>
            return this.cancelLoginButton;
        },
        set_cancelLoginButton: function(control) {
            this.cancelLoginButton = control;
        },

        get_logoutButton: function() {
            ///<value>The logout button element</value>
            return this.logoutButton;
        },
        set_logoutButton: function(control) {
            this.logoutButton = control;
        },

        get_loginUI: function() {
            ///<value>The login UI DOM element (div or span)</value>
            return this.loginUI;
        },
        set_loginUI: function(control) {
            this.loginUI = control;
        },

        get_loggedinUI: function() {
            ///<value>The logged in UI DOM element (div or span)</value>
            return this.loggedinUI;
        },
        set_loggedinUI: function(control) {
            this.loggedinUI = control;
        },

        get_loginFeedbackDiv: function() {
            ///<value>A feedback element, used for authentication failure</value>
            return this.loginFeedbackDiv;
        },
        set_loginFeedbackDiv: function(control) {
            this.loginFeedbackDiv = control;
        },

        cancelLogin: function(domEvent) {
            if (this.loginUI != null)
                this.loginUI.style.display = 'none';
        },

        dispose: function() {
            // Use this to clear any handlers.
            SOAjax.Application.callBaseMethod(this, 'dispose');
        }
    }
}

SOAjax.Application.registerClass('SOAjax.Application', Sys.Component);
Sys.Application.notifyScriptLoaded();
```

The initial application runtime isn't too useful. All it does is bind DOM elements to a component class. To make the application runtime more useful, we want to integrate authentication logic using *Sys.Services* Web services, bind to DOM events, and fire events such as *authenticated*. By firing the *authenticated* event, we can let the page class evolve according to the logged-in status of the user.

To add DOM event handlers to the component, use the *initialize* method to add handler methods to the DOM properties. You can also provide some basic validation logic to ensure required properties have been set. The following code demonstrates the addition of event handlers using *Function.createDelegate* within the *initialize* method:

```
initialize: function() {
    SOAjax.Application.callBaseMethod(this, 'initialize');

    if (this.loginButton == null || this.cancelLoginButton == null
        || this.logoutButton == null || this.passwordInput == null
        || this.loginUI == null || this.loggedinUI == null
        || this.loginFeedbackDiv == null) {
        throw Error.invalidOperation( 'The application component requires the DOM
            elements passwordInput,loginUI,loggedinUI,logoutButton,loginButton and
            loginFeedbackDiv');
    }
    $addHandler(this.loginButton, 'click',
        Function.createDelegate(this, this.login));
    $addHandler(this.cancelLoginButton, 'click',
        Function.createDelegate(this, this.cancelLogin));
    $addHandler(this.logoutButton, 'click',
        Function.createDelegate(this, this.logout));
}
```

We also want to create login functionality and the *authenticated* event. Because the application runtime is derived from the *Sys.Component* class, the event handler list is already defined using the *events* property. The following code demonstrates the implementation of the *authenticated* event:

```
add_authenticated: function(handler) {
    this.get_events().addHandler("authenticated", handler);
},
remove_authenticated: function(handler) {
    this.get_events().removeHandler("authenticated", handler);
}
```

When the component is successfully authenticated, it can call the following code to fire the *authenticated* event:

```
this.raisePropertyChanged('isAuthenticated');
var handler = this.get_events().getHandler("authenticated");
if (handler) {
    handler(this, Sys.EventArgs.Empty);
}
```

By firing the *authenticated* event and raising the *propertyChanged* event, we're letting client code handle the event. The event would be fired in response to the actual authentication from the server. Listing 7-12 shows the entire source code of the finished *SOAjax.ApplicationRuntime* component class, integrating the *Sys.Services* authentication logic, the *authenticated* event, and event bindings.

LISTING 7-12. The application runtime component defines events that can be handled from client code (*Web/Script/ApplicationRuntime.js*).

```
/// <reference name="MicrosoftAjax.js"/>
Type.registerNamespace('SOAjax');

SOAjax.Application = function() {
    /// <summary>
    /// A component that controls the page lifecycle, integrated with Sys.Services.
    /// </summary>
    SOAjax.Application.initializeBase(this);
}
SOAjax.Application.prototype = {
    usernameInput: null,
    passwordInput: null,
    loginUI: null,
    loggedinUI: null,
    logoutButton: null,
    loginButton: null,
    loginFeedbackDiv: null,

    initialize: function() {
        SOAjax.Application.callBaseMethod(this, 'initialize');
        // basic property validation:
        if (this.loginButton == null || this.cancelLoginButton == null
        || this.logoutButton == null || this.passwordInput == null
        || this.loginUI == null || this.loggedinUI == null
        || this.loginFeedbackDiv == null) {
        throw Error.invalidOperation( 'The application component requires the DOM
            elements passwordInput,loginUI,loggedinUI,logoutButton,loginButton and
            loginFeedbackDiv');
        }
        $addHandler(this.loginButton, 'click',
            Function.createDelegate(this, this.login));
        $addHandler(this.cancelLoginButton, 'click',
            Function.createDelegate(this, this.cancelLogin));
        $addHandler(this.logoutButton, 'click',
            Function.createDelegate(this, this.logout));
    },

    get_usernameInput: function() {
        ///<value>The authentication username text input element</value>
        return this.usernameInput;
    },
    set_usernameInput: function(control) { this.usernameInput = control; },

    get_passwordInput: function() {
        ///<value>The authentication password input element</value>
```

```
        return this.passwordInput;
    },
    set_passwordInput: function(control) { this.passwordInput = control; },

    get_loginButton: function() {
        ///<value>The login button element</value>
        return this.loginButton;
    },
    set_loginButton: function(control) {
        this.loginButton = control;
    },

    get_cancelLoginButton: function() {
        ///<value>The cancel login button element</value>
        return this.cancelLoginButton;
    },
    set_cancelLoginButton: function(control) {
        this.cancelLoginButton = control;
    },

    get_logoutButton: function() {
        ///<value>The logout button element</value>
        return this.logoutButton;
    },
    set_logoutButton: function(control) {
        this.logoutButton = control;
    },

    get_loginUI: function() {
        ///<value>The login UI DOM element (div or span)</value>
        return this.loginUI;
    },
    set_loginUI: function(control) {
        this.loginUI = control;
    },

    get_loggedinUI: function() {
        ///<value>The logged in UI DOM element (div or span)</value>
        return this.loggedinUI;
    },
    set_loggedinUI: function(control) {
        this.loggedinUI = control;
    },

    get_loginFeedbackDiv: function() {
        ///<value>A feedback element, used for authentication failure</value>
        return this.loginFeedbackDiv;
    },
    set_loginFeedbackDiv: function(control) {
        this.loginFeedbackDiv = control;
    },

    login: function(domEvent) {
        var userName = this.usernameInput.value;
        var password = this.passwordInput.value;
```

```
        var loginDelegate =
            Function.createDelegate(this, this.authenticateCallback);
        var faulureDelegate = Function.createDelegate(this, this.failureCallback);
        var context = new Object();
        Sys.Services.AuthenticationService.login(userName, password, true,
            null, null, loginDelegate, faulureDelegate, context);
    },

    cancelLogin: function(domEvent) {
        if (this.loginUI != null)
            this.loginUI.style.display = 'none';
    },

    logout: function(domEvent) {
        Sys.Services.AuthenticationService.logout(
            null,
            Function.createDelegate(this, this.onLogoutCompleted),
            Function.createDelegate(this, this.failureCallback),
            null);
    },

    onLogoutCompleted: function() {
        this.updateControls();
    },

    authenticateCallback: function(isLoggedIn, userContext, methodName) {
        if (this.passwordInput != null)
            this.passwordInput.value = '';
        if (!isLoggedIn) {
            this.get_loginFeedbackDiv().innerHTML = 'Unable to log in.';
            return;
        }
        else {
            this.get_loginFeedbackDiv().innerHTML = '';
            Sys.Services.RoleService.load(
                Function.createDelegate(this, this.rolesCompleted),
                Function.createDelegate(this, this.failureCallback), this);
        }
        this.updateControls();
    },

    rolesCompleted: function(roles, context, foo) {
        if (Sys.Services.AuthenticationService.get_isLoggedIn()) {
            this.raisePropertyChanged('isAuthenticated');
            var handler = this.get_events().getHandler("authenticated");
            if (handler) {
                handler(this, Sys.EventArgs.Empty);
            }
        }
    },
    rolesFailed: function() { },

    failureCallback: function(error, userContext, methodName) {
        debugger;
    },
```

```
    get_isAuthenticated: function() {
        /// <value type="Boolean">
        /// True if user is authenticated, false if anonymous.
        /// </value>
        return Sys.Services.AuthenticationService.get_isLoggedIn();
    },

    // events
    add_authenticated: function(handler) {
        /// <summary>Adds a event handler for the authenticated event.</summary>
        /// <param name="handler" type="Function">
        /// The handler to add to the event.
        /// </param>
        this.get_events().addHandler("authenticated", handler);
    },
    remove_authenticated: function(handler) {
        /// <summary>Removes a event handler for the authenticated event.</summary>
        /// <param name="handler" type="Function">
        /// The handler to remove from the event.
        /// </param>
        this.get_events().removeHandler("authenticated", handler);
    },

    updateControls: function() {
        var isLoggedIn = Sys.Services.AuthenticationService.get_isLoggedIn();
        if (!isLoggedIn) {    // show the login UI
            if (this.loggedinUI != null) this.loggedinUI.style.display = 'none';
            if (this.loginUI != null) this.loginUI.style.display = '';
        } else {              // show the logout UI.
            if (this.loggedinUI != null) this.loggedinUI.style.display = '';
            if (this.loginUI != null) this.loginUI.style.display = 'none';
        }
    },

    dispose: function() {
        // Use this to clear any handlers.
        this.usernameInput = null;
        this.passwordInput = null;
        if (this.loginButton != null)
            $clearHandlers(this.loginButton);
        this.loginButton = null;

        if (this.logoutButton != null)
            $clearHandlers(this.logoutButton);
        this.logoutButton = null;

        SOAjax.Application.callBaseMethod(this, 'dispose');
    }
}

SOAjax.Application.registerClass('SOAjax.Application', Sys.Component);
Sys.Application.notifyScriptLoaded();
```

With the code in Listing 7-12, we have a fully functional application runtime component that wraps the authentication logic of *Sys.Services* and fires events, enabling the component to be bound to page controls at run time. Next we'll create a page library that ties the logic from the page to the application components. Although this step can be performed in the HTML page itself, we'll define a page-based JavaScript file called Page.js that forms our page run-time. In the page JavaScript, we use the *$create* method to create an instance of the application run-time component we've built, which we bind to the page's DOM elements through properties.

Listing 7-13 contains the *Page.js* JavaScript file. This code creates an instance of *SOAjax. Application* and passes property and event objects. *Sys.Component* sets the properties and events in the *$create* method. For example, passing { *'authenticated' : Page.OnAuthenticated* } to the events parameter has the same effect as calling *component.add_authenticated(Page.OnAuthenticated)* after creating a new component. With this event binding, the page's *OnAuthenticated* method is bound to the application runtime's *authenticated* event. By using this event-driven approach, the code in the authentication class does not need to know about the application that hosts it, and the actual application implementation can still respond to authentication and authorization events.

LISTING 7-13. Page.js forms the JavaScript code behind for the application page (*Web/Script/Page.js*).

```
/// <reference name="MicrosoftAjax.js"/>
/// <reference path="ApplicationRuntime.js"/>

Type.registerNamespace('Page');
Page.load = function() {
    var isAuthenticated = Sys.Services.AuthenticationService.get_isLoggedIn();
    var appProperties = {
        usernameInput: $get('usernameInput'),
        passwordInput: $get('passwordInput'),
        loginButton: $get('ButtonLogin'),
        cancelLoginButton: $get('ButtonCancelLogin'),
        logoutButton: $get('ButtonLogout'),
        loginUI: $get('loginControl'),
        loggedinUI: $get('logoutControl'),
        loginFeedbackDiv : $get('loginFeedbackDiv')
    };

    var appEvents = { 'authenticated': Page.OnAuthenticated };
    Page.App = $create(SOAjax.Application, appProperties, appEvents, null, null);
    Page.App.updateControls();
    $addHandler($get('loginLink'), 'mouseover', Page.ShowLoginUI);
}

Page.OnAuthenticated = function(sender, eventArgs) {
    Sys.Debug.trace('Page.OnAuthenticated');
    if (Sys.Services.RoleService.isUserInRole('contributor')) {
        //show contributor controls on page
        $get('_EditControls').style.display = '';
    }
```

```
    if (Sys.Services.RoleService.isUserInRole('moderator')) {
        //instantiate moderator controls on page
    }
}

Page.unload = function() {
    if (Page.App != null)
        Page.App.dispose();
}

Sys.Application.add_load(Page.load);
Sys.Application.add_unload(Page.unload);

Page.ShowLoginUI = function(eventArgs) {
    $get('loginUI').style.display = '';
}

Sys.Application.notifyScriptLoaded();
```

Listing 7-13 demonstrates the basic JavaScript page implementation. Remember that the page doesn't need to be a component. We simply ran some functions as the application loaded to create our component instance. In the next chapter, when we build AJAX controls using *Sys.UI.Control* class implementations, we'll create control instances using this approach and bind the event handlers. This is a common development pattern and a best practice. The page class contains only enough logic to tie the application components together.

Summary

In this chapter you learned about object-oriented component development using the AJAX library component infrastructure. Components enable properties and events and can be bound together upon creation in the *Sys.Application init* and *load* events by using the *$create* method and event binding. Components are the foundation for AJAX controls. We'll build on the sample code in this chapter as we develop a control library that utilizes Web services for back-end data. In the next chapter we'll look at control development using *Sys.UI.Control*, and we'll develop a robust object-oriented library of client-side controls and components.

Chapter 8
Building AJAX Controls

After completing this chapter, you will

- Understand the control architecture of the Microsoft AJAX Library.

- Understand controls, events, and event-based control development.

- Understand and utilize AJAX behaviors.

- Utilize AJAX controls in your AJAX applications.

In Chapter 7, "Building an AJAX Class Library with Components," I introduced the Microsoft AJAX Library component implementation, in which components serviced by *Sys.Application* can be created and maintained by using event and property bindings through the *Sys.Component.Create* (*$create*) method. I also described how the component infrastructure supports event-driven programming and object disposal.

To provide component functionality that is tied to DOM elements, the AJAX library provides the base classes *Sys.UI.Behavior* and *Sys.UI.Control,* both of which inherit from *Sys.Component*. Behaviors are used to extend DOM elements with user interface functionality. Behaviors add functionality rather than replace it. Multiple behaviors can be added to a single DOM element, but the DOM element can be used by only a single *control* instance. A control can be used to replace a DOM element's functionality. Finally, the *Sys.UI.Control* class provides a JavaScript programming interface for a DOM element through both static and instance methods.

> **Tip** Nothing ties the JavaScript *Behavior* and *Control* classes to AJAX architecture, but the JavaScript *Behavior* and *Control* classes fit into the AJAX architecture nicely by wrapping client-side functionality that can be easily integrated with Web service data sources.

In this chapter we'll first look at the JavaScript *Sys.UI.Behavior* class and a behavior example that extends a DOM element with a simple tooltip. Next we'll look at the *Sys.UI.Control* base class and an example that extends an input control with custom functionality. Finally, we'll add more features and functionality to the case study knowledge base application by implementing a wiki control—a large-scale control implementation that ties control functionality to application components.

Figure 8-1 illustrates the role of controls in an AJAX application. They are central to the user interface and are based on the component system described in Chapter 7. In real-world applications you use discrete controls to build your own user interface library, as well as composite controls that implement major portions of functionality and call into the Web services back end.

The AJAX Application		
Custom AJAX Frameworks		AJAX Control Toolkit
Web Service Proxies		Control Infrastructure
Application Services		Component Infrastructure
Network Library		DOM Extensions
Type System (Namespace, Classes, Inheritance Model)		
Base Type Extensions		
JavaScript Language		
Browser DOM Model		

(Left margin label spanning the middle rows: Microsoft AJAX Library 3.5)

FIGURE 8-1. The control infrastructure and the AJAX Control Toolkit are used to build custom frameworks.

More Information The AJAX Control Toolkit is a collaboration between Microsoft and the ASP.NET AJAX community and contains a large variety of behavior and control implementations that are ready to use. I won't cover the AJAX Control Toolkit in this book because my focus is on development using the technology platform, but you might find the control toolkit useful in your applications. You can download the AJAX Control Toolkit from *http://codeplex.com/ ajaxcontroltoolkit*.

The Ajax Library *Behavior* Class

Behaviors are extensions to DOM elements that provide additional functionality for the user interface. Most often, however, an AJAX behavior doesn't alter the core functionality of the DOM element it references. Behaviors can alter the user interface by adding cascading style sheet (CSS) styles and different mouse-over actions, or they might provide functionality that extends controls, such as the drop down list extender, a behavior in the AJAX Control Toolkit that adds an auto-complete drop-down list to an element on the basis of an XML data source.

The *Sys.UI.Behavior* JavaScript class is used to implement behaviors. It provides a simple programming model by which to extend the *Component* class with support for lightweight DOM extensions. *Sys.UI.Behavior* is a base class that is used to provide common client-side behavior. Because behaviors are components, the *$create* method is used to create behavior instances.

Tip The *Behavior* class was originally written for server-side developers who wanted to extend server controls with JavaScript. You'll see this in the MSDN documentation, but I'll take a client-centric approach to behaviors here.

Behavior extends *Component* with the properties *element, name,* and *id*. By default, the *name* property is the name of the behavior type. For example, the behavior *SOAjax.Behaviors. TooltipBehavior* will have the value TooltipBehavior for its *name* property. The *id* property is generated by combining the name of the behavior with the DOM element's ID.

The *Behavior* class is similar to the *Control* class, but with a few distinctions. While the *Control* class can be defined only once per DOM element, a behavior is just a wrapper for event handlers that are added to an element, and multiple behaviors can be added. The following code sample shows the constructor from the *Behavior* class. Notice that the behavior is stored as an array named *_behaviors* on the element. The base class removes its reference from the element's *_behaviors* array in the *dispose* method.

```
// Behavior constructor, for reference only, implemented in the Microsoft AJAX Library:
Sys.UI.Behavior = function Sys$UI$Behavior(element) {
    Sys.UI.Behavior.initializeBase(this);
    this._element = element;
    var behaviors = element._behaviors;
    if (!behaviors)
        element._behaviors = [this];
    else
        behaviors[behaviors.length] = this;
}
```

Before we look at examples of behaviors, let's examine how the *Sys.UI.Behavior* class is implemented in the AJAX library. The *Behavior* class is abstract and is only a base class for control libraries to implement. It provides common functionality for DOM-based behaviors. Table 8-1 lists properties of the *Behavior* class, where properties are defined by *get_* and *set_* methods. *Sys.UI.Behavior* simply adds properties to the *Component* base class that associate the behavior instance with a DOM element. It also defines static methods that let client code access the behavior. Methods of the *Behavior* class, including the inherited methods from *Sys.Component*, are defined in Table 8-2. The *Behavior* class also contains the events defined in *Sys.Component*, and these are defined in Table 8-3. Events are handled by using the *add_* and *remove_* methods for each event to add or remove event handlers. Finally, *Sys.UI.Behavior* defines three static methods that let client code access behaviors from DOM elements. These static methods are listed in Table 8-4.

TABLE 8-1 *Behavior* **Class Properties**

Name	Description
element	Gets the DOM element that the *Behavior* instance is based on (read-only).
id	Gets or sets the ID of the *Behavior* instance.
name	Gets or sets the name of the *Behavior* instance.
events	Returns an instance of the *Sys.EventHandlerList* for the component (read-only).
isInitialized	Returns true if the control is initialized; otherwise false (read-only).
isUpdating	Returns true if the control is currently updating itself; otherwise false (read-only).

TABLE 8-2 *Behavior* **Class Methods**

Name	Description
beginUpdate	Called to set *isUpdating* to *true*. Called from the beginning of the *$create* method (*Sys.Component.create*).
endUpdate	Called to set *isUpdating* to *false*. Called from the end of the *$create* method (*Sys.Component.create*). Calls *initialize* if *isInitialized* is *false*, and finally calls the *updated* method.
updated	Called when the component is updated. Use to implement any custom post-update or post-initialization logic.
initialize	Used to initialize the behavior.
dispose	Removes the behavior from the DOM element. Use this method to clean up any event handlers.

TABLE 8-3 *Behavior* **Class Events**

Name	Description
propertyChanged	Raised when a property is changed.
disposing	Raised when the control is being disposed.

TABLE 8-4 **Static Methods of** *Sys.UI.Behavior*

Name	Description
getBehaviorByName	Gets a behavior instance with the specified name for a particular DOM element.
getBehaviors	Gets all behavior instances for a particular DOM element.
getBehaviorsByType	Gets all behavior instances of the specified type for a particular DOM element.

Implementing Custom Behaviors with the AJAX Library

In the following examples, we'll create the *SOAjax.Behaviors.ToolTipBehavior* class to add a simple tooltip to any DOM element. The tooltip is displayed when a user hovers the mouse over the element. To start creating a behavior, use the Ajax Client Behavior template in Visual Studio. The template creates the JavaScript namespace using the name of the Web application project it's created in, but a simple search and replace can be used to get a good starting point. Listing 8-1 shows a JavaScript class generated by using the AJAX Client Behavior template. After the initial code was generated, I replaced the default JavaScript namespace to use *SOAjax.Behaviors*.

 Tip Depending on the complexity of your behaviors, you might want to place them in a common file containing a library of behaviors and controls.

> **Tip** Code for this book is available online at *http://www.microsoft.com/mspress/companion/ 9780735625914*. The code for this chapter is in the file Chapter 8.zip.

LISTING 8-1. The AJAX Client Behavior template is used to begin behavior implementations (*Web/Script/ BehaviorTemplate.js*).

```
/// <reference name="MicrosoftAjax.js"/>

Type.registerNamespace("SOAjax.Behaviors");

SOAjax.Behaviors.ToolTipBehavior = function(element) {
    SOAjax.Behaviors.ToolTipBehavior.initializeBase(this, [element]);
}
SOAjax.Behaviors.ToolTipBehavior.prototype = {
    initialize: function() {
        SOAjax.Behaviors.ToolTipBehavior.callBaseMethod(this, 'initialize');
        // Add custom initialization here
    },
    dispose: function() {
        //Add custom dispose actions here
        SOAjax.Behaviors.ToolTipBehavior.callBaseMethod(this, 'dispose');
    }
}
SOAjax.Behaviors.ToolTipBehavior.registerClass('SOAjax.Behaviors.ToolTipBehavior',
Sys.UI.Behavior);

if (typeof(Sys) !== 'undefined') Sys.Application.notifyScriptLoaded();
```

As you can see from Listing 8-1, a behavior is simple to create using the Visual Studio template. To implement the behavior, add properties and delegates to modify the DOM as you want. To keep the example simple, I created a single property *toolTip* that is used to set the text of the tooltip. Remember that AJAX library properties are defined by convention as *get_* and *set_* methods. Here's the definition of the *toolTip* property:

```
SOAjax.Behaviors.TooltipBehavior.prototype = {
    _toolTipText: '',
    get_toolTip: function() {
        /// <value>Gets the tooltip text</value>
        return this._toolTipText;
    },
    set_toolTip: function(text) { this._toolTipText = text; },
    /* Code omitted for clarity.*/
}
```

To implement the tooltip, I created two handler methods in the prototype to handle events that trigger the tooltip's visibility. The following code demonstrates the handlers I created. The *_showTooltipHandler* method (a private method, inferred by the naming convention) creates a tooltip element if needed. The additional methods, *hide* and *show,* are defined to expose methods that client code can call to manually hide or show the tooltip.

```
_showTooltipHandler: function(event) {
    var _toolTipText = this.get_toolTip();
    if (_toolTipText == null || _toolTipText.length == 0) return;

    if (this.toolTipElement == null) {
        var toolTipElement = document.createElement('DIV');
        toolTipElement.style.zIndex = 999;
        document.body.appendChild(toolTipElement);
        var loc = Sys.UI.DomElement.getLocation(this.get_element());
        var bounds = Sys.UI.DomElement.getBounds(this.get_element());
        Sys.UI.DomElement.setLocation(
            toolTipElement, loc.x, loc.y + (bounds.height));
        Sys.UI.DomElement.setVisibilityMode(
            toolTipElement, Sys.UI.VisibilityMode.collapse);
        Sys.UI.DomElement.addCssClass(toolTipElement, 'ToolTip');
        this.toolTipElement = toolTipElement;
    }
    this.toolTipElement.innerHTML = _toolTipText;
    Sys.UI.DomElement.setVisible(this.toolTipElement, true);
},

show: function() {
    this._showTooltipHandler(null);
},

_hideTooltipHandler: function(event) {
    if (this.toolTipElement != null)
        Sys.UI.DomElement.setVisible(this.toolTipElement, false);
},

hide: function() {
    this._hideTooltipHandler(null);
}
```

By convention, private fields (methods or properties) are prefixed with an underscore. In the sample code, I declared the handlers as private following this convention, and as a result these handlers won't be shown by the Visual Studio IntelliSense engine outside the class. In this example, we're creating the DOM element for the tooltip as a floating DIV, and we're using static methods of *Sys.UI.DomElement* to position and style the element. Although we could make the CSS class another property, we're defining the class *ToolTip* on the tooltip element that is created, which means the element can be styled by a CSS style definition that is external to the behavior implementation.

After you define the handler methods, the next step is to create delegates and add DOM handlers to call the delegates on DOM events. The following code sample implements delegates to reference the *showTooltipHandler* and *hideTooltipHandler* methods and uses *$addHandler* to add the handler to the DOM element. The delegates are added in the *initialize* method defined in the prototype:

```
initialize: function() {
    var element = this.get_element();

    this._showTooltipDelegate =
        Function.createDelegate(this, this._showTooltipHandler);

    this._hideTooltipDelegate =
        Function.createDelegate(this, this._hideTooltipHandler);

    $addHandler(element, 'mouseover', this._showTooltipDelegate);
    $addHandler(element, 'focus', this._showTooltipDelegate);
    $addHandler(element, 'mouseout', this._hideTooltipDelegate);
    $addHandler(element, 'blur', this._hideTooltipDelegate);

    SOAjax.Behaviors.TooltipBehavior.callBaseMethod(this, 'initialize');
}
```

Whenever you add handlers, it's important to remove the handlers later to ensure references aren't left dangling, which can create memory leak problems or unexpected behavior. To remove the handlers, use the *Behavior* class's *dispose* method. You must also write code in the *dispose* function that is safe if it is called repeatedly. The following code sample demonstrates a *dispose* method that cleans up references created through the *initialize* method shown previously.

```
dispose: function() {
    var element = this.get_element();
    if (element) {
        if (this._showTooltipDelegate) {
            $removeHandler(element, 'mouseover', this._showTooltipDelegate);
            $removeHandler(element, 'focus', this._showTooltipDelegate);
            delete this._showTooltipDelegate;
        }
        if (this._hideTooltipDelegate) {
            $removeHandler(element, 'mouseout', this._hideTooltipDelegate);
            $removeHandler(element, 'blur', this._hideTooltipDelegate);
            delete this._hideTooltipDelegate;
        }
    }
    if (this.toolTipElement)
        this.toolTipElement.parentNode.removeChild(this.toolTipElement);
    this.toolTipElement = null;
    SOAjax.Behaviors.TooltipBehavior.callBaseMethod(this, 'dispose');
}
```

As you can see from the code samples, creating a behavior is a simple process with which you can implement powerful extensions to DOM elements. Simply define properties and events, and then implement delegates for event handlers within the *initialize* method. You might also want to provide additional methods that client code can use, such as the *hide* method in this example. Listing 8-2 contains the full code sample for *TooltipBehavior*.

LISTING 8-2. The *Behavior* class can be used to define simple user interface enhancements for DOM elements (*Web/script/tooltip.js*).

```
/// <reference name="MicrosoftAjax.js"/>
// A common control library for SOAjax Sample Code

Type.registerNamespace('SOAjax.Behaviors');

SOAjax.Behaviors.TooltipBehavior = function(element) {
    SOAjax.Behaviors.TooltipBehavior.initializeBase(this, [element]);
}
SOAjax.Behaviors.TooltipBehavior.prototype = {
    _showTooltipDelegate : null,
    _hideTooltipDelegate: null,

    _toolTipText: '',
    get_toolTip: function() {
        /// <value>Gets the tooltip text</value>
        return this._toolTipText;
    },
    set_toolTip: function(text) { this._toolTipText = text; },
    initialize: function() {
        var element = this.get_element();

        this._showTooltipDelegate =
            Function.createDelegate(this, this._showTooltipHandler);

        this._hideTooltipDelegate =
            Function.createDelegate(this, this._hideTooltipHandler);

        $addHandler(element, 'mouseover', this._showTooltipDelegate);
        $addHandler(element, 'focus', this._showTooltipDelegate);
        $addHandler(element, 'mouseout', this._hideTooltipDelegate);
        $addHandler(element, 'blur', this._hideTooltipDelegate);

        SOAjax.Behaviors.TooltipBehavior.callBaseMethod(this, 'initialize');
    },

    _showTooltipHandler: function(event) {
        var _toolTipText = this.get_toolTip();
        if (_toolTipText == null || _toolTipText.length == 0) return;

        if (this.toolTipElement == null) {
            var toolTipElement = document.createElement('DIV');
            toolTipElement.style.zIndex = 999;
            document.body.appendChild(toolTipElement);
            var loc = Sys.UI.DomElement.getLocation(this.get_element());
            var bounds = Sys.UI.DomElement.getBounds(this.get_element());
            Sys.UI.DomElement.setLocation(
                toolTipElement, loc.x, loc.y + (bounds.height));
            Sys.UI.DomElement.setVisibilityMode(
                toolTipElement, Sys.UI.VisibilityMode.collapse);
```

```
                    Sys.UI.DomElement.addCssClass(toolTipElement, 'ToolTip');
                    this.toolTipElement = toolTipElement;
                }
                this.toolTipElement.innerHTML = _toolTipText;
                Sys.UI.DomElement.setVisible(this.toolTipElement, true);
            },


            _hideTooltipHandler: function(event) {
                if (this.toolTipElement != null)
                    Sys.UI.DomElement.setVisible(this.toolTipElement, false);
            },

            hide: function() {
                this._hideTooltipHandler(null);
            },

            dispose: function() {
                var element = this.get_element();
                if (element) {
                    if (this._showTooltipDelegate) {
                        $removeHandler(element, 'mouseover', this._showTooltipDelegate);
                        $removeHandler(element, 'focus', this._showTooltipDelegate);
                        delete this._showTooltipDelegate;
                    }
                    if (this._hideTooltipDelegate) {
                        $removeHandler(element, 'mouseout', this._hideTooltipDelegate);
                        $removeHandler(element, 'blur', this._hideTooltipDelegate);
                        delete this._hideTooltipDelegate;
                    }
                }
                if (this.toolTipElement)
                    this.toolTipElement.parentNode.removeChild(this.toolTipElement);
                this.toolTipElement = null;
                SOAjax.Behaviors.TooltipBehavior.callBaseMethod(this, 'dispose');
            }
        }
        SOAjax.Behaviors.TooltipBehavior.registerClass(
            'SOAjax.Behaviors.TooltipBehavior', Sys.UI.Behavior);


        Sys.Application.notifyScriptLoaded();
```

Because *Behavior* inherits from *Component*, the *Sys.Component.create* (*$create*) method is used to create the behavior. To recap, *$create* has the following interface:

```
$create(type, properties, events, references, element)
```

A *Behavior* instance is attached to a specific DOM element. One instance of the behavior is created and used per DOM element. Listing 8-3 shows a simple test page for the tooltip behavior, with the behavior applied to both an INPUT and a DIV element.

LISTING 8-3. Behaviors are created and added to DOM elements with the *$create* method (*Web/Tooltip.aspx*).

```
<%@ Page Language="C#" %>
<html xmlns="http://www.w3.org/1999/xhtml">
<head id="Head1" runat="server">
    <title>SOAjax Controls Sample Page: Behaviors</title>
    <script type="text/javascript">
        function pageLoad() {
            var inputElement = $get('testInput');
            var inputProperties = { toolTip:
              'Behaviors are flexible and can do all sorts of cool things.' };
            $create(SOAjax.Behaviors.TooltipBehavior,
                inputProperties, null, null, inputElement);

            var divElement = $get('testDiv');
            var divProperties = { toolTip:
              'Behaviors can be added to any DOM element.'};
            $create(SOAjax.Behaviors.TooltipBehavior,
                divProperties, null, null, divElement);
        }
    </script>
</head>
<body>
    <form id="form1" runat="server">
        <asp:ScriptManager ID="ScriptManager1" runat="server">
            <Scripts>
                <asp:ScriptReference Path="~/Script/Tooltip.js" />
            </Scripts>
        </asp:ScriptManager>
        <input type="text" id="testInput" maxlength="255" />
            <br />
            <br />
        <div id="testDiv">Mouse over me!!!</div>
    </form>
</body>
</html>
```

Choosing Between *Behavior* and *Control*

As I mentioned at the outset, a behavior is based on the component infrastructure. The *Control* class builds on this concept but is more restrictive because only a single control can be created per DOM element, which makes a behavior more flexible if your needs are simple and the component isn't central to the application. If you're simply extending a user interface element through dynamic HTML, you should probably choose the *Behavior* class. However, if you're going to implement a component with application functionality, such as Web service integration or major user interface components, use the *Control* class. Because the classes are so similar, you can usually begin with a *Behavior* component and later "upgrade" to a *Control* component with little effort.

Behavior Class Static Methods

In addition to behavior component functionality, the *Behavior* class contains three methods for accessing behavior instances from an element. *Sys.UI.Behavior.getBehaviorByName* provides a way to get an instance of a typed behavior from an element. You can use this method to determine whether a behavior is already applied to an element. The *Sys.UI.Behavior.getBehaviors* method returns an array of all the behaviors of an element. Finally, the *Sys.UI.Behavior.getBehaviorsByType* method returns all behaviors that match the type specified for a given element. These static methods are shown in Listing 8-4 for your reference.

LISTING 8-4. The *Behavior* class contains static methods for accessing behaviors (from *MicrosoftAJAX.debug.js*).

```
// Static Sys.UI.Behavior methods for accessing behaviors on a DOM element
// Defined in MicrosoftAJAX.js

Sys.UI.Behavior.getBehaviorByName =
        function Sys$UI$Behavior$getBehaviorByName(element, name) {
    var b = element[name];
    return (b && Sys.UI.Behavior.isInstanceOfType(b)) ? b : null;
}

Sys.UI.Behavior.getBehaviors = function Sys$UI$Behavior$getBehaviors(element) {
    if (!element._behaviors) return [];
    return Array.clone(element._behaviors);
}

Sys.UI.Behavior.getBehaviorsByType =
        function Sys$UI$Behavior$getBehaviorsByType(element, type) {
    var behaviors = element._behaviors;
    var results = [];
    if (behaviors) {
        for (var i = 0, l = behaviors.length; i < l; i++) {
            if (type.isInstanceOfType(behaviors[i])) {
                results[results.length] = behaviors[i];
            }
        }
    }
    return results;
}
```

Tip An instance of *Behavior* is similar to an instance of *Control,* but a DOM element can have several behaviors attached to it but only one instance of *Control.*

The Ajax Library *Control* Class

Controls can be granular and represent a single user interface component such as a text box or a button, or they can be built as application controls and be based on container elements such as the HTML DIV or SPAN elements. For example, I might define a control to provide functionality for an input element (as you'll see in the next code sample) that will provide a discrete control implementation. However, when implementing major functionality, such as usage reports, user management, or the main collaborative user interface, I create a composite control much like the case study we'll examine at the end of the chapter.

Controls can contain multiple child controls, and child controls can bubble up events to parent controls. Typically, you should develop a library of generic controls that can be bound to DOM elements and back-end data sources.

Before we look at control examples, let's examine the *Sys.UI.Control* class as implemented in the AJAX library. Properties of the *Control* class are listed in Table 8-5, where properties are defined by *get_* and *set_* methods. *Control* adds properties and methods to the *Component* base class that manipulate the DOM element and include event-bubbling methods that allow child controls to bubble up events to parent controls. Methods of the *Control* class are defined in Table 8-6. Finally, the *Control* class contains the events defined in *Sys.Component*, and these are listed in Table 8-7. Events are handled by using the *add_* and *remove_* methods for each event to add or remove event handlers.

TABLE 8-5 *Control* Class Properties

Name	Description
element	Gets the DOM element that the *Control* instance is based on (read-only).
id	Gets the ID of the element (read-only).
parent	Gets or sets the parent control. If no parent control is explicitly set, *get_ parent* searches up the DOM hierarchy for the next control.
visibilityMode	Gets or sets the visibility mode of the control, either *VisibilityMode.hide* or *VisibilityMode.collapse*. *VisibilityMode.hide* specifies that the hidden element takes up space on the page and uses the style *visibility='hidden'* for hidden elements. *VisibilityMode.collapse* uses the style *display='none'*, and the hidden element uses no space on the page.
visible	Indicates whether the control's DOM element is visible or not. Setting the control to *hidden* uses the *visibilityMode* property to determine the style to use.
events	Returns an instance of the *Sys.EventHandlerList* for the component (read-only).
isInitialized	Returns *true* if the control is initialized, otherwise *false* (read-only).
isUpdating	Returns *true* if the control is currently updating itself, otherwise *false* (read-only).

TABLE 8-6 *Control* **Class Methods**

Name	Description
beginUpdate	Called to set *isUpdating* to *true*. Called from the beginning of the *$create* method (*Sys.Component.create*).
endUpdate	Called to set *isUpdating* to *false*. Called from the end of the *$create* method (*Sys.Component.create*). Calls *initialize* if *isInitialized* is *false*, and then calls the *updated* method.
updated	Called when the component is updated. Used to implement any custom post-update or post-initialization logic.
initialize	Used to initialize the control.
addCssClass	Adds a CSS class to the DOM element.
removeCssClass	Removes a CSS class from the DOM element.
toggleCssClass	Toggles a CSS class on the DOM element.
onBubbleEvent	Handles events bubbled from child controls.
raiseBubbleEvent	Raises an event to parent controls.
raisePropertyChanged	Raises a *propertyChanged* event for a specific property.

TABLE 8-7 *Control* **Class Events**

Name	Description
propertyChanged	Raised when a property is changed.
disposing	Raised when the control is disposing.

As I discussed in the section "Implementing Custom Behaviors with the AJAX Library," the main distinction between the *Control* and the *Behavior* classes is that an instance of *Control* can be defined only once per DOM element. To understand this concept, it's best to look at the source code for the *Control* class's constructor.

```
Sys.UI.Control = function Sys$UI$Control(element) {
    if (typeof (element.control) != 'undefined')
        throw Error.invalidOperation(Sys.Res.controlAlreadyDefined);
    Sys.UI.Control.initializeBase(this);
    this._element = element;
    element.control = this;
}
```

First the control saves a reference to the DOM element as *this._element* (exposed through the *element* property methods) and then adds a reference to itself to the DOM element's *control* expando property. This expando property is used by other methods that search the DOM for controls, and it's also used to ensure that only one *Control* instance is defined per DOM element. Only one *Control* instance can be defined per DOM element because the instance represents a one-to-one relationship between the script control and the DOM control. If you try to create an additional control based on the same DOM element, an error is thrown.

Because the control can be accessed through the DOM element's *.control* expando property, the control can easily be accessed by code through a reference to the DOM element. For example, the following code demonstrates how a control can be accessed through script from a reference to its DOM element, given that an HTML INPUT element ("passwordInput") exists as the DOM element of a *Sys.UI.Control*:

```
var inputElement = $get('passwordInput');
var inputControl = inputElement.control;
```

> **Note** An *expando* property describes an arbitrary property that is applied to a DOM element through script.

The *Control* class contains the read-only properties *element* and *id* that are used with the DOM element. You'll use the *element* property method frequently when writing custom controls. Following are the *element* and *id* property methods, which simply return the element passed into the constructor (or its ID).

```
// Methods from Control defined in MicrosoftAjax.js:
function Sys$UI$Control$get_element() {
    return this._element;
}
function Sys$UI$Control$get_id() {
    if (!this._element) return '';
    return this._element.id;
}
```

If you create a control that is added to a page as part of a composite control, you might want access to the control's parent. The parent is the next *Sys.UI.Control* instance up in the DOM hierarchy. For example, you might want to get the parent control when working with a custom gridview control that contains row controls. The *Control* class provides support for a parent relationship through the *parent* property. If the parent control is explicitly set, it returns with the *get_parent* method. If the parent has not been set, the code walks the DOM hierarchy until it locates a DOM element with a *control* expando property. The following code sample shows *get_parent* and *set_parent*:

```
// Methods from Control defined in MicrosoftAjax.js:
function Sys$UI$Control$get_parent() {
    if (this._parent) return this._parent;
    if (!this._element) return null;
    var parentElement = this._element.parentNode;
    while (parentElement) {
        if (parentElement.control) {
            return parentElement.control;
        }
        parentElement = parentElement.parentNode;
    }
    return null;
}
```

```
function Sys$UI$Control$set_parent(value) {
    var parents = [this];
    var current = value;
    while (current) {
        if (Array.contains(parents, current)) throw
            Error.invalidOperation(Sys.Res.circularParentChain);
        parents[parents.length] = current;
        current = current.get_parent();
    }
    this._parent = value;
}
```

Finally, the *Control* class contains methods for working with the DOM element. The following methods are defined in *Sys.UI.Control* as wrapper methods for *Sys.UI.DomElement* methods. These methods can be used to set visibility and to add, remove, or toggle CSS classes.

```
function Sys$UI$Control$get_visibilityMode() {
    return Sys.UI.DomElement.getVisibilityMode(this._element);
}
function Sys$UI$Control$set_visibilityMode(value) {
    Sys.UI.DomElement.setVisibilityMode(this._element, value);
}
function Sys$UI$Control$get_visible() {
    return Sys.UI.DomElement.getVisible(this._element);
}
function Sys$UI$Control$set_visible(value) {
    Sys.UI.DomElement.setVisible(this._element, value)
}
function Sys$UI$Control$addCssClass(className) {
    Sys.UI.DomElement.addCssClass(this._element, className);
}
function Sys$UI$Control$removeCssClass(className) {
    Sys.UI.DomElement.removeCssClass(this._element, className);
}
function Sys$UI$Control$toggleCssClass(className) {
    Sys.UI.DomElement.toggleCssClass(this._element, className);
}
```

Creating a Custom Control with the AJAX Library

Like the *Behavior* class, the *Control* class is an abstract class that provides functionality for working with a DOM element. To use controls in your application, you must develop your own control implementations that inherit from *Sys.UI.Control*. In this section we'll start with the Visual Studio template for the AJAX Client Control and develop a fully functional control based on the INPUT DOM element with properties, events, and custom functionality.

A common requirement for input elements in Web applications is that they respond to the Enter button on the keyboard so that a user can perform an action without having to click a button with the mouse. This type of functionality can improve the usability of the application by requiring fewer clicks. In the following code samples, we'll create an input control that extends the capability of the HTML input text box by adding support for the Enter button and simple validation. We can also provide a tooltip for these controls by using the tooltip behavior created earlier in the chapter. This control can be used throughout an application and in multiple contexts, wherever you have a need for simple validation and support for the Enter button.

We'll start with a simple Web page containing the ScriptManager control and an empty JavaScript library. The test Web page can be created using the AJAX Web Form template in Visual Studio. To create the JavaScript library, you can use the AJAX Client Control template. The template creates the JavaScript namespace by using the name of the Web application project it's created in, but a simple search and replace can be used to get a good starting point. Listing 8-5 shows a JavaScript class generated by the AJAX Client Control template. As I did with the AJAX Client Behavior template, I replaced the default JavaScript namespace after the initial code was generated to use *SOAjax.Controls*.

Tip You can use the code-generation tool CodeSmith to create JavaScript control instances with little effort. The tool generates a control class with properties, events, and delegates based on your input. This is my preferred method for generating complex JavaScript classes. CodeSmith 5.0 includes a rich set of templates for the Microsoft AJAX Library. For more information on CodeSmith, visit *www. codesmithtools.com*.

LISTING 8-5. The Ajax Client Control template in Visual Studio can be used to create a new JavaScript control class (*Web/Script/ClientControlTemplate.js*).

```javascript
/// <reference name="MicrosoftAjax.js"/>

Type.registerNamespace("SOAjax.Controls");

SOAjax.Controls.SmartInputControl = function(element) {
    SOAjax.Controls.SmartInputControl.initializeBase(this, [element]);
}

SOAjax.Controls.SmartInputControl.prototype = {
    initialize: function() {
        SOAjax.Controls.SmartInputControl.callBaseMethod(this, 'initialize');

        // Add custom initialization here
    },
    dispose: function() {
        //Add custom dispose actions here
        SOAjax.Controls.SmartInputControl.callBaseMethod(this, 'dispose');
    }
}
SOAjax.Controls.SmartInputControl.registerClass(
    'SOAjax.Controls.SmartInputControl', Sys.UI.Control);

Sys.Application.notifyScriptLoaded();
```

By examining the generated code in Listing 8-5, you can see that the *Control* class is ready
for custom implementation—the base class already contains the core control functionality,
and our class is set up to inherit from *Sys.UI.Control*. If your control implementation depends
on a specific DOM element type, you might want to add basic validation in the constructor,
as in the following sample:

```
SOAjax.Controls.SmartInputControl = function(element) {
    if (element.tagName != 'INPUT') {
        Sys.Debug.fail('Expected an input control!');
    }
    SOAjax.Controls.SmartInputControl.initializeBase(this, [element]);
}
```

Another common step you'll almost always want to take is to add disposal code for any handlers you add, using the *$clearHandlers* method to clear any handlers added to the DOM
element. The code in the following *dispose* method is useful in almost all control classes.
Notice that if the element contains child nodes that you added handlers to, you might need
to iterate recursively through its children. In the *Behavior* class example, we were particular
about removing only the handlers used by the behavior so that behaviors could be added
and removed during the page execution without disabling other functionality. However, it is
assumed that by design controls are used for the lifetime of the DOM element. The following
dispose method demonstrates the typical disposal logic for the control implementation:

```
dispose: function() {
    var element = this.get_element();
    if (element)
        $clearHandlers(element);
    SOAjax.Controls.SmartInputControl.callBaseMethod(this, 'dispose');
}
```

As with component and behavior implementations, the *dispose* method here must contain
conditional logic—the *dispose* method might be called multiple times, so it's important to
check whether a reference such as the element exists before using the method because the
element reference might have been removed in an earlier disposal pass.

> **Tip** As a rule, in JavaScript you should always check that objects are not null before using them.

For our text box control implementation, we'll implement the custom event *submit*, which
is fired from the control when a user presses the Enter key. Client code is able to handle the
submit event in external code through an event handler, which allows the control to be used
in multiple contexts without tying the control implementation to any given page or use.

The following code is used in the *SmartInputControl*'s prototype to define the *submit* event.

```
// Bind and unbind to custom submit event.
add_submit: function(handler) {
    this.get_events().addHandler('submit', handler);
},
remove_submit: function(handler) {
    this.get_events().removeHandler('submit', handler);
}
```

You'll notice that the event implementation uses the *get_events* method of the base *Component* class. (Remember that *Sys.UI.Control* inherits from *Sys.Component*.) Chapter 7 described the *Sys.Component* infrastructure in depth, including the *Sys.EventHandlerList* class that is used to support events.

To add a handler for the Enter button, use the *$addHandler* method to add a handler to the *keydown* DOM event. The handler is created by using a delegate—using *Function.create-Delegate* (discussed in Chapter 7) to create a delegate that refers to the class instance. The following code demonstrates a handler method for the *keydown* event that fires the *submit* event on the *enter* key event. To provide support for the *TooltipBehavior* behavior class, we can call *Sys.UI.Behavior.getBehaviorByName* to see whether an instance of the behavior is active on the control. If it is, we can hide the tooltip.

```
initialize: function() {
    var element = this.get_element();
    $addHandler(element, 'keydown',
        Function.createDelegate(this, this._keyDownHandler));
    SOAjax.Controls.SmartInputControl.callBaseMethod(this, 'initialize');
},

_keyDownHandler: function(event) {
    if (event == null) {
        event = new Sys.UI.DomEvent(null); throw Error.argumentNull();
    }

    // Check for the "submit" action (enter key)
    if (!event.keyCode) return;
    if (event.keyCode != Sys.UI.Key.enter) return;

    var handler = this.get_events().getHandler('submit');
    if (!handler) { Sys.Debug.trace('Handler is not defined for the enter key!'); }
    if (handler) handler(this, Sys.EventArgs.Empty);
    // If a tooltip behavior is active, hide it
    var element = this.get_element();
    var toolTipBehavior = Sys.UI.Behavior.getBehaviorByName(element, 'TooltipBehavior');
    if (toolTipBehavior)
        toolTipBehavior.hide();
}
```

Providing Visual Studio IntelliSense

To provide Visual Studio IntelliSense support, the following code is used in the method body of _keyDownHandler. Instantiating the *Sys.UI.DomEvent* type lets Visual Studio infer the type of *event*. We never expect this code to run because the *Sys.UI.DomEvent* instance is passed to the method, but the declaration allows Visual Studio to infer the type.

```
if (event == null) { event = new Sys.UI.DomEvent(null); throw Error.argumentNull(); }
```

The following screenshot demonstrates the effect of this code while using the Visual Studio IDE.

To handle the *submit* event from external code, declare an event handler method. The event handler uses the signature *handler(sender, eventArgs)*, where *sender* is the instance that fired the event and *eventArgs* is an instance of type *Sys.EventArgs*, which is used to pass extra information in certain cases. In this case, we don't need to pass any information other than the control instance, so we pass *Sys.EventArgs.Empty* from our control class. The following code can be placed in an HTML page to instantiate the control and test the Enter button functionality:

```
function onSubmit(control, eventArgs) {
    Sys.Debug.traceDump(control);
    var textValue = control.get_text();
    alert(textValue);
}

function pageLoad(){
    var events = { submit: onSubmit };
    var domControl = $get('testInput');
    $create(SOAjax.Controls.SmartInputControl, null, events, null, domControl);
}
```

Simple Validation and the *propertyChanged* Event

Sys.Component provides the *propertyChanged* event, which can be used to notify external clients of property changes. (I introduced this event in Chapter 7.) The *propertyChanged* event is a general purpose event that client code can subscribe to.

In our sample input control, simple input validation can be useful in developing a control library. For example, you might want to raise a *propertyChanged* event for *isValid* when an input passes simple validation and the validation status changes. To implement simple validation logic in the control, such as a minimum password length, you can add the properties *minLength* and *isValid* and raise the *propertyChanged* event when the status changes. You can also provide a *validationFailure* event that fires only when the user attempts a submission that includes invalid data.

Tip As an alternative, you could use a delegate property that implements validation, letting the external implementation code provide the validation. To keep the example simple, I used simple validation in the control itself.

The code in Listing 8-6 extends *SmartInputControl* with validation logic and raises the *propertyChanged* event when the *isValid* property changes. The *validationFailure* event is also defined in this listing. This event is fired from *_keyDownHandler* when validation failure occurs. (You can see the code for *_keyDownHandler* in Listing 8-7.)

LISTING 8-6. Properties and events can be used for simple validation logic (from *Web/Script/ SmartInputControl.js*).

```
// Simple validation logic for SmartInputControl,
// integrated with the raisePropertyChanged event:
minLength: null,
get_minLength: function() {
    ///<value>The minimum valid length of the user's input</value>
    return this.minLength;
},
set_minLength: function(length) {
    if (length) { // Only validate non-null values.
        if (typeof (length) != 'number') {
            throw Error.argumentType('length', typeof (length), typeof (1));
        }
    }
    this.minLength = length;
},
_lastKnownIsValid : false,
get_isValid: function() {
    ///<value>Returns true if this control passes minimal validation</value>
    var isValid;
    if (this.minLength && this.get_text().length < this.minLength)
        isValid = false;
```

```
        else
            isValid = true;
        if (this._lastKnownIsValid != isValid)
            this.raisePropertyChanged('isValid');
        return (isValid);
    }
    add_validationFailure: function(handler) {
        ///<value>The validationFailure event is fired when the user
        /// enters the enter key with invalid data.</value>
        this.get_events().addHandler('validationFailure', handler);
    },
    remove_validationFailure: function(handler) {
        this.get_events().removeHandler('validationFailure', handler);
    }
```

To further integrate validation into the control, we can check whether the control is valid on each key press, raise the *propertyChanged* event when the validation state changes, and conditionally fire the *submit* event on the Enter key press so that invalid submissions aren't fired. If the user tries to submit the control value and the validation fails, the *validationFailure* event is raised.

Listing 8-7 shows the modified *_keyDownHandler* with the integrated validation logic. On every key press the validation code is called, which raises the *propertyChanged* event in turn if the validation status has changed. Additionally, the *validationFailure* event is raised on failure to let the implementation code handle the event.

LISTING 8-7. The validation logic is applied to the key press event handler (from *Web/Script/ SmartInputControl.js*).

```
_keyDownHandler: function(event) {
    if (event == null) {
        event = new Sys.UI.DomEvent(null); throw Error.argumentNull();
    }

    // Check for the "submit" action (enter key)
    if (!event.keyCode || event.keyCode != Sys.UI.Key.enter) return;
    if (!this.get_isValid()) {
        var validationHandler = this.get_events().getHandler('validationFailure');
        if (validationHandler)
            validationHandler(Sys.EventArgs.Empty);
        else
            alert('This input isn\'t valid!');
        return;
    }
    var handler = this.get_events().getHandler('submit');
    if (!handler) { Sys.Debug.trace('Handler is not defined for the enter key!'); }
    if (handler) handler(this, Sys.EventArgs.Empty);
    this._hideTooltipHandler(null);
    // If a tooltip behavior is active, hide it
    var element = this.get_element();
```

```
        var toolTipBehavior = Sys.UI.Behavior.getBehaviorByName(
            element, 'TooltipBehavior');
        if (toolTipBehavior)
            toolTipBehavior.hide();
    }
```

With this simple validation logic in place, we can add the property *minLength* to the call to the *$create* method for *SmartInputControl*. The following code sample sets the *minLength* property through the *$create* method:

```
function pageLoad() {
    var element = $get('testInput');
    var events = { submit: onSubmit };
    var props = { minLength : 3};
    $create(SOAjax.Controls.SmartInputControl, props, events, null, element);
}
```

The test page for the control is shown in Listing 8-8, which assigns an event handler for the input control's *submit* event and assigns *TooltipBehavior* to the control. The complete code for the final *SmartInputControl* implementation is included in Listing 8-9.

LISTING 8-8. The *SmartInputControl* control class can be tested in an isolated page instance or integrated into more complex code (*Web/SmartInputControl.aspx*).

```
<%@ Page Language="C#" %>
<html xmlns="http://www.w3.org/1999/xhtml">
<head>
    <title>SOAjax Controls Sample Page</title>
    <script type="text/javascript">

        function pageLoad() {
            var element = $get('testInput');
            var events = { submit: onSubmit };
            var props = {minLength : 3};
            $create(SOAjax.Controls.SmartInputControl, props, events, null, element);

            var toolTipProps = { toolTip: 'Enter a value here!'};
            $create(SOAjax.Behaviors.TooltipBehavior, toolTipProps, null, null,
                element);
        }

        function onSubmit(control, eventArgs) {
            Sys.Debug.traceDump(control);
            var textValue = control.get_text();
            alert(textValue);
        }

    </script>
</head>
```

```
<body>
    <form id="form1" runat="server">
      <div>
        <asp:ScriptManager ID="ScriptManager1" runat="server" >
            <Scripts>
                <asp:ScriptReference Path="~/Script/SmartInputControl.js" />
                <asp:ScriptReference Path="~/Script/Tooltip.js" />
            </Scripts>
        </asp:ScriptManager>

        <input type="text" id="testInput" maxlength="255" />

      </div>
    </form>
</body>
</html>
```

LISTING 8-9. The *SmartInputControl* control class adds functionality to the HTML input text box (*Web/Script/ SmartInputControl.js*).

```
/// <reference name="MicrosoftAjax.js"/>
// A common control library for SOAjax Sample Code

Type.registerNamespace('SOAjax.Controls');


SOAjax.Controls.SmartInputControl = function(element) {
    if (element.tagName != 'INPUT') {
        Sys.Debug.fail('Expected an input control!');
    }
    SOAjax.Controls.SmartInputControl.initializeBase(this, [element]);
}
SOAjax.Controls.SmartInputControl.prototype = {

    // Simple validation logic:
    minLength: null,
    get_minLength: function() {
        /// <value>The minimum valid length of the user's input</value>
        return this.minLength;
    },
    set_minLength: function(length) {
        if (length) { // Only validate non-null values.
            if (typeof (length) != 'number') {
                throw Error.argumentType('length', typeof (length), typeof (1));
            }
        }
        this.minLength = length;
    },
    _lastKnownIsValid: false,
    get_isValid: function() {
        /// <value>Returns true if this control passes minimal validation</value>
        var isValid;
```

```
        if (this.minLength && this.get_text().length < this.minLength)
            isValid = false;
        else
            isValid = true;

        if (this._lastKnownIsValid != isValid)
            this.raisePropertyChanged('isValid');

        return (isValid);
    },

    add_validationFailure: function(handler) {
        /// <value>The validationFailure event is fired when the user
        /// enters the enter key with invalid data.</value>
        this.get_events().addHandler('validationFailure', handler);
    },
    remove_validationFailure: function(handler) {
        this.get_events().removeHandler('validationFailure', handler);
    },

    add_submit: function(handler) {
        /// <value>The submit event is fired when the user presses
        /// the enter key.</value>
        this.get_events().addHandler('submit', handler);
    },
    remove_submit: function(handler) {
        this.get_events().removeHandler('submit', handler);
    },

    get_text: function() {
        /// <value>Gets the text value of the control</value>
        return this.get_element().value;
    },
    set_text: function(text) { this.get_element().value = text; },

    initialize: function() {
        var element = this.get_element();
        if (!element.tabIndex) element.tabIndex = 0;

        $addHandler(element, 'keydown',
            Function.createDelegate(this, this._keyDownHandler));

        SOAjax.Controls.SmartInputControl.callBaseMethod(this, 'initialize');
    },

    _keyDownHandler: function(event) {
        if (event == null) {
            event = new Sys.UI.DomEvent(null); throw Error.argumentNull();
        }

        // Check for the "submit" action (enter key)
        if (!event.keyCode || event.keyCode != Sys.UI.Key.enter) return;
        if (!this.get_isValid()) {
```

```
                var validationHandler = this.get_events().getHandler('validationFailure');
                if (validationHandler)
                    validationHandler(Sys.EventArgs.Empty);
                else
                    alert('This input isn\'t valid!');
                return;
            }
        var handler = this.get_events().getHandler('submit');
        if (!handler) { Sys.Debug.trace('submit handler is not defined!'); }
        if (handler) handler(this, Sys.EventArgs.Empty);
        var element = this.get_element();
        var toolTipBehavior = Sys.UI.Behavior.getBehaviorByName(
            element, 'TooltipBehavior');
        if (toolTipBehavior)
            toolTipBehavior.hide();
    },

    dispose: function() {
        var element = this.get_element();
        if (element)
            $clearHandlers(element);
        if (this.toolTip)
            this.toolTip.parentNode.removeChild(this.toolTip);
        this.toolTip = null;
        SOAjax.Controls.SmartInputControl.callBaseMethod(this, 'dispose');
    }
}
SOAjax.Controls.SmartInputControl.registerClass(
    'SOAjax.Controls.SmartInputControl', Sys.UI.Control);

Sys.Application.notifyScriptLoaded();
```

After testing *SmartInputControl* on a sample page, it is easy to integrate the class into real code. For example, we can extend the login input elements from the application run-time component example in Chapter 7 simply by adding a script reference through the ScriptManager control and creating an instance of *SmartInputControl*. The code in Listing 8-10 demonstrates *SmartInputControl* as used by the application runtime component's *password-Input* property. The *set_passwordInput* property method in the component's prototype is used to create an instance of *SmartInputControl* for the password input element. This allows the user to press Enter rather than click the login button. The full code sample integrating the *SmartInputControl* control class in the JavaScript component *SOAjax.Application* is included in this chapter's code sample in the file *ApplicationRuntime.js*.

LISTING 8-10. *SmartInputControl* can easily be utilized in multiple contexts (*Web/Scripts/ApplicationRuntime.js*).

```
// Sample code excerpt from SOAjax.Application's prototype

set_passwordInput: function(element) {
    // Create a new SmartInputControl from the DOM element
    if (!element.control) {
        var properties = { minLength: 3 };
        var events = { submit: Function.createDelegate(this, this.login) };
        var passwordControl = $create(
            SOAjax.Controls.SmartInputControl, properties, events, null, element);

        $create(SOAjax.Behaviors.TooltipBehavior,
            { toolTip: 'Enter your password' }, null, null, element);
    }
    this.passwordInput = element;
}
```

Now that we've seen simple examples of creating and integrating discrete controls, let's look at a more complex example using the knowledge base wiki application and create a large-scale application control.

Case Study: Creating a Wiki Application Control

Controls can be used to apply JavaScript behavior and a rich, event-based API to DOM elements. However, in typical applications you want to develop controls that provide application functionality that is bound to server-side data sources. After all, without a Web service back end, AJAX components are only fancy JavaScript controls. To provide a rich AJAX user experience, you need to provide real-time data integration with back-end services.

An application control is usually a composite control or a DIV-based control that provides much of the functionality for a page. In the following example, we'll build an application control for the knowledge base application we've been developing throughout the book. First we'll develop a simple parsing library of static text-parsing functions that can be extended to provide full wiki capability. Then we'll develop a control for rendering, navigating, creating, and editing wiki content.

Figure 8-2 illustrates the wiki application. The *SOAjax.Application* component is used by the page to control the login elements as well as the wiki application control. The main content of the page is implemented by *SOAjax.Controls.WikiControl*, which we'll build in the following code samples. This control is browsable and editable using standard wiki markup.

FIGURE 8-2. The *SOAjax.Controls.WikiControl* control is used to implement the main user interface for a wiki application.

The wiki application in the following example is based on a wiki control that provides wiki rendering, editing, and navigation; the application runtime component from Chapter 7 that provides authorization and profile information; and a page class that creates the components and binds them to HTML elements. The application runtime that we developed and tested previously doesn't need to be rewritten for this application because we can add event handlers and respond to authentication events and properties from the page class, binding these properties to the wiki control. For example, we'll display a subset of the application for an anonymous user and provide editing capabilities when the user is authenticated.

Listing 8-11 displays the ASPX page for the wiki application (found in the ASPX file *wiki.aspx* in this chapter's sample code). The *_WikiContent* element is used to render the wiki, and the editing controls are used to switch editing modes. Because we support an anonymous user for read access, the editing controls are conditionally displayed by the page's JavaScript code. Notice that I included a reference to the Windows Communication Foundation (WCF) endpoint dataservice.svc in the ScriptManager. We use these Web service methods in the wiki control. In this sample we also use JSON-formatted data and the ASP.NET AJAX generated JavaScript proxies, incorporating much of the logic from earlier chapters but wrapping it in a *Control* class implementation.

LISTING 8-11. The wiki page elements are defined in the ASPX page and controls are defined in JavaScript libraries (*Web/Wiki.aspx*).

```
<%@ Page Language="C#" %>
<html xmlns="http://www.w3.org/1999/xhtml">
<head>
    <title>Service-Oriented AJAX</title>
    <link href="Style/StyleSheet.css" rel="stylesheet" type="text/css" />
</head>
<body>
  <form id="form1" runat="server">
    <asp:ScriptManager ID="AjaxScriptManager" runat="server"
            RoleService-LoadRoles="true"
            ProfileService-LoadProperties="startTopic">
        <Scripts>
            <asp:ScriptReference Path="~/Script/WikiLibrary.js" />
            <asp:ScriptReference Path="~/Script/SOAjax.js" />
            <asp:ScriptReference Path="~/Script/Tooltip.js" />
            <asp:ScriptReference Path="~/Script/SmartInputControl.js" />
            <asp:ScriptReference Path="~/Script/ApplicationRuntime.js" />
            <asp:ScriptReference Path="~/Script/WikiControl.js" />
```

```
                <asp:ScriptReference Path="~/Script/WikiPage.js" />
        </Scripts>
        <Services>
                <asp:ServiceReference Path="services/dataservice.svc" />
        </Services>
</asp:ScriptManager>
<div id="pageHeader">
    Service-Oriented AJAX on the Microsoft Platform

    <div id="logoutControl" class="loginControl" style="display: none;" >
        <button id="ButtonLogout" type="button" value="Logout">Logout</button>
    </div>

    <div style="display: none;" id="loginControl" class="loginControl">
        <div class="widgetTitle" id="loginLink">Login</div>
        <div class="lightPadding" id="loginUI" style="display: none;">
            Username <br />
            <input type="text" id="usernameInput" /><br /><br />

            Password <br />
            <input type="text" id="passwordInput" /><br /><br />

            <button id="ButtonLogin" value="Login" type="button"
            title="Login">Login</button>  
            <button id="ButtonCancelLogin" value="Cancel" type="button"
            title="Cancel">Cancel</button>
            <div id="loginFeedbackDiv">
            </div>
        </div>
    </div>
</div>


<div id="pageBody">
    <table style="width:100%; height:100%" cellpadding="0" cellspacing="0">
        <tr valign="top">
            <td width="150px" style="background-color:#EFEFEF; padding:15px;">

                <div id="_EditControls" style="display:none;">
                    <span id="_editButton" class="Button">Edit</span>
                    <span id="_saveButton"
                        style="display:none;" class="Button">Save</span>
                    <span id="_cancelButton"
                        style="display:none;" class="Button">Cancel</span>

                    <div style="padding:10px;">
                        Tag: <input type="text" id="tagInput" maxlength="50" />
                    </div>

                </div>
```

```
                  <div id="NavigationPlaceholder"
                      style="width:150px; background-color:#EFEFEF">
                      <!-- Navigation goes here -->
                  </div>
              </td>

              <td width="100%">
                  <div id="MainContent" style="overflow:auto;" >
                      <div id="_WikiContent"/>
                  </div>
              </td>
          </tr>
        </table>
      </div>
    </form>
  </body>
</html>
```

Usually in an AJAX application you use XSLT or JavaScript templates for rendering. In the next chapter we'll look more closely at AJAX rendering techniques and at the *XmlControl* implementation that binds a control to an XML data source. For the sample application, however, we need to develop a wiki parser for rendering HTML from wiki markup. We can use regular expressions in JavaScript to parse the wiki text and create HTML and add event handlers to handle navigation. Listing 8-12 contains the text-parsing methods to convert wiki syntax into HTML. To avoid writing more script to change HTML into wiki text, we store and edit the wiki text and only use the HTML conversion code in the rendering method.

Tip The wiki parsing in this example is very basic. For more information on wiki markup, search for "wiki creole". Additional parsing methods are included in the sample code downloads.

LISTING 8-12. JavaScript can be used to create simple wiki parsing methods (*Web/Scripts/WikiLibrary.js*).

```
/// <reference name="MicrosoftAjax.js"/>
Type.registerNamespace('SOAjax.Wiki');

// Simple Wiki parsing library:
// converts the HTML format to WIKI text
SOAjax.Wiki.convertToWiki = function(element){
  var links = element.getElementsByTagName('span');
  var placeholders = new Array();
  for(var i=0;i<links.length;i++){
    if (links[i].className=='WIKILINK')
      Array.add(placeholders, links[i]);
  }
  for(var ix=0;ix<placeholders.length;ix++){
    var wik = document.createTextNode(String.format('[[{0}]]',
        SOAjax.getText(placeholders[ix])) );
```

```
           var old = placeholders[ix].parentNode.replaceChild(wik, placeholders[ix]);
           placeholders[ix] = null;
       }
   }

   SOAjax.getText = function(node) {
       if (node == null) return '';
       if (node.innerText) return node.innerText;
       else if (node.textContent) return node.textContent;
       else return '';
   }

   // Converts WIKI text to HTML format
   SOAjax.Wiki.wikiToHtml = function(wikiText){
     var rex = new RegExp('\\[\\[([^\\]]+)\\]\\]',"mg");
     var match = rex.exec(wikiText);
     while (match){
         var linked = String.format("<span class=\"WIKILINK\">{0}</span>",match[1]);
         wikiText = wikiText.replace(match[0],linked);
         match = rex.exec(wikiText);
     }
     return wikiText;
   }

   // Adds click handlers to the WIKILINK spans
   SOAjax.Wiki.addWikiHandlers = function(element){
     var links = element.getElementsByTagName('span');
     for(var i=0;i<links.length;i++){
       if (links[i].className=='WIKILINK')
           $addHandler(links[i], 'click', SOAjax.Wiki.Link);
     }
   }

   SOAjax.Wiki.Link = function(clickEvent) {
       if (clickEvent == null) { clickEvent = new Sys.UI.DomEvent(); }
       var wiki = SOAjax.FindParentControl(clickEvent.target, SOAjax.Wiki.WikiControl);
       if (wiki == null) return;
       var link = null;
       if (clickEvent.target.innerText)
           link = clickEvent.target.innerText;
       else if (clickEvent.target.textContent)
           link = clickEvent.target.textContent;
       if (link != null && link != '')
           wiki.load(link);
   }
```

After creating a simple parsing library with JavaScript, we're ready to create a wiki control. The wiki control implements both the rendering and editing elements of the page and references button controls that are used to switch into editing mode or save content. Because we don't have special needs for buttons at the moment, we can use simple DOM elements for the buttons. Listing 8-13 shows the starter code for the wiki control, with the properties for DOM elements defined and placeholders for Web service event handlers.

LISTING 8-13. A *Control* class can be implemented to provide content rendering and editing capabilities (*Web/Script/WikiControl.js*).

```
/// <reference name="MicrosoftAjax.js"/>
/// <reference path="SOAjax.js"/>
/// <reference path="DataService.js"/>
/// <reference path="WikiLibrary.js"/>

SOAjax.Wiki.WikiControl = function(element) {
    SOAjax.Wiki.WikiControl.initializeBase(this, [element]);
}

SOAjax.Wiki.WikiControl.prototype = {
    _renderDiv: null,
    _titleDiv: null,
    _editControl: null,
    _editMode: false,
    _topic: null,
    _isLoading: false,
    _catalog: 'Default',
    _rawWiki: null,
    _tagInput: null,
    _editButton: null,
    _cancelButton: null,
    _saveButton: null,

    initialize: function() {
        Sys.Debug.trace('WikiControl:initialize');
        SOAjax.Wiki.WikiControl.callBaseMethod(this, 'initialize');
        // custom initialization
        var control = this.get_element();

        this._titleDiv = document.createElement('DIV');
        this._titleDiv.margin = '7px';
        this._titleDiv.style.padding = '7px';
        Sys.UI.DomElement.addCssClass(this._titleDiv, 'TitleHead');
        control.appendChild(this._titleDiv);

        this._renderDiv = document.createElement('DIV');
        control.appendChild(this._renderDiv);
        this._editControl = document.createElement('TEXTAREA');
        this._editControl.style.display = 'none';
        this._editControl.style.width = '100%';
        this._editControl.style.height = '100%';
        this._editControl.style.border = 'solid 0px';
        this._editControl.style.margin = '0px';
        this._editControl.style.padding = '0px';
        control.appendChild(this._editControl);
    },


    // child controls:
    get_editButton: function() { return (this._editButton); },
    set_editButton: function(button) {
        this._editButton = button;
```

```
    $addHandler(this._editButton,
        'click', Function.createDelegate(this, this.enterEditMode));
},

get_cancelButton: function() { return (this._cancelButton); },
set_cancelButton: function(button) {
    this._cancelButton = button;
    $addHandler(this._cancelButton,
        'click', Function.createDelegate(this, this.cancelEdits));
},
get_saveButton: function() { return (this._saveButton); },
set_saveButton: function(button) {
    this._saveButton = button;
    $addHandler(this._saveButton,
        'click', Function.createDelegate(this, this.save));
},

get_tagInput: function() { },
set_tagInput: function(input) {
    this._tagInput = input;
    this._tagInput.onkeydown =
        Function.createDelegate(this, this._onTagInputKeyDown);
},

get_isLoading: function() {
    return this._isLoading;
},

set_isLoading: function(isLoading) {
    this.raisePropertyChanged('loading');
    this._isLoading = isLoading;
},

enterEditMode: function(event) {
    if (event == null) event = new Sys.UI.DomEvent();
    event.stopPropagation();
    this.set_editMode(true);
},

load: function(topic) {/*Placeholder*/ },
save: function() { /*Placeholder*/ },
get_topic: function() { return this._topic; },
set_topic: function(topic) {
    if (this._topic !== topic) {
        this._topic = topic;
        this.raisePropertyChanged('topic');
    }
},

get_editMode: function() {
    /// <value type="Boolean">True if we're in edit mode,
    /// otherwise false.</value>
    return this._editMode;
},
```

```
    set_editMode: function(value) {
        Sys.Debug.trace('WikiControl:switching EditMode:' + value);
        if (value !== this.get_editMode()) {
            this._editMode = value;
            this.raisePropertyChanged('editMode');
            if (!this.get_isUpdating()) {
                // switch to edit if true, otherwise render
                Sys.UI.DomElement.setVisible(this._editControl, value);
                Sys.UI.DomElement.setVisible(this._cancelButton, value);
                Sys.UI.DomElement.setVisible(this._saveButton, value);
                Sys.UI.DomElement.setVisible(this._editButton, !value);
                Sys.UI.DomElement.setVisible(this._renderDiv, !value);
            }
        }
    },

    cancelEdits: function() {
        SOAjax.ClearHandlers(this._renderDiv);
        this._renderDiv.innerHTML = '';
        this.set_editMode(false);
        this._renderDiv.innerHTML = SOAjax.Wiki.wikiToHtml(this._rawWiki);
        SOAjax.Wiki.addWikiHandlers(this._renderDiv);
        this._editControl.value = this._rawWiki;
    },


    dispose: function() {
        Sys.Debug.trace('WikiControl:dispose');

        $clearHandlers(this._editButton);
        $clearHandlers(this._saveButton);
        $clearHandlers(this._cancelButton);

        SOAjax.Purge(this._renderDiv);
        SOAjax.Purge(this._editControl);
        var control = this.get_element();
        if (control) {
            control.removeChild(this._renderDiv);
            control.removeChild(this._editControl);
        }
        SOAjax.Wiki.WikiControl.callBaseMethod(this, 'dispose');
    }
}
SOAjax.Wiki.WikiControl.registerClass('SOAjax.Wiki.WikiControl', Sys.UI.Control);
Sys.Application.notifyScriptLoaded();
```

After defining the basic control shell, we can tie into the Web service methods we defined
in previous chapters and add the wiki text-parsing and rendering methods in the custom
wiki JavaScript library. In Listing 8-14, the *load* placeholder method is replaced with the Web
service *load* implementation, including the asynchronous callback handlers. After loading is
completed, the wiki library (defined earlier in Listing 8-12) is used to generate HTML from the
wiki text and is rendered in the control with wiki links.

LISTING 8-14. Controls can be implemented utilizing a Web service back end (*Web/Script/WikiControl.js*).

```
load: function(topic) {
    this.set_isLoading(true);
    this._topic = topic;
    this._titleDiv.innerHTML = topic;
    SOAjax.ClearHandlers(this._renderDiv);
    this._renderDiv.innerHTML = '';
    this._editControl.value = '';

    Sys.Debug.trace(String.format('WikiControl:load("{0}")', this._topic));
    //var control = this.get_element();

    knowledgebase.DataService.GetData(this._catalog, this._topic,
        Function.createDelegate(this, this.onLoadComplete),
        Function.createDelegate(this, this.onFailure),
        this);
},

onLoadComplete: function(wikiData, userContext, methodName) {
    var html = SOAjax.Wiki.wikiToHtml(wikiData.Body);
    this._editControl.value = wikiData.Body;
    this._rawWiki = wikiData.Body;
    SOAjax.ClearHandlers(this._renderDiv);
    this._renderDiv.innerHTML = html;
    SOAjax.Wiki.addWikiHandlers(this._renderDiv);
    this.set_isLoading(false);
}

onFailure: function(exception, userContext, methodName) {
    Sys.Debug.traceDump(exception, 'Failed callback!');
    Sys.Debug.fail(String.format("The method {0} failed miserably! ({1})",
        methodName, exception.get_message()));
    Sys.Debug.traceDump(this, 'Failed callback!');
}
```

Likewise, the *save* placeholder method is replaced with the Web service save operation and its callback handlers. When the user clicks the Save button (shown only in editing mode), the *save* method is called as the event handler. Listing 8-15 demonstrates the *save* method integrated into the wiki control.

LISTING 8-15. Controls can persist data against Web services using the Microsoft AJAX Library (*Web/Script/WikiControl.js*).

```
save: function() {
    Sys.Debug.trace(String.format('WikiControl:save("{0}")', this._topic));

    this._saveButton.style.display = 'none';
    this._cancelButton.style.display = 'none';
    this._editButton.style.display = '';
```

```
        var wikiObject = new Object();
        wikiObject.Body = this._editControl.value;
        wikiObject.Title = this._topic;

        knowledgebase.DataService.SaveData(wikiObject,
            Function.createDelegate(this, this.onSaveCallback),
            Function.createDelegate(this, this.onFailure),
            null); //usercontext

        SOAjax.ClearHandlers(this._renderDiv);
        this._renderDiv.innerHTML = SOAjax.Wiki.wikiToHtml(wikiObject.Body);
        this._rawWiki = wikiObject.Body;
        SOAjax.Wiki.addWikiHandlers(this._renderDiv);
        this.set_editMode(false);
},

onSaveCallback: function() {
    Sys.Debug.trace('Save success! ');
}
```

With the *load* and *save* AJAX methods integrated into the control, it's now fully functional. To sum up, the wiki control loads wiki text from a Web service in response to loading and navigation events. The wiki control switches from rendering to an edit control when the *editMode* property is set to true, and saves the data when the *save* event is fired from the DOM element that implements the Save button. The full code for the wiki control is shown in Listing 8-16.

LISTING 8-16. The final *WikiControl* control (*Web/Script/ WikiControl.js*).

```
/// <reference name="MicrosoftAjax.js"/>
/// <reference path="SOAjax.js"/>
/// <reference path="DataService.js"/>

Type.registerNamespace('SOAjax.Wiki');

SOAjax.Wiki.WikiControl = function(element) {
    SOAjax.Wiki.WikiControl.initializeBase(this, [element]);
}

SOAjax.Wiki.WikiControl.prototype = {
    _renderDiv: null,
    _titleDiv: null,
    _editControl: null,
    _editMode: false,
    _topic: null,
    _isLoading: false,
    _catalog: 'Default',
    _rawWiki: null,
    _tagInput: null,
    _editButton: null,
```

```
_cancelButton: null,
_saveButton: null,

initialize: function() {
    Sys.Debug.trace('WikiControl:initialize');
    SOAjax.Wiki.WikiControl.callBaseMethod(this, 'initialize');
    // custom initialization
    var control = this.get_element();

    this._titleDiv = document.createElement('DIV');
    this._titleDiv.margin = '7px';
    this._titleDiv.style.padding = '7px';
    Sys.UI.DomElement.addCssClass(this._titleDiv, 'TitleHead');
    control.appendChild(this._titleDiv);

    this._renderDiv = document.createElement('DIV');
    control.appendChild(this._renderDiv);
    this._editControl = document.createElement('TEXTAREA');
    this._editControl.style.display = 'none';
    this._editControl.style.width = '100%';
    this._editControl.style.height = '100%';
    this._editControl.style.border = 'solid 0px';
    this._editControl.style.margin = '0px';
    this._editControl.style.padding = '0px';
    control.appendChild(this._editControl);
},


// child controls:
get_editButton: function() { return (this._editButton); },
set_editButton: function(button) {
    this._editButton = button;
    $addHandler(this._editButton,
        'click', Function.createDelegate(this, this.enterEditMode));
},

get_cancelButton: function() { return (this._cancelButton); },
set_cancelButton: function(button) {
    this._cancelButton = button;
    $addHandler(this._cancelButton,
        'click', Function.createDelegate(this, this.cancelEdits));
},
get_saveButton: function() { return (this._saveButton); },
set_saveButton: function(button) {
    this._saveButton = button;
    $addHandler(this._saveButton,
        'click', Function.createDelegate(this, this.save));
},

get_tagInput: function() { },
set_tagInput: function(input) {
    this._tagInput = input;
    this._tagInput.onkeydown =
        Function.createDelegate(this, this._onTagInputKeyDown);
},
```

```
get_isLoading: function() {
    return this._isLoading;
},

set_isLoading: function(isLoading) {
    this.raisePropertyChanged('loading');
    this._isLoading = isLoading;
},

enterEditMode: function(event) {
    if (event == null) event = new Sys.UI.DomEvent();
    event.stopPropagation();
    // this._editControl.value = SOAjax.Wiki.convertToWiki(this._renderDiv);
    this.set_editMode(true);
},

load: function(topic) {
    this.set_isLoading(true);
    this._topic = topic;
    this._titleDiv.innerHTML = topic;
    SOAjax.ClearHandlers(this._renderDiv);
    this._renderDiv.innerHTML = '';
    this._editControl.value = '';

    Sys.Debug.trace(String.format('WikiControl:load("{0}")', this._topic));
    //var control = this.get_element();

    knowledgebase.DataService.GetData(this._catalog, this._topic,
        Function.createDelegate(this, this.onLoadComplete),
        Function.createDelegate(this, this.onFailure),
        this);
},

onLoadComplete: function(wikiData, userContext, methodName) {
    var html = SOAjax.Wiki.wikiToHtml(wikiData.Body);
    this._editControl.value = wikiData.Body;
    this._rawWiki = wikiData.Body;
    SOAjax.ClearHandlers(this._renderDiv);
    this._renderDiv.innerHTML = html;
    SOAjax.Wiki.addWikiHandlers(this._renderDiv);
    this.set_isLoading(false);
},

onFailure: function(exception, userContext, methodName) {
    Sys.Debug.traceDump(exception, 'Failed callback!');

    Sys.Debug.fail(String.format("The method {0} failed miserably! ({1})",
        methodName, exception.get_message()));
    Sys.Debug.traceDump(this, 'Failed callback!');

},

save: function() {
    Sys.Debug.trace(String.format('WikiControl:save("{0}")', this._topic));
```

```
            this._saveButton.style.display = 'none';
            this._cancelButton.style.display = 'none';
            this._editButton.style.display = '';

            var wikiObject = new Object();
            wikiObject.Body = this._editControl.value;
            wikiObject.Title = this._topic;

            knowledgebase.DataService.SaveData(wikiObject,
                Function.createDelegate(this, this.onSaveCallback),
                Function.createDelegate(this, this.onFailure),
                null); //usercontext

            SOAjax.ClearHandlers(this._renderDiv);
            this._renderDiv.innerHTML = SOAjax.Wiki.wikiToHtml(wikiObject.Body);
            this._rawWiki = wikiObject.Body;
            SOAjax.Wiki.addWikiHandlers(this._renderDiv);
            this.set_editMode(false);
        },

    onSaveCallback: function() {
            Sys.Debug.trace('Save success! ');
        },

    get_topic: function() { return this._topic; },
    set_topic: function(topic) {
            if (this._topic !== topic) {
                this._topic = topic;
                this.raisePropertyChanged('topic');
            }
        },

    get_editMode: function() {
            /// <value type="Boolean">True if we're in edit mode,
            /// otherwise false.</value>
            return this._editMode;
        },
    set_editMode: function(value) {
            Sys.Debug.trace('WikiControl:switching EditMode:' + value);
            if (value !== this.get_editMode()) {
                this._editMode = value;
                this.raisePropertyChanged('editMode');
                if (!this.get_isUpdating()) {
                    // switch to edit if true, otherwise render
                    Sys.UI.DomElement.setVisible(this._editControl, value);
                    Sys.UI.DomElement.setVisible(this._cancelButton, value);
                    Sys.UI.DomElement.setVisible(this._saveButton, value);
                    Sys.UI.DomElement.setVisible(this._editButton, !value);
                    Sys.UI.DomElement.setVisible(this._renderDiv, !value);
                }
            }
        },
```

```
    cancelEdits: function() {
        SOAjax.ClearHandlers(this._renderDiv);
        this._renderDiv.innerHTML = '';
        this.set_editMode(false);
        this._renderDiv.innerHTML = SOAjax.Wiki.wikiToHtml(this._rawWiki);
        SOAjax.Wiki.addWikiHandlers(this._renderDiv);
        this._editControl.value = this._rawWiki;
    },

    // events
    add_editModeChange: function(handler) {
        /// <summary>Adds a event handler for the editModeChange event.</summary>
        /// <param name="handler" type="Function">The handler to add to the event.
        /// </param>
        this.get_events().addHandler("editModeChange", handler);
    },
    remove_editModeChange: function(handler) {
        /// <summary>Removes a event handler for the editModeChange event.</summary>
        /// <param name="handler" type="Function">The handler to remove.</param>
        this.get_events().removeHandler("editModeChange", handler);
    },

    _editModeCallback: function() {
        var handler = this.get_events().getHandler("editModeChange");
        if (handler) {
            handler(this, Sys.EventArgs.Empty);
        }
    },

    dispose: function() {
        Sys.Debug.trace('WikiControl:dispose');

        $clearHandlers(this._editButton);
        $clearHandlers(this._saveButton);
        $clearHandlers(this._cancelButton);

        SOAjax.Purge(this._renderDiv);
        SOAjax.Purge(this._editControl);
        var control = this.get_element();
        if (control) {
            control.removeChild(this._renderDiv);
            control.removeChild(this._editControl);
        }
        SOAjax.Wiki.WikiControl.callBaseMethod(this, 'dispose');
    }
}
SOAjax.Wiki.WikiControl.registerClass('SOAjax.Wiki.WikiControl', Sys.UI.Control);
Sys.Application.notifyScriptLoaded();
```

With load, edit, and save functionality integrated in the wiki control, it's ready to be dropped onto the page and integrated with the application. In the application, the JavaScript page code instantiates the environment with components and creates controls and behaviors from DOM elements. Depending on the complexity of the script, this code may be inline or in a separate file (which can be more maintainable). In most cases, I prefer to keep the page JavaScript code in a separate file, typically in a *pages* subdirectory of *scripts*. In the sample code, I've created a page file named wikipage.js, which is like a JavaScript code-behind file for the wiki ASPX page. This script is shown in Listing 8-17.

LISTING 8-17. The wiki page code-behind JavaScript is used to instantiate and integrate the page, components, and control instances (*Web/Script/WikiPage.js*).

```
/// <reference name="MicrosoftAjax.js"/>
/// <reference path="ApplicationRuntime.js"/>
/// <reference path="CommonControls.js"/>
/// <reference path="SOAjax.js"/>
/// <reference path="WikiControl.js"/>

Type.registerNamespace('WikiPage');

WikiPage.load = function() {

    var isAuthenticated = Sys.Services.AuthenticationService.get_isLoggedIn();
    var startTopic = Sys.Services.ProfileService.properties.startTopic;
    if (startTopic == null || startTopic == '') startTopic = 'Default';

    var wikiElement = $get('_WikiContent');
    Sys.Debug.assert(wikiElement != null,
        '_WikiContent div must be present on page.');

    var wiki = $create(SOAjax.Wiki.WikiControl,
        { editButton: $get('_editButton'),
            saveButton: $get('_saveButton'),
            cancelButton: $get('_cancelButton'),
            tagInput: $get('tagInput')
        },
        null, null, wikiElement);

    wiki.load(startTopic);
    WikiPage.wiki = wiki;

    var appProperties = {
        usernameInput: $get('usernameInput'),
        passwordInput: $get('passwordInput'),
        loginButton: $get('ButtonLogin'),
        cancelLoginButton: $get('ButtonCancelLogin'),
        logoutButton: $get('ButtonLogout'),
        loginUI: $get('loginControl'),
        loggedinUI: $get('logoutControl'),
        loginFeedbackDiv : $get('loginFeedbackDiv')
    };

    var appEvents = { 'authenticated': WikiPage.OnAuthenticated };
    WikiPage.App = $create(SOAjax.Application, appProperties, appEvents);
```

```
        WikiPage.App.updateControls();
        $addHandler($get('loginLink'), 'mouseover', WikiPage.ShowLoginUI);
        $addHandler(window, 'resize', WikiPage.resizeElements);
        WikiPage.resizeElements();
    }

WikiPage.OnAuthenticated = function(sender, eventArgs) {
        Sys.Debug.trace('WikiPage.OnAuthenticated');

        if (Sys.Services.RoleService.isUserInRole('contributor')) {
            //show contributor controls on page
            $get('_EditControls').style.display = '';
        }
        if (Sys.Services.RoleService.isUserInRole('moderator')) {
            // instantiate moderator controls on page
        }
    }

WikiPage.unload = function() {
        wiki = WikiPage.wiki;
        WikiPage.wiki = null;

        if (wiki != null)
            wiki.dispose();
        if (WikiPage.App != null)
            WikiPage.App.dispose();
    }

Sys.Application.add_load(WikiPage.load);
Sys.Application.add_unload(WikiPage.unload);

// code from chapter 5, resize page elements to fill UI.
WikiPage.resizeElements = function() {
        var height;
        if (window.innerHeight) {
            height = window.innerHeight;
        }
        else if (document.body.parentNode.clientHeight) {
            height = document.body.parentNode.clientHeight;
        }
        else if (document.body.offsetHeight) {
            height = document.body.offsetHeight;
        }

        var pageHeader = $get('pageHeader');
        if (pageHeader) {
            var headerBounds = Sys.UI.DomElement.getBounds(pageHeader);
            var contentDivs = ['MainContent', 'NavigationPlaceholder'];
            for (var i = 0; i < contentDivs.length; i++) {
                var content = $get(contentDivs[i]);
                if (content)
                    content.style.height = height - headerBounds.height + 'px';
            }
        }
    }
Sys.Application.notifyScriptLoaded();
```

Summary

In this chapter we examined the Microsoft AJAX Library's *Behavior* and *Control* implementations and event-based programming of DOM elements. You learned how to create controls that aren't bound to implementation details and can be used in multiple contexts. We also looked at complex application controls with Web service integration.

Building on this foundation, we'll look at additional control techniques in the following chapters, including data rendering with XSLT, navigation, and page history with Back button support. Finally, in the last chapter of the book, we'll look at deploying service-oriented AJAX components into Microsoft's enterprise portal, Microsoft Office SharePoint Server.

Chapter 9
AJAX and XSLT

After completing this chapter, you will

- Understand client-side rendering with XSLT.

- Understand basic XSLT and general performance guidelines.

- Understand how to use event handlers for navigating XSLT-rendered data.

- Be able to implement XSLT in custom controls developed with *Sys.UI.Control*.

In the last few chapters, you learned about components and controls using *Sys.Component* and *Sys.UI.Control*. By this point, we've covered the basics of AJAX application programming, including data requests using *Sys.Net.WebRequest* and server-side implementations using Windows Communication Foundation (WCF) SOAP and REST endpoints. In the first part of this chapter, I'll describe XML and XSLT rendering using the AJAX library, and then in Chapter 10, "AJAX and Browser History," I'll examine AJAX navigation challenges and look at the Microsoft AJAX Library's support for managing browser history. I'll also show you how to integrate these principles into the case study application to give you an example of these technologies in action.

XML Rendering with XSLT

One of the most powerful tools in the AJAX toolkit is Extensible Stylesheet Language Transformations (XSLT). XSLT is a simple yet powerful language that transforms XML into HTML or other formats using an XSLT processor, which is built into all modern browsers and indirectly supported in the Microsoft AJAX Library.

I introduced XSLT rendering in Chapter 1, "Service-Oriented AJAX Fundamentals," using a basic XSLT transform. As you've seen in the book so far, XSLT is not required in the AJAX architecture pattern. In many cases, you might end up writing your own rendering logic, as I've done with the wiki case study application. However, in most applications, you need to render structured data in lists and provide additional collaborative functionality on top of the rendered data. To do this, you need a rendering technology that is fast, scales well, and is easy to implement and maintain. For special cases, such as advanced data grids, you might end up creating your own controls and creating control instances for each data row in an aggregate control. But for common rendering tasks, creating a control for each instance doesn't scale well. Instead, templates are ideal for rendering the user interface. These templates can be implemented in a variety of ways, either through JavaScript templates, HTML fragments, or XSLT. In this chapter, we'll take a deeper look at using XSLT to render data on the client.

Although I can't possibly cover XSLT in full in a chapter, I'll cover enough to get you started. With the examples I show and some online documentation, you should have no trouble in beginning to use XSLT in your AJAX applications.

> **More Information** As an alternative to XSLT, you can use JavaScript client-side template rendering, which is part of the ASP.NET AJAX 4.0 future release. For more information, see *http://www.codeplex.com/aspnet*. However, it's my opinion that XSLT is the best choice for client-side rendering for most cases.

From my experience over the past few years, XSLT is a simple approach that makes use of modern tools for developing and debugging, including full support in Microsoft Visual Studio. It's also a faster approach from a performance perspective because string manipulation in JavaScript can be a relatively slow operation, whereas an XSLT transform happens in native code. XSLT is just one option for client-side rendering, however. Choose whichever technology works best for you and your application.

> **Real World** At NewsGator, we've used XML and XSLT in production AJAX code for several years and have found it to be the fastest, simplest, and most powerful and supportable rendering technology for AJAX applications. We use this chapter's technique extensively in the NewsGator Enterprise and NewsGator Social Sites product lines.

Although the Microsoft AJAX Library has no direct support for XSLT, XSLT is supported either through Microsoft XML Core Services technology (*MSXML*) or native browser technology in non-Microsoft browsers. This means that XML code must account for two XML processing models, either MSXML or the native browser's implementation. Internet Explorer 8 will also use native browser methods for XSLT, so very soon MSXML will be used only for backward compatibility in Internet Explorer 6 and 7. The interfaces for both XML models are similar, with a few distinctions that I'll cover in this section. Both XML models are encapsulated in the *Sys.Net.XMLDOM* object in the Microsoft AJAX Library, which is used in the network stack when receiving XML from Web services. However, you need to write a few methods for cross-browser XSLT support for use with the Microsoft AJAX Library.

Figure 9-1 illustrates the role of XSLT in the AJAX application. XSLT is an XML markup language that we'll use to transform XML into HTML that will be added to the browser. For example, you might get a list of products in XML format from a REST service endpoint implemented with WCF.

Keep in mind that client-side XSLT transform files should be simple and should not contain any compiled XSLT extensions, external references, or linked XSLT files. The supported client-side XSLT library is a subset of what you can do in .NET code, so keep it simple. XSLT can also be confusing to developers who are not used to it, so keeping it simple helps the rest of your development team as well.

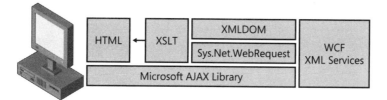

FIGURE 9-1. XSLT can be used to provide rendering logic in the AJAX application architecture.

Keeping your XSLT code simple will address most compatibility issues, but you should also test your XSLT logic in the browsers you want to support. The following guidelines will help you write an XSLT that can run successfully across multiple browsers:

- Avoid external references, and use self-contained XSLT files. Linked XSLT files will not be loaded in the browser, and this is not a technique you can use with an AJAX application. As an alternative, you can merge XSLT files on the server to implement shared XSLT resources.

- Test any XSLT functions you use in all supported browsers. Only the simplest XSLT functions are universally supported in the browser. Specifically, string functions are not universally implemented.

- Don't include JavaScript in the XSLT output. If you do, there's a high likelihood of generating invalid JavaScript when you use real data.

- Create one XSLT file for each supported view of a data schema.

- Above all, keep your XSLT small and lightweight. Ideally, the XSLT file should be less than 200 lines of code, although this is just a guideline from my experience.

 More Information Although I've found the browser's built-in XSLT support to be sufficient, Google has a robust XSLT library for AJAX available under a BSD-style license. You might want to look at Google's AJAXSLT project at *http://goog-ajaxslt.sourceforge.net/*.

XSLT Basics

XSLT, also referred to as *XSL*, is a simple XML-based language for transforming XML into other formats. In its most common use, XSLT transforms XML into HTML, but XSLT can also be used for any output format, including text or XML. In contrast to HTML, XSLT is a procedural language in that you can develop templates and rules for specific XML formats and nodes. XSLT is run through an XSL processor, either a server-side framework such as the .NET Framework, a client library such as MSXML, or the native Web browser.

Although Visual Studio has an item template for XSLT files, we'll use a simpler syntax. Before we go further, let's look at a basic Hello World XSLT file. Listing 9-1 shows an XSLT file that outputs the text "Hello, World!" while matching the root XML element.

Note Code for this book is available online at *http://www.microsoft.com/mspress/companion/ 9780735625914*. The code for this chapter is in the file Chapter 9.zip.

LISTING 9-1. A simple XSLT file matches the root node and applies further processing instructions (*Web/ XML/HelloWorld.xslt*).

```
<?xml version="1.0" encoding="UTF-8" ?>
<xsl:stylesheet version="1.0" xmlns:xsl="http://www.w3.org/1999/XSL/Transform">
    <xsl:output omit-xml-declaration="yes" method="html" encoding="utf-16" />

    <xsl:template match='/'>
        Hello, World!
    </xsl:template>

</xsl:stylesheet>
```

Tip While Visual Studio does include an item template for an XSLT document, the template uses the advanced expanded XSLT syntax, which can be difficult to follow unless you're an experienced XSLT developer. When developing XSLT resources in my AJAX libraries, I'll start by replacing the contents of the XSLT file generated by Visual Studio with a root template match, as shown in Listing 9-1.

XSLT is based on XPath (*XML Path Language*), a simple way to select nodes in an XML document. The slash character (/) delimits XML elements, and a single slash is used to select the root element. Therefore, the XSL template defined in Listing 9-1 always matches any root element with the root template definition and inserts the contents of the template ("Hello, World!") into the output.

Tip Because XSLT is based on XPath, it's important to understand basic XPath notation. There are two XPath notation styles, an abbreviated notation and an expanded notation. To keep matters simple, I'll use the abbreviated notation in this book. In fact, I recommend always using the abbreviated syntax in AJAX applications because it is a simpler format.

XSLT has two basic constructs as its building blocks: the *template* and *value-of* elements. The *xsl:template* element defines a template that is processed in response to a match in the XML file. The *template* element has a *match* attribute that causes the element to be processed when a match from the XML document is found. Basically, the XML document starts at the root node and processes any matches found in the XSLT. Each *template* generally defines some output text or HTML and nested *select* statements, which cause additional elements to be processed recursively.

The *xsl:value-of* element outputs the text value of the XPath expression it defines. Also of importance is the *apply-templates* element, which instructs the XSLT processor to process any additional matches at the current level. The XSLT processor always processes the XML document as it traverses the node set—that is, it starts at the root element and recursively processes any matches that are defined by the XSLT document.

> **Tip** I'll cover the basics of XSLT and XPath in this book, but you might want to pick up an additional reference or simply use MSDN online documentation.

For the following XSLT examples, we'll use the following XML document as the input data. The document defines a simple data structure for a list of books that I've written, with two books defined so far. Each book has an *id* attribute and elements that define its authors.

```
<books>
  <book id="soAJAX">
    <title>Service Oriented AJAX on the Microsoft Platform</title>
    <author>
      <name>Daniel Larson</name>
      <url>http://daniellarson.spaces.live.com</url>
    </author>
  </book>
  <book id="insideWSS">
    <title>Inside Microsoft Windows SharePoint Services 3.0</title>
    <author>
      <name>Ted Pattison</name>
      <url>http://tedpattison.com</url>
    </author>
    <author>
      <name>Daniel Larson</name>
      <url>http://daniellarson.spaces.live.com</url>
    </author>
  </book>
</books>
```

When processing XSLT, you must always start at the root of the document because the XSLT processor always starts with the root XML element and processes it. The processor only processes matches, so if you include only a rule matching a *book* element, the rule will not be processed. To select the root of the document, use a slash. You can also specify a match only for a specific root element by using the slash, such as */books*. In the sample document, you would want to select the */books* element and then process each *book* node. The following rules would be used to match books in the sample document. Keep in mind that the rule for */books* will only match the root element for books.

```
<xsl:template match='/books'>
  <xsl:apply-templates />
</xsl:template>

<xsl:template match='book'>
  <!-- Process each book element here. -->
</xsl:template>
```

> **Tip** You might want to create an alternative root match rule for error handling so that you can render friendly error messages for known errors.

You can select child elements from the currently selected node simply by using their name. For example, while the code is processing the XSL template that matches the */books* element, you can select the child *book* nodes by defining a rule for *book*. For example, to select the XML element *<book>*, define a template with the rule *match='book'*. Within the *book* template, you would use *value-of* elements, which select the value of the given XPath expression. For example, to match the XML element *title*, select *'title'*. To select attributes, use the @ sign. For example, to select the *id* attribute, select *'@id'*. The following code sample demonstrates a simple *select* statement for the *title* element and the *id* attribute.

```
<xsl:template match='book'>
    Book: <xsl:value-of select='title'/>
    (<xsl:value-of select='@id'/>)
</xsl:template>
```

> **Tip** To select elements, use the slash (/) to delimit named element nodes. A preceding slash indicates the document root element. For example, the path */foo/bar* would select the *bar* node under the *foo* root element.

XML and XPath expressions are namespace sensitive. Namespaces in XML documents are used to disambiguate data schemas. When using WCF technologies such as the Data Contract Serializer, namespaces are implemented automatically in the generated XML and are based on the namespace defined on the data contract. For example, the preceding code sample might be a specialized book library schema for your custom application. In that case, you might not be able to understand all XML formats for *books*, but you do know how to handle the book schema that you've defined. To create a namespace in an XML element, define it on the root node as in the following example:

```
<books xmlns="http://mylibrary" />
```

The addition of the *xmlns* attribute specifies the default namespace for the document. This also changes the XPath expressions for the document. In the sample XML document, with the XML namespace added, the root node *books* is represented by the XPath expression

/lib:books, assuming that the XML namespace *http://mylibrary* has been assigned to the prefix *lib*. Namespaces are used in XSLT documents to define known elements. You'll see more examples of XML namespaces in the next section when we implement a real-world use case.

Creating an XSLT View

In the XSLT-based AJAX architecture, you might want to create one or more views per data schema. Each view is implemented through a template and used to render data based on a data schema. The data schema you use is defined by the WCF service's data contract. In the following example, I'll create a navigational control based on a list of topics. The Catalog service defined at the endpoint *http://localhost:8080/Web/Services/CatalogService. svc/Default/Topics* produces an XML document similar to Listing 9-2. It's important to have a source XML document when you develop the XSLT so that you can test the output as you work. Listing 9-3 demonstrates the output document from the sample application's Catalog service.

LISTING 9-2. To begin developing XSLT files, save an XML sample data file.

```
<ArrayOfLink xmlns="http://knowledgebase"
     xmlns:i="http://www.w3.org/2001/XMLSchema-instance">
  <Link>
    <Title>AJAX</Title>
    <Catalog>Default</Catalog>
  </Link>
  <Link>
    <Title>Default</Title>
    <Catalog>Default</Catalog>
  </Link>
</ArrayOfLink>
```

To start creating an XSLT view, begin with a simple XSLT file using the Visual Studio XSLT template as previously described. In the root *xsl:stylesheet* element, you need to define any XML namespaces that your document uses. For the sample application, the XML namespace *http://knowledgebase* is used. In the XSLT document, assign a prefix to the namespace in the root node. This prefix is used to alias the XML namespace. The XML namespace definition *xmlns:kb="http://knowledgebase"* is used in the sample code, so *kb* can be used in XPath expressions to alias the namespace *http://knowledgebase*.

You also need to define the output type of the XSLT file. To declare an HTML fragment, use the following tag inside the root *xsl* element. The use of this tag prevents an XML declaration from being included in the output, and it instructs the XSLT processor to render HTML.

```
<xsl:output omit-xml-declaration="yes" method="html" encoding="utf-16" />
```

One advantage of using XSLT is that you can use Visual Studio to debug your XSL logic against a source file. In your Visual Studio project, save the sample XML file from the input. Next, to debug the XSLT, open the XSLT file and choose Debug XSLT from Visual Studio's XML menu. You might be prompted to choose a source file for the XML input, which is saved in the project as a property of the XSLT file. You can set break points in the XSLT file to examine the XML nodes at the selected path. Figure 9-2 demonstrates the Visual Studio XSLT debugging process.

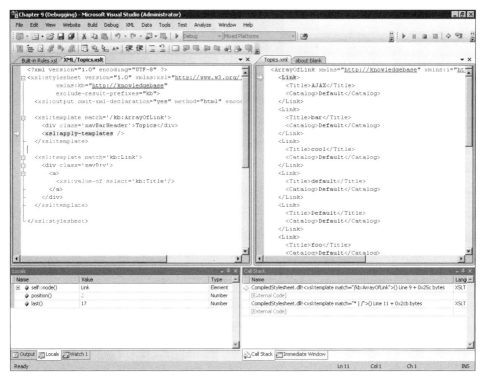

FIGURE 9-2. Visual Studio provides debugging support for XSLT code.

After generating and testing the basic XSLT structure, you're ready to start defining template rules. A *template rule* is a processing instruction for a given XPath path, and it usually defines a block of markup to render and any child template rules to process. In our example, we're expecting a root element with the XPath expression */kb:ArrayOfLink*. This XPath rule matches the root *ArrayOfLink* element defined in the *http://knowledgebase* namespace. The following XSL template will match the root node of our expected XML document and include the test "Topics" before continuing to process any child nodes. The processing command *<xsl:apply-templates />* instructs the XSLT engine to process any other matches at the currently selected document element.

```
<xsl:template match='/kb:ArrayOfLink'>
    <div class='navBarHeader'>Topics</div>
    <xsl:apply-templates />
</xsl:template>
```

As a best practice, include any styles in a CSS definition, defined either in the page or in a global CSS file (although not all of my code samples will reflect this, for simplicity's sake).

Finally, for each link, we'll include an HTML anchor element inside of a DIV element. You should avoid writing JavaScript in the XSLT because it's too easy to create invalid JavaScript from user input. Instead, you should use post-processing to attach event handlers to the anchor elements by using *Sys.UI.DomEvent.addHandler*, as first introduced in Chapter 5, "The Microsoft AJAX Library." Listing 9-3 displays the final XSLT file we'll use for the topics list in the navigation element.

LISTING 9-3. The XSLT file can be very simple (*Web/XML/Topics.xslt*).

```
<?xml version="1.0" encoding="UTF-8" ?>
<xsl:stylesheet version="1.0" xmlns:xsl="http://www.w3.org/1999/XSL/Transform"
        xmlns:kb="http://knowledgebase"
        exclude-result-prefixes="kb">
    <xsl:output omit-xml-declaration="yes" method="html" encoding="utf-16" />

    <xsl:template match='/kb:ArrayOfLink'>
        <div class='navBarHeader'>Topics</div>
        <xsl:apply-templates />
    </xsl:template>

    <xsl:template match='kb:Link'>
        <div class='navDiv'>
            <a><xsl:value-of select='kb:Title' disable-output-escaping='yes'/></a>
        </div>
    </xsl:template>

</xsl:stylesheet>
```

Listing 9-3 also shows a new attribute on the *stylesheet* element: *exclude-result-prefixes*. This attribute prevents the namespace from being rendered in the output HTML. Without this attribute, you end up with the HTML containing *xmlns:kb="http://knowledgebase"*. You can specify a space-delimited list of prefixes to exclude in the *exclude-result-prefixes* attribute.

If the text you are transforming is to include HTML markup (rather than plain text), be sure to include the processing instruction *disable-output-escaping="yes"*. Without this attribute, the XSLT processor might output escaped HTML. For example, the following XSLT rule for the *title* XML element allows the processor to output HTML rather than escaped HTML:

```
<xsl:value-of select='kb:title' disable-output-escaping="yes" />
```

After validating the XSLT, you are ready to use it in the AJAX application. I prefer saving the XSLT files in an XML directory for the application, although you can save them anywhere in the Web application. These XSLT files can be loaded as needed by the AJAX client application. Loading files on this basis doesn't add considerable overhead because XSLT loads very quickly on the client, as fast as loading an additional CSS file or image.

XML on the Client

To create a new XML document using the Microsoft AJAX Library, you can use the class *Sys.Net.XMLDOM*. This class is included in the AJAX library and is used internally to create XML documents from Web service calls made through classes defined in the *Sys.Net* namespace.

> **Tip** Prior to the Microsoft AJAX Library 3.5, ASP.NET AJAX Extensions 1.0 implemented the XML object in the class *XMLDOM* (without the *Sys.Net* namespace). In the 3.5 library, this class is part of the *Sys.Net* namespace, a breaking change if you used the class in legacy applications. To write JavaScript that runs on the ASP.NET AJAX Extensions 1.0, include the following line in your code:
>
> ```
> if (Sys$Net$XMLDOM)  XMLDOM = Sys$Net$XMLDOM;
> ```

By examining the source code of *Sys.Net.XMLDOM* you can get a better understanding of the XML processing engine. All non-Microsoft browsers include the native browser object *window.DOMParser,* which is used to implement an XML object. Microsoft browsers (Internet Explorer 5.5, 6.0, and 7.0) use the MSXML library to implement the XML parser. The MSXML 3.0 library is used consistently for all Windows operating systems since Windows 2000 SP4, including Windows XP, Windows Server 2003, Windows Vista, and Windows Server 2008. Listing 9-4 contains the *Sys.Net.XMLDOM* function from the Microsoft AJAX Library. By examining the code, you can see more clearly how the framework provides support for the MSXML library in Internet Explorer or just uses *window.DOMParser* in other modern browsers.

LISTING 9-4. *Sys.Net.XMLDOM* provides support for MSXML in Internet Explorer and for the browser's native XML technology for non-Microsoft browsers (excerpt from *MicrosoftAjax.debug.js.*).

```
// Excerpt from the Microsoft AJAX Library
Sys.Net.XMLDOM = function Sys$Net$XMLDOM(markup) {
    if (!window.DOMParser) {
        var progIDs = ['Msxml2.DOMDocument.3.0', 'Msxml2.DOMDocument'];
        for (var i = 0, l = progIDs.length; i < l; i++) {
            try {
                var xmlDOM = new ActiveXObject(progIDs[i]);
                xmlDOM.async = false;
                xmlDOM.loadXML(markup);
                xmlDOM.setProperty('SelectionLanguage', 'XPath');
                return xmlDOM;
            } catch (ex) {}
        }
    } else {
        try {
            var domParser = new window.DOMParser();
            return domParser.parseFromString(markup, 'text/xml');
        } catch (ex) {}
    }
    return null;
}
```

As I've mentioned before, while Internet Explorer uses the MSXML implementation, other browsers, including Mozilla Firefox, Apple Safari, Google Chrome, and Opera, use native browser objects for processing XML. When writing XML support into your application, it's important to check between the ActiveX model and the native browser model, which we'll demonstrate in the following example.

A simple method for transforming XML with XSLT is shown in Listing 9-5. In the sample code, this method is included in the utility library SOAjax.js. You'll notice that the XSLT transform is a simple one-line command using MSXML in Internet Explorer, which is the only browser that doesn't implement the *XSLTProcessor* method. Other browsers implement the same interface for XSLT, letting you use common code for all other cases. With browsers other than Internet Explorer, you might end up with encoded output in certain cases, for example RSS feeds with encoded HTML. In this case, you need to decode the escaped HTML characters, as implemented in the *SOAjax.HtmlDecode* method, also shown in Listing 9-5.

LISTING 9-5. A simple method for transforming XML with XSLT (from *SOAjax.js*).

```
// XML TOOLKIT
SOAjax.XmlTransform = function(xml, xsl, control, decode) {
    var decode; if (decode == null){decode = true;}
    if (decode == null) decode = true;
    if (!window.XSLTProcessor) // ie, using MSXML:
        control.innerHTML = xml.transformNode(xsl);
    else {  // MOZZILA
        Sys.Debug.trace('XSLT using XSLTProcessor');
        Sys.Debug.trace(typeof (XSLTProcessor));
        var processor = new XSLTProcessor();
        processor.importStylesheet(xsl);
        var content = processor.transformToFragment(xml, document);
        if (decode) {
            var div = document.createElement('div');
            div.appendChild(content);
            control.innerHTML = SOAjax.HtmlDecode(div.innerHTML);
        } else {
            control.appendChild(content);
        }
    }
}
//   client side version of the useful Server.HtmlDecode method
//   takes an encoded string and returns the decoded string.
SOAjax.HtmlDecode = function HtmlDecode(enc) {
    return enc.replace(/&quot;/gi, String.fromCharCode(0x0022))
        .replace(/&amp;/gi, String.fromCharCode(0x0026))
        .replace(/&lt;/gi, String.fromCharCode(0x003c))
        .replace(/&gt;/gi, String.fromCharCode(0x003e));
}
```

XML processing can be a fundamental building block for your AJAX library. In fact, you can implement nearly all the code for an application's user interface by using client-side XSLT and a little bit of JavaScript. As mentioned earlier, however, it is important to keep your stylesheets compact, simple, and maintainable. If several views use the same data structure, use a common XSLT file. For example, you can use the same XSLT file for lists of people whether they're online users, site contributors, or friends. The user interface is best designed by data views coded against a schema, not the relationship of the data. This strategy helps you reuse common XSLT assets in your application.

Building an XML Control

To implement XSLT in a control, you can create a control class that loads data and XSLT on demand. This class can be used as a building block throughout multiple applications, either as a base class or to provide full functionality. An XML control implementation is a very powerful component in your AJAX toolkit and can be used to build entire applications. In the next section, I'll walk through the creation of an XML control and then show how to integrate it into the sample application. To build a control for XML loading and rendering, you want to build a control class with the interface defined in Table 9-1.

TABLE 9-1. The XML Control Interface

Methods	Description
loadXML(url)	Loads the XML data from the specified URL.
loadXSLT(url)	Loads the XSLT data from the specified URL.
reload	Causes the data to be reloaded from the server.
reloadInterval	When set, causes the control to reload on an interval.
Properties	**Description**
xml	The XML source data.
xslt	The XSLT used for rendering.
Events	**Description**
error	Raised when an error occurs in the data load or XSLT transform.
prerender	Raised before rendering. Used to pre-process the rendered HTML by clearing any DOM event handlers from the prior render.
render	Raised after the XSLT render. Used to add any DOM event handlers to the rendered HTML.
xmlLoaded	Raised when the XML is loaded from the data source.
xsltLoaded	Raised when the XSLT is loaded from the XSLT URL.

The significant methods of the XML control will be for data loading and transformation. We can also implement a timer function so that the control can refresh itself at arbitrary intervals and present live data to the user. To load the data, we'll implement fairly standard logic to load XML from an arbitrary endpoint that will be set from client code. Listing 9-6 demonstrates the methods used to load the XML.

LISTING 9-6. To implement a client-side XML control, create methods to load XML data at will (from *Web/ Script/Controls/XmlControl.js*).

```
_loadXml: function(url) {
    if (this._timeoutID) window.clearTimeout(this._timeoutID);
    this.xmlUrl = url;
    if (url == null || url == '') return;
    var request = new Sys.Net.WebRequest();
    var context = new Object();
    request.add_completed(Function.createDelegate(this, this._loadXmlComplete));
    request.set_userContext(context);
    request.set_url(url);
    request.invoke();
},

_loadXmlComplete: function(response) {
    if (response == null) { response = new Sys.Net.WebRequestExecutor(); }
    var context = response.get_webRequest().get_userContext();
    var status = response.get_statusCode();
    var url = response.get_webRequest().get_url();
    var xml;
    if (status == 200) {
        try {
            var lastMod = response.getResponseHeader('Last-Modified');
            if (lastMod && lastMod != '' && this._lastMod == lastMod) {
                this.queueReload();
                return;
            }else this._lastMod = lastMod;
            xml = response.get_xml();
            if (xml == null)
                xml = response.get_responseData();
            if (!xml) throw Error.create(
                'We could not load the XML data at the URL ' + url);
            var xmlLoadedHandler = this.get_events().getHandler('xmlLoaded');
            if (xmlLoadedHandler) xmlLoadedHandler(this, Sys.EventArgs.Empty);
            this.set_xml(xml);
        } catch (e) {
            Sys.Debug.fail('Could not process callback method.');
        }
    }
    else if (status == 304) { // not modified, not handled by the browser.
        this.queueReload();
    }
    else { // Process the status. Could be 401, 404 (not found), 410 (gone)
        var statusText = response.get_statusText();
        Sys.Debug.trace(String.format('ERROR: {0} replied "{1}" ({2}).',
            url, statusText, status));
        var errorHandler = this.get_events().getHandler('error');
        if (!errorHandler) {   // Default error handler
            switch (status) {
                case 410: // HttpStatusCode.Gone:
                    alert('Content has been removed.');
                    break;
```

```
                    case 404: // HttpStatusCode.NotFound:
                        alert('Could not find resource.');
                        break;
                    default:
                        alert(String.format('ERROR: {0} replied "{1}" ({2}).',
                            url, statusText, status));
                }
            } else {
                errorHandler(response, Sys.EventArgs.Empty);
            }
        }
    }
},
```

As with the XML logic, we need to implement a method for loading XSLT. The method for
loading XSLT is simpler because we won't implement error handling for the Web request.
These errors will be caught during development rather than in production code. Listing 9-7
demonstrates the logic for loading XSLT in the XML control.

LISTING 9-7. Client-side AJAX code must be able to load XSLT on the client on demand (from *Web/Script/
Controls/XmlControl.js*).

```
loadXslt: function(url) {
    this.xslUrl = url;
    if (url == null || url == '') return;
    var request = new Sys.Net.WebRequest();
    Sys.Debug.trace("XSLT Load: " + url);
    request.add_completed(Function.createDelegate(this, this._loadXsltComplete));
    request.set_url(url);
    request.invoke();
},


_loadXsltComplete: function(response) {
    var context = response.get_webRequest().get_userContext();
    var status = response.get_statusCode();
    var xml;
    if (status == 200) {
        try {
            xml = response.get_xml();
            if (xml == null)
                xml = response.get_responseData();
            var xsltLoadedHandler = this.get_events().getHandler('xsltLoaded');
            if (xsltLoadedHandler) xsltLoadedHandler(this, Sys.EventArgs.Empty);
            if (xml) this.set_xslt(xml);
        } catch (e) {
            var errorHandler = this.get_events().getHandler('error');
            if (errorHandler) errorHandler(response, Sys.EventArgs.Empty)
            else
                Sys.Debug.trace('Could not process callback method.');
        }
    }
},
```

For both the *xml* and *xslt* properties, when the XML content is set we can call the *render* method. The *render* method can be private, which is inferred by prefixing the method name with an underscore. The following logic is in both the *xml* and *xslt* properties.

```
if (this._xml && this._xslt) this._render();
```

The *render* method simply wraps the *SOAjax.XmlTransform* utility method (previously shown in Listing 9-3) with prerender and postrender handlers. These handlers call the handlers for the *prerender* event and the *render* event. The following code shows the *render* method, which is called as soon as both the XML and XSLT are loaded:

```
_render: function() {
    Sys.Debug.trace('XmlControl Render');
    var control = this.get_element();
    if (control == null || this._xml == null || this._xslt == null)
        return;

    var prerenderHandler = this.get_events().getHandler('prerender');
    if (prerenderHandler) prerenderHandler(this, Sys.EventArgs.Empty);

    SOAjax.XmlTransform(this._xml, this._xslt, control);
    control.style.display = '';
    this._rendered = true;

    var renderHandler = this.get_events().getHandler('render');
    if (renderHandler) renderHandler(this, Sys.EventArgs.Empty);
}
```

The full *XmlControl* class is shown in Listing 9-8. With this control, you can implement very rich applications using XML source data and client-side rendering on demand. In the following code samples, we'll utilize *XmlControl* in the case study application while adding more functionality to the rendered HTML through DOM events.

LISTING 9-8. The *XmlControl* class is a standard control used for XML loading and rendering (*Web/Script/Controls/XmlControl.js*).

```
/// <reference name="MicrosoftAjax.js"/>
Type.registerNamespace('SOAjax.Controls');

SOAjax.Controls.XmlControl = function(element) {
    /// <summary>
    /// A component that loads and renders XML using XSLT on the client.
    /// </summary>
    SOAjax.Controls.XmlControl.initializeBase(this, [element]);
}

SOAjax.Controls.XmlControl.prototype = {
    _xml: null,
    _xslt: null,
    _xsltUrl: null,
    _xmlUrl: null,
```

```
_reloadInterval: null,
_interval: null,
_timeoutID: null,
_lastMod: null,

get_xml: function() {
    /// <value>Gets or sets the XML data for the control.</value>
    return this._xml;
},
set_xml: function(value) {
    if (this._xml !== value) {
        this._xml = value;
        this.raisePropertyChanged('xml');
    }
    if (this._xml && this._xslt) this._render();
},

get_xslt: function() {
    /// <value>Gets or sets the XSLT for the control.</value>
    return this._xslt;
},
set_xslt: function(value) {
    if (this._xslt !== value) {
        this._xslt = value;
        this.raisePropertyChanged('xslt');
    }
    if (this._xml && this._xslt) this._render();
},

get_xsltUrl: function() {
    /// <value>The URL to load the XSLT from.</value>
    return this._xsltUrl;
},
set_xsltUrl: function(value) {
    if (this._xsltUrl !== value) {
        this._xsltUrl = value;
        this.raisePropertyChanged('xsltUrl');
        if (this._xsltUrl && !this.get_isUpdating())
            this._loadXslt(this._xsltUrl);
    }
},

get_xmlUrl: function() {
    /// <value>The URL to load the data from.</value>
    return this._xmlUrl;
},
set_xmlUrl: function(value) {
    if (this._xmlUrl !== value) {
        this._lastMod = null;
        this._xmlUrl = value;
        this.raisePropertyChanged('xmlUrl');
        if (this._xmlUrl && !this.get_isUpdating())
            this._loadXml(this._xmlUrl);
    }
},
```

```
get_reloadInterval: function() {
    /// <value>The interval at which we'll reload the control.</value>
    return this._reloadInterval;
},
set_reloadInterval: function(value) {
    if (this._reloadInterval !== value) {
        if (value != 0 && value < 99) {
            throw Error.argumentOutOfRange('reloadInterval',
                value, 'The reload interval must be 0 or over 100 milliseconds.');
        }
        this._reloadInterval = value;
        this.raisePropertyChanged('reloadInterval');
    }
},

reload: function() {
    if (this._timeoutID) window.clearTimeout(this._timeoutID);
    this._reload();
},

_reload: function() {
    var xmlUrl = this.get_xmlUrl();
    if (xmlUrl != null) { this._loadXml(xmlUrl); }
},

// Events -------------------------------------------------------
add_xmlLoaded: function(handler) {
    /// <value>Bind and unbind to the xmlLoaded event.</value>
    this.get_events().addHandler('xmlLoaded', handler);
},
remove_xmlLoaded: function(handler) {
    this.get_events().removeHandler('xmlLoaded', handler);
},

add_xsltLoaded: function(handler) {
    /// <value>Bind and unbind to the xsltLoaded event.</value>
    this.get_events().addHandler('xsltLoaded', handler);
},
remove_xsltLoaded: function(handler) {
    this.get_events().removeHandler('xsltLoaded', handler);
},

add_render: function(handler) {
    /// <value>Bind and unbind to the render event.</value>
    this.get_events().addHandler('render', handler);
},
remove_render: function(handler) {
    this.get_events().removeHandler('render', handler);
},

add_prerender: function(handler) {
    /// <value>Bind and unbind to the prerender event.</value>
    this.get_events().addHandler('prerender', handler);
},
```

```
remove_prerender: function(handler) {
    this.get_events().removeHandler('prerender', handler);
},

add_error: function(handler) {
    /// <value>Bind and unbind to the error event.</value>
    this.get_events().addHandler('error', handler);
},
remove_error: function(handler) {
    this.get_events().removeHandler('error', handler);
},

initialize: function() {
    SOAjax.Controls.XmlControl.callBaseMethod(this, 'initialize');
    if (this._xsltUrl && !this.get_isUpdating())
        this._loadXslt(this._xsltUrl);
    if (this._xmlUrl && !this.get_isUpdating())
        this._loadXml(this._xmlUrl);
},

_loadXml: function(url) {
    if (this._timeoutID) window.clearTimeout(this._timeoutID);
    this.xmlUrl = url;
    if (url == null || url == '') return;
    var request = new Sys.Net.WebRequest();
    var context = new Object();
    request.add_completed(Function.createDelegate(this, this._loadXmlComplete));
    request.set_userContext(context);
    request.set_url(url);
    request.invoke();
},

_loadXmlComplete: function(response) {
    if (response == null) { response = new Sys.Net.WebRequestExecutor(); }
    var context = response.get_webRequest().get_userContext();
    var status = response.get_statusCode();
    var url = response.get_webRequest().get_url();
    var xml;
    if (status == 200) {
        try {

            var lastMod = response.getResponseHeader('Last-Modified');
            if (lastMod && lastMod != '' && this._lastMod == lastMod) {
                this.queueReload();
                return;
            }
            else this._lastMod = lastMod;

            xml = response.get_xml();
            if (xml == null)
                xml = response.get_responseData();
            if (!xml) throw Error.create(
                'We could not load the XML data at the URL ' + url);
```

```
                    var xmlLoadedHandler = this.get_events().getHandler('xmlLoaded');
                    if (xmlLoadedHandler) xmlLoadedHandler(this, Sys.EventArgs.Empty);
                    this.set_xml(xml);
                } catch (e) {
                    Sys.Debug.fail('Could not process callback method.');
                }
            }
            else if (status == 304) { // not modified, not handled by the browser.
                this.queueReload();
            }
            else { // Process the status. Could be 401, 404 (not found), 410 (gone)
                var statusText = response.get_statusText();
                Sys.Debug.trace(String.format('ERROR: {0} replied "{1}" ({2}).',
                    url, statusText, status));
                var errorHandler = this.get_events().getHandler('error');
                if (!errorHandler) {    // Default error handler
                    switch (status) {
                        case 410: // HttpStatusCode.Gone
                            alert('Content has been removed.');
                            break;
                        case 404: // HttpStatusCode.NotFound
                            alert('Could not find resource.');
                            break;
                        default:
                            alert(String.format('ERROR: {0} replied "{1}" ({2}).',
                                url, statusText, status));
                    }
                } else {
                    errorHandler(response, Sys.EventArgs.Empty);
                }
            }
        }
    },

    _loadXslt: function(url) {
        this.xslUrl = url;
        if (url == null || url == '') return;
        var request = new Sys.Net.WebRequest();
        Sys.Debug.trace("XSLT Load: " + url);
        request.add_completed(Function.createDelegate(this,
            this._loadXsltComplete));
        request.set_url(url);
        request.invoke();
    },
    _loadXsltComplete: function(response) {
        var context = response.get_webRequest().get_userContext();
        var status = response.get_statusCode();
        var xml;
        if (status == 200) {
            try {
                xml = response.get_xml();
                if (xml == null)
                    xml = response.get_responseData();
                var xsltLoadedHandler = this.get_events().getHandler('xsltLoaded');
```

```
                if (xsltLoadedHandler) xsltLoadedHandler(this, Sys.EventArgs.Empty);
                if (xml) this.set_xslt(xml);
            } catch (e) {
                var errorHandler = this.get_events().getHandler('error');
                if (errorHandler) errorHandler(response, Sys.EventArgs.Empty)
                else
                    Sys.Debug.trace('Could not process callback method.');
            }
        }
    },

    _render: function() {
        var control = this.get_element();
        if (control == null || this._xml == null || this._xslt == null)
            return;
        var prerenderHandler = this.get_events().getHandler('prerender');
        if (prerenderHandler) { prerenderHandler(this, Sys.EventArgs.Empty); }
        SOAjax.XmlTransform(this._xml, this._xslt, control);
        this._rendered = true;
        var renderHandler = this.get_events().getHandler('render');
        if (renderHandler) renderHandler(this, Sys.EventArgs.Empty);
        this.queueReload();
    },

    queueReload: function() {
        if (this._timeoutID) window.clearTimeout(this._timeoutID);
        // Only queue a reload if we have a valid reload interval (over 100 ms):
        if (this._reloadInterval && this._reloadInterval > 100) {
            this._timeoutID = window.setTimeout(
                String.format("SOAjax.Controls.XmlControl.Refresh('{0}')",
                    this.get_element().id),
                    this._reloadInterval);
        }
    },
    dispose: function() {
        ///<summary>Release resources before control is disposed.</summary>
        var element = this.get_element();
        if (element) { try { $clearHandlers(this.get_element()); } catch (e) { } }
        SOAjax.Controls.XmlControl.callBaseMethod(this, 'dispose');
    }
}
SOAjax.Controls.XmlControl.registerClass(
    'SOAjax.Controls.XmlControl', Sys.UI.Control);

SOAjax.Controls.XmlControl.Refresh = function(elementID) {
    var xmlControl = $find(elementID);
    if (xmlControl && xmlControl.reload)
        xmlControl.reload();
}
Sys.Application.notifyScriptLoaded();
```

To create an instance of *XmlControl* on a page, you can use the *$create* method of *Sys.Component*, passing in the *xmlUrl* and *xsltUrl* properties. (We discussed the *$create* method in depth in Chapter 8, "Building AJAX Controls.") In the following examples, we'll use the Topics.xslt file (defined earlier in Listing 9-3), which transforms the topics from the Catalog service into a repeating list of DIV elements with an anchor tag. Each topic is rendered as the following HTML:

```
<div><a>AJAX</a></div>
```

The generated link for each topic will fire a navigation event for the wiki control. The approach we'll take is to add an AJAX event handler for the *click* event rather than generate JavaScript code in the XSLT file.

> **Tip** When rendering JavaScript in the XSLT, there's a high likelihood of error. One common point of error is introduced with the apostrophe. One of the bugs that occurs most often in software is the result of invalid output when a user's name contains an apostrophe, which is common in Irish names such as O'Brien. Regardless, *whenever* users can input text, there's a high likelihood of error. For example, if a topic was based on Dave O'Brien and the JavaScript method was rendered by XSLT, the following HTML, with an invalid JavaScript method, would be output, and this would cause an error when added to the page:
>
> ```
> <a onclick="javascript:alert('Dave O'Brien')">AJAX</a>
> ```
>
> Instead, it's best to render pure HTML with no JavaScript in AJAX XSLT implementations and instead attach an event handler to process the *click* event.

Listing 9-9 demonstrates a test page for the *XmlControl* class that adds a handler to the *prerender* and *render* events of *XmlControl* to add functionality to the rendered HTML. In a real-world use case we would fire a navigation event. The typical use for the dynamic *XmlComponent* class is a data set that is navigable or that might be updated frequently, instead of data that is rendered once. Because you might have previously attached event handlers, if you are re-rendering the control, you need to clear them to prevent memory leaks. Any time you add handlers, you need to remove them when the content is removed from the page or when the page is closed or reloaded. For example, in the XML control's *prerender* handler, you need to remove any handlers you might have added in a prior rendering before the content is cleared and rendered again.

In the example in Listing 9-9, the handler itself simply processes the innerHTML of the target element as in the following code, which simply alerts the content of the link element that was clicked. In the following section, we'll convert this to a navigational link:

```
function topicHandler(domEvent, eventArgs){
    alert(domEvent.target.innerHTML);
}
```

As an alternative to the innerHTML of the element, you can also access attributes of the HTML element. This approach is useful if you are using database-generated unique identifiers as method parameters. The following source code demonstrates a simple handler that is added to the *click* event. In the next sample, we'll integrate the *XmlControl* class into the case study wiki application to see a real-world use with object orientation.

LISTING 9-9. *XmlControl* is a staple in the AJAX Web application and is instantiated with an XML data source URL, an XSLT URL, and a DOM element (*Web/XmlControl.aspx*).

```
<%@ Page Language="C#" %>
<html xmlns="http://www.w3.org/1999/xhtml">
<head runat="server">
    <title>Service Oriented AJAX: XmlControl test page</title>
    <script type="text/javascript">

        function preRenderHandler(sender, eventArgs){
            var element = sender.get_element();
            var links = element.getElementsByTagName('A');
            for (var i = 0; i < links.length; i++) {
                $clearHandlers(links[i]);
            }
        }
        function renderHandler(sender, eventArgs){
            var element = sender.get_element();
            var links = element.getElementsByTagName('A');
            for (var i = 0; i < links.length; i++) {
                $addHandler(links[i], 'click', topicHandler);
            }
        }

        function topicHandler(domEvent, eventArgs){
            // add intellisense to domEvent
            if(domEvent == null){
                domEvent = new Sys.UI.DomEvent(null);
                throw Error.argumentNull();
            }
            alert(domEvent.target.innerHTML);
        }

        function pageLoad() {
            initDebug();
            var props = {
                xmlUrl: '/Web/Services/CatalogService.svc/Default/Topics',
                xsltUrl : '/Web/XML/Topics.xslt'
            };
            var events = { prerender: preRenderHandler, render: renderHandler };
            var xmlElement = $get('testControl');
            var xmlControl =
                $create(SOAjax.Controls.XmlControl, props, events, null, xmlElement);
        }

    </script>
</head>
```

```
<body>
    <form id="form1" runat="server">
        <asp:ScriptManager ID="ScriptManager1" runat="server">
            <Scripts>
                <asp:ScriptReference Path="~/Script/Controls/SOAjax.js" />
                <asp:ScriptReference Path="~/Script/Controls/XmlControl.js" />
            </Scripts>
        </asp:ScriptManager>
        <div id="testControl" />
    </form>
</body>
</html>
```

Case Study: Implementing Navigation in the Wiki Application with an Xml Control

Xml controls can be used to render the main content or navigational controls in a typical AJAX application. In the following code samples, I explain how to implement a navigational control from XML entries listing the contents of the knowledge base. We've already developed the XSLT based on the topics list from the Catalog service. All that is left is to wire up navigation events between the navigation control and the wiki control.

When you are rendering links for navigation, you might want to make it clear to the user that the link is indeed clickable. To do that, you can add the following style rule to the CSS for the application:

```
a { color:Blue; text-decoration:'underline'; cursor:pointer; }
```

XmlControl is a great example of object-oriented programming in JavaScript, where a simple object can be used to perform complex tasks. The *XmlControl* class can be extended through static utility methods for complex functionality, as you'll see in the following examples.

To create a navigational control in the wiki page, we use the *$create* method to create an instance of *XmlControl*. The *XmlControl* JavaScript source file must also be added to the page. The following code can be added to the *WikiPage.load* method, which is called on the *Sys.Application.load* event.

```
var props = {
    xmlUrl: '/Web/Services/CatalogService.svc/Default/Topics',
    xsltUrl: '/Web/XML/Topics.xslt'
};
var events = { prerender: WikiPage.clearWikiNavLinks, render: WikiPage.addWikiNavLinks };
var xmlElement = $get('NavigationPlaceholder');
var xmlControl = $create(SOAjax.Controls.XmlControl, props, events, null, xmlElement);
```

To implement the navigation method, the *WikiPage* class defines a utility method that finds the wiki component by using *Sys.Application.findComponent ($find)* and then calls the *load* method, which causes the wiki to load new data for the selected topic. Listing 9-10 demonstrates the *wikiNav* function that is called from delegates attached to DOM events.

LISTING 9-10. A navigation event handler must be created to handle navigation DOM events (from *Web/Script/WikiPage.js*).

```
WikiPage.wikiNav = function(domEvent, eventArgs) {
    // Find the wiki:
    var wiki = $find('_WikiContent');
    wiki.load(domEvent.target.innerHTML);
}
```

To implement the navigation delegates that call *WikiPage.wikiNav*, the *WikiPage* class defines two utility methods that add and remove navigation handlers to the *click* DOM event. To add handlers, we simply look for all the *A* elements in *XmlControl* and attach a DOM handler. In this example, the innerHTML of the *A* element contains all the data we need to load the new data set. Listing 9-11 shows the *XmlControl* handlers that are used to manage navigational links.

LISTING 9-11. Event handlers for prerender and postrender events are used to attach DOM event handlers (from *Web/Script/WikiPage.js*).

```
WikiPage.addWikiNavLinks = function(sender, eventArgs) {
    var element = sender.get_element();
    var links = element.getElementsByTagName('A');
    for (var i = 0; i < links.length; i++) {
        $addHandler(links[i], 'click', WikiPage.wikiNav);
    }
}

WikiPage.clearWikiNavLinks = function(sender, eventArgs) {
    var element = sender.get_element();
    var links = element.getElementsByTagName('A');
    for (var i = 0; i < links.length; i++) {
        $clearHandlers(links[i]);
    }
}
```

As you can see from these code samples, a trivial amount of code is required to implement rich AJAX functionality in an application based on the *XmlControl* class, making it a favorite in my AJAX development toolkit. The full source code for *XmlControl* and *WikiControl* is available in this chapter's sample code.

Summary

In this chapter we examined XSLT support by using methods from the Microsoft AJAX Library as well as custom code and native browser support for XSLT. Using these techniques, we developed a custom control class that implements XML loading and XSLT operations, and we looked at a real-world use of *XmlControl* for a navigational control in the wiki application.

 At this point, you should be able to implement XSLT rendering in your own JavaScript components based on *Sys.UI.Control*. In the next chapter, I'll expand on *XmlControl* and navigation as we look at navigation and history support in the Microsoft AJAX Library.

Chapter 10
AJAX and Browser History

After completing this chapter, you will

- Understand the importance of navigational history and Back button support.

- Understand the Microsoft AJAX Library's support for history using *Sys.Application*.

- Be able to implement history in your AJAX application.

- Be able to support the Back and Forward buttons in the Web browser.

In the last few chapters we've examined the Microsoft AJAX Library in depth, along with its support for components, behaviors, controls, and rendering. Throughout the book, you've seen how to implement an AJAX application from the ground up using Web services for application functionality. As page-based navigation has been replaced with AJAX navigation, the overall usability of the Web application has increased, but the navigational usability of the Web application has decreased. In this chapter we'll look at navigation and history support that lets users navigate in an AJAX Web application with ease.

The History Problem

In traditional Web applications, the URL of the page identifies its content, which is static for the lifetime of the page instance. After the page is loaded, either a form post (a *postback*) or a refresh is required to get new data. The Web browser remembers these actions in its history, and a user can navigate backward and forward.

When you remove URL-based navigation, replace it with JavaScript navigation, and load data on demand from the client rather than on page loading, you lose support for browser history. Worse, users still expect history support, which means that when they click the Back button in the browser, they expect to go back to the previously loaded context rather than the page they were viewing before logging on to your application.

Consider this scenario: A user opens her Web browser and sees her home page. Then she enters the URL of your application, logs on, and navigates around. After several minutes of activity, browsing and creating content, the user clicks the Back button expecting to go to the previous page of data. But because you implemented your application as one physical page with an AJAX data model, the user navigates back to her home page. It's now difficult and confusing for that user to navigate to the context she was looking for and expecting.

 Tip Supporting browser history and navigation adds a tremendous amount of usability and polish to your AJAX application.

History Support in the Microsoft AJAX Library

You can implement history in JavaScript by serializing the current state of the page or a control and storing that object as a history point. As a user performs actions, history points are saved in the *Sys.Application* object. These history points are accessed as the user navigates with the Back or Forward button, allowing the user to return to previous application contexts.

To enable history support in the *Sys.Application* object, you need to set the ScriptManager control to enable history. The property *EnableHistory* enables AJAX history support for all modern browsers by using a combination of a hidden IFrame, form actions, the URL, and the browser's native history API. Because different browsers implement history differently, the actual implementation can vary depending on what browser you're using, but the interface stays the same. The constant interface is a huge benefit of the AJAX library because you don't have to worry about developing code for each browser—the fine folks at Microsoft have done this for you and will continue to support future browsers in service packs and future frameworks.

Note Some modern browsers, including Internet Explorer 8 and Firefox 3.0, support history through a native JavaScript API, but older browsers require intricate programming to implement history support in JavaScript. Fortunately, as browsers continue to evolve, future releases and service packs of the .NET Framework will add support for new browsers using the current API of the *Sys.Application* object.

History Support with the ScriptManager Control

To support browsing history, a page must have an instance of the ScriptManager server control with *EnableHistory* set to *true*. Certain browsers, such as FireFox, might not need this property enabled through the server control, but it is a requirement for Internet Explorer versions 6 and 7. The following ScriptManager instance allows history support, although this example only adds *support* for history—you have to add history points and handle the *navigate* event through custom code.

```
<asp:ScriptManager runat="server" EnableHistory="true" />
```

When *EnableHistory* is set in the ScriptManager, the page elements required to support history for the current browser are included, and the method *Sys.Application._enableHistoryInScriptManager* is added to the page, setting the *enableHistory* property of the *Sys.Application* JavaScript object to *true*.

Tip The ScriptManager's property *EnableSecureHistoryState* has no effect on a client-side history implementation. It only encrypts history using partial postbacks with the UpdatePanel. To hide history on the client, you need to implement your own client-side encryption or encoding, but this would only obfuscate the history at best.

History Support with the Client-Side *Sys.Application* Object

Sys.Application includes the following property, event, and method for history support:

- **enableHistory**   This property gets or sets history support through the *Sys.Application* framework. This property isn't usually set from custom code; instead it is set by the ScriptManager control during page loading. Custom code can detect whether history is enabled by calling the *get_enableHistory* method. As a standard AJAX library property, *enableHistory* is accessed through the methods *Sys.Application.get_enableHistory* and *Sys.Application.set_enableHistory(bool)*.

- **navigate**   This event is fired from *Sys.Application* when a user navigates to a history point. This event is always fired with an instance of *Sys.HistoryEventArgs* containing the state of the history point. To add or remove an event handler for the *navigate* event, use the methods *Sys.Application.add_navigate(handler)* and *Sys.Application. remove_navigate(handler)*.

- **addHistoryPoint**   This method is used by custom code to add history points. To add a history point, call the method *Sys.Application.addHistoryPoint(state, title)*, where the *state* parameter must be a dictionary of strings that is used to serialize the state of the object, and the *title* parameter is a string used to set the title of the page in the browser's history.

To add a history point, use the method *Sys.Application.addHistoryPoint* with a *state* parameter that includes a dictionary of key-value pairs that identify the current state of the application. The *state* parameter will be serialized and stored after the hash (#) in the browser's URL. The following sample serializes three simple values in history, creating three history points that are accessible via the Web browser's Back and Forward buttons.

```
var state = { message : "Hello World!" };
Sys.Application.addHistoryPoint(state, "Welcome");

var italianState = { message : "Ciao mondo!" };
Sys.Application.addHistoryPoint(italianState, "Benvenuto");

var frenchState = { message : "Bonjour monde!" };
Sys.Application.addHistoryPoint(frenchState, "Bienvenue");
```

By creating these history points with *Sys.Application*, the browser creates three history entries, titled "Welcome," "Benvenuto," and "Bienvenue." When the user clicks Back or Forward, these *state* objects are sent in the *HistoryEventArgs* instance to the *navigate* event handler. The *HistoryEventArgs* class is a simple class with one property, *state*. To create a handler for the *navigate* event, use the standard AJAX library event handler signature:

```
function handler(sender, eventArgs){}
```

The *eventArgs* parameter is an instance of the *HistoryEventArgs* class. You can then use the *state* property to access the serialized state. Because any code could have created the entry point (not necessarily the class you're currently coding in), be sure to check whether it's a serialized *state* object that you want to handle. The following code sample demonstrates a handler for the *navigate* event, adding Visual Studio IntelliSense support to the method body.

```
function onHistoryNavigate(sender, eventArgs) {
    if (eventArgs == null) {
        eventArgs = new Sys.HistoryEventArgs();
        throw Error.invalidOperation('Expected Sys.HistoryEventArgs');
    }
    var state = eventArgs.get_state();
    if (state.message) {
        Sys.Debug.trace(state.message);
    }
}
```

To add the handler to the *navigate* event, use the *add_navigate* method as follows:

```
Sys.Application.add_navigate(onHistoryNavigate);
```

As an alternative to adding an event handler through JavaScript, you can define a global history event handler in the ScriptManager control by setting the *ClientNavigateHandler* property, although this approach isn't a best practice. Regardless, the following code sample demonstrates how to add the static JavaScript function *SOAjax.Examples.OnHistoryNavigate* as a global history event handler:

```
<asp:ScriptManager runat="server" EnableHistory="true"
    ClientNavigateHandler="SOAjax.Examples.OnHistoryNavigate" />
```

When you add a history point, the *navigate* event is immediately raised and calls any handlers added to the event. Because the *navigate* event is raised, you most likely want to use the same event handler that implements history to process the user action—or you might end up with your code being called twice.

Listing 10-1 shows the complete code sample for a very simple history implementation. Keep in mind that when the *addHistoryPoint* method is called, the *navigate* method is also immediately called. This means that the *onHistoryNavigate* handler is also called for each history point. After the code runs, the page displays "Bonjour monde!" with two prior history points, and the user is able to navigate through the three application states using the Back and Forward buttons on the browser.

 Tip Code for this book is available online at *http://www.microsoft.com/mspress/companion/ 9780735625914*. The code for this chapter is in the file Chapter 10.zip.

LISTING 10-1. To implement history, add history points and handle the *navigate* event (*Web/ SimpleHistoryDemo.aspx*).

```
<%@ Page Language="C#" %>
<html xmlns="http://www.w3.org/1999/xhtml">
<head>
    <title>A simple history demo</title>

    <script type="text/javascript">
        function pageLoad() {
            Sys.Application.add_navigate(onHistoryNavigate);

            var state = { message: "Hello World!" };
            Sys.Application.addHistoryPoint(state, "Welcome");

            var italianState = { message: "Ciao mondo!" };
            Sys.Application.addHistoryPoint(italianState, "Benvenuto");

            var frenchState = { message: "Bonjour monde!" };
            Sys.Application.addHistoryPoint(frenchState, "Bienvenue");
        }

        function onHistoryNavigate(sender, historyEventArgs) {
            if (historyEventArgs == null) {
                historyEventArgs = new Sys.HistoryEventArgs();
                throw Error.invalidOperation('Expected Sys.HistoryEventArgs');
            }
            var state = historyEventArgs.get_state();
            if (state.message) {
                $get('Greeting').innerHTML = state.message;
            }
        }
    </script>
</head>
<body>
    <form id="form1" runat="server">
    <div>
        <asp:ScriptManager runat="server" EnableHistory="true" />
        <div id="Greeting"></div>
    </div>
    </form>
</body>
</html>
```

Listing 10-1 demonstrates a simple history implementation using an event handler and history points. To add history support to an instance of an AJAX control, you need to create a *state* object that serializes its state and identifies the state with the control, because multiple controls could exist on the page, each implementing history points.

To demonstrate history in a control instance, Listing 10-2 shows an example of a control defined as the *SOAjax.Examples.DataControl* class. This control adds AJAX navigation links to the *A* elements defined in the control's DOM element and simulates data loading and rendering by rendering the navigation value in a DIV. The code in Listing 10-3 instantiates the control on page loading.

LISTING 10-2. The *DataControl* is a simple control simulating a more complex AJAX component (*Web/Script/ DataControl.js*).

```
/// <reference name="MicrosoftAjax.js"/>
Type.registerNamespace ('SOAjax.Examples');

SOAjax.Examples.DataControl = function (element) {
    /// <summary>A control to demonstrate history.</summary>
     SOAjax.Examples.DataControl.initializeBase (this, [element]);
}

SOAjax.Examples.DataControl.prototype = {
    onHistoryNavigate: function(sender, historyEventArgs) {
        ///<summary>Handles browser navigation through history points</summary>

        // Adds intellisense to the method body:
        if (historyEventArgs == null) {
            historyEventArgs = new Sys.HistoryEventArgs();
            throw Error.argumentNull(); }

        // State is a dictionary of params that serialize the current state.
        var state = historyEventArgs.get_state();

        // Only handle history for this control instance
        if (state.controlID && state.controlID == this.get_id()) {
            this.loadData(state.data);
        }
    },

    loadData: function(id) {
        ///<summary>Simulates an AJAX method that would load & render data</summary>
        $get('data', this.get_element()).innerHTML = id;
    },

    onNavigate: function(domEvent, eventArgs) {
        ///<summary>Handles navigation through the AJAX page links</summary>
        var id = domEvent.target.getAttribute('nav');
        if (Sys.Application.get_enableHistory()) {
            var title = domEvent.target.innerHTML;
            var state = { controlID: this. get_id(), data: id};
            Sys.Application.addHistoryPoint(state, title);
        } else
        this.loadData(id);
    },

    initialize: function() {
        ///<summary>Initialize the component.</summary>
        Sys.Application.set_enableHistory(true);
        SOAjax.Examples.DataControl.callBaseMethod(this, 'initialize');
```

```
        this.historyDelegate = Function.createDelegate(
            this, this.onHistoryNavigate);
        Sys.Application.add_navigate(this.historyDelegate);

        this.navigationDelegate = Function.createDelegate(this, this.onNavigate);
        var element = this.get_element();
        var links = element.getElementsByTagName('A');
        for (var i = 0; i < links.length; i++) {
            $addHandler(links[i], 'click', this.navigationDelegate);
        }
    },

    dispose: function() {
        ///<summary>Release resources before control is disposed.</summary>
        var element = this.get_element();
        if (element) {
            $clearHandlers(this.get_element());
            var links = element.getElementsByTagName('A');
            for (var i = 0; i < links.length; i++) {
                $clearHandlers(links[i]);
            }
        }

        if (this.historyDelegate) {
            Sys.Application.remove_navigate(this.historyDelegate);
            delete this.historyDelegate;
        }
        if (this.navigationDelegate) delete this.navigationDelegate;
        SOAjax.Examples.DataControl.callBaseMethod(this, 'dispose');
    }
}
SOAjax.Examples.DataControl.registerClass(
    'SOAjax.Examples.DataControl', Sys.UI.Control);

Sys.Application.notifyScriptLoaded();
```

By examining the code in Listing 10-2, you can see several details. The *onNavigate* event handler method is added through a delegate to the DOM element's *click* event, a technique we discussed in Chapter 9, "AJAX and XSLT." This method parses the relevant data from the control that fires the event and serializes it into the *state* object. This object is then passed to the *Sys.Application.addHistoryPoint* method to create a history point for this action and a page title for the history point. Because *Sys.Application*'s *addHistoryPoint* method fires the *navigate* event, you don't need to call the control's *loadData* method—the *onHistoryNavigate* event handler calls it. If you were to add a history point and call *loadData* from the DOM element's handler, the *loadData* method would be called twice. To be sure that your code works even when history support is not enabled, wrap the history code in an *if* block that checks the *enableHistory* property of *Sys.Application*.

The code in Listing 10-3 demonstrates a simple page with two DOM elements, each of which creates an instance of the sample *DataControl* in the page load method. Because the control is coded to handle history only for the current instance, each instance handles its own history.

LISTING 10-3. The ScriptManager supports history through the *EnableHistory* attribute (*Web/History.aspx*).

```
<%@ Page Language="C#" %>
<html xmlns="http://www.w3.org/1999/xhtml" >
<head>
    <title>History Demo</title>
    <style type="text/css">
        a { color:Blue; text-decoration:'underline'; cursor:pointer; }
        #display { font-size:larger; padding:10px; border:solid 2px black;}
    </style>
    <script language="javascript" type="text/javascript">
        function pageLoad() {
            $create(SOAjax.Examples.DataControl,
                null, null, null,
                $get('HistoryTestControl'));

            $create(SOAjax.Examples.DataControl,
                null, null, null,
                $get('HistoryTestControl2'));
        }
    </script>
</head>
<body>
    <form id="form1" runat="server">
    <asp:ScriptManager runat="server" EnableHistory="true" >
        <Scripts>
            <asp:ScriptReference Path="script/DataControl.js" />
        </Scripts>
    </asp:ScriptManager>

    <div id="HistoryTestControl">
        <span id="display">
            JavaScript Data: <span id="data">[]</span>
        </span>
        <br /><br />
        <div>
            <a nav="1">Test 1</a><br />
            <a nav="2">Test 2</a><br />
            <a nav="3">Test 3</a><br />
            <a nav="4">Test 4</a><br />
            <a nav="5">Test 5</a><br />
        </div>
    </div>

    <div id="HistoryTestControl2">
        <span id="display">
            JavaScript Data: <span id="data">[]</span>
        </span>
        <br /><br />
        <div>
```

```
                <a nav="6">Test 6</a><br />
                <a nav="7">Test 7</a><br />
                <a nav="8">Test 8</a><br />
                <a nav="9">Test 9</a><br />
                <a nav="10">Test 10</a><br />
            </div>
        </div>

        </form>
    </body>
    </html>
```

Case Study: Adding History to the Wiki Application

The wiki knowledge base application we've worked on in previous chapters is a larger-scale application than the simple code samples present. The main functionality for the application is provided in a *WikiControl* instance that implements the *Sys.UI.Control* class and renders content that is loaded on demand from Windows Communication Foundation (WCF) back-end services. The *WikiControl* instance also lets users edit and save content through Web services. Additionally, the application includes authentication logic and an external navigation component that lets users navigate through links in the content or through an external catalog of topics that is rendered as an *XmlControl* (a control that loads XML data and renders it using client-side XSLT), which we implemented in Chapter 9.

In the application, we don't want to implement history support for user actions such as logging in or out, or even actions such as editing data. Instead we want to support history wherever users perform navigational actions. Although a user can browse through the wiki content by performing one of several navigational actions, the *WikiControl* itself is responsible for loading the data. The *load* method, which is called to cause the wiki to load data for the specified topic, is called by several code paths and is the most appropriate place to add history support. Here is the code for the *load* method:

```
load: function(topic) {
    this.set_isLoading(true);
    this._topic = topic;
    this._titleDiv.innerHTML = topic;
    SOAjax.ClearHandlers(this._renderDiv);
    this._renderDiv.innerHTML = 'Loading...';
    this._editControl.value = '';

    Sys.Debug.trace(String.format('WikiControl:load("{0}")', this._topic));

    knowledgebase.DataService.GetData(this._catalog, this._topic,
        Function.createDelegate(this, this.onLoadComplete),
        Function.createDelegate(this, this.onFailure),
        this);
}
```

To add history support, we can break the *load* method into three methods. These new methods are defined in Listing 10-4. First we'll change the *load* method to a private method called *_load*. Next we'll add a method named *load* that simply creates a history point. Upon creation of the history point, the *navigate* event is raised, and this event will be handled by the newly created *onHistoryNavigate* method. The *onHistoryNavigate* method in turn determines whether the event's history is from this control instance by comparing the *controlID* that identifies the history state with its own ID. If it is, *onHistoryNavigate* calls the private *_load* method. This strategy ensures that the *WikiControl* does not handle history state that was generated by another control.

LISTING 10-4. The *WikiControl* demonstrates the design pattern for history support (*Web/Script/Controls/ WikiControl.js*).

```
load: function(topic) {
    if (Sys.Application.get_enableHistory()) {
        var state = { controlID: this.get_id(), topic: topic };
        Sys.Application.addHistoryPoint(state, topic);
    } else {
        this._load(topic);
    }
},

onHistoryNavigate: function(sender, historyEventArgs) {
    var state = historyEventArgs.get_state();
    if (state.controlID == this.get_id()) {
        this._load(state.topic);
    }
},

_load: function(topic) {
    this.set_isLoading(true);
    this._topic = topic;
    this._titleDiv.innerHTML = topic;
    SOAjax.ClearHandlers(this._renderDiv);
    this._renderDiv.innerHTML = 'Loading...';
    this._editControl.value = '';

    Sys.Debug.trace(String.format('WikiControl:load("{0}")', this._topic));

    knowledgebase.DataService.GetData(this._catalog, this._topic,
        Function.createDelegate(this, this.onLoadComplete),
        Function.createDelegate(this, this.onFailure),
        this);
}
```

After implementing the *navigate* handler as demonstrated in Listing 10-4, the next step is to add the *navigate* event handler to the actual *navigate* event. In the *WikiControl*'s *initialize* method, the following code can be used to create a delegate to the event handler and add it to *Sys.Application*'s *navigate* event:

```
this.historyDelegate = Function.createDelegate(this, this.onHistoryNavigate);
Sys.Application.add_navigate(this.historyDelegate);
```

When adding the handler to the *initialize* event, it's also important to remove it in the *dispose* event. The following sample code removes and deletes the *historyDelegate* in the *dispose* method of the *WikiControl*:

```
if (this.historyDelegate) {
    Sys.Application.remove_navigate(this.historyDelegate);
    delete this.historyDelegate;
}
```

With this technique, you can add history support to an existing AJAX control with minimal coding effort. You simply serialize the control's state in an object and add it as a history point. The framework handles creating the history point, and the control loads the data—whether it's coming from a direct user action such as a navigation click or the user clicks the Back or Forward button.

 Tip The entire code sample for the AJAX wiki application is available online at *http://www.microsoft.com/mspress/companion/9780735625914*.

Summary

In this chapter, you learned about the importance of supporting the Back button in the AJAX application. We looked at the Microsoft AJAX Library's support for browser history through history points and *Sys.Application*. We looked at some simple examples and a control implementation, demonstrating how to support history in multiple independent controls. Finally, we added history support to the knowledge base case study application without affecting the application's overall architecture.

At this point, you should be able to add history support to AJAX controls and components using *Sys.Application* history points, and you should be able to handle the *navigate* event to implement navigation.

By this point in the book, you should be comfortable building back-end data services using WCF and you should be proficient at creating AJAX components and controls using the Microsoft AJAX Library to implement AJAX applications. In the last chapter, I'll show how you can apply these techniques to enterprise portal development using Microsoft's portal server technology, Microsoft Windows SharePoint Services 3.0.

Chapter 11
Extending SharePoint with Service-Oriented AJAX

After completing this chapter, you will

- Understand Windows SharePoint Services as an application platform.

- Understand the basic SharePoint programming model of sites and services.

- Be able to implement Web services that are integrated with the SharePoint site context.

- Implement contract-based Web services using HTTP handlers and WCF technologies.

- Understand the Web Part programming model and how to deploy AJAX controls in Web Parts.

- Understand how to integrate and deploy AJAX application code to the SharePoint server.

Introducing the SharePoint Application Platform

The SharePoint application platform is a portal server that runs natively on the ASP.NET framework, providing sites and services for developing and delivering large-scale collaborative Web applications in the enterprise and on the Internet. While SharePoint development can't be fully explained in a chapter, I'll provide a brief overview in the following sections and then focus on service development and AJAX integration in the portal environment. As in previous chapters, the examples I provide will use a service-oriented API as the core of the application.

 More Information For an in-depth look at SharePoint as a development platform, see my other book, with Ted Pattison, *Inside Microsoft Windows SharePoint Services 3.0* (Microsoft Press, 2007). This chapter, and in fact this book, is based on the architectural principles introduced in our chapter on AJAX Web Parts.

The term *SharePoint* applies to both Microsoft Office SharePoint Server, also known as MOSS or SharePoint Server, and Windows SharePoint Services 3.0 (WSS), the core platform. WSS is included in Windows Server 2003 and Windows Server 2008, making it an ideal platform for ASP.NET portal applications. WSS is a site-provisioning platform in which application provisioning components are built by a developer and instantiated and customized by the business user. Provisioning components include site templates, page layouts, list definitions, Web Part applications, and Web service extensions. SharePoint Server builds on the WSS platform by adding enterprise search, a social platform that includes colleagues and user profiles, My Site personal site templates, and publishing and content management components.

> **Tip** In the rest of the chapter, I'll refer to SharePoint as a generic term that applies to WSS and SharePoint Server.

SharePoint has gained tremendous momentum in the market and is deployed in virtually every Fortune 500 company, even when a company has invested in competing portal servers. Both its ease of use and the SharePoint developer community have contributed to its success. Its widespread deployment makes SharePoint an ideal platform for the ASP.NET AJAX developer to learn.

While SharePoint is basically just an ASP.NET application, it does have some nuances that make it challenging to work with. To soften the learning curve, the following steps will get you up and running with SharePoint in no time. If you're a seasoned SharePoint developer, you may want to skip over the next section.

The SharePoint Virtualized Web Application

SharePoint sites are virtualized in a Web application that is managed by the WSS runtime, which is based on an IIS Web application, file system templates, and Microsoft SQL Server database content. SharePoint sites exist entirely in the database as records of site instances.

One SharePoint *Web application* is created for each Internet Information Services (IIS) Web site through the SharePoint Central Administration Web site (available by choosing Start, Administrative Tools, SharePoint 3.0 Central Administration), and each Web application can have one or more *site collections*. Each site collection can contain one or more *sites*, which correspond to virtual directories and contain the main context for the application. A SharePoint site can be created by any user (with appropriate rights) and contains the social, task, and security contexts that the application executes in. The site can contain pages and lists, and lists can contain list items.

Each site is based on a file system template, which exists in the Program Files directory. The ASPX pages exist in the database based on these templates and can be customized with Web Parts that exist in DLLs. Pages can also be created and deployed to SharePoint sites through site features that add an instance of a file to the site's virtualized file system.

The default Web application is typically located at *C:\inetpub\wwwroot\wss\VirtualDirectories\80*. We'll use this path in text and in this chapter's sample code, but this path may vary depending on your installation. This application directory is where the main Web.config file is located that you will edit for your Web application, although all other content in the site exists in the SharePoint virtual file system.

The SharePoint virtual file system is implemented in SQL Server. This virtual file system is used for content in SharePoint sites, including pages and files that are stored in the application.

The Layouts Directory

SharePoint's _layouts directory is an ideal place to deploy code that extends every SharePoint site. This path is virtualized and exists as a subpath to every SharePoint site's URL. For example, a SharePoint site that exists at the URL http://mysharepointserver/myorg/myteam would be able to access the *layouts* virtual directory through the URL *http://mysharepointserver/ myorg/myteam/_layouts/.* This directory is served entirely through the file system and is mapped to the file path \Program Files\Common Files\Microsoft Shared\Web Server Extensions\12\TEMPLATE\LAYOUTS. SharePoint uses files in this location for managing sites and for any resource or Web page that is part of every site. The *layouts* directory is also an ideal place to serve JavaScript files, CSS files, images, and Web service endpoints such as WCF SVC files.

In the sample code in this chapter, we'll create the folder SOAjax.Services in the *layouts* directory to host our WCF endpoints and the folder SOAjax.Script to host the client runtime for our AJAX applications. Code that is run in the *_layouts* directory should be deployed to the global assembly cache (GAC).

> **Tip** A similar directory to *layouts* is the *_vti_bin* directory, which is virtualized just as *layouts* and is used by the SharePoint Web service API. This directory is located at \Program Files\Common Files\Microsoft Shared\Web Server Extensions\12\ISAPI\ and is available through the Web-relative URL *http://sharepointserver/mysharepointsite/_vti_bin/.* As with code deployed to the *layouts* folder, you should create subdirectories for custom code and include your own web.config file for WCF configuration. Although some developers prefer *_vti_bin*, I'll use *_layouts* in this chapter.

Web Service Options for SharePoint

SharePoint includes support for ASMX services and has a relatively complete set of ASMX Web services. Unfortunately, these Web services aren't AJAX enabled, and in many cases they aren't very JavaScript friendly either. SharePoint also includes a URL protocol that implements a Web-style API. (For details on this, search on the Web for "SharePoint URL Protocol.")

To create a custom Web service API in SharePoint, there are three recommended options: WCF, ASMX, and HTTP handlers. Each option has its own benefits and drawbacks. ASMX Web services are used throughout the product itself, but this option isn't recommended for developing new code. WCF is particularly challenging to integrate into the SharePoint environment. It might not be the best approach for commercial applications built on the current release of the SharePoint platform (as of service pack 1), but it is the best long-term approach. WCF is the most flexible option for developing service-oriented APIs for SharePoint. While WCF is not fully supported in the current release, it will be included in future releases.

To support WCF, additional configuration must be deployed to the SharePoint runtime. If you have full control over the SharePoint server, WCF is an option to consider. However, if you are creating and reselling third-party solutions, be cautious about taking a WCF approach within the SharePoint environment. If you are creating REST service endpoints serving XML content, you can still use WCF attributes to define the contract and simply wrap the service in an ASP.NET handler. This is the approach we'll take in this chapter, and with this approach, you gain the benefits and flexibility of the WCF Web programming model without any configuration changes to the SharePoint runtime.

With an HTTP handler wrapping the WCF endpoint, you can easily move from HTTP handlers to WCF endpoints using the Web programming model without any change in functionality. HTTP handlers and handler factories can be registered through web.config, in the *httpHandlers* node. Using this technique (which was demonstrated at the end of Chapter 2, "The AJAX Application Server: Service Orientation and the Windows Communication Foundation"), an *IHttpHandlerFactory* is created in an assembly and registered to a handler mapping in web.config. HTTP handlers can be used to wrap WCF Web service classes, giving you a great future-proof solution. I'll demonstrate this technique throughout this chapter. First, you will see how to create a WCF service, including the data contract. Then you will wrap the service implementation with an HTTP handler using *DataContractSerializer*. With this technique, it's trivial as to which technology services the request (HTTP handlers or WCF) because it is processed in the same manner.

To run WCF in the SharePoint application, you must alter the SharePoint runtime through a custom virtual path provider. This technique and instructions for integrating WCF with full access to the SharePoint site context is described in the document "WCF Support in SharePoint" available on the book's companion content Web site at *http://www.microsoft. com/mspress/companion/9780735625914*. After WCF support is enabled, WCF must be run in ASP.NET compatibility mode as documented in Chapter 2. Because of this, I favor using an HTTP handler and wrapping the service implementation in the handler, but I'll also demonstrate the WCF approach. You can run the same code samples through WCF endpoints by deploying an SVC file that utilizes *WebServiceHostFactory*.

More Information In the code download for this chapter, support for WCF can be added to SharePoint by adding a specialized *VirtualPathProvider* to the SharePoint runtime through a custom HTTP module. The document "WCF Support in SharePoint," included in the book's companion content, provides instructions for configuring WCF support in SharePoint.

The Web Part Application

The most common way to extend SharePoint is by adding Web Parts. (You can also add pages without Web Parts using SharePoint Features, which is the recommended approach for full-page AJAX applications, but I won't cover Features in this book.) Web Parts exist as classes that inherit from *System.Web.UI.Controls.WebPart* and are a pre-AJAX technology deeply rooted in the SharePoint platform. Code for Web Part applications must be deployed to the GAC or the Web application's *bin* directory, just as you would deploy code to a typical ASP.NET Web application. Web Part assemblies and namespaces must also be registered in web.config, and they can be added to the Web Part gallery through the Sites Settings link from the root-level SharePoint site.

If you're new to SharePoint, you'll want to read the sidebar "Setting up the SharePoint Developer Environment," but seasoned SharePoint developers probably want to skip to the section "Deploying Code Through Web Parts."

Setting up the SharePoint Developer Environment

The recommended SharePoint development environment is an instance of Windows Server 2008 or Windows 2003 Server running Windows SharePoint Services 3.0 or MOSS. While WSS is available as a free download from *http://microsoft.com/SharePoint*, Windows Server is required to run it. Before you get started, identify an instance of Windows Server for your development environment, either in a virtual environment or a dedicated computer, with Visual Studio 2008 installed as your development environment. The following steps apply to an environment with Windows SharePoint Services 3.0 fully installed.

> **Tip** While you can run Windows Server as a virtual environment on a product such as Virtual PC, I prefer to run Windows Server 2008 as my main development operating system. This can be an ideal platform for development and everyday use if you have access to a license through the Microsoft Developer Network.

After installing SharePoint and configuring a default Web application (which is done for you in a basic installation), the following steps configure the SharePoint instance for development by enabling debugging and full trust. These steps are intended for development only. Experienced SharePoint developers will not want to run in full trust but to configure CAS (code access security) from an installation package.

First you should enable error messages in the *layouts* directory. (I'll talk about the *layouts* directory soon). To do this, open \Program Files\Common Files\Microsoft Shared\ Web Server Extensions\12\TEMPLATE\LAYOUTS\Web.config, and set *customErrors* to *"Off"*:

```
<customErrors mode="Off" />
```

Next open the Web application's Web.config file. This file will exist in the root of your SharePoint Web application. By default, it is located at *\inetpub\wwwroot\wss\VirtualDirectories\80*, although this could be a different path depending on your configuration. There will be multiple directories in this path, with one that is used for the SharePoint Central Administration application. The folder you want to edit is the one used by the Web application you are targeting. To verify the location of the Web application, view the Web site properties in IIS Manager. Make the following changes to the SharePoint Web application's web.config file:

1. Set *trust* to *Full*. For production applications, you should create a custom trust level for your code, although that is outside the scope of this book.

   ```
   <trust level="Full" originUrl="" />
   ```

2. Set customErrors to Off:

   ```
   <customErrors mode="Off" />
   ```

3. Enable full error messages by enabling the call stack in the *SafeMode* element:

   ```
   <SafeMode MaxControls="200" CallStack="true" DirectFileDependencies="10"
   TotalFileDependencies="50" AllowPageLevelTrace="false">
   ```

4. Enable AspNetCompatibilityMode for WCF. Add the following element at the end of Web.config, just before the close of the *configuration* tag:

   ```
   <system.serviceModel>
       <serviceHostingEnvironment aspNetCompatibilityEnabled="true" />
   </system.serviceModel>
   ```

   Because the SharePoint object model is designed to run as an ASP.NET Web application with full code impersonation, enabling ASP.NET compatibility mode allows the WCF code to run and behave just as native SharePoint code.

5. Add the following handler element to the *httpHandlers* node, which is used by ASP.NET to serve the Microsoft AJAX Library script files:

   ```
   <add verb="GET,HEAD" path="ScriptResource.axd"
       type="System.Web.Handlers.ScriptResourceHandler, System.Web.Extensions,
       Version=3.5.0.0, Culture=neutral, PublicKeyToken=31bf3856ad364e35"
   validate="false"/>
   ```

6. Finally, for all projects that contain Web Parts or controls that will be added to an ASP.NET page, you need to add a *SafeControls* entry. The *SafeControls* entry allows your code to execute. Because anyone with rights can create page content in SharePoint, SharePoint adds this safeguard to ensure that users don't create content that bypasses security and runs arbitrary code on the server. The virtualized SharePoint application runs in *safe mode*, meaning that only controls that are registered on the server through a *SafeControls* entry can execute.

   ```
   <SafeControl Assembly="SOAjax.SharePoint" Namespace="SOAjax.SharePoint"
       TypeName="*" Safe="True" AllowRemoteDesigner="True" />
   ```

Tip Code for this book is available online at *http://www.microsoft.com/mspress/companion/ 9780735625914*. The code for this chapter is in the file Chapter 11.zip. This chapter's code requires Windows SharePoint Services 3.0 either on Windows Server 2003 or Windows Server 2008. On Windows Server 2008, you will need to run Visual Studio as an administrator to work with this chapter's code samples.

Deploying Code Through Web Parts

Tip If you are already familiar with Web Parts in SharePoint, you may want to skip ahead to the section "Deploying the AJAX Runtime Through the ScriptManager Control."

A typical application in SharePoint is developed through the use of Web Parts. A Web Part can be added to a page through configuration or by an end user and is serialized into the application's database by the Web Part framework. A Web Part is a class that derives from the class *System.Web.UI.WebControls.WebParts.WebPart*, which is a special type of *WebControl* that runs in the ASP.NET Web Part framework.

The only reason to deploy code as a Web Part is to give end users the capability to add and configure the Web Part in any page. If the code is tied to a page location or you need to develop a full-page user interface, you're better off deploying code in a page context. My commercial products at NewsGator employ both of these techniques, pages and Web Part applications, using the same common JavaScript library and Web service API. AJAX code is developed independently of its deployment target, although Web Part applications require a different deployment strategy, as I'll discuss in this section.

Utilizing the Web Part framework in an ASP.NET application can be complex, but SharePoint includes support for Web Parts in almost all its pages and includes a built-in Web Part gallery from which users can select Web Parts at run time.

More Information For full MSDN documentation on the Web Part class, see *http://msdn.microsoft.com/system.web.ui.webcontrols.webparts.webpart.aspx*. Avoid using code in the *Microsoft.SharePoint.WebPartPages* namespace; this namespace is included for backward compatibility.

As I mentioned previously, to create a Web Part, you create a public class that inherits from *System.Web.UI.WebControls.WebParts.WebPart*. The Hello World Web Part is shown in Listing 11-1. This Web Part simply writes the text "Hello, World!" to the page during the *Render* method. The main methods that you override to provide custom functionality are *CreateChildControls*, which is used to add controls to the *Controls* collection, and *RenderContents*, which is used to render the output to the page. Note that the outer *Render* method is used by the Web Part framework to render "chrome" that wraps the Web Part with an administrative interface that allows an end user to customize the Web Part.

LISTING 11-1. To create a Web Part, derive from *System.Web.UI.WebControls.WebParts.WebPart* (*SOAjax. SharePoint/HelloWorldWebPart.cs*).

```
using System;
using System.Web.UI.WebControls.WebParts;

namespace SOAjax.SharePoint
{
    /// <summary>A very simple Web Part</summary>
    public class HelloWorldWebPart : WebPart
    {
        protected override void CreateChildControls()
        {
            // Add any child controls here, such as the Script Manager.
            base.CreateChildControls();
        }

        protected override void RenderContents(System.Web.UI.HtmlTextWriter writer)
        {
            // Use this to write HTML directly to the page
            writer.Write("Hello World!");
        }
    }
}
```

To get the Web Part to the Web Part page, the DLL must be deployed in the *bin* directory or in the GAC, and the namespace must be registered in web.config. To review, the following entry must be included in web.config inside the *SafeControls* element. This entry allows execution of any Web Part code in the namespace *SOAjax.SharePoint* in the assembly SOAjax. SharePoint.dll. If the assembly is strongly named and deployed to the GAC, the assembly name must include the full strong name of the assembly.

```
<SafeControl Assembly="SOAjax.SharePoint" Namespace="SOAjax.SharePoint"
    TypeName="*" Safe="True" AllowRemoteDesigner="True" />
```

After adding the web.config entry, you can add the Web Part to the Web Part gallery, which makes it easy to add to pages. This step is done by going to the Site Settings page (available from the Site Actions link on the page) and navigating to the Web Part gallery. From the gallery, click the New button, which takes you to the New Web Parts page at *http://localhost/_layouts/NewDwp.aspx*. This page lists every public Web Part type that is available in the *bin* directory or the GAC and that is in a namespace registered through a *SafeControls* entry. You will use this page during development to add every Web Part class that you want to make available in the Web Part gallery.

> **Tip** For production applications, you export the .webpart file generated by the Web Part gallery, edit it, and deploy it through a SharePoint Feature. Again, this information is detailed in *Inside Microsoft Windows SharePoint Services 3.0.*

After adding the Web Part gallery entry, on the SharePoint Web page click Site Actions, Edit Page. From here you can add any Web Part in the Web Part gallery to the page within Web Part Zones. A Web Part Zone is a special container control on the page that supports the addition of Web Parts. You can only add Web Parts at run time to Web Part Zones that are defined on the page. Web Part Zones save their serialized Web Part states into the SharePoint database. The interface for adding Web Parts to Web Part Zones is shown in Figure 11-1.

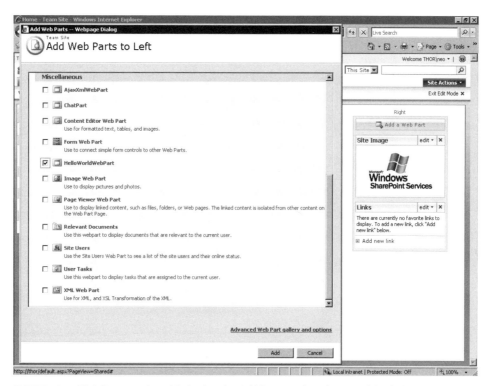

FIGURE 11-1. Web Parts can be added using the Add button when the page is in design mode.

To add properties that will be stored by the Web Part framework, add the *Personalizable* attribute to a property. The *Personalizable* attribute is defined in the *System.Web.UI.WebControls.WebParts* namespace. When it is applied to a public property along with the *WebBrowsable* attribute, SharePoint displays an interface for editing the property in the Web Page when the user edits the Web Part. Listing 11-2 demonstrates a simple property. Figure 11-3 shows the Edit Web Part interface for this Web Part instance, demonstrating the user interface for the custom property *Message*.

LISTING 11-2. To add persistent properties to a Web Part, use the *Personalizable* attribute (*SOAjax. SharePoint/HelloWorldWebPart.cs*).

```
using System;
using System.Web.UI.WebControls.WebParts;
using System.ComponentModel;

namespace SOAjax.SharePoint
{
    /// <summary>A very simple Web Part</summary>
    public class HelloWorldWebPart : WebPart
    {
        [WebBrowsable]
        [WebDescription("The message we want to render.")]
        [WebDisplayName("Message")]
        [Personalizable(PersonalizationScope.Shared)]
        [Category("Text")]
        public string Message {get; set;}

        protected override void CreateChildControls()
        {
            // Add any child controls here, such as the Script Manager.
            base.CreateChildControls();
        }

        protected override void RenderContents(System.Web.UI.HtmlTextWriter writer)
        {
            // Use this to write HTML directly to the page
            writer.Write("Hello World! ");
            writer.Write(this.Message);
        }
    }
}
```

To edit the Web Part, use the Edit Web Part menu and choose Modify Shared Web Part, as shown in Figure 11-2. This will display the Web Part Properties dialog box, as shown in Figure 11-3.

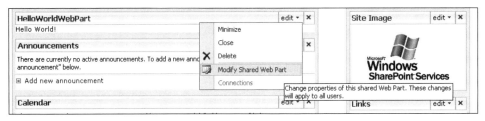

FIGURE 11-2. To edit a Web Part, select Modify Shared Web Part from the Web Part's Edit menu while you are editing the page.

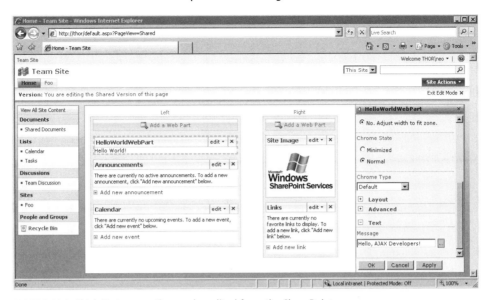

FIGURE 11-3. Web Part properties can be edited from the SharePoint page.

While the Web Part framework itself isn't AJAX-enabled, we'll use the Web Part framework to deploy placeholder DIV elements and JavaScript to the page. We will then use the JavaScript to create AJAX controls in the Web Part Zone. In the following section, I'll describe a custom server control that programmatically includes and configures the ASP.NET ScriptManager control and can be included in multiple Web Parts. This technique was also covered in detail in Chapter 4, "The AJAX Runtime with the Microsoft AJAX Library." Then we'll look at using this control in Web Parts to implement AJAX controls deployed through Web Parts.

Deploying the AJAX Runtime Through the ScriptManager Control

In a typical ASP.NET application the script manager is declared in the page, but SharePoint is not your typical Web application. In a typical SharePoint project, you develop Web Parts that can be placed on customer pages alongside existing functionality and other people's code. It's important that your code doesn't break existing code, Microsoft's functionality, or even third-party functionality. This means that your Web Part code must coexist with existing application code, and you may or may not "own" the page that the Web Part is deployed to. With Web Part applications, you must not break functionality in other Web Parts. The AJAX-enabled Web Part must deploy a ScriptManager control only if there isn't one already in the page. Listing 11-3 demonstrates a ScriptManager control that can be included as a child control of a Web Part. (Note that this class was shown earlier in the book, as Listing 4-3. This code sample has simply been renamed and included in this assembly.)

LISTING 11-3. The *ScriptRuntimeControl* is a critical component in a Web Part–deployed AJAX application (*SOAjax.SharePoint/ScriptRuntimeControl.cs*).

```
using System;
using System.Web.UI;
using System.ComponentModel;
using System.Web;
using System.Drawing.Design;
using System.Globalization;
using System.Security.Permissions;
using System.Reflection;

namespace SOAjax.SharePoint
{
    public class ScriptRuntimeControl : Control
    {
        private ScriptReferenceCollection _scripts;
        public ScriptReferenceCollection Scripts
        {
            get
            {
                if (this._scripts == null)
                    this._scripts = new ScriptReferenceCollection();
                return this._scripts;
            }
        }

        private ServiceReferenceCollection _services;
        public ServiceReferenceCollection Services
        {
            get
            {
                if (this._services == null)
                    this._services = new ServiceReferenceCollection();
                return this._services;
            }
        }

        private ScriptManager scriptMan;
        // A null-safe reference to the page's script manager.
        public ScriptManager ScriptManager
        {
            get
            {
                EnsureScriptManger();
                return scriptMan;
            }
        }

        protected override void CreateChildControls()
        {
            base.CreateChildControls();
            EnsureScriptManger();
        }
```

```csharp
// Make sure there is only 1 script manager on the page.
private void EnsureScriptManger()
{
    if (scriptMan == null)
    {
        scriptMan = ScriptManager.GetCurrent(this.Page);
        if (scriptMan == null)
        {
            scriptMan = new ScriptManager();
            this.Controls.Add(scriptMan);
        }
    }
}


private string cacheKey;
/// <summary>A cache key for script paths</summary>
/// <remarks>Ideally, this would be generated from the build.</remarks>
public string CacheKey
{
    get
    {
        if (cacheKey == null)
            cacheKey =
  Assembly.GetExecutingAssembly().ManifestModule.ModuleVersionId.ToString();
        return cacheKey;
    }
}


// Add any scripts and service references to the real script manager.
protected override void OnPreRender(EventArgs e)
{
    base.OnPreRender(e);
    this.EnsureChildControls();
    // Add a cache key to every script in the manager.
    foreach (ScriptReference script in this.ScriptManager.Scripts)
    {
        if (!string.IsNullOrEmpty(script.Path) &&
            !script.Path.ToLowerInvariant().Contains("cache"))
        {
            char seperator = script.Path.Contains("?") ? '&' : '?';
            script.Path = string.Format("{0}{1}cache={2}",
                script.Path, seperator, this.CacheKey);
        }
    }
    foreach (ScriptReference script in this.Scripts)
    {
        if (!string.IsNullOrEmpty(script.Path)){
            char seperator = script.Path.Contains("?") ? '&' : '?';
            script.Path = string.Format("{0}{1}cache={2}",
                script.Path, seperator, this.CacheKey);
        }
        this.ScriptManager.Scripts.Add(script);
    }
```

```
            foreach (ServiceReference proxy in this.Services)
                this.ScriptManager.Services.Add(proxy);

            // Common scipt manager configuration:
            this.ScriptManager.EnableHistory = true;
        }
    }
}
```

ScriptRuntimeControl can be included in any Web Part by adding it to the *Controls* collection in the *CreateChildControls* method. Listing 11-4 demonstrates a simple base class for an AJAX Web Part that registers the *ScriptRuntimeControl*.

LISTING 11-4. The *ScriptRuntimeControl* is a critical component in a Web Part–deployed AJAX application (*SOAjax.SharePoint/AjaxWebPart.cs*).

```
using System.Web.UI.WebControls.WebParts;

namespace SOAjax.SharePoint
{
    /// <summary>A base class for AJAX Web Parts.</summary>
    public abstract class AjaxWebPart : WebPart
    {
        private ScriptRuntimeControl ajaxRuntime = new ScriptRuntimeControl();

        /// <summary>Gets the ScriptManager for this page </summary>
        public ScriptRuntimeControl ScriptManager
        {
            get
            {
                return this.ajaxRuntime;
            }
        }

        /// <summary>Includes the ajax runtime components.</summary>
        protected override void CreateChildControls()
        {
            base.CreateChildControls();
            this.Controls.Add(this.ajaxRuntime);
        }
    }
}
```

The technique to create an AJAX control in SharePoint is similar to the technique used in previous chapters—you simply render a DIV that is a placeholder and create the AJAX control instance in the page initialization through the *Sys.Application.init* event.

In the Web Part, you render a DIV that is used as the element of the control. However, with Web Parts, you want to support multiple instances of the Web Part, so you need unique IDs for each placeholder DIV element. You won't know these until the Web Part renders, and because of this, you won't be able to use statically named items in the JavaScript page initialization code. To account for this and to make your code even more portable, you need to render JSON-serialized object templates that can be read during the page initialization. This lets you map Web Part properties to AJAX control properties.

To demonstrate this technique, we'll create a Web Part implementation of the JavaScript AJAX control *XmlControl* that was built in Chapter 9, "AJAX and XSLT." First we need to implement the page initialization method that is added to the XmlControl.js file. Then we'll implement a control template in the Web Part class *AjaxXmlControl* and include the necessary script library through the previously explained *ScriptRuntimeControl*.

> **Tip** The AJAX Xml Web Part architecture can be used to produce very complex AJAX Web Part applications with little effort. It is the main architecture behind commercial products we've built at NewsGator.

To review, the *XmlControl* has the properties *xmlUrl*, *xsltUrl*, and *reloadInterval*. When an *XmlControl* is initialized with *xmlUrl* and *xsltUrl*, it loads XML data and the XSLT transform file from these locations and performs a client-side render.

The JavaScript object template that we will use for the *XmlControl* looks like the following JavaScript object. In the Web Part, we'll render this in the page in a JavaScript array with a known naming convention, which we'll pick up in the AJAX *Sys.Application.init* event.

```
var template = {
    elementID: ElementID,
    properties : {
        xmlUrl : URL,
        xsltUrl : XSLT_URL,
        reloadInterval : '3000'
    }
};
```

To add a page initialization script, look for the JavaScript array of control templates with your given naming convention. A uniquely named array should be used for each type of AJAX control. The following JavaScript method adds a page initialization script that creates instances of *XmlControl* based on the templates added to the *window._XmlControlTemplates* variable.

```
// Initializes the XmlControl templates during the page load.
SOAjax.Controls.XmlControl.OnPageInit = function() {
    if (window.__XmlControlTemplates != 'undefined' &&
            window.__XmlControlTemplates != null) {
        while (window.__XmlControlTemplates.length > 0) {
            var template = Array.dequeue(window.__XmlControlTemplates);
            var element = $get(template.elementID);
            var control = $create(SOAjax.Controls.XmlControl,
```

```
                    template.properties, template.events, template.references, element);
        }
        window.__XmlControlTemplates = null;
    }
}
Sys.Application.add_init(SOAjax.Controls.XmlControl.OnPageInit);
```

To create a Web Part that utilizes *XmlControl*, we need to write a simple Web Part that creates a JavaScript template and a placeholder, while including the ASP.NET ScriptManager and
the custom library that contains the XmlControl.js JavaScript file. Listing 11-5 demonstrates a
simple Web Part that includes the properties *XmlUrl*, *XsltUrl*, and *RefreshInterval*, all of which
are written to the JavaScript template. In the sample code, a default XML and XSLT file are
included that supply the initial render. *AjaxXmlWebPart* can be used to implement views of
any XML data source, including RSS feeds that are included out of the box with SharePoint.

LISTING 11-5. The *AjaxXmlWebPart* class is a Web Part wrapper for *XmlControl* (*SOAjax.SharePoint/
AjaxXmlWebPart.cs*).

```csharp
using System;
using System.Collections.Generic;
using System.ComponentModel;
using System.Web.UI;
using System.Web.UI.WebControls.WebParts;
using Microsoft.SharePoint.Utilities;


namespace SOAjax.SharePoint
{
    public class AjaxXmlWebPart : AjaxWebPart, IXmlWebPart
    {
        /// <summary>
        /// Gets a string specifying the client ID of the XmlControl
        /// </summary>
        public string XmlControlID
        {
            get{return (@"XmlControl_" + this.ClientID);}
        }

        /// <summary>Defines the client data refresh interval in seconds</summary>
        [WebBrowsable]
        [WebDescription("Defines the client data refresh interval in seconds")]
        [WebDisplayName("Refresh Interval (seconds)")]
        [Personalizable(PersonalizationScope.Shared)]
        [Category("AJAX")]
        public uint RefreshInterval { get; set;}

        /// <summary>Xml Url defines the client Xml data source URL </summary>
        [WebBrowsable(true)]
        [WebDisplayName("Xml Url")]
        [Personalizable(PersonalizationScope.Shared)]
        public string XmlUrl { get; set; }

        /// <summary>Xslt Url defines the client XSLT source URL</summary>
        /// <remarks>If empty the SharePoint.AJAX RSS XSLT will be used.</remarks>
```

```
[WebBrowsable(true)]
[WebDisplayName("Custom Xslt Url Override")]
[Personalizable(PersonalizationScope.Shared)]
public string XsltUrl { get; set; }

protected override void CreateChildControls()
{
    base.CreateChildControls();
    this.ScriptManager.Scripts.Add(
        new ScriptReference("/_layouts/soajax.script/xmlcontrol.js"));
    this.ScriptManager.Scripts.Add(
        new ScriptReference("/_layouts/soajax.script/soajax.js"));
}


/// <summary>
/// Renders the contents of this control.
/// This is where we will register the XmlComponent instances.
/// </summary>
/// <param name="writer">HtmlTextWriter</param>
protected override void RenderContents(HtmlTextWriter writer)
{
    var xml = this.XmlUrl;
    // Only provide a default for the XmlWebPart-- not inherited parts.
    if (this.GetType() == typeof(AjaxXmlWebPart)
            && string.IsNullOrEmpty(xml))
        xml = @"/_layouts/soajax.script/Sample.xml";
    var xsl = this.XsltUrl;
    if (xsl == null)
        xsl = @"/_layouts/soajax.script/Sample.xslt";

    writer.Write(@"<div id=""XmlControl_{0}"" style=""display:block;"">",
        this.ClientID);
    this.RenderInitialContents(writer);
    writer.Write(@"</div>");

    var scriptFormat =
        @"if (window.__XmlControlTemplates == null){{
            window.__XmlControlTemplates = new Array();
            }}
            var template = {{
                elementID: 'XmlControl_{0}',
                properties : {{   xmlUrl : '{1}',
                    xsltUrl : '{2}',
                    reloadInterval : '{3}'
                }}
            }};
            window.__XmlControlTemplates.push(template);
        ";

    var script = string.Format(scriptFormat,
        this.ClientID,
        SPEncode.ScriptEncode(this.XmlUrl),
        SPEncode.ScriptEncode(xsl),
        this.RefreshInterval * 1000);
```

```
        writer.Write(@"<script type=""text/javascript""
            language=""javascript"">");
        writer.Write(script);
        writer.Write(@"</script>");
    }

    /// <summary>
    /// Used to write the inside part of the XmlComponent.
    /// By default, it will render "Loading"
    /// </summary>
    /// <param name="writer">HtmlTextWriter</param>
    protected virtual void RenderInitialContents(HtmlTextWriter writer)
    {
        writer.Write(@"<div style=""margin:3px;"" class=""SOAjaxLoading"">
                    <span style=""font-size:smaller;"">Loading...</span>
                    </div>");
    }
  }
}
```

The full *XmlControl* JavaScript class is included in Listing 11-6. This control dynamically loads and renders XML data sources with XSLT files that are loaded from the client as well. The *XmlControl* class implements logic for reloading where it can reload on an interval or through the *reload* method. This control can be used as the core run-time component for AJAX applications.

LISTING 11-6. The *XmlControl* class is used to dynamically load and render XML data sources from the client (*SOAjax.SharePoint\SOAjax.Script\XmlControl.js*).

```
/// <reference name="MicrosoftAjax.js"/>
Type.registerNamespace('SOAjax.Controls');

SOAjax.Controls.XmlControl = function(element) {
    /// <summary>
    /// A component that loads and renders XML on the client.
    /// </summary>
    SOAjax.Controls.XmlControl.initializeBase(this, [element]);
}

SOAjax.Controls.XmlControl.prototype = {
    // ------------ Private fields ---------
    _xml: null,
    _xslt: null,
    _xsltUrl: null,
    _xmlUrl: null,
    _reloadInterval: null,
    _active: true,
    _interval: null,
    _timeoutID: null,
    _lastMod: null,
```

```
// ------------- Properties -------------
get_active: function() {
    /// <value>Gets or sets the XML data of the control.</value>
    return this._active;
},
set_active: function(value) {
    if (this._active !== value) {
        this._active = value;
        this.raisePropertyChanged('active');
        if (this._active && _reloadInterval > 100) {
            window.setTimeout(
                String.format("SOAjax.Controls.XmlControl.Refresh('{0}')",
                    this.get_element().id),
                this._reloadInterval);
        }
    }
},

get_xml: function() {
    /// <value>Gets or sets the XML data of the control.</value>
    return this._xml;
},
set_xml: function(value) {
    if (this._xml !== value) {
        this._xml = value;
        this.raisePropertyChanged('xml');
    }
    if (this._xml && this._xslt) this._render();
},

get_xslt: function() {
    /// <value>Gets or sets the XSLT rendering logic for the control.</value>
    return this._xslt;
},
set_xslt: function(value) {
    if (this._xslt !== value) {
        this._xslt = value;
        this.raisePropertyChanged('xslt');
    }
    if (this._xml && this._xslt) this._render();
},

get_xsltUrl: function() {
    /// <value>The URL to load the XSLT from.</value>
    return this._xsltUrl;
},
set_xsltUrl: function(value) {
    if (this._xsltUrl !== value) {
        this._xsltUrl = value;
        this.raisePropertyChanged('xsltUrl');
        if (this._xsltUrl && !this.get_isUpdating())
            this._loadXslt(this._xsltUrl);
    }
},
```

```
get_xmlUrl: function() {
    /// <value>The URL to load the data from.</value>
    return this._xmlUrl;
},
set_xmlUrl: function(value) {
    if (this._xmlUrl !== value) {
        this._lastMod = null;
        this._xmlUrl = value;
        this.raisePropertyChanged('xmlUrl');
        if (this._xmlUrl && !this.get_isUpdating())
            this._loadXml(this._xmlUrl);
    }
},

get_reloadInterval: function() {
    /// <value>The interval at which we'll reload the control.</value>
    return this._reloadInterval;
},
set_reloadInterval: function(value) {
    if (this._reloadInterval !== value) {
        if (value != 0 && value < 99) {
            throw Error.argumentOutOfRange('reloadInterval',
                value, 'The reload interval must be 0 or over 100 milliseconds.');
        }
        this._reloadInterval = value;
        this.raisePropertyChanged('reloadInterval');
    }
},

reload: function() {
    if (this._timeoutID) window.clearTimeout(this._timeoutID);
    this._reload();
},

_reload: function() {
    var xmlUrl = this.get_xmlUrl();
    if (xmlUrl != null) { this._loadXml(xmlUrl); }
},

// Events -------------------------------------------------------
add_xmlLoaded: function(handler) {
    /// <value>Bind and unbind to the xmlLoaded event.</value>
    this.get_events().addHandler('xmlLoaded', handler);
},
remove_xmlLoaded: function(handler) {
    this.get_events().removeHandler('xmlLoaded', handler);
},

add_xsltLoaded: function(handler) {
    /// <value>Bind and unbind to the xsltLoaded event.</value>
    this.get_events().addHandler('xsltLoaded', handler);
},
remove_xsltLoaded: function(handler) {
    this.get_events().removeHandler('xsltLoaded', handler);
},
```

```
add_render: function(handler) {
    /// <value>Bind and unbind to the render event.</value>
    this.get_events().addHandler('render', handler);
},
remove_render: function(handler) {
    this.get_events().removeHandler('render', handler);
},

add_prerender: function(handler) {
    /// <value>Bind and unbind to the prerender event.</value>
    this.get_events().addHandler('prerender', handler);
},
remove_prerender: function(handler) {
    this.get_events().removeHandler('prerender', handler);
},

add_error: function(handler) {
    /// <value>Bind and unbind to the prerender event.</value>
    this.get_events().addHandler('error', handler);
},
remove_error: function(handler) {
    this.get_events().removeHandler('error', handler);
},

initialize: function() {
    SOAjax.Controls.XmlControl.callBaseMethod(this, 'initialize');
    if (this._xsltUrl && !this.get_isUpdating())
        this._loadXslt(this._xsltUrl);
    if (this._xmlUrl && !this.get_isUpdating())
        this._loadXml(this._xmlUrl);
},

_loadXml: function(url) {
    if (this._timeoutID) window.clearTimeout(this._timeoutID);
    this.xmlUrl = url;
    if (url == null || url == '') return;

    var request = new Sys.Net.WebRequest();
    //Sys.Debug.trace("XML Data load: " + url);
    var context = new Object();
    request.add_completed(Function.createDelegate(this, this._loadXmlComplete));
    request.set_userContext(context);
    if (this._lastMod)
        request.get_headers()['If-Modified-Since'] = this._lastMod;
    request.set_url(url);
    request.invoke();
},

_loadXmlComplete: function(response) {
    if (response == null) { response = new Sys.Net.WebRequestExecutor(); }
    var context = response.get_webRequest().get_userContext();
    var status = response.get_statusCode();
    var url = response.get_webRequest().get_url();
    var xml;
```

```
        if (status == 200) {
            try {
                var lastMod = response.getResponseHeader('Last-Modified');
                if (lastMod && lastMod != '' && this._lastMod == lastMod) {
                    this.queueReload();
                    return;
                }
                else this._lastMod = lastMod;

                xml = response.get_xml();
                if (xml == null)
                    xml = response.get_responseData();
                if (!xml) throw Error.create(
                    'We could not load the XML data at the URL ' + url);
                var xmlLoadedHandler = this.get_events().getHandler('xmlLoaded');
                if (xmlLoadedHandler) xmlLoadedHandler(this, Sys.EventArgs.Empty);
                this.set_xml(xml);
            } catch (e) {
                Sys.Debug.fail('Could not process callback method.');
            }
        }
        else if (status == 304){
            // not modified.
            this.queueReload();
        }
        else { // Process the status. Could be 401, 404 (not found), 410 (gone)
            var statusText = response.get_statusText();
            Sys.Debug.trace(
          String.format('ERROR: {0} replied "{1}" ({2}).', url, statusText, status));
            var errorHandler = this.get_events().getHandler('error');
            if (!errorHandler) {    // Default error handler
                switch (status) {
                    case 410: // HttpStatusCode.Gone:
                        alert('Content has been removed.');
                        break;
                    case 404: // HttpStatusCode.NotFound:
                        alert('Could not find resource.');
                        break;
                    default:
                        alert(String.format('ERROR: {0} replied "{1}" ({2}).',
                            url, statusText, status));
                }
            } else {
                errorHandler(response, Sys.EventArgs.Empty);
            }
        }
    },

    _loadXslt: function(url) {
        this.xslUrl = url;
        if (url == null || url == '') return;
        var request = new Sys.Net.WebRequest();
        Sys.Debug.trace("XSLT Load: " + url);
        request.add_completed(Function.createDelegate(
            this, this._loadXsltComplete));
```

```
            request.set_url(url);
            request.invoke();
        },
        _loadXsltComplete: function(response) {
            var context = response.get_webRequest().get_userContext();
            var status = response.get_statusCode();
            var xml;
            if (status == 200) {
                try {
                    xml = response.get_xml();
                    if (xml == null)
                        xml = response.get_responseData();

                    var xsltLoadedHandler = this.get_events().getHandler('xsltLoaded');
                    if (xsltLoadedHandler) xsltLoadedHandler(this, Sys.EventArgs.Empty);
                    if (xml) this.set_xslt(xml);
                } catch (e) {
                    var errorHandler = this.get_events().getHandler('error');
                    if (errorHandler) errorHandler(response, Sys.EventArgs.Empty)
                    else
                        Sys.Debug.trace('Could not process callback method.');
                }
            }
        },

        _render: function() {
            Sys.Debug.trace('XmlControl Render');
            var control = this.get_element();
            if (control == null || this._xml == null || this._xslt == null)
                return;

            var prerenderHandler = this.get_events().getHandler('prerender');
            var needsRendering = true;
            if (prerenderHandler) needsRendering = prerenderHandler(this, Sys.EventArgs.
Empty);

            if (needsRendering)
                SOAjax.XmlTransform(this._xml, this._xslt, control);
            //control.style.display = '';
            this._rendered = true;

            var renderHandler = this.get_events().getHandler('render');
            if (renderHandler) renderHandler(this, Sys.EventArgs.Empty);
            this.queueReload();
        },

        queueReload: function() {
            if (!this._active) return;
            if (this._timeoutID) window.clearTimeout(this._timeoutID);
            this._timeoutID = window.setTimeout(
                String.format("SOAjax.Controls.XmlControl.Refresh('{0}')",
                    this.get_element().id), this._reloadInterval);
        },
        dispose: function() {
```

```
        ///<summary>Release resources before control is disposed.</summary>
        var element = this.get_element();
        if (element) $clearHandlers(this.get_element());
        SOAjax.Controls.XmlControl.callBaseMethod(this, 'dispose');
    }
}
SOAjax.Controls.XmlControl.registerClass(
    'SOAjax.Controls.XmlControl', Sys.UI.Control);

SOAjax.Controls.XmlControl.Refresh = function(elementID) {
    var xmlControl = $find(elementID);
    if (xmlControl && xmlControl.reload)
        xmlControl.reload();
}

// Initializes the XmlControl templates during the page load.
SOAjax.Controls.XmlControl.OnPageInit = function() {
    Sys.Debug.trace('SOAjax.Controls.XmlControl.OnPageInit.');
    if (window.__XmlControlTemplates != 'undefined' &&
            window.__XmlControlTemplates != null) {
        while (window.__XmlControlTemplates.length > 0) {
            var template = Array.dequeue(window.__XmlControlTemplates);
            try {
                var element = $get(template.elementID);
                var control = $create(SOAjax.Controls.XmlControl,
                template.properties, template.events, template.references, element);
            } catch (e) {
                Sys.Debug.trace(
                    'Could not create XmlControl instance from template.');
                Sys.Debug.traceDump(template, 'invalid XmlControl template');
                if (Sys.Debug.isDebug)
                    Sys.Debug.fail('Error in XmlControl onpageinit.');
            }
        } // end while
    }
}
Sys.Application.add_init(SOAjax.Controls.XmlControl.OnPageInit);
Sys.Application.notifyScriptLoaded();
```

Sample Application: Creating a Site Chat

In the following code samples, we'll use the *AjaxXmlWebPart* and the *XmlControl* to develop a chat application that runs on a SharePoint site. The first step in the process is to create a chat protocol that runs as a REST-ful service through a simple XML endpoint.

Creating the Chat Protocol

Because WCF is not fully supported on the current SharePoint platform, we'll follow an approach that uses HTTP handlers—however, we'll make use of the WCF platform so that we can maintain a consistent API. By implementing the service using WCF technology, we can serve the same code through a WCF endpoint or through an HTTP handler wrapper class. We will also register the HTTP handler endpoint with the path *chat.svc* so that client code is completely neutral about whether the service is implemented in WCF or not. And whether the Web service is served through WCF or ASP.NET is trivial—we can easily convert the service to WCF if we want, which is demonstrated later in the chapter in Listing 11-17.

The chat data itself will be implemented in a simple SharePoint list that is served through our Web service. However, we want to keep our protocol neutral with respect to the hosting platform, and we don't want to tie our chat implementation to the SharePoint platform. To create a clean API, we can create our own XML schema that simplifies the interface and implements a data schema that isn't tied to SharePoint. By creating a data contract, we have standard XML serialization in the Web service regardless of the service implementation. We can use the *DataContractSerializer* class in the HTTP handler instance, which will output the same XML as the WCF endpoint. The classes *ChatData* and *Author* will be used in the *Chat* data contract that wraps a list of chat entries in a common format. These data contracts are defined in Listing 11-7, which will output XML in the following format:

```
<chat xmlns="http://soajax" xmlns:i="http://www.w3.org/2001/XMLSchema-instance">
    <lastModified>datetime last modified</lastModified>
    <chats>
        <chatData>
            <message>message text</message>
            <pubDate>datetime published</pubDate>
            <author>
                <name>author display name</name>
                <email>author email</email>
                <id>chat ID</id>
                <url>profile page URL</url>
                <picture>picture URL</picture>
            </author>
        </chatData>
    </chats>
</chat>
```

LISTING 11-7. The *Chat* data contract defines the XML schema for the custom chat protocol (*SOAjax. SharePoint.Services/ChatData.cs*).

```
using System;
using System.Runtime.Serialization;

namespace SOAjax.SharePoint.Services
{
    [DataContract(Name = "chat", Namespace = "http://soajax")]
    public class Chat
    {
        [DataMember(Name = "lastModified", Order = 1)]
        public DateTime LastModified { get; set; }
```

```
        [DataMember(Name = "chats", Order = 2)]
        public ChatData[] Chats { get; set; }
    }

    [DataContract(Name = "chatData", Namespace = "http://soajax")]
    public class ChatData
    {
        [DataMember(Name = "message", Order = 1)]
        public string Message { get; set; }

        [DataMember(Name = "pubDate", Order = 2)]
        public DateTime PostedDate { get; set; }

        [DataMember(Name = "author", Order = 3)]
        public Author Author { get; set; }
    }

    [DataContract(Name = "author", Namespace = "http://soajax")]
    public class Author
    {
        [DataMember(Name = "name", Order = 1)]
        public string Name { get; set; }

        [DataMember(Name = "email", Order = 2)]
        public string Email { get; set; }

        [DataMember(Name = "id", Order = 3)]
        public int UserID { get; set; }

        [DataMember(Name = "url", Order = 4)]
        public string Url { get; set; }

        [DataMember(Name = "picture", Order = 5)]
        public string Picture { get; set; }
    }
}
```

To create a service that implements the *Chat* data contract, create a WCF service class that implements a service contract and returns the *Chat* object. If the service class is exposed through a WCF endpoint, it requires ASP.NET compatibility mode to run in the SharePoint context. In this example, we'll create a WCF service and wrap it in an HTTP handler, which gives us the consistency of the WCF platform and the stability of SharePoint's supported platform. You can also deploy the service as a WCF *svc* endpoint if you want to without changing any code or breaking any external contracts. Creating the WCF service, even for an HTTP handler implementation, helps you create a more logical API by clearly defining the contracts, rather than just stream operations as you define with HTTP handlers.

The next step in creating the service is to define the service contract. In this example, the only methods supported are *View* and *Post*, where *View* returns only the current conversation and *Post* accepts a simple message from the calling identity. The *Post* operation accepts a single string as the message parameter and creates the chat entry by using the identity of the caller. Listing 11-8 shows the service contract for the chat service, including support for WCF web binding with the *GET* and *POST* HTTP verbs.

LISTING 11-8. The *Chat* data contract defines the XML schema for the custom Chat protocol (*SOAjax. SharePoint.Services/IChatService.cs*).

```
using System;
using System.ServiceModel;
using System.ServiceModel.Web;

namespace SOAjax.SharePoint.Services
{
    [ServiceContract]
    public interface IChatService
    {
        [OperationContract]
        [WebGet(UriTemplate="")]
        Chat View();

        [OperationContract]
        [WebInvoke(BodyStyle = WebMessageBodyStyle.Bare, UriTemplate = "")]
        void Post(string chat);
    }
}
```

To implement the service, we need to include some simple access code for SharePoint lists. The chat service could interface with external systems and proxy the chat across the network or store the results in a database, but in this example we'll use the SharePoint list-storage mechanism. When programming the service, we don't want to tie the service to the SharePoint implementation. We want to create a generic protocol that is platform neutral and use SharePoint as a data-storage mechanism. This is a key principle of service orientation; the protocol is defined independently of the implementation.

The *GetChatList* method in Listing 11-9 includes a mechanism to get an instance of the Chat list. This sample code will create an instance of the chat list if the list does not exist.

LISTING 11-9. The *GetChatList* method wraps the SharePoint list API and retrieves the *SPList* reference (excerpt from *SOAjax.SharePoint.Services/ChatService.cs*).

```
private SPList GetChatList()
{
    SPList list;
    try{
        list = SPContext.Current.Web.Lists["chat"];
    }
    catch{
        // Only a user with rights to create the list will be able to run this code.
        SPContext.Current.Web.AllowUnsafeUpdates = true;
```

```
        Guid listGuid =
            SPContext.Current.Web.Lists.Add("chat", "A persisted chat",
            SPListTemplateType.GenericList);
        list = SPContext.Current.Web.Lists[listGuid];
        list.ReadSecurity = 1; // All users can read all items.
        list.WriteSecurity = 4; // Users cannot modify any list item.
        list.Update();
        SPContext.Current.Web.Update();
    }
    return list;
}
```

To get a list of recent chat list items with which we can create the *ChatData* item, we use the
SharePoint API to perform a query on the list. The helper method *GetRecentChats,* shown
in Listing 11-10, encapsulates the SharePoint API call to get a list of the last ten chat entries,
ordered in reverse chronological order.

LISTING 11-10. The *GetRecentChats* method returns list items from the SharePoint list API (excerpt from
SOAjax.SharePoint.Services/ChatService.cs).

```
protected SPListItemCollection GetRecentChats(SPList list)
{
    var chats = new List<ChatData>();
    SPQuery query = new SPQuery();
    query.RowLimit = 10;
    query.ViewFields =
        @"<FieldRef Name='Title'/><FieldRef Name='Author'/>
            <FieldRef Name='Created'/>";
    query.Query = @"<OrderBy>
                        <FieldRef Name='Created' Ascending='FALSE'/>
                    </OrderBy>";
    return list.GetItems(query);
}
```

With the method to retrieve recent chat data in place, the next step is to create a helper
method for converting the list item to a *ChatData* item. The helper method is part of the
data contract we return to the client. The method in Listing 11-11 demonstrates the conversion of the generic SharePoint *SPListItem* object into a *ChatData* object. While the SharePoint
list item is powerful and able to implement many capabilities, it isn't the ideal data format for
our external chat protocol.

Tip While I won't attempt to explain the SharePoint list API in this book, we cover it in depth in
Inside Microsoft Windows SharePoint Services 3.0.

LISTING 11-11. *GetChatItem* converts the *SPListItem* to a *ChatData* object (excerpt from *SOAjax.SharePoint. Services/ChatService.cs*).

```
private ChatData GetChatItem(SPListItem listItem)
{
    // Common fields, exist in EVERY list:
    var createdByFieldID =
        new Guid("1df5e554-ec7e-46a6-901d-d85a3881cb18");
    var createdFieldID =
        new Guid("8c06beca-0777-48f7-91c7-6da68bc07b69");

    var created = (DateTime)listItem[createdFieldID];
    var link = new Uri(
        string.Format("{0}/{1}",
        SPContext.Current.Web.Url, listItem.ParentList.DefaultViewUrl));
    var authorField = listItem.ParentList.Fields[createdByFieldID];
    var userValue =
        (SPFieldUserValue)authorField.GetFieldValue(
        (string)listItem[createdByFieldID]);
    var author = userValue.User;
    var users = SPContext.Current.Site.GetCatalog(
        SPListTemplateType.UserInformation);
    var userItem = users.GetItemById(author.ID);
    var pict = (string)userItem["Picture"];
    if (!string.IsNullOrEmpty(pict))
        pict = pict.Split(',')[0];

    return new ChatData
    {
        Author = new SharePointAuthor
        {
            Name = author.Name,
            Email = author.Email,
            UserID = author.ID,
            Picture = pict,
            Url = string.Format("{0}/_layouts/userdisp.aspx?ID={1}",
                SPContext.Current.Site.Url, author.ID)
        },
        Message = listItem.Title,
        PostedDate = (DateTime)listItem[createdFieldID]
    };
}
```

To post an item, the logic to create a list item is very simple. We create a list item with the call to *list.Items.Add*() and then simply assign the Title field with the value of the chat. SharePoint picks up the current authentication principal as the author of the item, so we don't need to include any identity code. We can also assume that the list inherits permissions from the site context, so there's no real security code we need to implement. Listing 11-12 demonstrates the simplicity of the SharePoint list API for creating a new entry within the *Post* method.

LISTING 11-12. The SharePoint list API is simple to use in creating a new item (excerpt from *SOAjax.SharePoint.Services/ChatService.cs*).

```
public void Post(string chat)
{
    if (string.IsNullOrEmpty(chat)) return;
    SPContext.Current.Site.CatchAccessDeniedException = false;
    SPContext.Current.Web.AllowUnsafeUpdates = true;
    var list = this.GetChatList();
    var newItem = list.Items.Add();
    newItem["Title"] = chat;
    newItem.Update();
}
```

Because we will call the chat service frequently to poll for new data, we want to implement a conditional response. As I described in Chapter 3, "The AJAX Application Server: Windows Communication Foundation's Web Programming Model," the HTTP protocol supports conditional response with the *Last-Modified* and *If-Modified-Since* HTTP headers, as well as the *ETag* and *If-None-Match* headers. In this example, the *Last-Modified* HTTP header is used to implement a conditional response. If the chat list hasn't been modified since the last response, the server returns an empty response with the NOT MODIFIED (304) HTTP status. To implement the conditional response, the View method checks for the Last-Modified string from the HTTP context. For code that works in WCF or in an HTTP handler, you can implement a conditional check for *WebOperationContext.Current*, which will be null outside the WCF runtime. The following code will get the If-Modified-Since string from either WCF or ASP.NET:

```
var lastModClientString =
    (WebOperationContext.Current != null) ?
    WebOperationContext.Current.IncomingRequest.Headers
    [HttpRequestHeader.IfModifiedSince]
    : HttpContext.Current.Request.Headers["If-Modified-Since"];
```

To implement a conditional response that works both in WCF and in an HTTP handler, you can use the following code within the *View* method. This code checks the HTTP header *If-Modified-Since* using the previous conditional logic and will set the status to 304 only in the case of the WCF runtime. If the current WCF *WebOperationContext* is null, we let the calling code (the HTTP handler) process the 304 response.

```
var list = this.GetChatList();
var lastModClientString =
    (WebOperationContext.Current != null) ?
    WebOperationContext.Current.IncomingRequest.Headers
    [HttpRequestHeader.IfModifiedSince]
    : HttpContext.Current.Request.Headers["If-Modified-Since"];
```

```
if (!string.IsNullOrEmpty(lastModClientString))
{
    var lastMod = DateTime.MinValue;
    var tempDateTime = DateTime.MinValue;
    if (DateTime.TryParse(lastModClientString,
            CultureInfo.InvariantCulture,
            DateTimeStyles.AssumeUniversal, out tempDateTime))
        lastMod = tempDateTime.ToUniversalTime();

    if (lastMod >= list.LastItemModifiedDate)
    {
        if (WebOperationContext.Current != null)
            WebOperationContext.Current.OutgoingResponse.StatusCode =
                System.Net.HttpStatusCode.NotModified;
        return null;
    }
}
```

The complete code for the *ChatService* class is included in Listing 11-13. This code is compatible with the WCF service host. It is designed to run through the *WebServiceHostFactory* and can also be wrapped in an HTTP handler, as you'll see in the next example.

LISTING 11-13. The *Chat* data contract defines the XML schema for the custom Chat protocol (*SOAjax.SharePoint.Services/ChatService.cs*).

```
using System;
using System.Collections.Generic;
using System.Text;
using Microsoft.SharePoint;
using System.ServiceModel.Activation;
using System.Diagnostics;
using System.Web;
using System.ServiceModel.Web;
using System.Net;
using System.Globalization;

namespace SOAjax.SharePoint.Services
{
    [AspNetCompatibilityRequirements(RequirementsMode =
        AspNetCompatibilityRequirementsMode.Required)]
    public class ChatService : IChatService
    {
        // Common fields, exist in EVERY list:
        static readonly Guid createdByFieldID =
            new Guid("1df5e554-ec7e-46a6-901d-d85a3881cb18");
        static readonly Guid createdFieldID =
            new Guid("8c06beca-0777-48f7-91c7-6da68bc07b69");

        private SPList GetChatList()
        {
            SPContext.Current.Site.CatchAccessDeniedException = false;
            SPList list;
            try
```

```
            {
                list = SPContext.Current.Web.Lists["chat"];
            }
            catch
            {
                SPContext.Current.Web.AllowUnsafeUpdates = true;
                Guid listGuid =
                    SPContext.Current.Web.Lists.Add("chat", "A persisted chat",
                    SPListTemplateType.GenericList);
                list = SPContext.Current.Web.Lists[listGuid];
                list.ReadSecurity = 1; // All users can read all items.
                list.WriteSecurity = 4; // Users cannot modify any list item.
                list.Update();
                SPContext.Current.Web.Update();
            }
            return list;
        }

        public void Post(string chat)
        {
            SPContext.Current.Site.CatchAccessDeniedException = false;
            SPContext.Current.Web.AllowUnsafeUpdates = true;
            var list = this.GetChatList();
            var newItem = list.Items.Add();
            newItem["Title"] = chat;
            newItem.Update();
        }

        private SPListItemCollection GetRecentChats(SPList list)
        {
            var chats = new List<ChatData>();
            SPQuery query = new SPQuery();
            query.RowLimit = 25;
            query.ViewFields = @"<FieldRef Name=""Title""/><FieldRef Name=""Author""/
><FieldRef Name=""Created""/>";
            query.Query = @"<OrderBy><FieldRef Name=""Created"" Ascending='FALSE' /></
OrderBy>";
            return list.GetItems(query);
        }

        public Chat View()
        {
            var list = this.GetChatList();
            var lastModClientString =
                (WebOperationContext.Current != null) ?
                WebOperationContext.Current.IncomingRequest.Headers
                [HttpRequestHeader.IfModifiedSince]
                : HttpContext.Current.Request.Headers["If-Modified-Since"];

            if (!string.IsNullOrEmpty(lastModClientString))
            {
                var lastMod = DateTime.MinValue;
                var tempDateTime = DateTime.MinValue;
```

```
        if (DateTime.TryParse(lastModClientString,
            CultureInfo.InvariantCulture,
            DateTimeStyles.AssumeUniversal, out tempDateTime))
        lastMod = tempDateTime.ToUniversalTime();

    if (lastMod >= list.LastItemModifiedDate)
    {
        if (WebOperationContext.Current != null)
            WebOperationContext.Current.OutgoingResponse.StatusCode =
                System.Net.HttpStatusCode.NotModified;

        return null;
    }
}

var chats = new List<ChatData>();
var listItems = this.GetRecentChats(list);
foreach (SPListItem listItem in listItems)
{
    var created = (DateTime)listItem[createdFieldID];

    Uri link = new Uri(
        string.Format("{0}/{1}",
        SPContext.Current.Web.Url, list.DefaultViewUrl));
    SPField authorField = list.Fields[createdByFieldID];
    SPFieldUserValue userValue =
        (SPFieldUserValue)authorField.GetFieldValue(
        (string)listItem[createdByFieldID]);
    SPUser author = userValue.User;
    var users = SPContext.Current.Site.GetCatalog(
        SPListTemplateType.UserInformation);
    var userItem = users.GetItemById(author.ID);
    var pict = (string) userItem["Picture"];
    if (!string.IsNullOrEmpty(pict))
        pict = pict.Split(',')[0];

    var item = new ChatData
    {
        Author = new SharePointAuthor{
            Name = author.Name,
            Email = author.Email,
            UserID = author.ID,
            Picture = pict,
            Url = string.Format("{0}/_layouts/userdisp.aspx?ID={1}",
                SPContext.Current.Site.Url, author.ID)
            },
        Message = listItem.Title,
        PostedDate = (DateTime)listItem[createdFieldID]
    };
    chats.Add(item);
}
```

```
                    // Process this only for WCF code:
                    if (WebOperationContext.Current != null)
                    {
                        WebOperationContext.Current.OutgoingResponse.Headers
                        [HttpResponseHeader.CacheControl] = "Private";

                        // Expire the content to force a request
                        WebOperationContext.Current.OutgoingResponse.Headers
                            [HttpResponseHeader.Expires] =
                            list.LastItemModifiedDate.ToString("r");
                            DateTime.UtcNow.AddYears(-1).ToString("r");

                        WebOperationContext.Current.OutgoingResponse.LastModified =
                            list.LastItemModifiedDate.ToLocalTime();
                    }
                    return new Chat {
                        LastModified=list.LastItemModifiedDate, Chats = chats.ToArray() };
                }
            }
        }
```

Next, we'll create a lightweight HTTP handler that wraps the WCF service method. The *ChatHandler* class defined in Listing 11-14 acts as a simple HTTP handler that delegates the method to the *ChatService* class for its implementation. Note that the *ChatService* class does not execute in the WCF runtime it executes entirely in the ASP.NET runtime.

LISTING 11-14. The *ChatHandler* HTTP handler can be used to call the service class as an HTTP handler (*SOAjax.Services/ChatHandler.cs*).

```
using System;
using System.IO;
using System.Net;
using System.Xml;
using System.Xml.Serialization;
using System.Runtime.Serialization;
using System.Web;

namespace SOAjax.SharePoint.Services
{
    public class ChatHandler : IHttpHandler
    {
        public bool IsReusable{ get { return false; }}

        public void ProcessRequest(HttpContext context)
        {
            if (context.Request.HttpMethod.Equals("GET"))
            {
                context.Response.ContentType = "text/xml";
                ChatService chat = new ChatService();
                Chat chatData = chat.View();
```

```
        if (chatData == null)
        {
            HttpContext.Current.Response.ClearContent();
            HttpContext.Current.Response.StatusCode =
                (int)HttpStatusCode.NotModified;
        }
        else
        {
            var wcfSerializer = new DataContractSerializer(typeof(Chat));
            wcfSerializer.WriteObject(context.Response.OutputStream,
                chatData);
            context.Response.StatusCode = (int)HttpStatusCode.OK;

            HttpContext.Current.Response.Cache.SetCacheability(
                HttpCacheability.Private);

            HttpContext.Current.Response.Cache.SetExpires(
                chatData.LastModified.ToLocalTime());

            HttpContext.Current.Response.Cache.SetLastModified(
                chatData.LastModified.ToLocalTime());
        }
    }
    else if (context.Request.HttpMethod.Equals("POST"))
    {
        var message =
            new StreamReader(context.Request.InputStream).ReadToEnd();
        if (message.Length > 0 && message.Length < 1024)
        {
            ChatService chat = new ChatService();
            chat.Post(message);
            context.Response.StatusCode = (int)HttpStatusCode.OK;
        }
        else
        {
            context.Response.StatusDescription = "Bad request";
            context.Response.StatusCode = (int)HttpStatusCode.BadRequest;
        }
    }
    else
    {
        context.Response.StatusCode = (int)HttpStatusCode.BadRequest;
        context.Response.StatusDescription = "Method not supported.";
        context.Response.Write("Method not supported.");
    }
        }
    }
}
```

To serve the chat service from an HTTP handler in the virtualized *Layouts* directory, we need to include the web.config file shown in Listing 11-15. This web.config file is deployed to the file location \Program Files\Common Files\Microsoft Shared\Web Server Extensions\12\ TEMPLATE\LAYOUTS\SOAjax.Services\web.config.

By registering this handler in the *layouts* directory, you identify the URL of the chat service to be *http://[server]/[site]/_layouts/soajax.services/chat.svc*.

LISTING 11-15. The Chat Web service is implemented through the HTTP handler registered with ASP.NET through the web.config file (*SOAjax.SharePoint.Services/SOAjax.Services/web.config*).

```xml
<?xml version="1.0" encoding="UTF-8" standalone="yes"?>
<configuration>

    <system.web>
        <httpHandlers>
            <add verb="*" path="chat.svc"
                type="SOAjax.SharePoint.Services.ChatHandler" validate="false"/>
        </httpHandlers>
    </system.web>

</configuration>
```

As an alternative, you could remove the HTTP handler from the web.config and include an SVC file that utilizes *WebServiceHostFactory*, as demonstrated in Listing 11-16. However, this requires modifications to the SharePoint runtime as described in the document "WCF Support in SharePoint," available with the book's companion content.

LISTING 11-16. The Chat Web service can easily be deployed using a WCF endpoint through *WebServiceHostFactory* (*SOAjax.SharePoint.Services/SOAjax.Services/chat.svc*).

```
<%@ Assembly Name="SOAjax.SharePoint.Services, Version=1.0.0.0, Culture=neutral,
  PublicKeyToken=5716b00ea413c97d"%>
<%@ServiceHost Service="SOAjax.SharePoint.Services.ChatService"
    Factory="System.ServiceModel.Activation.WebServiceHostFactory" %>
```

With the service in place, we can access the chat service from any site-relative URL, such as *http://sharepoint/development/_layouts/SOAjax.Services/chat.svc*, which would return the chat data stream that is specific to the *http://sharepoint/development* site context.

By using *.svc* as the file extension for the HTTP handler, you can later remove the HTTP handler registration from web.config and include an SVC file that implements *WebServiceHostFactory* after adding WCF support to the SharePoint Web application. The SVC file that implements the service is shown in Listing 11-17.

LISTING 11-17. An SVC file can host the WCF endpoint natively if WCF is supported on the SharePoint Server.

```
<%@ Assembly Name="SOAjax.SharePoint.Services, Version=1.0.0.0, Culture=neutral,
    PublicKeyToken=5716b00ea413c97d"%>
<%@ServiceHost Service="SOAjax.SharePoint.Services.ChatService"
    Factory="System.ServiceModel.Activation.WebServiceHostFactory" %>
```

To implement a read-only view of the chat, we can use the AJAX XML Web Part defined earlier, using an XSLT file and by hard-coding the chat service URL. This is generally a great first step in developing more complex XML-based AJAX components. In the following section we'll create a specific implementation of the *AjaxXmlWebPart* that will add bidirectional chat functionality.

As discussed in Chapter 9, when you're creating XML-based AJAX components, you typically create an XSLT file for each view of the data that you want to define. For example, you might want to create compact and full views of the chat control. In this example, we'll create a single view for the *Chat* data contract. The chat XSLT file, shown in Listing 11-18, can be used by the AJAX XML Web Part and demonstrates the simplicity and flexibility of the XML-based AJAX architecture.

LISTING 11-18. The chat view is implemented in XSLT (*SOAjax.SharePoint/SOAjax.Script/ChatView.xslt*).

```
<?xml version='1.0' encoding='utf-8'?>
<xsl:stylesheet xmlns:xsl="http://www.w3.org/1999/XSL/Transform"
    xmlns:dc="http://purl.org/dc/elements/1.1/"
    xml:space="default"
    xmlns:sa="http://soajax" version="1.0">

    <xsl:strip-space elements="true"/>
    <xsl:output omit-xml-declaration="yes" method="html" />

    <xsl:template match='/sa:chat'>
        <xsl:apply-templates select='sa:chats' />
    </xsl:template>

    <xsl:template match='sa:chats'>
        <xsl:apply-templates select='sa:chatData' />
    </xsl:template>

    <xsl:template match='sa:chatData'>
        <div class="" style="border-bottom:1px solid #87ceeb;margin:7px;">

            <table>
                <tr valign="top">
                    <td width="48">
                        <xsl:choose>
                            <xsl:when test="sa:author/sa:picture">
                                <a href="{sa:author/sa:url}">
                                    <img src="{sa:author/sa:picture}"
                                        border="0" width="48" height="48" />
                                </a>
                            </xsl:when>
                            <xsl:otherwise></xsl:otherwise>
                        </xsl:choose>
                    </td>
```

```
                <td>
                    <span style="margin-bottom:5px; color:gray;
                        font-weight:bold;">
                        <xsl:value-of select='sa:author/sa:name'/>
                    </span>
                    <xsl:text
                        disable-output-escaping="yes"> </xsl:text>
                    <xsl:value-of select='sa:message' />
                </td>
            </tr>
        </table>
    </div>
  </xsl:template>
</xsl:stylesheet>
```

To create a control that can post data to the chat service, we'll create a second AJAX control that wraps an input control and a post button and includes a reference to the *XmlControl* class. To instantiate the control, you can use the same initialization logic as shown with the *XmlControl* script, looking for the *window._ChatControlTemplates* array.

To post the data, we'll use the following instance method of the Ajax control, which is added as an event handler. In the *onChatInput* method, we create an HTTP POST to the site-relative URL of the chat service. On the return call of the post, we tell the *XmlControl* instance to re-load, which will update the user interface.

```
onChatInput: function(sender, eventArgs) {
    var input = this.get_chatInput();
    var chat = input.value;
    input.value = '';
    var post = new Sys.Net.WebRequest();
    post.set_httpVerb('post');
    post.set_url(window._spweb + '/_layouts/soajax.services/chat.svc');
    var json = Sys.Serialization.JavaScriptSerializer.serialize(chat);
    post.set_body(json);
    post.get_headers()["Content-Type"] = "application/json";
    post.add_completed(Function.createDelegate(this, this.onPostComplete));
    post.invoke();
},

onPostComplete: function(response, context, args) {
    var xmlControl = this.get_xmlControl();
    if (xmlControl) xmlControl.reload();
},
```

The complete code sample for the ChatControl AJAX control is shown in Listing 11-19. This control is programmed against the chat protocol defined by our WCF chat service.

LISTING 11-19. The *Chat* data contract defines the XML schema for the custom Chat protocol
(*SOAjax.SharePoint/SOAjax.Script/ChatControl.js*).

```
/// <reference name="MicrosoftAjax.js"/>
/// <reference path="XmlControl.js"/>

Type.registerNamespace('SOAjax.Controls');

SOAjax.Controls.ChatControl = function(element) {
    /// <summary>
    /// A component that implements chat with the chat service.
    /// </summary>
    SOAjax.Controls.ChatControl.initializeBase(this, [element]);
}

SOAjax.Controls.ChatControl.prototype = {
    // ----------- Private fields ---------
    //_chatPostedDelegate: null,
    _chatInput: null,
    _chatButton: null,
    _xmlControl: null,

    // ------------- Properties -------------
    get_chatInput: function() {
        /// <value></value>
        return this._chatInput;
    },
    set_chatInput: function(value) {
        if (this._chatInput !== value) {
            this._chatInput = value;
            this.raisePropertyChanged('chatInput');
        }
    },

    get_chatButton: function() {
        /// <value></value>
        return this._chatButton;
    },
    set_chatButton: function(value) {
        if (this._chatButton !== value) {
            this._chatButton = value;
            this.raisePropertyChanged('chatButton');
        }
    },

    get_xmlControl: function() {
        /// <value>Gets or sets the XmlControl that implements the chat.</value>
        if (this._xmlControl.control)
            return this._xmlControl.control;
        else
            return this._xmlControl;
    },
```

```
set_xmlControl: function(value) {
    if (typeof (value) == 'string') {
        value = $get(value);
    }
    if (value == null) { throw Error.argument('xmlControl',
        'Expected an XmlControl.') }
    this._xmlControl = value;
},


get_chatButton: function() {
    /// <value>Gets or sets the chat button.</value>
    return this._chatButton;
},
set_chatButton: function(value) {
    if (typeof (value) == 'string') {
        value = $get(value);
    }
    this._chatButton = value;
    $addHandler(this._chatButton, 'click',
        Function.createDelegate(this, this.onChatInput));
},
_chatInput: null,
get_chatInput: function() {
    /// <value>Gets or sets the Input control.</value>
    return this._chatInput;
},
set_chatInput: function(value) {
    if (typeof (value) == 'string') {
        value = $get(value);
    }
    this._chatInput = value;
},


onChatInput: function(sender, eventArgs) {
    var input = this.get_chatInput();
    var chat = input.value;
    input.value = '';
    var post = new Sys.Net.WebRequest();
    post.set_httpVerb('post');
    post.set_url(window._spweb + '/_layouts/soajax.services/chat.svc');
    //post.set_userContext(chatPost);
    var json = Sys.Serialization.JavaScriptSerializer.serialize(chat);
    post.set_body(json);
    post.get_headers()["Content-Type"] = "application/json";
    post.add_completed(Function.createDelegate(this, this.onPostComplete));
    post.invoke();
},


onPostComplete: function(response, context, args) {
    String.format('Status: {0} ({1}) ',
        response.get_statusText(), response.get_statusCode()
        );
```

```
            var xmlControl = this.get_xmlControl();
            if (xmlControl) xmlControl.reload();
        },
        dispose: function() {
            ///<summary>Release resources before control is disposed.</summary>
            var element = this.get_element();
            if (element) $clearHandlers(this.get_element());
            SOAjax.Controls.ChatControl.callBaseMethod(this, 'dispose');
        },

        initialize: function() {
            ///<summary>Initialize the component.</summary>
            var element = this.get_element();
            SOAjax.Controls.ChatControl.callBaseMethod(this, 'initialize');
        }
    }
}

SOAjax.Controls.ChatControl.registerClass(
    'SOAjax.Controls.ChatControl', Sys.UI.Control);

// Initializes the ChatControl templates during the page load.
SOAjax.Controls.ChatControl.OnPageInit = function() {
    if (window.__ChatControlTemplates != 'undefined' &&
            window.__ChatControlTemplates != null) {
        while (window.__ChatControlTemplates.length > 0) {
            var template = Array.dequeue(window.__ChatControlTemplates);
            try {
                var element = $get(template.elementID);
                var control = $create(SOAjax.Controls.ChatControl,
                    template.properties, template.events,
                    template.references, element);
            } catch (e) {
                Sys.Debug.trace(
                    'Could not create ChatControl instance from template.');
                Sys.Debug.traceDump(template, 'invalid ChatControl template');
                if (Sys.Debug.isDebug)
                    Sys.Debug.fail('Error in SOAjax.Controls.ChatControl.OnPageInit.');
            }
        } // end while
    }
}
Sys.Application.add_init(SOAjax.Controls.ChatControl.OnPageInit);
Sys.Application.notifyScriptLoaded();
```

After creating the Chat Control JavaScript library, we can create a specialized instance of *AjaxXmlWebPart* that includes the XML and XSLT paths, adds an HTML input control with a POST button, and includes the *ChatControl* JavaScript library. The code for *ChatWebPart* is included in Listing 11-20. The Web Part will be rendered as the chat control shown in Figure 11-4.

LISTING 11-20. The ChatPart Web Part implements a chat control based on *XmlControl*.

```csharp
using System;
using Microsoft.SharePoint;
using System.Web.UI.WebControls.WebParts;
using Microsoft.SharePoint.Utilities;
using System.Web.UI;

namespace SOAjax.SharePoint
{
    public class ChatPart : AjaxXmlWebPart
    {
        /// <summary>Don't return the base editor parts.</summary>
        /// <returns>null</returns>
        public override EditorPartCollection CreateEditorParts()
        {
            // DO NOT: return base.CreateEditorParts(),
            // as Xml and XSLT are predefined for this part.
            return null;
        }

        /// <summary>Override the base part by adding XML endpoints.</summary>
        protected override void OnPreRender(EventArgs e)
        {
            base.OnPreRender(e);
            this.XmlUrl = SPContext.Current.Web.Url +
                "/_layouts/SOAjax.Services/chat.svc"; ;
            this.XsltUrl = SPContext.Current.Web.Url +
                "/_layouts/SOAjax.Script/chatview.xslt";
            if (this.Title == this.GetType().Name) this.Title = "Site Chat";
        }

        protected override void CreateChildControls()
        {
            base.CreateChildControls();
            this.ScriptManager.Scripts.Add(
                new ScriptReference("/_layouts/soajax.script/chatcontrol.js"));
            this.RefreshInterval = 3;
        }ddan

        protected override void RenderContents(System.Web.UI.HtmlTextWriter writer)
        {
            writer.Write(
              @"<div id=""ChatControl_{0}"" style=""display:block; padding:5px;"">",
              this.ClientID);
            writer.Write(
                @"<input id='ChatInput_{0}' maxlength='200' type='text' />",
                this.ClientID);
            writer.Write(@"<span id='ChatButton_{0}'
                style='background-color:gray;border:1px solid black; cursor:pointer;
                padding: 3px; color:white; font-weight:bold;'>chat</span>",
                this.ClientID);
            writer.Write(@"</div>");

            base.RenderContents(writer);
```

```
            string scriptFormat =
                @"if (window.__ChatControlTemplates == null){{
                    window.__ChatControlTemplates = new Array();
                    }}
                    var template = {{
                        elementID: 'ChatControl_{0}',
                        properties : {{
                            xmlControl : 'XmlControl_{0}',
                            chatButton : 'ChatButton_{0}',
                            chatInput : 'ChatInput_{0}'
                        }}
                    }};
                    window.__ChatControlTemplates.push(template);
                ";

            string script = string.Format(scriptFormat, this.ClientID);
            writer.Write(
                @"<script type=""text/javascript"" language=""javascript"">");
            writer.Write(script);
            writer.Write(@"</script>");
        }
    }
}
```

The Chat Web Part will appear like the image shown in Figure 11-4. Because the *XmlControl*
is checking for new data every second in a lightweight call that returns 304 (NOT MODIFIED)
in most cases, the Web application maintains a responsive user interface while enabling real-
time socializing within the SharePoint site context.

FIGURE 11-4. The Chat Web Part renders a custom chat interface, programmed against the custom
WCF chat protocol.

While we implemented the Chat Service using SharePoint data storage, it's common to build services that integrate external data sources that run within the SharePoint site context. You could easily swap out the data access code from the *ChatService* class in the previous example to access data from an external system such as a chat server running the Jabber XMPP protocol (*www.jabber.org*). To do this, you would use a SharePoint site context to identify the site's identity and the caller's identity before making a call to the external system, delegating the credentials using Kerberos or a custom delegation scheme.

With the techniques used in this example, you can build complex and powerful collaborative applications that run in the SharePoint site context and can easily be extended and consumed through external systems that use the same Web service APIs that the JavaScript AJAX application uses.

Summary

In this chapter you learned about the SharePoint application platform and simple SharePoint programming techniques. You learned about the SharePoint virtual file system and how to integrate custom WCF endpoints into SharePoint by implementing a specialized virtual path provider. You learned how to write and deploy WCF services that take advantage of the SharePoint site context and how to deploy WCF services in the virtualized *LAYOUTS* directory.

Next, you learned how to write a basic Web Part and how to include AJAX controls in a Web Part by rendering a placeholder and JavaScript template that is initialized in AJAX page initialization code.

By now, we've covered complex AJAX programming techniques in ASP.NET and in SharePoint and have programmed AJAX components using XSLT and custom rendering methods. At this point you should be able to create complex APIs with simple WCF endpoints, and complex AJAX applications written with very simple AJAX code. There's no need to create complex JavaScript code to implement most AJAX applications; most applications can be built with a very simple framework and multiple XSLT view components.

Index

Symbols and Numbers

A

About the Author

Daniel Larson is known for his work developing social software and enterprise AJAX applications. He's a software architect at NewsGator Technologies in Denver, Colorado, on the enterprise development team. When he's not with his family, he can be found speaking or writing about AJAX, enterprise development, or social applications using AJAX technologies and Microsoft enterprise servers. He is also a coauthor of the best-selling SharePoint developer book *Inside Microsoft Windows SharePoint Services 3.0*. Daniel lives in Centennial, Colorado, with his beautiful wife Sallina and their two children. Keep up with Daniel at *http://daniellarson.spaces.live.com*.

Best Practices for Software Engineering

Software Estimation: Demystifying the Black Art

Steve McConnell

ISBN 9780735605350

Amazon.com's pick for "Best Computer Book of 2006"! Generating accurate software estimates is fairly straight-forward—once you understand the art of creating them. Acclaimed author Steve McConnell demystifies the process—illuminating the practical procedures, formulas, and heuristics you can apply right away.

Code Complete, Second Edition

Steve McConnell

ISBN 9780735619678

Widely considered one of the best practical guides to programming—fully updated. Drawing from research, academia, and everyday commercial practice, McConnell synthesizes must-know principles and techniques into clear, pragmatic guidance. Rethink your approach—and deliver the highest quality code.

Agile Portfolio Management

Jochen Krebs

ISBN 9780735625679

Agile processes foster better collaboration, innovation, and results. So why limit their use to software projects—when you can transform your entire business? This book illuminates the opportunities—and rewards—of applying agile processes to your overall IT portfolio, with best practices for optimizing results.

Simple Architectures for Complex Enterprises

Roger Sessions

ISBN 9780735625785

Why do so many IT projects fail? Enterprise consultant Roger Sessions believes complex problems require simple solutions. And in this book, he shows how to make simplicity a core architectural requirement—as critical as performance, reliability, or security—to achieve better, more reliable results for your organization.

The Enterprise and Scrum

Ken Schwaber

ISBN 9780735623378

Extend Scrum's benefits—greater agility, higher-quality products, and lower costs—beyond individual teams to the entire enterprise. Scrum cofounder Ken Schwaber describes proven practices for adopting Scrum principles across your organization, including that all-critical component—managing change.

ALSO SEE

Software Requirements, Second Edition
Karl E. Wiegers
ISBN 9780735618794

More About Software Requirements: Thorny Issues and Practical Advice
Karl E. Wiegers
ISBN 9780735622678

Software Requirement Patterns
Stephen Withall
ISBN 9780735623989

Agile Project Management with Scrum
Ken Schwaber
ISBN 9780735619937

microsoft.com/mspress

Collaborative Technologies—
Resources for Developers

Inside Microsoft® Windows® SharePoint® Services 3.0
Ted Pattison, Daniel Larson
ISBN 9780735623200

Get the in-depth architectural insights, task-oriented guidance, and extensive code samples you need to build robust, enterprise content-management solutions.

Inside Microsoft Office SharePoint Server 2007
Patrick Tisseghem
ISBN 9780735623682

Led by an expert in collaboration technologies, you'll plumb the internals of SharePoint Server 2007—and master the intricacies of developing intranets, extranets, and Web-based applications.

Inside the Index and Search Engines: Microsoft Office SharePoint Server 2007
Patrick Tisseghem, Lars Fastrup
ISBN 9780735625358

Customize and extend the enterprise search capabilities in SharePoint Server 2007—and optimize the user experience—with guidance from two recognized SharePoint experts.

Working with Microsoft Dynamics® CRM 4.0, Second Edition
Mike Snyder, Jim Steger
ISBN 9780735623781

Whether you're an IT professional, a developer, or a power user, get real-world guidance on how to make Microsoft Dynamics CRM work the way you do—with or without programming.

Programming Microsoft Dynamics CRM 4.0
Jim Steger *et al.*
ISBN 9780735625945

Apply the design and coding practices that leading CRM consultants use to customize, integrate, and extend Microsoft Dynamics CRM 4.0 for specific business needs.

ALSO SEE

Inside Microsoft Dynamics AX 2009
ISBN 9780735626454

6 Microsoft Office Business Applications for Office SharePoint Server 2007
ISBN 9780735622760

Programming Microsoft Office Business Applications
ISBN 9780735625365

Inside Microsoft Exchange Server 2007 Web Services
ISBN 9780735623927

microsoft.com/mspress